17.95

**Economics of Engineering
and Social Systems**

Economics of Engineering and Social Systems

Edited by

J. MORLEY ENGLISH

Professor of Engineering, University of California, Los Angeles

WILEY–INTERSCIENCE, a Division of John Wiley & Sons, Inc.
New York • London • Sydney • Toronto

Library of Congress Catalog Card Number: 73–37644

ISBN 0–471–24180–6

Printed in the United States of America.

10 9 8 7 6 5 4 3 2 1

PREFACE

This book is based on a series of lectures presented during the spring of 1969 by University Extension of the University of California under the "Statewide Lecture Series" program. Each lecture was repeated in four locations within California—San Francisco, Los Angeles, Fullerton, and San Diego.

The series was planned and presented in recognition of a growing emphasis both in engineering and management circles on the "systems approach" to major problems of our age. This emphasis on systems arises from the need to attack large-scale socioeconomic problems—water and air pollution, water supply, power networks, transportation, space and undersea exploration, urban redevelopment, and economic development.

Solutions to problems of such scope involve many specialists—economists, sociologists, engineers, and managers. The engineer designing the system and the executive implementing it must understand the importance and relationship of other disciplines to the total effort—the key one perhaps being economics.

In many systems problems, both engineers and managers work closely with economists in defining objectives but often find their positions in conflict due to misunderstanding of economic principles or to lack of communication. On the other hand, engineers have successfully applied engineering approaches to solve economic systems problems.

The purpose of the series was to provide a greater awareness of economic concepts and disciplines relevant to engineering and management problems of the future and to generate concern for the complexities of the economic considerations in design of new systems. In particular it was intended to provide insight into economic concepts and models as perceived by professional economists, and to demonstrate application of economic principles to the evaluation of proposed engineering and social systems. The lectures were presented by men operating in the interdisciplinary field of engineering economics. Several lectures were specifically designed as examples of the economic evaluation of new or proposed systems.

Assistance in the organization of the lectures and selection of the guest speakers was generously provided by an advisory committee, some members of which also contributed lectures. The committee members were as follows.*

Helen Barry, Continuing Education in Engineering, University of California, Berkeley
J. C. Dillion, Engineering and Physical Sciences Extension, University of California, Los Angeles
J. Morley English, Engineering, University of California, Los Angeles
Ole I. Franksen, Electric Power Engineering Department, Technical University of Denmark, Lyngby, Denmark
Raoul J. Freeman, Manager, Special Programs, Center for Advanced Studies, General Electric Company, Santa Barbara
Thomas H. Hazlett, Continuing Education in Engineering, University of California, Berkeley
Marvin Hoffenberg, Political Sciences, University of California, Los Angeles
Willian Linvill, Institute in Engineering—Economic Systems, Stanford University
Daniel L. McFadden, Economics, University of California, Berkeley
Wesley L. Orr, Engineering, University of California, Los Angeles
Alan M. Schneider, Aerospace Engineering, University of California, San Diego
William F. Sharpe, Economics, University of California, Irvine
David Sternlight, Director, Cost and Economic Analysis, Advanced Marine Technology Division, Litton Industries, Culver City
H. L. Tallman, Engineering and Physical Sciences Extension, University of California, Los Angeles
Andrew Vazsonyi, Consultant, North American Rockwell Corporation El Segundo

The coordination of the lecture presentations required considerable detail work. I am grateful to the following for the assistance which they unstintingly gave me in this effort.

E. C. Keachie, Associate Professor of Industrial Engineering and Operations Research, University of California, Berkeley
Ernst S. Valfer, Chief, Management Sciences Staff, U.S. Forest Service, Berkeley
William F. Sharpe, Professor of Economics, University of California, Irvine
Alan M. Schneider, Professor of Aerospace Engineering University of California, San Diego, La Jolla

Unfortunately, three of the lecturers were unable to provide manuscripts for their lectures and so are not included in the book. The first of these was given by Dr. Roy Radner, Professor of Economics, University of California, Berkeley. It addressed the problem of "The Market as a Principle of Organization" and emphasized the need for exploiting the market as a means for allocating resources. The second lecture was by Dr. Harry Markowitz, Professor of Business Administration, UCLA. This lecture was focused on

* Affiliations of the committee members are those at the time the program was presented. Some have changed since then.

the development of "Models and Simulation for System Evaluation." The third was that of Mr. Blair Bower of Resources for the Future, Inc. His lecture was on "The Diseconomy of Waste." I am most appreciative of their excellent contributions to the success of the series.

Los Angeles, California   J. MORLEY ENGLISH
October 1971

CONTENTS

Economics of Engineering
and Social Systems

I Prospective: J. Morley English

The last thirty years of the twentieth century are being ushered in with a sudden change in the public attitude in the United States toward priorities that should be assigned to our national goals. There is evidence of a new concern for the quality of environment at home. This is accompanied by a lessened interest in providing the traditional form of aid for foreign development. Also there is a new awareness of a need to rebuild cities, to clean polluted water and air, and to reduce congestion, along with a sudden disinterest in space exploration and a reduced concern over national defense.

These new attitudes are strong, and if persistent, will result in a rather dramatic reallocation of our resources from one that has been accompanied by long-term economic stability to a very different one. The transient effect must be somewhat disequilibrating so that a number of years may elapse before the United States economy will approach some new equilibrium. The resulting changes that will be induced in our social, political, and economic institutions will require a great deal of understanding on the part of those responsible for making policy decisions. In no small way a profound knowledge of underlying economic principles will be needed by the engineers called on to design the needed new systems. The problems are systems problems, whose solutions will require a systems approach rather than the evolutionary or the piecemeal component approach that has largely characterized engineering for the economic development of the past. The new designs must take into account technical performance, management control, and the planning needed for implementing the system as an operational reality. They must satisfy essentially social and economic objectives as well as meet the technical requirements.

THE SYSTEMS VIEWPOINT

A system may be regarded as a collection of elements or components arranged or organized to achieve some recognized objective. To analyze a

1

system one must consider it in isolation from its environment which estab-lishes the constraints on the system including all inputs to it as well as the outputs from it. In any real system the outputs feed back through complex and often unknowable interactions with elements of the environment to modify the inputs. To the extent that one is able to define the system to keep the interfaces with the environment few and the characteristic of the inter-actions between the system and its environmental or external systems across these interfaces simple, he enhances his chances of accurate prediction of the system performance (outputs). However, the system performance can only be predicted in terms of the perceived and defined inputs. Any that are intention-ally or unintentionally excluded from consideration will not be reflected in the predicted systems characteristics. In many cases the neglecting of certain inputs will not significantly impair the predicted systems performance. How-ever, the more complex the system the more difficult it becomes to perceive what the final effects of such simplifications may be. There is a danger in simplification that the model will not represent reality.

Every system may be viewed in terms of some objective that is subordinate to that of a larger system of which it is a component or subsystem. A molecule is a complex system comprised of atoms which in turn are complex systems of more elemental particles. The molecule in turn builds up into systems of materials that form structures and so on to the ultimate system—the universe. In consideration of any system one must accept certain components as being elemental and therefore needing no further consideration of their internal behavior. In engineering systems these independent components are often referred to as *black boxes*. Systems become complex when the number and variety of the elements become large. This complicates the kind and extent of interactions. What then characterizes the systems approach is really an expansion of the concept of a system to encompass greater degrees of complexity and the consideration of higher levels of super systems along with a greater variety of subsystems. In part *systems analysis* or *systems engineering* is an outgrowth of the modern tools of analysis including the computer.

Not only is a larger systems viewpoint possible today but also the develop-ment of new systems for societal needs may only be possible by taking a systems viewpoint. The economic evaluation that was traditionally employed by engineers for comparing alternatives disregarded interactions with the economic environment. The scale of the many new systems that now must be designed will be such that economic interaction with other systems will be much too important to ignore.

The experience gained from the space program may afford one of the most important assets for attacking new systems problems. It is conceivable that without such background the possibility of effecting solutions for the new systems problems, and doing this on a reasonably short time scale, would not be possible. Such a pay-off from the space program may, in retrospect, ultimately prove to have been its most significant economic justification. This is not to imply that because of the systems engineering of the space program the systems engineering for the new civil systems will be easy. The space program had an extremely simple objective—a man on the moon by 1970. The new systems have very complex objectives that escape precise and invariant definition. The single purpose space system did require the development of a large and complex management system and it is this experience that may be transferable. In other words, it may have been the proper order to develop the complex management system first while holding to the straightforward objective that the space program afforded and only then extending the systems engineering methodology to handle the more complex objectives of social systems.

THE NEW SYSTEMS

One common characteristic of the needed new systems of society is one of scale. They are large by any measure. In a relative sense they will demand larger increment investments as represented by proportion of GNP than we as a society are used to considering. This enlarged scale of commitment makes the problem somewhat frightening and could lead to an inability to act. A second characteristic is that the time required for the full realization of the pay-off may be expected to be longer than that required for past investments with which we are more accustomed.

Systems could be classified in many ways. One is chosen to illustrate certain economic considerations discussed later; it is as follows.

- Expansion of existing systems on a larger scale and with more complex interactions.
- Entirely new systems.
- Replacement systems that require abandonment or significant alteration of existing systems.

In the case of expansion of existing systems, the scale of new increments will usually be much larger than for previous units. This introduces questions of economy of scale but also may introduce the need for structural changes within the system itself. Such an effect might be exemplified by the growth of electrical power systems. The size of both power stations and generators is increasing. For example, at present approximately 3000 power plants provide 300,000 MW of capacity in the United States. It is projected that by 1980 an addition of approximately 600 plants will be needed to furnish 1,000,000 MW of new capacity needed then. This change in power-generating systems in turn affects the economics of distribution and transmission networks.

Examples of entirely new systems that may emerge in the future are computer utilities, new cities that are completely separated from existing metropolitan complexes, ocean transport by surface-effects machines, submarine freight, desalting of water, waste disposal, and the like. Satellite communication is one such system that has already been implemented. In each case the scale for the threshold for starting such systems is very large. While such new systems will grow in an evolutionary way, they must be designed at the outset as complete systems with initial operations on a large scale.

It is the third category that presents the most difficulty. Here the major impact of meeting either expanded demand, or an entirely new demand impinges on both an industry and a public that have become committed to some existing system. The new system will either obsolete the existing system or seriously change its form. A good example of an existing system so threatened is that of automobile transportation. A very large fraction of the GNP is now represented in the automobile and its related support systems of fuel supply and distribution, maintenance and repair services, insurance, roads, and freeways, as well as all other industry that is in some way related to the automobile. No new system for transporting people on a scale of several times the present automobile travel demand could conceivably replace the automobile without a new investment comparable to that already in existence for the automobile industry today. Furthermore, even if such replacement is ever made it would still take a very long time to effect a transition. During this time the existing system could continue to grow for some time. The immensity of just the idea of replacing the automobile is so great that most people would be inclined to reject even its consideration out of hand. Yet soon the transportation demand may be as much as four times the present demand. Could any automobile system with normal evolutionary change handle this load at all, let alone economically? Therefore it may be imperative that we at least consider such seemingly incredible alternatives.

The relative economy of competing systems depends on the scale of the demand. With reference to Figure 1, system A is more economical than B for demand level I. Since demand level I was the limit of public vision when the choice was made, A is the system that evolved. However, for demand level II, B is the more economical. If the system had been designed to meet demand level II originally, B most assuredly would have been selected. However, if level II had not been visualized, so that A came into existence, then a change from A to B can only be made by abandonment of A. It is true that Figure 1 does not depict the whole story because, given A exists, the economy of B relative to the existing A must be calculated on the basis of the marginal

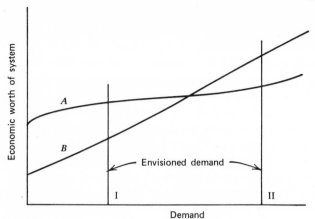

Fig. 1. Economic worth versus envisioned demand.

economy for continuing *A*. Nevertheless many systems may continue to operate even when the marginal economy relative to a new system of comparable scale may be more economical.

Systems that need to be reexamined from this point of view include nearly all of the existing large-scale systems on which society depends heavily today. Starting with transportation, chosen only to illustrate the point above, one can include the following as examples of broader systems areas.

New city concepts.
Waste disposal and pollution control.
Water supply.
Electrical power.
Crime prevention.
Food preparation and distribution.
Education.
Communications.
Health care.

PROFESSIONAL INVOLVEMENT

The solutions of the new systems problems will require the combined efforts of all the professions. The expertise of specialists in all fields of sociology, economics, physical sciences, and technology will be required. In addition to specialists, many generalists who have the skills to design, organize, and manage will be needed. These men are the entrepreneurs, engineers, and managers of the systems. They must be integraters of specialized knowledge.

As such they need a broad background in specialized fields. The University of California Statewide Lecture Series on "Economics of Social and Engineering Systems" was designed primarily for them, and most of the lectures comprise chapters in this book.

A common characteristic of any system today is its strong dependence on technology and science. For this reason the design of a new system requires engineers, who because of education and experience can be expected to do the job. These men must also be thoroughly grounded in economics.

However, the engineer's approach to economics can be expected to differ from that of the economist. The economist is basically a scientist. As such, his primary interest is to observe how economic systems behave. He often will be called on to advise the policy makers about the consequences of various policy decisions. Still his approach has largely developed from the scientific interest in observation and analysis of systems. In this respect he tends to have the same point of view as a physicist who, in observing the natural world, attempts to generalize various laws and principles. He is not really interested in putting them to use.

The engineer on the other hand starts from the established bodies of knowledge as generalized by scientists. He *uses* knowledge from all relevant sources to design some new system. In other words, he proceeds from the general to the specific. This can be an airplane design or a freeway system. For this reason he is interested in using economics as a design tool. He must establish criteria for evaluating the prospective worth of his new system. His point of view of economics tends to reflect this concern for the system within a broader economic environment in contrast to the economist's tendency to be more concerned about the economic environment. This dichotomy of viewpoint has often led to conflicting opinions about the worth of some proposed new venture. Often such differences may have been more apparent than real. Nevertheless, there is one other aspect of the difference that is worthy of comment. Historically, economic models of society have been developed by economists from the concepts of equilibrium. The market is a good example of this. Essentially equilibrium models are static models. The engineer's *free body* concept is an equilibrium device too. By means of d'Alembert's principle a dynamic nonequilibrium situation may be transformed into an equilibrium model. In economics, there is no equivalent for the d'Alembert principle. Furthermore, the engineer in designing new systems is not only not content to accept the equilibrium condition but also is deliberately attempting to upset the equilibrium model of the economist. He wants change, not equilibrium.

The economist sometimes perceives the engineer's use of average rather than marginal cost analysis as an error. Yet the engineer, although more interested in considering total cost functions rather than unit costs that represent a more popular mode of the economist's analysis, does base his evaluations on marginal costs. Where the engineer is more often in error is in an unawareness of externalities and the diseconomies that they may induce. This error is explainable in his tendency to take a more local point of view than the economist. He may be more interested in whether a decision is profitable for his client, whereas the economist is more inclined to perceive the gain from a more global social point of view.

What is indicated by these difficulties is the necessity for establishing more dialogue between the professions and better team efforts in working on the systems problems of the future. The possibility of improved communication requires a broader understanding.

ECONOMIC IMPLICATIONS OF THE NEW SYSTEMS

The public demand for the new systems described above arises from a complex of reasons. In the first place the systems that we have evolved up to now are creating other new needs for their continuing operation. However, the possibility of satisfying new demands derives from our affluence and fundamental production efficiency. Changing personal and social tastes are influenced by the trappings of society and at the same time people react to these environmental factors to produce still new demands. In total effect, however, these new demands represent extensions to our standard of living.

A standard of living grows naturally from an elementary survival level in consumption of food and shelter to consumption of all the hardware that we find necessary for increasing physical and psychological comfort. As we approach limits to the quantity of *gadgets* we can use, we understandably proceed to a search for improved quality of existence. This naturally leads to a greater demand for more *social* goods relative to *private* goods. The characteristic of social goods is that they require societal decisions to produce them. They are not *divisible and scarce* in the sense of private goods. The use of a park, or pleasure in viewing a beautiful landscape, by one person does not detract from that of another. For this reason the market can fail as a mechanism for allocating wealth for the purchase of social goods.

Private goods on the other hand are scarce. The restriction of use by one person excludes that of others. This produces the competitive situation that is an essential condition for a market. A society in its development moves from agriculture toward manufacturing industry largely on the basis of expanding supply of private goods and services. It was only natural then that economists perceived economic activity in relation to value arising out of the exchange of private goods. The market was the ideal. Fred Hoffman amplifies many of these concepts in Chapter II.

It is appropriate that a series of lectures addressing the consideration of engineering and social systems should start from the already accepted concepts of value and description of the economic influences operative in our society up to the present. Professor Lind does this in Chapter III. While he builds his exposition on the traditional market model, he clearly recognizes its limitations and offers suggestions for efficient pricing of goods for which the market works imperfectly. One such class of goods that has its own peculiarities and for which the market has certain limitations is that of information.

The role of information in the economy is unique. In some cases it takes on the characteristics of social goods in that there is virtually no limit in the distribution of a piece of information. Its use by one individual in no way limits its use by another. It can be disseminated as widely as desired or restricted to a very few. Certain kinds of information will become more valuable to each individual the more widely it is disseminated. On the other hand, the more some information is restricted in its availability the more valuable it becomes to those who are privy to it. For example, a company will guard certain process secrets very closely because knowledge of them will permit competitors to deprive it of an economic advantage innate in the information. Patent and copyright laws recognize this in protecting the use of information to reward innovators.

The importance of information in the more advanced economies is increasing. Proportionately, more and more of economic activity is in one way or another represented by value of information. One aspect alone, education, represents a greater proportion of an individual's lifetime activity. People not only enter the labor force at an older age, but also they spend a great deal of time continuing education; then they may retire earlier. Therefore the economics of information that does not fit the market ideal must be more seriously considered in future systems.

This trend to a demand for goods for which the market does not operate well raises serious philosophical questions. Traditionally we have looked to government to provide our social goods. Usually this has meant that government that was equipped to make the purchase of such goods also went into the business of producing them. The implications of a trend to greater proportion of total goods being social goods is clear. If we do not change from the traditional mechanisms for providing these goods, then it follows that we *must* have more government business—not less. Thus while we say we want less government involvement, we inevitably take the actions that demand more.

On the other hand, dependence on government may not be the only way. Certainly if government is the accepted purchasing agent for social goods, then proportionately more of our income must be channeled through some taxing system to government for the payment of the things we desire. This does not mean necessarily that government should also be the producer. For defense and space the engineering and manufacturing has been provided by large but private corporations. This has created a market under conditions of monopsony on the production side. For social goods, other than defense hardware, governments may have been much more involved in the production process. For example, state highway departments may do the engineering and subcontract only the production of the components—earth moving, concrete, steel, and such.

A second far reaching question, which will require hard policy decisions, relates to the changed nature of capital expenditure required for many of the new large systems. In Chapter IV, it is shown that capital derives from the lag between the initiation of production and the final consumption. Certain resources must flow into intermediate goods for production, in other words tools. This capital is justified by reason of its increased productivity. Essentially our economic growth comes from employment of this production capital. It requires postponement of consumption or *saving* to obtain it. A second kind of capital is consumer capital. Resources here flow into goods over a short time period required to produce them but their consumption takes place over a long time span. For example, a house is essentially a consumer good, but from the standpoint of the time lag between production and consumption it is truly a capital investment and is properly considered as such either by its owner or the mortgager who finances it. However, unlike production capital it does not represent a contribution to production efficiency. Saving is required for the formation of either kind of capital. Now the emphasis on new systems may represent a major shift in demand for consumer capital. At the same time the need for production capital likely will not diminish. This effect will mean a significantly increased need for saving. Specifically this will represent curtailment in consumption of many of the gadgets that we are now accustomed to having. Concomitantly, the full realization of a new consumption pattern—the enjoyment of our improved environment—will have to be postponed. This will be done, in effect, by spreading consumption out in time. Such changing patterns may well be expected to occasion dislocations and strife; people will resist reductions of perceived standards of living, particularly when such changes are difficult to associate with the promised returns. Also, not all those deprived by the process will necessarily benefit later.

One other aspect of this question cannot be totally ignored. There is a certain amount of risk in such changes. We must first deprive ourselves in anticipation of later returns. There can be no positive assurance that there will be a pay-off. The pay-off will depend on the skill and wisdom of our investment decisions. If we do not design the systems well and if our political sophistication does not match our aspirations, the expected improvement in our standard of living might turn out to be illusion.

MEASURES OF ECONOMIC ACTIVITY

The design of any physical system depends on ability to predict perform-ance. We observe physical phenomena and note that when certain measurable influences act on a system other measurable effects are obtained. By estab-lishing invariant relationships we can organize new systems to achieve some desired result. The same argument may be extended to the economic conse-quences of new systems. The difficulty in economics that is much greater than in engineering is the problem of quantifying measurements.

In Chapter V Dr. Franksen starts with some very fundamental philosophies of measurement of physical systems. He extends the concepts used in the physical sciences to show how in principle they apply in exactly the same way for economic systems. The problem of measurement, hence of prediction, is several orders of magnitude more difficult in economics. In physical systems we always have an external system which we are able to use for comparison. We do this by measuring something that goes through from one point to another as a flow—an *intervariable* (or through-variable)—or a difference between one point and another—*transvariable* (or across-variable). In either case an instrument that can be calibrated by comparison with a standard is employed. This cannot be so in economics for the very simple fact that there can be no way of isolating the system in order to compare it with a standard measure even if such existed.

If we recall the perceptual origin of science on the one hand and economics on the other, it is readily seen how this dilemma comes about. Our perception of the physical world initially was macroscopic. We felt the effects of force and heat; we could compare one force system with another. Only after considerable insight gained from observing macrophenomena did we develop the averaging laws that relate the activities of molecules to pressures and temperatures which we had learned to measure and predict long before we knew the laws that explained the observed macroeffects. Much of the behavior of particles is inferred from macromeasurements.

In economics the situation is reversed. The individual's perception of economic phenomena is atomistic at the outset. He perceives the effects of his trades with other individuals. He does not perceive the *economy*. This is inferred. Thus all economic measurement is built up from the microobserva-tion. For this reason, economic measurements are statistical aggregates. There probably is also a fundamental uncertainty principle similar in concept to the Heisenberg uncertainty principle in physics. This principle is a funda-mental concept that the very fact of taking a micromeasurement disturbs the thing that you wish to measure and so you can only make a probability statement about the state. A parallel to this in economics may be observed in the difficulty of using a single commodity as a reference of value or *numeraire* to which all exchanges may relate. The very fact of choosing a commodity, such as gold, once so highly regarded for this purpose, disturbs its value as a commodity relative to the commodities with which it is to be compared.

In spite of these difficulties significant strides are being made in economic measurement, but these are based on aggregation concepts. The basic elements of this developing science is covered by Dr. Intrilligator in Chapter VI.

A significant aid to economic analysis was provided by the input-output model of Wassily Leontief.* While the model has been used for analysis of whole economies on rather highly aggregated data, it has potential for the analysis of the operations of individual systems. As a result it holds promise as a design tool for engineering and social systems. One such approach for a water resource system is discussed in some detail by Dr. Lofting in Chapter IX. In addition to the illustrative use of an input-output model for water resource development, Dr. Lofting offers an interesting history of its development and its theoretical basis.

Input-output models have useful application in problems of economic development. Dr. Kendrick in Chapter VIII discusses this problem and approaches to its solution by use of a number of mathematical models. The advantages and limitations of each is discussed in some depth.

In addition to the penetrating discussion of measurements, Dr. Franksen in Chapter V develops the fundamental relationships that apply for physical networks in terms of the first and second laws of thermodynamics. He demonstrates how the same laws apply to the Walrasian economic model on which the Leontief input-output model is based. In all of these approaches considerable progress has been made by reason of the availability of the computer and the techniques of mathematical programming.

INVESTMENT DECISIONS

The economic models discussed in Chapters III, V, and VII largely ignore the question of capital investment. In Dr. Franksen's development the technical coefficients are fixed and constant. The production process described can include the production of capital goods but these become outputs from the system considered. No provision is made for feedback. Yet it is precisely the nature of capital that may be expected to change the technical coefficients. The control model described by Dr. Kendrick in Chapter VIII does recognize the importance of capital investment. In fact in economic development problems capital formation is an extremely important variable. Nevertheless

* W. W. Leontief, "Input-Output Economy," *Sci.-Amer.*, October 1951.

its inclusion in his models is only introduced by providing somewhat artificially imposed constraints. Specifically the question of capital consumption by use of depreciation allowances is subject to serious misinterpretation if not to actual error. He recognizes that an optimal policy for either a multiperiod or finite horizon plan would result in the consumption of the physical capital at the horizon time. To overcome this difficulty some arbitrary level of capital is introduced as a constraint at the horizon time and some defined percentage of existing capital (represented by depreciation) considered as a year by year cost. While such arbitrary quantities may be necessary to obtain tractable computable models, their use is theoretically questionable.

In a rapidly growing economy or firm, much of the capital employed in the initial time period will not require replacement until many years beyond the horizon time. While a depreciation allowance is needed in an accounting sense, it should not be a factor in investment decisions. Only the resources allocated to capital expenditures in each period are of concern. For example, a hydroelectric power development may be there for all time. Certainly its replacement may not be a factor for another 50 or 100 years. Therefore, once its demand for capital from the economy has been satisfied, what follows will be a pay-off. If this same development has been financed by external loans, these may have to be repaid. This repayment schedule may result in some form of export that would be included in the model. In an indirect sense this takes care of the depreciation and to include depreciation in addition could amount to a duplication.

Failure to take account of capital spending decisions in any really satisfactory way is understandable. The problem of capital allocation is a difficult one. In the first place it requires long-range forecasts. Under the best of situations these are not easily made. In Chapter IV, I offer an approach, which, as far as I am aware, is new. It may hold some promise for a development of a better methodology for long range investment analysis.

A second difficulty arises out of the intertemporal nature of investment. A limited budget, constrained by the savings flow of society, can be assigned for each period. Some expenditures made in one year condition a sequence of follow-on expenditures in subsequent years and in each case the effects extend far beyond what are usually taken as reasonable planning horizons.

Certain types of capital decisions are mutually exclusive. The selection of one machine for a particular job excludes the need for some other alternative equipment or process. The comparison often is not between alternatives requiring comparable capital allocations. This decision to accept the alternative that requires the greater capital expenditure based on an independent analysis of the equipment alternatives automatically reduces the capital available for other projects that may appear to be quite unrelated to that one particular decision.

Within the capital budgeting problem are the subclasses of complementary and competitive investments. Most investments in a single enterprise are made for building a complete production system. Under such circumstances it is impossible to ascribe any discernable return to any one component because the system depends on the harmonious interaction of all of them. Thus the question of establishing priorities for capital expenditures within the single plant becomes one of assessing effects on the total system.

In competitive substitutive investments, the problem ranges from the mutually exclusive special case described above to the one of diversification between opportunities. This arises out of a need to trade-off some expected return against risk. It is recognized as the portfolio problem. Usually this problem is treated as a continuous allocation type of situation since investment in securities, for example, may be varied almost continuously between securities over the capital budget available. By contrast the capital budgeting problem requires the allocation of capital to discrete projects. The decision becomes one of accepting a given lump sum allocation or rejecting it. This leads to a special class of techniques known as integer programming. It is discussed in an elementary sense by Dr. Freeman in Chapter VII. However, the problem can become far more complex than he has described it.

Most major new systems will require capital allocations over a number of years. In the early stages relatively small but significant amounts may be allocated to engineering investigations. The program will be planned in a number of phases. At each step the decision to abandon, modify, or proceed to the next planned step must be made. Thus each year's capital budget must allow for continuing projects and this requires budget planning for a number of years. While the decision to allocate certain monies may only need to be made for the following budget year, such a decision can be substantiated by the forecast of many more years. This in essence is the program planning and budgeting system, PPBS, that Fred Hoffman discusses in Chapter II.

A further complication to the capital budgeting problem arises from the fact that capital requirements are really not discrete. A certain threshold level of capital may be needed for the project to be feasible. However, given that the threshold has been reached there may be a continuous allocation function which extends beyond the threshold and which would result in some optimal allocation. Again this optimal should be considered in relation to the total budget that is to be allocated for all projects. This may not be practicable at present and indeed it probably is not done. The funding to be considered for each opportunity at best may have to remain a suboptimal estimate.

In most cases, capital budgeting either for the firm or for a state enterprise is done on the basis of complementary investments. In other words the candidate projects are all directly related to the objectives of the particular enterprise. They do not represent diversification. On the other hand, they may be diversification type ventures. This means that the returns to be realized will not be completely correlated with the success of the other activities of the particular enterprise. At the same time, neither will they be completely independent in a probabilistic sense. At a minimum there will be some tendency to correlate with the external economic environment and within that to an industry group. Thus at one end of the spectrum of capital budgets, the problem approaches the portfolio problem.

DYNAMICS AND CONTROL

Economic systems are dynamic. If the forces operating on them may interact with the system in a way that the system will tend to some steady state, it may decay or become unstable. The basic concept of control is that whatever the system is tending toward, that information can be sensed and fed back as a signal to redirect it toward some recognized objective. It is questionable that a system as complex as our society can be well enough understood that it could be centrally controlled. Indeed this would be contrary to our basic social mores even if it were possible. Nevertheless, we do by adaptation arrive at environmental conditions that permit many millions of individual decisions to be made that implicitly control the system. To the extent that the process of feedback control can be more generally understood, the individual decisions will tend to be better ones.

On a smaller scale a particular activity may well be modeled on the basis of feedback systems with conscious controls designed into them. Dr. Koenig in Chapter X models just such an approach. Not only does he bring out the principles but also develops some interesting examples.

OTHER EXAMPLES

In Chapter XII Dr. Mood points up some of the difficulties in using sophisticated mathematical tools on highly unstructured situations for which at best data are very limited and subject to considerable error. With all the difficulties that are innate to such situations there are ways of going about the analysis of such problems as the educational system and still providing better answers than that of pure intuition.

A second more highly developed example is that of Dr. George Hoffman who describes the nature of the engineering considerations and their relationship to economic evaluation that must be taken into account in such a project as a new high speed transit system.

SUMMARY

The reader should keep in mind that the book is a compendium of independent contributions. As such, there is a certain amount of overlap of a number of topics. On the other hand, where this does occur it represents different viewpoints, sometimes with different conclusions. Furthermore, it permits the reader to select the order of reading subsequent chapters and to omit any one that may not be commitant with his interest.

II The Analysis and Evaluation of Public Expenditures: The PPB System: Fred S. Hoffman*

The planning, programming, and budgeting (PPB) system, as the name suggests, was conceived as a system of interrelated elements. The system was intended to improve Federal decision-making about resource allocation in several important ways. The system is designed to:

- Compare the efficiency of alternative ways of carrying on government resource-using or resource-affecting activities, as the market tests the efficiency of private resource-using activities.
- Relate tests of efficiency to the proper objectives of public action (not necessarily the historical or organizational objectives of government agencies).
- Present major issues for decision in a useful way to high officials who have no time to be specialists on even a fraction of the matters they must decide.

To accomplish the desired improvements in governmental decision-making, PPB has strived to introduce or strengthen three aids to the making of choices about resource allocations:

1. *Analysis.* Comparisons of the cost and effectiveness of alternative ways of achieving the objectives of public policy.
2. *Program budgeting.* Presentation of the agency budget in a classification system related to the major program choices to be made.
3. *Planning.* Presentation of information about the future implications of current program choices for cost and effectiveness beyond the budget year.

Analysis, program budgeting, and planning are distinct elements of PPB,

---

* This chapter, under the title of "Public Expenditure Analysis and the Institutions of the Executive Branch," was originally published from the hearings before the Joint Economic Committee of the Congress of the United States, prior to the reorganization of the Executive Office of the President when the name of the Bureau of the Budget was changed to Office of Management and Budget.

and might have been introduced separately. Moreover, their development has proceeded at different rates during the 3 years since the introduction of PPB, and in response to different stimuli and impediments.

Although analysis, in my view, is at the heart of PPB, I believe that there were good reasons for linking the three elements. The reasons are related to the nature of systems analysis and to the nature of decision-making in a large organization such as the Federal Government. The chapter first reviews the nature and origin of systems analysis and then turns to the relations among the three elements as they have developed in PPB.

THE ORIGINS OF SYSTEMS ANALYSIS IN NATIONAL SECURITY PLANNING

The PPB system is extending to the other major departments and agencies of the Executive the approach to resource management developed by Secretary McNamara in the Department of Defense. Systems analysis played a central role in the system that evolved in the Defense Department, and an understanding of its salient characteristics is necessary to understand the PPB system.

Systems analysis is a term whose meaning has been eroded by very wide and diverse usage. The sense of the term most relevant to PPB is the one that describes the approach to national security problems developed during the early 1950s. The approach evolved in response to the planning problems of the early post-World War II period; it was not the result of a grand intellectual design.

Operations analysis in World War II provided the immediate antecedents for systems analysis. The successful application of applied mathematics, physical science, and systematic data collection to tactical problems of increasing complexity created the presumption that people trained in these activities could contribute to postwar planning. The Air Force, in 1946, at the urging of Mr. Lovett, Secretary of War for Air (later to become Secretary of Defense) and under the leadership of General H. H. Arnold, created Project RAND, later to become the RAND Corp., to bring together people of the sort who had done wartime operations analysis, to advise the Air Force on its research and development activities.

The nature of the problem facing the Air Force in 1946 was vastly different and more difficult than the wartime operations analysis problems had been. The postwar problem was one of maintaining for an indefinite period, peace-time readiness for combat, rather than conducting ongoing combat operations. After 1946, the problem became one of making decisions that would shape our military forces for many years in the future, subject to the resource constraints encountered in a peacetime economy. This was a far less determinate problem than that of choosing the best search tactics for a destroyer hunting a submarine, or firing tactics for a fighter in pursuit of a bomber.

The indeterminacy of the postwar planning problem was augmented by the postwar technological revolution. In addition to increasing the urgency of national security questions and the cost of providing and maintaining military forces, the flood of new technology so changed the character of prospective conflict that very little past military experience could be considered relevant to the problem of deterring World War III, or of protecting the United States if conflict should come. Under the circumstances, it was necessary to gather such data as might be available from physical science, engineering analysis, and past military operations, and from these, to synthesize by analytic means, predictions, and comparisons that would be useful for policy decisions.

The analysis that developed in response to this need could be no respecter either of organizational boundaries or of the limits of traditional disciplines. The analysis of air defense could not stop within the limits of a fighter squadron, for fighter aircraft became dependent on information provided by a radar network connected by an elaborate communications system. In the choice of bombers, also, the wide range of alternative bomber designs offered by technology made it necessary to take account of the overseas bases or tanker aircraft needed in larger quantities by the shorter range aircraft, and also of the greater vulnerability to enemy attack involved in operating from overseas bases. Also, as the linkages among elements of the problem forced the boundaries of the analysis outward, more and more diverse skills were required in intimate interaction during the course of an analysis.

One important effect of the systems approach is to call into question the narrower, organizationally oriented objectives of many programs. During the 1950s, for example, there was an important reorientation of air defense to take account of the growing importance of protecting the country by deterrence of attack rather than by defeating the attack if it came. Under the conditions of that period, the highest priority tasks of the air defense system became the provision of warning to the strategic bombing forces, permitting them to survive a surprise attack and retaliate. Such reorientations of objectives have generally followed a long series of analyses with steadily widening perspectives. Thus the neat, logical characterization of analysis as beginning with a clarification of objectives is somewhat misleading.

In reality, systems analysts have more often than not begun by accepting current objectives and later proposed changes in them only after repeated analyses of broadening scope have shown objectives to be in conflict with one another. Certainly, the most fruitful systems analyses have not indulged in argument about objectives for argument's sake, but have been forced to review existing objectives and priorities as inconsistencies among them have appeared or because they proved to be inappropriate under changing conditions. The analytical process is an educational process revealing new objectives and often new means of achieving them.

In summary, then, systems analysis was a response to the complexity of the national security planning problems encountered after World War II. It is not a discipline or a technique, but rather a style for dealing with complex problems of choice. The style is characterized by two salient characteristics:

Explicitness. From its origins in the application of scientific method to the analysis of military operations, systems analysis has emphasized explicit treatment of objectives, assumptions of fact, criteria for choice, and above all, the alternatives among which choice is to be made. Explicit statement permits reproducibility of results, and by isolating points of disagreement, permits the policy process to converge to agreement.

Orientation to decision. The scope of the analysis is determined by the scope of the decision. The systems analyst attempts to include all those elements which interact strongly in determining the implications of a choice among the alternatives, regardless of the boundaries of academic disciplines or of bureaucratic organization. Such an approach inevitably calls into question existing objectives from time to time and suggests new policies for inclusion among the set of alternatives. It also calls for consideration of effects that go beyond a 1-year budget period.

THE APPLICABILITY OF SYSTEMS ANALYSIS TO DOMESTIC PROGRAM CHOICES

A Misleading Distinction

Those who question the relevance of the experience in the Department of Defense to the analysis of domestic programs have often done so on the grounds that quantitative analysis is appropriate for programs that are essentially concerned with *things* such as aircraft, missiles, and radar, but that it is not appropriate for programs which deal with *people*.

This distinction is misleading, first of all, because it is not true that domestic programs are concerned entirely with people any more than that national security programs are devoid of such considerations. Deterrence of war, the central concern of national security policy, is a question of how people and governments will react. Analysis has been useful in decision-making about the requirements to maintain deterrence, despite the fact that no one has devised a quantitative, objective measure of deterrence. Similarly, analysis can be useful in allocating resources among programs to combat disease, despite the fact that no way exists to establish a socially accepted dollar value for a human life.

Second, domestic programs are far from devoid of questions involving large, expensive, and long-lived items of equipment for capital. Schools, hospitals, dams, air traffic control radars, and highways are all objects of decision-making about domestic programs.

There are, nevertheless, real and important distinctions between domestic and national security programs from the point of view of analysis. These differences stem largely, I believe, from differences in the basis for the government's role.

The Basis for the Role of Government in Resource Allocation

Economists call national security a "public good." A public good is one that is either consumed in common or not consumed at all. Either nuclear war is deterred for all of us, or it is deterred for none of us. In the case of a private good, like shoes, for example, if I buy a pair of shoes there is one less pair available for use by everyone else. In the case of national security, my enjoyment of the benefits of peace does not detract from that of others. It is therefore impossible to use a private market mechanism to determine the amount of a public good to be provided. Everyone would sit back and wait for everyone else to pay for his security. The decision about the level of spending on national security must, consequently, be made by government.

Examples of public goods may be found also in domestic programs, although national security is probably the purest and most extreme example of a public good. Education provides an example of a good that has both public and private elements. Individuals want education for themselves and for their children to increase the quality of themselves and their earning power. However, there is also a variety of public motives for education. In particular, the requirement that a self-governing electorate achieve certain minimal educational standards, establishes education as at least partly a public good and one about which public decisions are, therefore, required.

In the domestic area, there are several additional government roles in resources allocation decisions. Since 1946, the government has had a statutory responsibility for the maintenance of full employment. More recently, the maintenance of a suitable growth rate without excessive inflation has become a widely recognized responsibility of government. There are, however, numerous more specific roles for government which bear upon the analysis of government programs.

Dealing with Spillover Effects. Spillover effects exist when the consequence of a decision affect not only the individual making the decision, but also others as well, and the decision-maker need not or cannot take into account his effect on others. Spillovers become more important as we live ever closer to our fellow citizens. When John Doe burns leaves with a prevailing wind toward Richard Roe's garden party down the street, a spillover effect exists. The two individuals have conflicting interests if John Doe finds burning leaves preferable to having them removed; but this is not the essence of the problem. Richard Roe may be bothered enough by the smoke to be willing to have the leaves removed, but if there exists no social mechanism which will permit this, the spillover situation is an appropriate subject for governmental action. (In the case of near neighbors there exists a variety of informal mechanisms by which this situation may be resolved; in the more general case, this is not so.)

In the particular example, the government might either subsidize the removal of the leaves until removal is so cheap that John Doe will prefer it to burning, or it might tax their burning. In place of monetary incentives, government often resorts to regulatory action to deal with spillover effect. Each way will induce John Doe to act in a way that takes account of the effect of his actions on others. Less trivial examples than leaf burning are actual environmental pollution, traffic congestion, and such.

The effects that spill over need not always be bad. Examples of beneficial spillovers occur in unpatentable research activities, social welfare programs which not only benefit the individual but reduce the costs to society by making him less of a public charge and less likely to break the law, and so on. Spillover effects it can be seen, are closely related to public goods, and like them, require public action.

Making the Distribution of Income and Opportunity More Equal.   For the last 35 years Government has become more and more concerned to increase the equality of income and especially of opportunity, to limit the risks of old age or ill health, and to compensate for the handicaps of poverty, racial discrimination, or disability. There has been a great variety of programs with these objectives, including direct transfers of income, food subsidy programs, social insurance programs, training programs, programs to provide social services, and more recently, medical insurance and assistance.

Managing Publicly Owned Resources.   As a result of history, political preferences, or economic factors, the government owns a wide variety of resources and provides to the public many different kinds of services. The publicly owned resources range from the electromagnetic frequency spectrum to the highways and federally owned mineral and forest lands. The services provided include such large-scale and diverse activities as the post office, the Federal health service establishments, and the FAA's air traffic control facilities. Government is expected to manage its resources and provide the services it is engaged in in an efficient manner. However, there is very rarely, if ever, a market test of the efficiency of the government's activities, and since the government is very often a monopolist, profit-maximizing behavior would not lead to a socially desirable result.

Large-Scale Risk-Bearing and Innovation.   There are many activities which would be socially desirable but which involve operation on a scale beyond that which is feasible for private enterprise, or that involve risks that are too large for an individual decision-maker to assume but that may be tolerable when spread over society as a whole. Examples that illustrate both the problems of scale and risk are attempts to stem the decay of central cities (urban renewal requires in addition to the scale and risk-spreading available to the government, the exercise of the government's power of eminent domain) and attempts to open major new areas of technology such as nuclear power. These activities must be carefully examined and periodically reviewed to insure that they do not merely provide windfalls for private activities that would be undertaken even without government subsidies.

Increasing the Efficiency of Private Markets.   The government attempts to increase the efficiency of private economic activity in a number of ways, including the strengthening of competition, and the regulation of injurious trade practices. Especially important in this role, however, is the provision of information to labor, businessmen, and consumers, permitting them to behave more efficiently.

Significant Differences Between the Analysis of National Security Programs and Domestic Programs

The principal difference between the application of systems analysis to domestic programs and to national security programs is to be found in the differences between the government's role in these two areas. The overriding objective in national security, as discussed above, is the provision of a public good. Most domestic programs of any significance, however, are involved in more than one of the several government roles discussed above. The multiplicity of government's roles in domestic programs is reflected in a multiplicity of objectives for individual programs, greatly complicating the analysis of the program and the comparison among alternatives.

Consider, as an extreme example, programs for the education for the disadvantaged, such as title I of the Elementary and Secondary Education Act of 1964. Virtually all of the government roles are involved. Like other educational programs, this one is intended to provide the public good of a better educated electorate; it is clearly an attempt to redistribute resources in a way that will equalize the opportunity of the children involved; to the extent that it leads them to become more productive members of the labor force, it will increase the efficiency of private markets; and, to the extent that it results in less dependence on social services and less frequent criminal behavior, reducing the cost of social services and law enforcement, it will realize spillover benefits. Moreover, it is likely that aid furnished to local school districts to improve the education of the disadvantaged partly displaces local resources for that purpose (although such is counter to the intent of the legislation). Therefore, it represents a contribution to a developing role of the Federal Government not discussed above, that of supporting state and local governments with Federal revenues.

Clearly this large program has very complicated objectives. Some of them are joint products, others are in conflict with each other. However, whether they are mutually reinforcing or in conflict, the comparison of an alternative way of improving the status of disadvantaged children with the title I programs, would involve comparisons in many dimensions. Since there is no hope of finding a common unit to measure the public good of a better-educated electorate against the benefits due to redistribution of income or increases in individual productivity, it is highly unlikely that an analysis of alternatives will result in a conclusive preference for one program over another.

This complexity is also encountered in the analysis of national security programs, but to a lesser degree. Although the objectives of national security programs are simpler, there are some respects in which analysis in that area encounters more severe limitations than in the domestic area. Since the predominant objective in national security programs is the provision of a public good, and since a public good cannot be evaluated in the marketplace, it follows that the outputs of national security programs cannot be measured in terms of dollars. Consequently, the Department of Defense has developed cost-effectiveness analysis. Cost is used as a measure of the inputs to the program, but the outputs are measured in physical terms. This means, for example, that one cannot compare the efficiency of resources spent on improving our Strategic Air Command against resources spent on improving our forces for guerrilla war. It also means that analysis must be supplemented by judgment to arrive at the desirable level of spending on national security programs as a whole.

To the extent that government domestic programs are involved in the provision of public goods, or the redistribution of income or opportunity, the same limitations apply. However, many Government programs are predominantly concerned with spillover effects, with the provision of marketable goods or services by the government, or with improvements in the efficiency of private markets. In these cases, analysis can aspire to go beyond cost-effectiveness analysis to measure both costs and at least some benefits in dollars. Even in such cases, however, the analysis is limited by a variety of conceptual problems and data gaps.

The lack of sound theory and data with which to analyze most domestic programs points to another difference between systems analysis in the national security and domestic program areas. For over 20 years, the Department of Defense and the military services have spent large sums of money on systems analysis of national security choices. As a result, there exist substantial analytic organizations within the Department of Defense as well as large independent ones outside. Large numbers of highly trained people from many disciplines have for years been working together on the analysis of national security programs. They have developed the data and analytic models needed to evaluate programs. Prior to 1965 this situation was a very rare exception in most domestic agencies. As a result, the newly developing analytic organizations in the domestic agencies must begin with very little in the way of accumulated knowledge or experience in the program areas concerned.

Finally, and in some way perhaps the most pervasive of the differences between the analysis of national security and domestic programs, is the greater political sensitivity of decisions about domestic programs. Although individuals, special interest groups, and sectional interests do sometimes play a role in national security decisions, that role is circumscribed by the overriding common interest in providing the nation's security. In most domestic programs the question of who benefits is much more important. Analysis can shed light on the distribution of the benefits among the beneficiaries, but the resolution of conflicts among individual interests must be done by the political process. In the leaf-burning example above, analysis may reveal that either a tax on leaf burning or a subsidy to leaf removal would be a more efficient solution than allowing the leaf burning to continue, but analysis will not be able to choose between a subsidy for leaf removal, borne by the community at large, or a tax on leaf burning, which will be borne by the man who has to get rid of the leaves. Thus analysis, properly conceived, complements the political process and cannot replace it.

PROGRAM BUDGETING IN PPB

Program budgeting is, of course, a good deal older than either PPB or systems analysis. Students of budgeting assert that the basic ideas have been in evidence since at least the early part of the 20th century, and the idea received powerful support from the postwar Hoover Commission.

Program budgeting is often described as involving the presentation of budget data in a classification system based on output categories rather than input categories. Sometimes it is described instead as involving categories based on objectives. When the PPB system was introduced, agencies were asked to review their objectives and to devise program categories that were based on the systems of objectives resulting from the review. In particular, to free the so-called program structure from the traditional budget classification schemes, agencies were instructed to disregard traditional classification systems in developing their program structures.

The attempt to construct program structures that cut across organizational lines and existing appropriations accounts is closely related to the tendency of systems analysis to ignore predetermined definitions of a problem and follow instead the boundaries of the decision. Thus it was natural for an alliance to occur between systems analysis and program budgeting. The program budget was to show *all* the costs and outputs relevant to each program decision.

The alliance has, however, resulted in some confusion and excesses in abandoning the older classification systems. To begin, there were some who confused the presentation of costs and outputs in the program budget with the analyses themselves. A program budget does not directly assist in choosing among alternatives, for it shows only the cost of outputs of one specific set of choices. It does not present a comparison among alternative choices, which is the essence of program analysis. The program budget serves instead as a standard reference document displaying the costs and output implication of the approved programs. It also serves as a base for subsequent reviews of the program. Thus the program budget provides the link between the analysis and the budget.

In doing so, however, it imposes significant administrative costs which need to be considered in the design of the program structure. These costs arise because the program structure supplements rather than replaces the older classification systems based on appropriations and organizational lines. So long as the Appropriations Committees of Congress choose to enact the budget into law in terms of the older appropriations structure, it will be necessary for the Executive branch to continue to prepare the budget in those terms. Moreover, apart from the preferences of the Appropriations Committees, so long as there is divergence between organizational structure and the structure imposed by the analysis of program decisions, it will be necessary to have separate classification systems for planning and for program execution. Execution must, of course, be manageable mainly within organizational boundaries or a reorganization is indicated.

For these reasons, it appears that most agencies will have to develop and maintain at least two distinct classification systems for their activities and must sustain the workloads of doing so. This being the case, divergence between the classification systems should be justifiable on the grounds of contribution to program analysis, and should not be undertaken merely in a spirit of innovation.

PLANNING IN THE PPB SYSTEM

An unsophisticated approach to Federal planning would simply attempt to prejudge, in its entirety, the budget for each year of the planning period. Such an approach ignores the uncertainties inherent in planning. It would also raise arguments concerning decisions which need not yet be taken. A more realistic approach to planning treats the projection of programs as having several tiers.

The bottom tier of the planning structure is the projection of the cost and output implications of decisions *already made* or *currently proposed.* A second tier consists of the cost and output implications of those future decisions necessary to achieve *currently approved* goals in *specific* programs, such as the 10-year housing goal adopted by President Johnson. And, finally, it is possible to project the aggregate level of agency budgets by working from the top down, estimating a likely or desirable level of future government expenditure as determined by fiscal policy, and then allocating portions to agencies on the basis of broad priorities. Estimates of the output implications of this tier may not be possible since the program activities will not generally be sufficiently defined.

A multitiered approach is essential to planning in a bureaucratic environment. If upper levels of an organization request plans from subordinate levels without specification of several distinct tiers as indicated above and without imposing future resource constraints, they will get blue-sky estimates. Or, if budget ceilings are imposed, the subordinate levels will often omit some high-priority programs from the plan to bring pressure to bear to restore them and thus to raise the budget.

We might call this response "Portia's ploy" from its resemblance to the way in which Portia protected her client against Shylock in Shakespeare's *Merchant of Venice.* Shylock, it will be recalled, after proving his case at law, was told to take his pound of flesh—but only flesh and no blood and from the victim's heart—and he was threatened with execution if the victim died. The analog, when the Budget Bureau plays Shylock, is that the agency will all too often offer up that program which is closest to the President's heart in response to a request for their priorities within a budget ceiling. This device plays hob with the development of a decentralized planning process.

In addition to problems like Portia's ploy, planning must cope with uncertainties about the general state of budget stringency in future years and about future priorities. Because of these problems, attempts to develop *overall* agency and the government budget *totals* for a period as long as 5 years are more valuable for the stimulation derived from the process of developing them than for their reliability as a guide to future activities. Consequently, a planning process that deals only with the total of the three tiers discussed above is likely to intensify bureaucratic bargaining unnecessarily and embarrass an administration that must defend future budget totals with little basis in analysis or fact.

A multitiered approach, on the other hand, offers several useful contributions. The projection of commitments resulting from past or currently contemplated decisions is essential to preserve the future flexibility of the President and to avoid the problem of starting a number of programs which later will not only absorb the resources that might be wanted for future new program starts, but which themselves may be underfunded as a result of failure to take account of the future growth in the resource demands implied by current program decisions. In some cases, the future growth is obvious but is nevertheless not systematically taken into account without a formal planning process. "Commitments" in the sense intended here is a broader term than contractual or statutory commitments. It also embraces commitments that arise as a logical consequence of program decisions. When we buy a hospital or a truck there is no legal commitment to operate it over a period of years, but there is a clear, logical implication that we will do so. In fact, for the Government to walk away from a newly built hospital would be a very embarrassing act. Commitment projections offer a way to take such implications into account.

In other cases, the implied commitment may be less obvious but is, nonetheless, real. For example, if the Federal Aviation Agency were to request funding for a new ground control radar system at one or two heavy traffic airports on a demonstration basis, it would be difficult to withhold subsequent installation at other airports with equally heavy traffic. The commitment to install systems at other similar airports implied by the decision to install the first one or two should be considered in deciding whether to proceed at all. The projection is also necessary to test whether the aggregate of currently contemplated decisions will exceed any likely or desirable level of commitment of future resources.

The second tier of projection, comprising the costs and outputs necessary to reach selected future goals, permits the President to espouse high-priority goals, gain public support for them, and provide guidance to the bureaucracy to achieve them in an orderly fashion. Such commitments to major future goals should require the approval of the President to avoid the tendency for each agency to rush in with its high-priority programs with the likelihood of overcommitment of resources.

Finally, if the first two tiers of projection are clearly identified, agencies may usefully be requested to propose an overall plan for the expenditure of likely levels of total budget resources to permit them to display their priorities to the President and the Budget Bureau. In my view, however, the political and administrative costs of attempting to arrive at an approved set of govern-ment-wide agency budgets for a 5-year period is not worth the cost.

PROBLEMS ENCOUNTERED IN THE INTRODUCTION OF PPB TO DOMESTIC AGENCIES

This section will recapitulate some of the problems mentioned in the dis-cussion above, and also introduce some new ones. The problems are largely related to the differences between PPB in the domestic and the national security areas already discussed. They fall into three main groups:

The lack of trained and experienced people, conceptual frameworks, and data.
Bureaucratic problems.
Problems arising from conflict of individual interest among the public.

The first of these has been adequately discussed above. The other two are taken up in turn.

Problems Arising out of the Operation of a Bureaucracy

Perhaps the root problem besetting the operation of the PPB system during its first 3 years of operation has been the inability, except in a relatively small number of cases, to state issues for decision in terms of a range of rele-vant alternatives. Most often, issues will be stated in terms of acceptance or rejection of a specific program proposal. When alternatives are stated they are very often a mere mechanical compliance with the requirement to do so imposed by the Budget Bureau.

An almost classical style for the statement of alternatives has evolved. The alternatives most often will be stated in terms of three possible levels of funding for a given program—zero, quadrupling of the current program level, and a 10% increase. It is not terribly difficult to guess which alternatives the agency wants chosen. Issues involving a reorientation of the objectives of the program, or the mix of the programs intended to serve a given purpose are much less frequently encountered.

The absence of realistic, relevant alternatives is related to both the dearth of experienced analysts outside the government and to the way in which a hierarchical bureaucracy like that of the executive branch normally tends to operate. Each level wants to receive alternatives from those below—and to pass only the preferred course of action to those above. To rely on a bureau-cracy to generate alternatives is to encounter a dilemma.

Most of the operational experience necessary to suggest a practical new approach to the problem is to be found at relatively low levels in the line organizations of the agencies. On the other hand, people at that level may lack the breadth of view as well as the incentives to suggest changes. As one moves toward the peak of the hierarchy, in the White House and the Budget Bureau, the breadth of view increases, and certainly the general level of ability is high, but the familiarity with operational details is missing. Even though the people involved at those levels may have had substantial experience in one or another part of the government, their experience is too selective and their exposure not recent enough to afford the kind of familiarity that generates approaches that are both new and practical.

Moreover, the conflict of interest between higher and lower levels of the government, and the resulting bargaining situation, has affected the overall development of PPB. The decision to introduce PPB comprehensively, to all of the major domestic agencies at once, made inevitable the assumption of a major role by the Bureau of the Budget. There were both advantages and disadvantages of this decision and it is not my purpose now to evaluate it in retrospect.

The resulting identification of PPB as a system, of, by, and for the Bureau of the Budget has, however, been a substantial disadvantage in the development of PPB. If, instead, the system had developed in a way that led agency and department heads to identify themselves with the system more, I believe that some of the bureaucratic problems would have been alleviated. It is true, of course, that bargaining occurs not only between departments and the Budget Bureau, but also between the office of the secretary of a department and his bureau chiefs. Nevertheless, the responsibility of a department head is more direct than that of the Budget Bureau and it is possible for him and his staff to provide more continuous, better informed, and more forceful guidance for the activities of his agency.

Bureaucratic bargaining also manifests itself in attempts to make agencies establish priorities. The usual response to a request for a ranking of activities by priority is that all agency activities are vital to the welfare of the country and would not be otherwise undertaken. If a more operational approach is taken, and the agency is given a budget planning figure within which it must make allocation decisions, the response described above as Portia's ploy is often the result.

Finally, bargaining within the Government is not restricted to internal jockeying in the Executive. Relations between the Executive and the Congress are, of course, also a mixture of cooperative and adversary proceedings. Moreover, whereas the Executive is organized, at least roughly, in a hierarchical way, the Congress represents a much more complex set of arrangements of diverse interests and responsibilities.

The problems that have arisen between the Congress and the Executive in the development of PPB are correspondingly diverse. They are characterized under three headings: lack of PPB output, lack of congressional access to the existing PPB output, and lack of interest (or actual antipathy) in some quarters of Congress to the things that PPB is striving to do.

Of the outputs of PPB, the Congress probably is and should be most concerned with the alternatives and the comparisons among them that PPB is to generate. Because of separation from the operations of government agencies (even more so than in the case of the White House and the Bureau of the Budget), and because of staff limitations relative to the executive branch, the Congress will probably continue to be dependent upon the information and analyses generated by the Executive. The presentation of decisions in terms of choices among relevant alternatives, together with analyses comparing the alternatives and presenting the basis for the choice proposed by the Executive, should permit the Congress and its staff to ask more relevant questions, and should provide the data base to make it possible for even a small staff to test the sensitivity of the conclusions reached by the Executive to changes in key assumptions. Thus when PPB has overcome the problems of generating alternatives and of making systematic comparisons among them, it should offer output of high value to the Congress.

There is, however, a further problem, the problem of congressional access. With the exception of data concerning the current budget year, the executive branch has preferred not to release PPB material for either congressional or public examination. The reluctance of large organizations to make explicit the basis for their choices would result in sterilization of PPB material if it were all to be released routinely for scrutiny outside the Executive. As it is, the discussion above indicates that it is very difficult to get a high degree of candor even within the executive family.

An answer to this problem may be found in distinguishing the degree of sensitivity of the different kinds of PPB materials. The most sensitive documents of all are the program memorandums which are intended to present, for review by the White House and the Budget Bureau, the choices recommended by the heads of the agencies and departments, together with the basis for those recommendations. Less sensitive are the analytic comparisons among alternatives which often are far short of conclusive with regard to policy choices. Because of the limitations of quantitative analysis, especially in regard to the treatment of conflicts among individual interests, the results of the analytic comparisons will require a considerable mixture of judgment and advocacy before a decision will emerge. However, it is precisely in regard to the quantitative analysis that the Congress needs most to rely upon the Executive. A possible solution, therefore, would be to continue to treat the program memorandums as documents privileged to the Executive, to but make the analytic studies available for public use.

Planning data for future years beyond the budget year has also been a sensitive item of PPB output. So long as the 5-year plan was comprehensive and appeared to commit the Executive to decisions which the President had not yet either considered or resolved, the data on costs, outputs, and budget totals for the future years was also considered highly sensitive. If, however, the kind of multitiered planning discussed above is developed and applied, there should be much less sensitivity about making public the commitments implied by decisions already taken by the executive. Moreover, in the case of selected future program goals, the President will have positive reasons for wanting to make them public to mobilize public understanding and support.

Conflicts among Individual Interests

Apart from, but related to, the bargaining among the various elements of the government, is the bargaining that goes on to resolve conflicts among the interests of the public. In the example discussed above, it is quite likely that John Doe, the leaf burner, would attempt to resist by political means, any attempt to impose a tax on leaf burning. Richard Roe, on the other hand, the unwilling inhaler of John Doe's smoke, would probably resist an increase in taxes to subsidize the collection of leaves. As indicated above, analysis cannot say whether it is preferable to deal with the spillover effect by a tax or a subsidy. It can, however, say that either would be preferable to a situation in which John Doe goes on burning leaves, and Richard Roe goes on inhaling the smoke. All too often, an impasse is reached because John Doe merely sees the impending tax on leaf burning and Richard Roe sees the tax to support a subsidy on leaf removal and neither is clearly aware of the implication of one course or the other or of the possibility of some compromise that might be acceptable to both.

Analysis cannot be expected to replace the political horse-trading by which many conflicts are resolved in our society. Rather, it has great potential for making that horse-trading a more effective process by clarifying the implications of alternative choices or by generating new and more effective alternatives, and where there is an over-riding common interest, by helping to clarify and present the case for that interest.

Another limitation of analysis is its inability to establish, without the aid of the political process, desirable priorities among such broad aggregates as health, education, economic development, conservation, and national security. To make analytic comparisons among alternative patterns of resource-allocation, it is necessary that costs and outputs of the various activities be comparable. Obviously, there is no unit of measure that will establish the relative benefits of education against those of health or national security. No computer, therefore, will ever produce an allocation of resources among these activities that has any claim to optimality, let alone compelling appeal to the electorate. Choices at this high level of aggregation must be developed on the basis of public preferences that largely find their expression in the political process.

Nevertheless, analysis does have an important role to play in the making of such decisions. All too often, at present, the choice between spending an additional billion dollars on urban transportation as opposed to, say, the education of disadvantaged children, is a choice between putting resources into one black box as opposed to another. For public preferences to find intelligent expression, it is necessary that the public know something about the benefits to be gained from an increment of expenditure on urban transportation and an increment to education. The comparison will still have to be made in the minds of individual citizens and elected officials, but the factual basis for making such a comparison can be greatly improved.

SOME DIRECTIONS FOR THE IMPROVEMENT OF PPB

Greater Involvement by Department and Agency Heads

The interest and attention of the head of each department or agency or of his deputy are crucial to the success of PPB. The prototype of PPB was created by Secretary McNamara who considered the job of managing the resources of the Defense Department as among his prime responsibilities. Other cases where PPB has taken hold almost all show some similar pattern of interest on the part of the agency head or his immediate deputy. Although the President expects his cabinet officers and their immediate subordinates to assist him in many capacities, he must accord high priority to the role of resource manager if Government resources are to be used more efficiently. The Bureau of the Budget will continue to have an important role to play in monitoring the development of PPB, but steps should be taken to make PPB responsible to the needs of department and agency heads, and to encourage initiatives on their part in developing the system further. Increasing the ability of the Budget Bureau to do independent analysis can help to stimulate the departments and agencies to improve their own analyses.

More and Better Analysis and Data

If we are to improve our understanding of the program choices open to us, it will be necessary to devote much larger resources on a long-term, continuing basis to efforts to improve our conceptual understanding and to increase and improve the data available. Some significant steps in this direction have already been taken.

In particular, a start has been made on the systematic evaluation of the performance of programs already in existence. In several recent pieces of legislation, the statute contains authorization and direction to the secretary of the agency involved to spend up to 1% of the authorized funds on evaluation of the program, either in his own office, in the field organization of the Federal department, or (in the case of grant-in-aid programs) at the state and local level. Such provisions should be contained in more legislation, perhaps in all new authorizing legislation, and other methods should be sought to indicate the intent of the Congress to encourage and support program evaluation.

Improvement is also needed in our ability to evaluate new programs that have no existing counterparts. An example of an attempt to do this is the OEO experiment to determine the effects of a negative income tax on such aspects of behavior as labor force participation and consumption patterns. Imaginative, controlled experiments of this sort are essential to improving our ability to design new programs. However, it is also essential that both the Executive and Congress require more systematic presentation of the implications of proposed new legislation and comparisons with alternative ways to accomplish the desired ends.

Most of all, it is necessary to assemble groups of people who are technically trained in analysis and who have an understanding of the substantive areas which they are to analyze. Because of the twin problems of institutional blinders on those currently involved in operations, and lack of relevant experience on the part of outsiders, a pattern of rotation from analytic positions to operating positions should be developed. Such rotation between program analysis and program operation could occur within the government between an agency line organization and the office of the secretary, between line organizations and an expanded program evaluation staff either in the Budget Bureau or elsewhere in the Executive Office of the President, or between government line organizations and private independent research organizations of the sort that have proven useful in the national security area. A start has been made in increasing outside expertise, but much more needs to be done, and the domestic agencies must develop patterns of long-term continuing funding of research like those in the Defense Department. To the extent that the problems encountered are interagency problems, it will be especially necessary to develop groups of analysts either in the Executive Office of the President or outside the government.

To help meet the requirements for trained people, the government should encourage universities, through graduate fellowships, to develop curricula that combine analytic training and substantive courses in the applied fields of health services, urban transportation, the evaluation of education, and so on.

Increased Accessibility to PPB Material

Although the program memorandums should continue to be privileged documents if they are to be useful at all, analytic studies displaying alternative programs and comparing their costs and benefits should routinely be made available to the Congress and to the public. Such analyses need not and should not attempt to be conclusive and reach definite program recommendations. That can be left to the program memorandums in the executive branch and to the legislative process in Congress. The analyses should, however, provide a common basis in fact for making program choices. In addition, as the Executive develops the projection of the commitments implied by decisions that have been made, it should make these projections available, together with the projection of selected programs to realize future goals approved by the President.

The Further Development of Program Budgeting

Since the maintenance and development of program budgets will be super-imposed on the requirement to maintain budgets along traditional lines in many cases, the existing program structures should be reviewed to determine whether the added workload is justified by their contribution to the under-standing of the agency's program activities. The criterion by which the program structure should be judged should correspond to the lines of definition of the analyses required to assist in making program choices. Other things being equal, ease of translation between program structure and appropriation structure or organizational structure should be considered in reviewing the program structure. Wherever possible, of course, a single, integrated classification system should be devised and proposed for acceptance by the Executive and the Congress.

As yet, little has been done to establish a government-wide program structure. In the many areas where departmental responsibilities overlap, the development of departmental program structures that are consistent with one another and that will correspond to the program decisions is necessary to improve our understanding of resource allocation and to provide a common starting point for analyzing subsequent program decisions. A substantial interagency effort, led by the Bureau of the Budget, should be undertaken to develop a Government-wide program structure and consistent definitions of costs and outputs in areas where agency programs overlap.

Improving the PPB Process

One of the purposes of PPB is to permit program evaluation to go on continuously during the year rather than under the crisis atmosphere of fall budget review. The schedule for development of PPB material and its submission to the Budget Bureau has been extremely late in each of the three PPB cycles so far completed. In part, this has been the result of changes in the process from year to year, but more fundamentally, it has stemmed from lack of interest on the part of the department heads and unwillingness to commit themselves to decisions in the spring. Greater interest on the part of the Secretary will help to alleviate this situation, but it is also necessary to distinguish the analysis preparatory to decision-making from the decision itself. The spring review should concentrate on reaching an understanding of the costs and benefits of the alternatives. Formal choices among them by high-level officials should be separated from this process in order to avoid delaying the analytic process. Such choices can be made in the fall if their implications are understood as a result of the spring review.

III   Optimal Resource Allocation, Markets, and Public Policy: An Introduction: Robert C. Lind

INTRODUCTION

The allocation of resources is central to the operation and planning of any economic system. The question of resource allocation arises because, given the existing resources and technology, it is not possible to satisfy all human wants. Therefore, choices have to be made as to what will be produced and to whom it will be distributed. The interest in resource allocation arises from the desire to make these production and distribution decisions so as to maximize, in some sense, the fulfillment of human wants. Therefore, resource allocation is a problem of constrained maximization where the objective is to maximize the fulfillment of human wants, and the constraints are the state of technology and the stocks of available resources.

The first task is to select a criterion by which one allocation can be judged as better than another. In principle, every individual could rank all possible allocations according to his own preferences; however, there would be wide differences among the rankings. More specifically, individuals would almost certainly prefer the allocations that favored them. To obtain a social ranking of alternative allocations, value judgments have to be introduced.

One value judgment which commands wide acceptance is that the social ranking should be based on individual rankings. A related value judgment is that one allocation is better than another if, given this allocation, every individual is at least as well off and some individual is better off than he would have been, given the other allocation. This proposition leads to the concept of Pareto optimality. An allocation is said to be Pareto optimal if there is no other feasible allocation which would make at least one person better off without making someone else worse off.

The concept of Pareto optimality plays a central role in the literature on economic efficiency and optimal resource allocation. One reason for its importance is that the proposition on which it is based commands wide acceptance. However, this concept generally does not determine a unique optimum. Additional value judgments are required to select the best allocation from among the set of Pareto-optimal allocations. These value judgments relate to the distribution of income. A second reason for the importance of Pareto optimality is that, although the concept does not define a unique optimum, the overall optimum will be Pareto optimal. Pareto optimality is therefore a necessary but not sufficient condition for optimal resource allocation.

The theory of optimal resource allocation and the theory of competitive equilibrium are closely related. Specifically, given the requisite conditions for an equilibrium in a perfectly competitive economy, the resulting allocation will be Pareto optimal. However, the theory of optimal resource allocation is in no way dependent upon perfect competition. The theory is developed without reference to any specific institution for allocating resources. The necessary conditions for optimality apply to socialist economies as well as to capitalist economies.

In this chapter the basic conditions for Pareto optimal resource allocation are presented without reference to institutional arrangements for production and distribution. It is then demonstrated that under certain conditions a competitive equilibrium will correspond to a Pareto optimal allocation. In the course of the discussion it will become apparent that the competitive allocation will be one of many allocations which satisfy the conditions for Pareto optimality. To choose among these allocations, value judgments are formally introduced into the analysis by means of a social welfare function. The theoretical and practical difficulties of using a social welfare function to compare allocations are discussed briefly.

The analysis of efficiency is based on an exceedingly simple model economy predicated on certain simplifying assumptions. These assumptions are analyzed and the importance of each assumption is indicated. The model presented does not account for time or uncertainty; however, extensions of the model are outlined which do incorporate these considerations. Also, problems caused by inequalities in wealth and opportunity are discussed.

In addition it is demonstrated that if economies of scale and externalities are present, competitive markets fail to effect a Pareto optimal allocation of resources. In both cases some form of government intervention is required to bring about a Pareto optimal allocation of resources. It will also be shown that markets will fail to bring about a Paretooptimal allocation when there are monopoly elements in the economy.

The presentation of the theory of optimal resource allocation is traditional in that production and utility functions are defined and a diagrammatic device, the Edgeworth-Bowley box diagram, is used to demonstrate the basic conditions for optimal resource allocation. The advantage of this approach is that it requires only the basic mathematical tool of calculus, and it is consistent with the presentation in most standard economic texts (Bator, 1957;

Henderson and Quandt, 1958; Little, 1950). Therefore, the background of most readers will be sufficient for this presentation. It should be pointed out, however, that an alternative formulation in terms of set theory is in some ways more elegant and more powerful than the one presented. The disadvantage of this alternative is that it requires the use of mathematical concepts which are unfamiliar to a large segment of this audience. For an excellent geometric presentation of this second formulation see Koopmans (1957), and Quirk and Saposnik (1968). For a complete statement and rigorous proof of the basic theorems see Debreu (1959). The presentation is divided into three major sections. The first considers the optimal conditions for productive efficiency; the second, the optimal conditions for distribution of the production. The third considers selection of the commodities to be produced.

OPTIMAL RESOURCE ALLOCATION

Production

To demonstrate the basic ideas of optimal resource allocation consider a hypothetical economy containing two individuals, denoted by A and B, two factors of production, capital and labor, K and L, and two goods for final consumption, X and Y. In addition, suppose that the total amount of capital and labor available is fixed at $\bar{K}$ and $\bar{L}$, respectively, and that these factors are used exclusively to produce consumption goods X and Y. Furthermore, suppose that the amounts of K, L, X, and Y can be varied continuously, that is, they are perfectly divisible.

Now consider the production of the good X. Given any combination of inputs (K, L) applied to the production of X and given the existing technology, there is some maximum amount of X which can be produced. Therefore, we can define a production function for X, f_x, on the space of ordered pairs (K, L), where $f_x(K, L)$ is the maximum amount of X which can be produced with inputs K and L, given the technical possibilities for production. Note that the definition of the production function specifies that the chosen technique of production will be that one which maximizes the output of a commodity given fixed inputs. Upon reflection the reader should see that this condition is necessary for optimal resource allocation if individuals prefer more of a commodity to less of it. It should also be noted that f_x is defined only where K and L are positive because negative inputs of capital and labor do not make sense in this context. In addition we assume that f_x has continuous second derivatives with respect to both K and L. This assumption permits the use of the standard tools of calculus without seriously limiting the validity of the results. If we select a particular value of X, say $\bar{X}$, then we can implicitly define a locus of points in the input space by the equation $f_x(K, L) = \bar{X}$. This locus of points is called an isoquant or equal output curve. For every value of X we can plot such an isoquant in the input space thereby forming a family of isoquants. Such a family is illustrated in Figure 1. Successively higher isoquants are associated with the production of larger amounts of X.

The shape of the isoquants is of particular importance for the analysis of optimal resource allocation and the theory of competitive markets. If we assume that by increasing either factor of production independently it is possible to increase output, then it follows that each isoquant will be negatively sloped. Furthermore, it is assumed that isoquants are convex to the origin as shown in Figure 1. This assumption has been the subject of much discussion among economists. The basic rationale for the assumption is that the marginal rate at which unit increments in one factor can be substituted for decrements in another, while maintaining the same output, diminishes as the amount of first factor employed increases. More formally, the marginal rate of substitution which is defined to be the absolute value of the slope of the isoquant is assumed to be diminishing. This concept of a diminishing marginal rate of substitution between two factors of production can be illustrated with a simple example. Suppose we consider an earthmoving operation which can be carried out by employing labor and capital in the form of machines. If we were to undertake the job without using any capital, it would require a great deal of labor. Now consider the amount of labor which could be replaced by one machine such that the same output was maintained. The contention is that the first machine can be substituted for

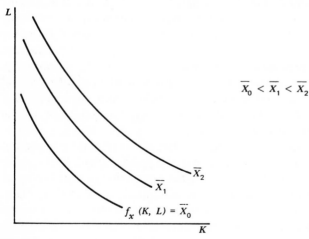

$\bar{X}_0 < \bar{X}_1 < \bar{X}_2$

$\bar{X}_2$

$\bar{X}_1$

$f_x (K, L) = \bar{X}_0$

Fig. 1

more labor than can the second machine, the second for more than the third, and so on. Given a large number of machines and very little labor it may be virtually impossible to substitute additional machines for labor while maintaining the same output. Whether a production function is such that there is a diminishing marginal rate of substitution between factors of production depends on the particulars of the specific situation; however, if this condition is not satisfied, competitive markets may fail to allocate resources efficiently. This point is developed subsequently.

To summarize, it will be assumed that there are two production functions f_x and f_y for X and Y, respectively, which are defined on ordered pairs $(K, L) \geq 0$. In addition

$$\frac{\partial f_x}{\partial K}, \quad \frac{\partial f_x}{\partial L}, \quad \frac{\partial f_y}{\partial K}, \quad \text{and} \quad \frac{\partial f_y}{\partial L}$$

are positive, and for any positive outputs $\bar{X}$ and $\bar{Y}$ the loci defined by $f_x(K, L) = \bar{X}$ and $f_y(K, L) = \bar{Y}$ are convex to origin. Furthermore, given an isoquant defined by $f_x(K, L) = \bar{X}$, the marginal rate of substitution (MRS) between factors at a point is defined by

$$\text{MRS} = \left| \frac{dL}{dK} \right| = \frac{\partial f_x / \partial K}{\partial f_x / \partial L}$$

An analogous definition applies to f_y.

Given these concepts and given the simplifying assumption of two outputs and two factor inputs available in fixed supply, it is possible to demonstrate diagramatically the conditions for productive efficiency by use of an Edgeworth-Bowley box diagram.

In Figure 2 the horizontal edge of the rectangle is of length $\bar{K}$ and represents the total supply of capital available for the production of goods X and Y; the vertical edge is of length $\bar{L}$ and represents the total supply of labor. From the lower left-hand corner of the box are measured the amounts of capital and labor allocated to the production of X, denoted by K_x and L_x, respectively. Similarly, from the upper right-hand corner are measured amounts of capital and labor allocated to the production of Y. Therefore, each point in the box represents an allocation of the total supply of capital and labor to the production of X and the production of Y.

Furthermore, since every point in the box diagram represents an allocation of K and L between the production of X and of Y, isoquants of X and Y can be drawn onto the diagram. The origin for the production of X is the lower left-hand corner of the box and isoquants of X are convex to this origin. Movements upward to the right are associated with ascending levels of the output of X, for example, $\bar{X}^1$, $\bar{X}^2$, $\bar{X}^3$ represent ascending levels of production of X. Similarly, the upper right-hand corner of the box is the origin for Y;

isoquants of Y are convex to this origin. The $\overline{Y}^1$, $\overline{Y}^2$, $\overline{Y}^3$ and so on represent ascending levels of the production of Y. Therefore, each point in the box corresponds to a level of production of X and Y; the levels can be determined by looking at the isoquants for X and Y which pass through that point. For example, point R in Figure 2 is associated with outputs of goods X and Y of $\overline{X}^5$ and $\overline{Y}^1$.

Pareto optimality requires the factors of production to be allocated to the production of X and Y in such a way that it is not possible to increase the output of both X and Y by simply reallocating factor inputs. An allocation is said to be productively efficient if there exists no other allocation which produces at least as much of all outputs and more of one output. Clearly, if consumers prefer more rather than less of a commodity, productive efficiency is a necessary condition for Pareto optimality.

Consider again point R in Figure 2. This point does not represent an efficient allocation of the factors of production because more of both X and Y can be produced by any allocation represented by points lying within the shaded area below R. That is, the isoquants of X and Y which pass through any point of the shaded area represent larger amounts of output than do the isoquants passing through R. Furthermore, upon reflection it is clear that the only efficient points in the box are those points at which an isoquant for X is tangent to an isoquant for Y. Point S in Figure 2 represents such a point. A move in any direction from point S will be associated with a decrease in the production of X, Y, or both X and Y. Therefore, the condition for productive efficiency is that the marginal rate of substitution between any two factors of

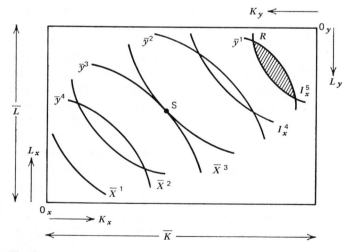

Fig. 2

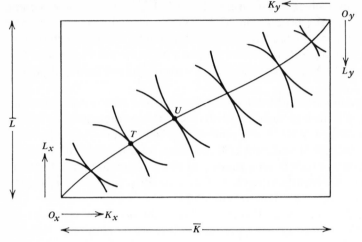

Fig. 3

production is the same in all productive processes which use positive quantities of both factors.* Intuitively one can see that if the factors of production can be substituted at different rates in the two industries, then an opportunity exists for trading factors between the industries so as to increase the production of one good without decreasing the production of the other. Therefore, the efficient points are points of tangency between the isoquants for X and Y. The locus of such points is represented in Figure 3.

From the information contained in Figure 3, it is a simple task to develop the production possibility frontier. Each point on the locus $0_x 0_y$ corresponds to a point in the output space of ordered pairs (X, Y). For example, corresponding to the point T is an output of X and an output of Y. Similarly, the point U corresponds to another pair of outputs, and we know that the output of X associated with U will be greater than that associated with T. The converse is true for Y. Therefore, if we begin at 0_x and proceed to 0_y we can develop a corresponding locus of points in the output space. This production possibility frontier is shown in Figure 4. Point $0'_x$ corresponds to 0_x and point $0'_y$ corresponds to 0_y. Because the points on $0'_x 0'_y$ correspond to efficient allocations of factor inputs this curve must have a negative slope. Otherwise, it would be possible to increase the production of both X and Y and one of

* It is possible for an allocation to be efficient even though the marginal rates of substitution of K for L are not the same in the production of X as in the production of Y if this inequality occurs at an allocation on the boundary of the box where one factor is not used in the production of X or Y. Such an allocation does not violate the condition above since the production of either X or Y does not use positive quantities of both K and L.

the points on $0'_x0'_y$ would not correspond to a point on 0_x0_y. The shaded area inside $0'_x0'_y$ represents the set of feasible outputs; however, optimal resource allocation requires that we produce somewhere on the production possibility frontier. This requirement follows from the assumption, which subsequently will be discussed, that people prefer to have more of goods X and Y rather than less.

The absolute value of the slope of $0'_x0'_y$ represents the marginal rate at which X can be transformed into good Y by optimally reallocating factors from the production of X to the production of Y. The absolute value of the slope of $0'_x0'_y$ at a point (X, Y) is commonly referred to as the marginal rate of transformation of X into Y. In addition to having a negative slope the production possibility frontier has been drawn in Figure 4 so that

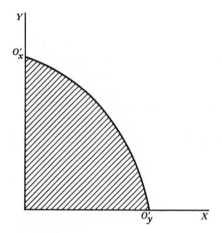

Fig. 4

it is concave to the origin. The concavity means that the marginal rate of transformation of X into Y is increasing as the production of X increases.

This condition can be summarized mathematically. Suppose the locus $0'_x0'_y$ were defined implicitly by the function $Q(X, Y) = C$ where C is a constant or by $Y = q(X)$. Then the marginal rate of transformation is

$$\text{MRT} = \left| \frac{dY}{dX} \right| = -q'(x) = \frac{\partial Q/\partial X}{\partial Q/\partial Y}$$

It is assumed that the marginal rate of transformation is an increasing function of X.

If different factors are differently suited to the production of different goods then it is reasonable to argue that the marginal rate of transformation between two goods is increasing. This can be explained intuitively in terms of an example.

Suppose there are two goods, wheat and rice, and that the wheat requires a dry climate and one type of land, and rice requires a wet climate and a second type of land. Furthermore, assume that all labor used in the production of both wheat and rice has the same characteristics, and that all land and labor were used in the production of wheat. Now consider the optimal reallocation of land and labor to produce one unit of rice. Obviously, the land which is best suited to rice production would be withdrawn from wheat production. Since this land was not well suited to wheat production a large increase in rice production could be obtained at the cost of a small decrease in the output of wheat. As more land is reallocated from the production of wheat to the production of rice each additional unit will produce a smaller increment of rice while it will cause a greater decrement in wheat production. Therefore, the amount of wheat which must be foregone to produce an additional unit of rice increases with increases in rice production.

If different factors were not better suited to the production of some goods than to others we might have obtained the opposite result. For example, if the factors of production were equally well suited to the production of both X and Y and if there were economies of scale in the production of both goods, the production possibility frontier would be convex to the origin as illustrated in Figure 5. This case is discussed later in the chapter as it creates problems for the efficient operation of competitive markets.

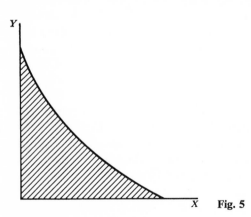

Fig. 5

Distribution

At this point we have considered the problem of allocating factors of production. The total allocation problem involves two additional questions:

first, what bundle of goods should be produced; and second, how should this bundle be distributed between the two consumers. Equivalently, we must consider what point on the production possibility frontier should be selected and how the goods should be distributed between individual A and individual B.

We proceed by assuming that the first choice has been made and discuss the optimal distribution of a fixed bundle of goods. Before we can proceed with the analysis we must introduce the notion of a preference ordering and the concept of a utility function. We assume that each individual is concerned only with the goods he receives. We further assume that his preferences are such that for any two commodity bundles (X^1, Y^1) and (X^2, Y^2) either (X^1, Y^1) is preferred to (X^2, Y^2), (X^2, Y^2) is preferred to (X^1, Y^1), or he is indifferent between (X^1, Y^1) and (X^2, Y^2).

These three alternatives are mutually exclusive and collectively exhaustive. In addition, the individual's preferences are assumed to be transitive. Transitivity means that if (X^1, Y^1) is preferred to (X^2, Y^2) and (X^2, Y^2) is preferred to (X^3, Y^3), then (X^1, Y^1) is preferred to (X^3, Y^3). In addition if $X^1 \geq X^2$ and $Y^1 \geq Y^2$ and if the strict inequality holds for either case, then (X^1, Y^1) is assumed to be preferred to (X^2, Y^2) on the grounds that people prefer to consume more goods to less. A complete discussion of the logical properties of preference orderings is beyond the scope of this chapter; however, for the interested reader a concise and readable treatment of this subject is presented in Quirk and Saposnik (1968).

Given certain conditions the preference ordering of an individual can be represented by a utility function. A function U_A defined on ordered pairs of commodities is a utility function for individual A if for (X^1, Y^1) preferred to (X^2, Y^2), $U_A(X^1, Y^1) > U_A(X^2, Y^2)$ and for (X^1, Y^1) indifferent to (X^2, Y^2), $U_A(X^1, Y^1) = U_A(X^2, Y^2)$. Clearly, U_A is an increasing function of X and Y. However, the utility function is not uniquely determined. If $h(\cdot)$ is any strictly increasing function of a real variable, then the function V_A also satisfies the conditions for a utility function for individual A where $V_A(X, Y) = h[U_A(X, Y)]$. Therefore, it is clear that only the ordinal properties of a utility function are central to the analysis. If $U_A(X^1, Y^1) > U_A(X^2, Y^2)$, this means that (X^1, Y^1) is preferred to (X^2, Y^2) by individual A; however, no other significance can be attached to the difference $U_A(X^1, Y^1) - U_A(X^2, Y^2)$. This difference is not invariant under all strictly increasing transformations of U_A.

Suppose we have a utility function U_A for individual A. Then the relationship $U_A(X, Y) = C$, where C is a constant, implicitly defines a locus of points among which individual A is indifferent. This locus is called an indifference curve. A family of indifference curves for individual A is presented in Figure 6. Points on higher indifference curves are preferred to points on lower curves by individual A. From the assumption of transitivity and the

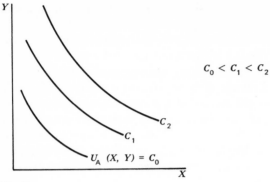

$C_0 < C_1 < C_2$

Fig. 6

assumption that individuals prefer more goods rather than less, it follows that indifference curves must be downward sloping from left to right. It also follows that no two indifference curves can cross each other. Furthermore, it follows that indifference curves are invariant to any strictly increasing transformation of the utility function. Again let $U_A(X, Y)$ be a utility function. Let $V_A(X, Y) = h[U_A(X, Y)]$ be a second utility function where $h(\cdot)$ is a strictly increasing function of a real variable. Let $U_A(X, Y) = C$ define an indifference curve under the first utility function. Then for all (X, Y) on this indifference curve, $V_A(X, Y) = h[U_A(X, Y)] = h[C]$, another constant. Therefore, the indifference curves under the first utility function are identical to the indifference curves under the second utility function.

In addition, the indifference curves in Figure 6 have been drawn convex to the origin. This requirement means that the marginal rate at which increments of Y can be substituted for decrements of X so that utility is kept constant decreases as the consumption of X increases. In other words if an individual has an initial endowment of food and clothing he is willing to trade less food for additional clothing as his clothing supply is increased by trading food for clothing. The absolute value of the slope of the indifference curve for individual A is the marginal rate at which he is willing to substitute Y for X given some initial endowment (X, Y). It is generally assumed that this marginal rate of substitution is decreasing as X increases so that indifference curves are convex to the origin as in Figure 6. In addition we assume, for convenience, that the utility function has continuous second-order derivatives.

To summarize, each consumer is assumed to have a preference ordering for commodity bundles (X, Y), and these preference orderings can be expressed in terms of utility functions U_A and U_B. Furthermore, individual utility is assumed to be a function only of the goods allocated to that individual. The indifference curves for each individual are assumed to be

convex to the origin as pictured in Figure 6. Finally, only the ordinal properties of the utility function are significant.

We can now address the problem of how to distribute efficiently a fixed
bundle of goods between individual A and individual B. In Figure 7 we have
drawn the production possibility curve $0'_x 0'_y$, have selected a point, β, on this
curve, and have denoted the total output at this point by (X_β, Y_β). To demonstrate the conditions for optimal distribution of the fixed output (X_β, Y_β),
we have drawn an Edgeworth-Bowley box diagram in Figure 7. The horizon-

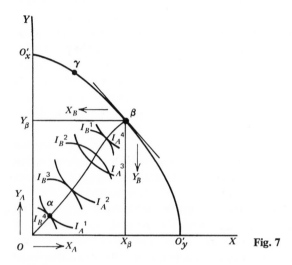

Fig. 7

tal edge of the box is of length X_β; the vertical edge, Y_β. The amount of X
and Y allocated to individual A is measured from the origin 0; the amount
of X and Y allocated to individual B is measured from the origin β. Every
point in the box, $0 Y_\beta \beta X_\beta$ represents an allocation of X_β and Y_β between
individuals A and B. In addition we can draw in the indifference curves for
individuals A and B. The $I_A{}^1, I_A{}^2, I_A{}^3$, and so on are indifference curves which
represent increasing levels of utility for individual A, and $I_B{}^1, I_B{}^2, I_B{}^3$, and
so on represent increasing levels of utility for individual B.

The question that arises is how to allocate (X_β, Y_β) between A and B so
that it is not possible for both individuals to move to higher utility levels
through trading. By an argument analogous to that for productive efficiency,
it can be shown that the locus of efficient points corresponds to the locus of
tangency points of the indifference curves for A and B. The locus of efficient
distributions is represented by the locus 0β in Figure 7. Therefore, the
condition for efficiency in distribution is that, given a particular distribution

of X and Y, the marginal rate of substitution is the same for all individuals who consume positive quantities of both X and Y.* Intuitively one can see that if one individual is willing to trade X for Y at a different rate than is another, there exists an opportunity for a trade which redistributes X and Y so as to make both individuals better off. If this opportunity exists, the initial distribution was not efficient in the Pareto sense.

Choice of Outputs

At this point efficiency has been discussed in terms of allocation of factors of production and of distribution of a fixed bundle of goods. In both cases there was an infinite number of points which satisfied the efficiency conditions. Two questions remain: (1) what bundle of goods should be produced; and (2) which distribution among the efficient distributions of that bundle should be chosen. The answer to these questions involves an introduction of additional value judgments into the analysis. The concept of a social welfare function is introduced to incorporate these value judgments into the analytical framework.

Consider Figure 7 again. Every point on the efficient locus corresponds to a utility level for individual A and a utility level for individual B. By plotting utility levels for A and B for each point on the efficient locus, we can construct a utility possibility frontier. Such a frontier represents a mapping into utility space of efficient distributions of fixed quantities of output. Of course the utility possibility frontier for one output bundle is different from the frontier for another output bundle. In Figure 8 are plotted utility possibility frontiers for several output bundles on the production possibility frontier. The locus $\beta\beta$ corresponds to the output bundle β; the locus $\bar{\gamma}\bar{\gamma}$ corresponds to another output bundle γ. Note that each utility possibility frontier must have a negative slope because each point on the locus corresponds to an efficient distribution of a fixed bundle of goods. The grand utility frontier is the outer envelope of all utility possibility frontiers and is represented by UU in Figure 8.

Since an allocation may correspond to a point on a utility possibility frontier while not corresponding to a point on the grand utility frontier, the two efficiency conditions developed previously are not sufficient to guarantee Pareto optimality. In particular, even though resources are allocated optimally for the chosen levels of outputs and though the outputs are optimally distributed, the chosen outputs themselves may not be optimal. Therefore, we must derive conditions to assure that it is impossible to make both individuals better off by reallocating resources from the production of X to the production

---

* As in the case of productive efficiency, this condition may not hold for points on the boundary of the box.

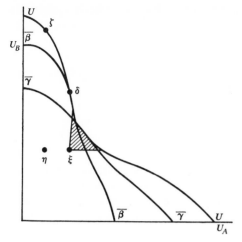

Fig. 8

of Y or vice versa. A condition relating production to distribution must be developed. This condition is that the marginal rate of transformation of X into Y must equal the marginal rates at which A and B are willing to substitute Y for X. This condition is pictured in Figure 7. The only points on the efficient locus 0β which correspond to points on the grand utility frontier are those such as α where the slopes of the indifference curves for A and B at α equal the slope of the production possibility frontier at β.

A simple example will demonstrate that this condition is necessary for Pareto optimality. Suppose that individuals A and B were both willing to substitute two units of X for one unit of Y, and that it was possible to reallocate the factors of production so that one additional unit of Y could be produced at the expense of one unit of X. Then if we produced two more units of Y and two fewer units of X and gave each individual one more unit of Y and one less unit of X, both individuals would prefer this new bundle of goods to the initial one. This conclusion can be drawn from the fact each individual would have been willing to give two units of X for one unit of Y; each, in fact, had to sacrifice only one unit of X for an additional unit of Y; therefore, each is better off with the new allocation than with the old.

To summarize, the conditions which must be satisfied for an allocation of resources to be Pareto optimal are (1) the marginal rate of substitution between any two factors of production must be the same in all productive processes which use positive quantities of both factors, (2) the marginal rate of substitution between two goods in consumption must be the same for all individuals who consume positive quantities of both goods, and (3) the marginal rate of substitution between two goods in consumption must equal the marginal rate of transformation between these two goods. These conditions along with the assumptions about the shapes of the isoquants and indifference curves constitute the necessary conditions for Pareto optimality. The conditions are also sufficient for Pareto optimality except in certain cases where there are corner solutions and the equalities above must be replaced by inequalities. This refinement is discussed in Bator (1957), Debreu (1959), and Quirk and Saposnik (1968).

Again consider the grand utility frontier in Figure 8. It is clear that the points on this frontier correspond to Pareto optimal resource allocations; however, there is an infinite number of such allocations. The problem is how to choose among them. Consider the point at which the utility frontier intersects the vertical axis. Here the allocation of resources is such that the utility of individual B is maximized while individual A has nothing. As we move down the utility frontier individual A's utility increases and individual B's utility decreases until we reach the horizontal axis where the utility for A is the maximum possible while B has nothing. Therefore, resource allocation may be Pareto optimal even though one individual gets everything that is produced. Furthermore, it is clear that the choice of the optimal point on the grand utility frontier is essentially a choice of how income should be distributed between A and B. This choice requires the introduction of a value judgment regarding the appropriate distribution of income.

One tempting line of argument would be to choose that point on UU at which $U_A + U_B$, the sum of the utilities of the two individuals is maximized. However, this procedure could be justified only if we could assign to each individual a cardinal utility function which measured the intensity of his preferences and if the utility functions for both individuals measured intensity of preference on a common scale. While this kind of social calculus once formed the basis of welfare economics, no satisfactory conceptual procedure has been devised to measure intensity of preference. Furthermore, inter-personal comparisons of this type have been abandoned for this reason. To get around these difficulties modern welfare economics assumes only that individuals can rank alternatives in a consistent manner.

Consider again the grand utility frontier in Figure 8. The choice among the points on this frontier involves making a value judgment as to the appropriate utility levels to be assigned to individuals A and B. The social processes by which such a decision might be made and the related question of proper definition of the social welfare function have been discussed in the literature; however, this discussion is beyond the introductory treatment of the subject presented here (Arrow, 1963; Graaf, 1957; Little, 1950; Quirk and Saposnik, 1968).* For the present discussion, assume that alternative points (U_A, U_B)

---

* Social welfare functions commanding general consent cannot as a practical matter be defined. The concept, however, is useful as a tool in analyzing the issues that are central to optimal resource allocation and to public policy. There exists a special body of

in Figure 8 can be ranked according to some ethical criterion. Furthermore, assume that this ranking is transitive and can be expressed by a social welfare function, W, such that if $(U_A{}^1, U_B{}^1)$ is socially preferred to $(U_A{}^2, U_B{}^2)$ then $W(U_A{}^1, U_B{}^1) > W(U_A{}^2, U_B{}^2)$. The only condition imposed on W is that it be a strictly increasing function of U_A and U_B. The justification for imposing this condition is the value judgment that social preferences should relate positively to individual preferences. If, given two points η and ξ in Figure 8, such that ξ provides a higher level of utility for individual A and the same level for individual B as does alternative η, then ξ should be socially preferred to η. The assumption that W is an increasing function of U_A and U_B implies that the social optimum among the attainable allocations will correspond to a point on the utility frontier such as a point δ in Figure 8. An allocation of productive factors, a production of a particular bundle of goods, and a distribution of goods, corresponds to δ.

Now consider the relationship of Pareto optimality to the optimal allocation of resources from an overall social point of view. Given that the social welfare function has been postulated to be a strictly increasing function of U_A and U_B it follows that the overall social optimum will lie on the grand utility frontier. Therefore, Pareto optimality is a necessary condition for overall welfare maximization or social optimality. At the same time it is important to make it clear that Pareto optimality is not sufficient for social optimality. In fact allocations which are Pareto optimal may be inferior from a social point of view to allocations which are non-Pareto optimal. This fact can be illustrated in Figure 8. The point ξ which lies inside the utility frontier may be superior to the point ζ which lies on the frontier, but which distributes most of the output produced to individual B. That is, ξ may be preferred to ζ because the distribution of income at ξ is considered socially more desirable than at ζ. At the same time it is clear that there are feasible allocations of resources which are superior to ξ; these allocations are represented by the shaded area lying to the right of ξ in Figure 8.

From the foregoing discussion it should be clear that Pareto optimality is desirable, but that other factors such as the distribution of income must be considered in choosing among various resource allocations. In addition it is

---

literature dealing with questions of how in principle one might construct a social welfare function. The classic work on this topic is Arrow (1963). As a practical matter, policy decisions of this type are made through the political process where bargaining and voting procedures are a central element. No complete model of the political decision making process has been developed with which one could explore the properties of this process, and there is no reason to believe that this process leads to decisions or choices which satisfy any of the properties postulated for social welfare functions. Therefore, while the concept of a social welfare function is instructive, it does not provide an operational tool for choosing among allocations nor does it necessarily correspond to any actual decision process.

clear that an allocation is either Pareto optimal or it is not. The concept of Pareto optimality generally does not provide a basis for choosing among allocations which are not Pareto optimal. In practice this problem often arises since it may be impossible to bring about an allocation of resources that satisfies all the conditions required for Pareto optimality and, at the same time, meets the requirements for an equitable distribution of the income. One is often faced with the task of evaluating alternative policies which are associated with resource allocations which are not Pareto optimal, but which are feasible given all the constraints faced in the real world. The concept of Pareto optimality is of little use for choosing among such allocations. If, however, one accepts the distribution of income as optimal, Pareto optimality becomes a sufficient condition for a social optimum. This last point is expanded in the discussion of optimality and competitive markets.

OPTIMUM RESOURCE ALLOCATION AND COMPETITIVE EQUILIBRIUM UNDER PERFECT COMPETITION

The development of a theory of optimal resource allocation has closely paralleled the development of the theory of perfectly competitive markets. In particular it can be demonstrated that given the conditions which are assumed to hold in perfectly competitive markets, the allocation of resources associated with competitive equilibrium will be Pareto optimal. Furthermore, under appropriate assumptions it can be demonstrated that any Pareto-optimal allocation of resources corresponds to the equilibrium allocation of a perfectly competitive economy given some initial distribution of wealth. In this section the basic assumptions underlying the model of perfectly competitive markets are presented, the argument that competitive equilibrium brings about a Pareto optimal allocation of resources is sketched, and the conditions under which market competition fails to bring about an efficient allocation of resources are discussed.

It is assumed that each producer operates his firm to maximize profit, and that each individual buys goods and sells his services to maximize his utility. From the assumption that producers are profit maximizers it follows that for any fixed bundle of inputs the producer will employ these inputs so as to produce the maximum output. Therefore, a production function defines the relationship between inputs and outputs for each production unit.

In addition it is assumed that each production unit and each individual behaves as a price taker in the sense that market prices are taken as given by each consumer and by each producer. This assumption is based on a concept of markets in which there is a large number of buyers and sellers in each market and in which the transactions of any buyer or seller are an inconsequential fraction of the total transactions of that market. For example, a farmer selling wheat in a national market would not be in a position to influence the market price. Neither would a consumer buying shoes. There has been wide debate over the minimum number of participants and the maximum relative size of the participants consistent with the assumption that prices are taken as given. Clearly, in markets where the industrial giants account for a major fraction of the sales, this assumption is not valid.

A further assumption of the theory of perfectly competitive markets is that the output of any productive unit depends only on the quantity of inputs it uses and on its technical capabilities. The output does not depend upon the production decisions of other firms. This assumption is implicit in the definition of a production function which relates inputs to outputs and which does not depend on the level of production of other commodities. Similarly, the utility of each individual is assumed to depend only on his own consumption. These assumptions were also implicit in the presentation of optimal resource allocation.

Finally, it is assumed, as before, that production functions are such that the isoquants are convex to the origin and that preferences are such that indifference curves are convex to the origin. Production functions are also assumed to exhibit decreasing returns to scale* at some point. This assumption is related to the condition that the production possibility curve be concave to the origin as pictured in Figure 4. This assumption assures that at some level of output the incremental costs of producing an additional unit of output begin to increase. This increase in incremental or marginal costs is a necessary condition for the size and number of firms to be consistent with competitive markets, a point which will subsequently be discussed.

Consider an individual firm which produces a single product X using capital and labor, K and L. Let the production function for this firm be $X = f(K, L)$. In addition the prices for X, K, and L are P_X, P_K, and P_L respectively. The profit of the firm is equal to $P_X X - P_K K - P_L L$. Therefore, the problem of the firm is to maximize $P_X X - P_K K - P_L L$ subject to the constraint that $f(K, L) = X$. The problem of profit maximization can be decomposed into two parts: one is selection of that bundle of inputs which minimizes cost for the chosen level of output; the other is a selection of that level of output which maximizes profit.

It will be demonstrated that if all production units individually were to maximize their profits given a fixed set of prices consistent with the equation of supply and demand in every market, the total production of all commodities would represent a point on the production possibility curve.

Suppose that the production unit under consideration were to produce an

---

* Technically, decreasing returns to scale means that a proportionate increase in factor inputs will lead to a less than proportionate increase in output.

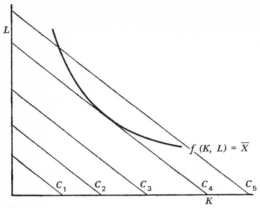

Fig. 9

output $\overline{X}$ at minimum costs. The various combinations of K and L which can be used to produce this output are represented by the isoquant in Figure 9. Equal cost lines have been also plotted in Figure 11. Each line is defined by a cost equation of the form $P_K K + P_L L = C$ where C represents a constant level of cost. The slope of each equal cost line is $-P_K/P_L$. The input combination which minimizes the cost of producing $\overline{X}$ is represented by the point at which the isoquant is tangent to the equal cost line C_4. The absolute value of the slope of the isoquant at any point is the marginal rate of substitution between K and L. Therefore, at the point where costs are minimized the marginal rate of substitution between K and L is equal to the price ratio P_K/P_L.

In Figure 9, we see that the minimum cost of producing $\overline{X}$ is C_4. By using the same procedure, we could find the minimum cost of producing any other level of output X. Therefore, we can represent the minimum cost of producing a given level of X as a function of X, $C(X)$. The revenue derived from the sale of the output X is also a function of X. This revenue is equal to $P_X X$. Therefore, profits will be maximized at that level of output at which $\pi(X) = P_X X - C(X)$ is maximized. Clearly, a necessary condition for X to maximize $\pi(X)$ is that $P_X = dC/dX$. That is, the profit maximizing level of output is that level at which the marginal or incremental cost of producing the last unit produced just equals the price at which that unit can be sold. This condition is illustrated in Figure 10. Notice that the maximum occurs at the point where marginal cost (MC) equals price only if $C(X)$ is concave upward at that point. Notice, also, that if the profit maximizing level of output is to be finite, then the marginal cost of production must at some point become greater than the price. Otherwise, a firm could continue to increase its profit by increasing its output. In such a case, one firm would

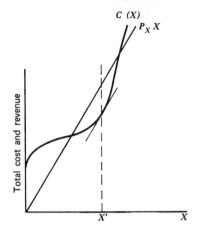

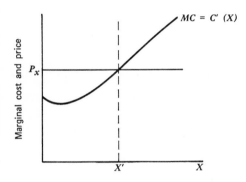

Fig. 10

eventually drive out the competition and would produce for the entire market. This is a basic reason why increasing returns to scale are incompatible with perfect competition.

Now consider the overall allocation of resources in terms of the results of this discussion. Consider a producer of commodity X and a producer of any other commodity Y. If each producer uses both K and L as inputs, the marginal rate of substitution between K and L will equal P_K/P_L for each producer. Therefore, the marginal rate of substitution between K and L will be the same in the production of both X and Y. This equality is one condition required for optimal resource allocation. In addition each firm will produce up to the point at which its marginal cost is just equal to the price of the good that it produces. Therefore, $MC_X = P_X$ and $MC_Y = P_Y$. It follows that if resources were diverted from the production of X to the production of Y, at the margin the rate of transformation between X and Y would be given by

P_X/P_Y. For example, suppose $P_X = \$2$ and $P_Y = \$1$. Then a decrease in the production of one unit of X would free \$2 worth of resources. These resources would produce 2 units of Y. Therefore, the marginal rate of transformation is 2 for 1. This rate of transformation is just equal to the price ratio, P_X/P_Y.

Now consider the behavior of individual consumers. Each consumer begins with a certain quantity of capital and labor which he can sell. He simultaneously decides on how much capital and labor to sell and how much of the commodities X and Y to buy. This decision is made to maximize his utility. To facilitate a graphical presentation in two dimensions, suppose the individual has decided to sell K' units of capital and L' units of labor so that his income is given by

$$I = P_K K' + P_L L'$$

His decision is now to choose a bundle of goods (X', Y') within his budget. In Figure 11, the budget constraint is the line defined by having $I = P_X X' + P_Y Y'$ having a slope P_X/P_Y. All points below the budget line represent bundles the cost of which is less than his total income; all points on the budget line represent bundles the cost of which equals his income. It is assumed that he will choose that combination of goods within his budget which will maximize his utility. Clearly, this combination is represented by point λ in Figure 11, the point at which the budget line is just tangent to the highest indifference curve which contains a point (X', Y') such that $P_X X' + P_Y Y' = I$. Therefore, at λ the marginal rate at which the individual is willing to trade Y for X equals the price ratio P_X/P_Y.

Since everyone faces the same set of prices, it follows that the marginal

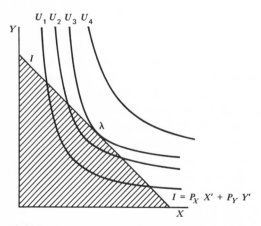

Fig. 11

rate of substitution between X and Y will be the same for every individual who consumes both X and Y. This equality is one of the conditions for Pareto optimality. In addition, since the marginal rate of transformation between X and Y equals P_X/P_Y, it follows that the marginal rate of substitution between X and Y in consumption equals the marginal rate of transformation between X and Y in production as shown in Figure 7. Therefore under the assumptions of perfect competition, the equilibrium resource allocation which obtains through competitive markets will be Pareto optimal and will correspond to a point on the grand utility frontier in Figure 8.

The point on the grand utility frontier which actually will be obtained under perfect competition will depend on the initial distribution of wealth. Recall that an individual's income was determined by the equation $I = P_L L + P_K K$. Therefore, the level of utility that an individual can attain will depend on his original endowment of capital and labor and upon the prices of these two factors. It can be demonstrated that each point on the grand utility frontier corresponds to an allocation of resources which will prevail in competitive equilibrium given some initial distribution of wealth. Therefore, by some redistribution of the initial wealth it is possible to attain any point on the grand utility frontier. It is in this sense that a choice among points on the utility frontier is essentially a choice among different distributions of income.

The discussion to this point has employed the concept of general equilibrium without defining its meaning. The behavior of individuals and of production units has been discussed on the assumption that individuals and production units can buy and sell any amount of each commodity they choose at the given set of prices. Clearly, for an arbitrary set of prices the sum of individual choices will not be consistent with resource endowments. Demands will exceed supplies in some markets and supplies will exceed demands in others. An equilibrium set of prices is one, such that demand and supply are equated simultaneously in all markets. A competitive equilibrium is an allocation of resources associated with an equilibrium set of prices.

One of the primary functions of a competitive market is that it directs production and consumption decisions toward an equilibrium. The process of adjustment toward equilibrium takes place through price changes. If supply exceeds demand for a commodity the price of that commodity will fall; the price decline will effect an increase in the amount demanded by buyers and a decrease in the amount supplied by producers. Both changes will reduce the amount by which the supply exceeds the demand. In the case of an excess of demand over supply the price will be driven up, thereby reducing the excess demand. In summary, competitive markets operate so as to guide production and distribution not only toward an equilibrium state where supplies equal demands, but also toward a Pareto optimal allocation of resources. If one were to accept the premise that the initial distribution of wealth was ideal from a social point of view, then in equilibrium the competitive market would produce the socially optimal allocation of resources.

The significance of several obvious simplifications must be clarified. First, it was assumed that there were two factors of production, two individuals, and two goods which were produced. This assumption made it possible to present the results graphically. The results can be generalized to the case where there are any finite number of factors, individuals, and consumption goods. Second, it was assumed that the factors of production were in fixed supply and that these factors could not be consumed directly; there were no intermediate goods and no goods which were both consumed and used in production. Again, this assumption was made to facilitate a graphical presentation and does not affect the validity of the results. Third, there were no joint products, that is, each production unit was assumed to produce a single product. This assumption too can be dropped without changing the basic results of the analysis. Fourth, it was assumed that the isoquants and the indifference curves were smooth and convex to the origin. The assumption of a smooth curvature can be relaxed with the result that the conditions for Pareto optimality become a set of inequalities instead of equalities, but this relaxation does not significantly alter basic results. The assumptions concerning the convexity of the indifference curves and the isoquants and the concavity of the production possibility frontier are, however, critical to the analysis. These shapes are related to the mathematical concept of convexity which plays a central role in the formal proof of the general theorems presented. A complete discussion of convexity as it relates to competitive markets and Pareto optimality is beyond the scope of this chapter. The interested reader should refer to Bator (1957), Debreu (1959), and Quirk and Saposnik (1968) for a basic discussion of this issue. One can get an idea of the difficulties which can arise, however, if the assumptions regarding the shapes of various curves are violated. Suppose that isoquants instead of being convex to the origin were concave to the origin. Then the tangency points in Figure 2 would not be optimal. Similarly, the tangency point between the equal cost line and the isoquant, in Figure 9, would not represent the least cost combination for producing that output, but would instead represent the most costly combination. One particularly important situation associated with nonconvexity is that of increasing returns to scale. This situation is discussed in the final section of the chapter.

The analysis of resource allocation has been presented as if production and distribution were carried out under conditions of certainty at a given point in time and space. Clearly, however, production takes place over time, at different locations, under uncertain conditions; the factors of time, location, and uncertainty are critical. The analysis which has been developed can be extended so as to handle these factors with no effect of the basic results. This extension is accomplished by distinguishing commodities by time, location, and states of the world. Suppose that economic activity takes place over time and that time can be divided into T periods. Then if X is a given commodity, X_t would represent a quantity of commodity X in period t. Similarly, one could index the commodity by location so that X_{tl} would represent a quantity of commodity X at time t at location l. Since from an economic point of view, commodities at different locations or at different points in time are not interchangeable, they are treated as different commodities each with its own price.

It is fairly easy to see how one can incorporate time and space into the analysis by differentiating commodities by time and location. The treatment of uncertainty while it is analogous to that of time and location is conceptually more difficult. To introduce uncertainty into the analysis the concept of a state of nature is employed. A state of nature is a complete description of the world such that if the state of nature is known, then the outcomes of all actions are known with certainty. Therefore, given a state of nature, a deterministic model of the economy can be applied. In general, however, there are many possible states of nature and only one will be the true state of nature. Individuals are assumed to assess subjective probabilities as to which state of nature does in fact obtain. Therefore, production and consumption decisions are made on the basis of expectations about the future. Under this analysis commodities are differentiated by time, location, and the state of nature. Individuals are assumed to buy and sell claims much like insurance policies which yield different bundles of commodities given different states of the world. For example, suppose there are two possible states of the world, one in which a given individual will be alive and another in which he will be dead. A life insurance policy is a claim contingent on the state of the world. If the first state obtains, then the policy pays nothing; if the second state obtains and the man dies, the claim pays the amount prescribed by the policy.

The extensions of the model to cover multiple time periods, spatial considerations, and uncertainty simply increase the number of commodities in the economy. This increase creates no analytical problems. However, the difficulty illuminated by the analysis of the extensions is that markets are required for the purchase and sale of contingent claims on commodity bundles at different locations and times. Conceptually, at the beginning of each time period individuals would contract a complete set of transactions for future as well as present production and consumption. Clearly, the set of markets required for the complete set of transactions does not exist. One reason that markets do not exist is that the cost of establishing and carrying out some transactions is so high that markets do not develop.

A more complete discussion of time, space, and uncertainty is beyond the scope of this introductory treatment of resource allocation; however, the interested reader is referred to Debreu (1969) and Radner (1968). The basic conclusion of much of the discussion is that once time, space, and uncertainty have been introduced into the model, the case for the Pareto optimality of competitive markets is weakened because of the difficulties in setting up the requisite markets. Similarly, the economic system which exists in the United States today may fail to achieve optimality not only because of market imperfections to be discussed in the next section, but also because certain markets for insurance and for intertemporal transactions do not exist. When the markets for insurance and capital do exist they often do not meet the conditions of perfect competition.

The theory of resource allocation even as extended to cover a number of periods of time is basically static and does not consider the dynamic aspects of capital formation and economic growth. Recently economists have developed a dynamic theory of optimal resource allocation analogous to the static theory presented here. This work has gone under the heading of optimal economic growth and has employed many of the results of control theory. While the theory of optimal economic growth has been an important contribution to our understanding of efficiency over time, it has not provided a full blown model of economic growth. In particular, processes of innovation and of technical change are not adequately incorporated into this work. In addition, at the present state of development these models are of little value for practical planning.

MARKET FAILURE, EXTERNALITIES, AND INCREASING RETURNS TO SCALE

In addition to problems presented by time and uncertainty, there are two important situations in which competitive markets fail to effect a Pareto optimal allocation of resources. It is in these situations that we find government action which is designed to redress the misallocations. The first case is one in which there are increasing returns to scale in the production of a specific product. The second is the situation in which there are direct, non-market interactions between units. Such interactions are referred to as externalities.

Consider the situation in which there are increasing returns to scale in the production of one commodity. In this case the per unit or average cost of production of the commodity falls as the level of output increases. As a result the marginal cost curve will lie below average cost curve at all levels of output as illustrated in Figure 12. If the firm could sell any level of output at a fixed price, then the profit maximizing level of output would be either zero or infinity depending upon the price level. Clearly, however, an infinite output is impossible since the market for any product is finite. In such a situation, an aggressive firm will tend to expand rapidly and drive smaller firms out of the market by selling at a lower price based on lower per unit production costs. Once competitors are driven from the market, the remaining firm will behave as a monopolist and the resulting allocation of resources will not be Pareto optimal. More specifically, the price fixed by the monopolist will be above that consistent with Pareto optimality and production will be below the optimum level. This situation is shown in Figure 12.

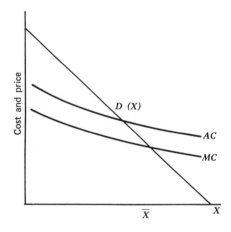

Fig. 12

In Figure 12 the demand curve for a product, represented by $D(X)$, gives that price which will clear the market as a function of the quantity produced. A basic theorem in welfare economics is that for Pareto optimality goods must be priced so that the marginal cost of the last unit produced is equal to the price. If this equality does not hold, then there exists someone who is willing to pay more for an additional unit of production than the additional cost of that production. If the firm were to produce that unit and to sell it at marginal cost the consumer would be better off and the producer would be made no worse off. Therefore, the initial allocation would not have been Pareto optimal. However, if a producer must charge one price for all units sold, a profit maximizing producer facing increasing returns to scale will not set price equal to marginal cost. It can be seen from Figure 12 that whenever there are increasing returns to scale a price equal to marginal cost will result in losses being incurred by the producer. In Figure 12 the demand curve and the marginal cost curve intersect at $\overline{X}$; at this point price is less than average cost and the producer incurs losses. Clearly, no private monopoly would operate at such a point. In fact, it is clear from Figure 12 that a profit-maximizing monopoly will produce at an output below that which is Pareto optimal and will charge a price above marginal cost.

The case of increasing returns can be illustrated with two examples. First consider the case of supplying water. It would not be efficient for competing companies to serve the same market since there are economies of scale. At the same time a private monopoly may pursue a pricing policy which is contrary to the public interest. In a large number of cases this difficulty has been resolved through public ownership of water companies. A second example is that of the telephone industry. In this case the solution has been to allow a private monopoly to own and operate the system, but for the government to regulate prices.

The second situation in which competitive markets fail to effect a Pareto optimal allocation of resources is where there are externalities, or direct nonmarket interactions of the economic units. In the development of the basic results of this paper, it was assumed that the production relationships in one firm were independent of production decisions by other firms and that the utility levels of one individual were independent of consumption decisions of other individuals. These independence assumptions were implicit in the way production functions and utility functions were defined. Where interdependencies exist, they are called externalities. Pollution is a classical example of an externality. Production which results in pollution may affect both the production function of other firms and the well being of individuals. This nonmarket, direct interaction, between the firm causing pollution and other firms and individuals, violates the independence assumptions of perfect competition. Externalities cause misallocation of resources because the person who creates a cost or a benefit for someone else does not take this cost or benefit into account in planning his production and consumption decisions. For this reason, prices will not direct the market system toward a resource allocation in which the marginal rate of substitution in consumption between any two goods is equal to the marginal rate of transformation in production for the two goods.

An extreme case of an externality in consumption is the case of "public goods." A public good is one where if one person can consume this good, everyone can consume it. National defense is a public good since it is practically impossible to defend only certain individuals. Clean air is a public good since everyone can enjoy it if it exists. Thus the nature of public goods is such that it is impossible to exclude individuals from consuming the good if they do not pay for it. Therefore, it is impossible to sell such goods in the market. There would be no incentive for private firms to produce these goods which cannot be sold. Clearly, many such goods are of value and should be produced. One way around the dilemma is for a governmental unit to purchase these goods publicly and to require that everyone pay for them through taxation.

To summarize, markets will fail to allocate resources efficiently when there are economies of scale or when there are externalities. Most cases in which the government intervenes directly in the allocation of resources involve either externalities or increasing returns to scale. However, the third reason for government intervention is not related to economic efficiency but to income distribution. When the existing distribution of wealth diverges greatly from the socially optimal distribution of wealth, government action may be required to bring the actual distribution closer to the ideal distribution.

REFERENCES

Arrow, K. J. (1963), *Social Choice and Individual Values*, Wiley, New York.

Arrow, K. J., L. Hurwicz, and H. Uzawa (1958), *Studies in Linear and Non-Linear Programming*, Stanford University Press, Stanford, Calif.

Bator, F. M. (1957), "The Simple Analytics of Welfare Maximization," *American Economic Review*, March, pp. 22–59.

Debreu, G. (1959), *Theory of Value*, Wiley, New York.

Graaff, J. de V. (1957), *Theoretical Welfare Economics*, University Press, Cambridge.

Henderson, James M., and Richard E. Quandt (1958), *Microeconomic Theory*, McGraw-Hill, New York.

Koopmans, Tjalling C. (1957), *Three Essays on the State of Economic Science*, McGraw-Hill, New York.

Little, I. M. D. (1950), *A Critique of Welfare Economics*, Clarendon Press, Oxford.

Quirk, James, and Rubin Saposnik (1968), *Introduction to General Equilibrium Theory and Welfare Economics*, McGraw-Hill, New York.

Radner, R. (1968), "Competitive Equilibrium under Uncertainty," *Econometrica*, Vol. 36, No. 1, pp. 31–58.

IV

Some Investment Concepts in Engineering Systems with Particular Emphasis on Long-Range Investment: J. Morley English

This chapter deals with some new concepts as well as with some subtle aspects of investments in large-scale systems. It is assumed that the reader has some familiarity with how investment analyses of engineering projects are actually accomplished at present.*

The Nature of Investment

Before considering the question of investment in large-scale engineering and social systems, it might be well to establish clearly what is meant by investment. Then from this point investment might be examined in a macroeconomic sense to establish the environment in which investment decisions are made. This leads to an examination of how investment decisions are actually made and finally to the question of whether the methods of analysis on which decisions are based are indeed correct.

Investment can be defined as the allocation of resources in the present to some activity in anticipation that such use will result in a greater return of benefits at some later time. The fact that such allocation requires foregoing a present consumption benefit implies saving. Individuals tend to consider the employment of their savings as investments. However, in most cases savings do not flow directly into investment but rather through some intermediary financial system that channels them into investment. When one buys stock in a company on the stock market he may regard this as investment of his savings, but strictly speaking no net investment has occurred. He has merely traded places with someone else in the ownership of shares that represent equity in already existing investment. In this case, one man's investment is another's disinvestment. When this occurs, the market mechanism only establishes relative values of various investment opportunities; it *does not* create new investment. Only when a corporation through new stock issues takes money out of the market and spends it for new plant and equip-

* Refer to any current text in engineering economy, for example, Eugene L. Grant and Grant Ireson, *Engineering Economy*, Ronald Press, New York, 1970.

ment does investment occur. In an economic sense then, investment only occurs when the physical resources flow into constructing new assets.

In a similar way, savings may flow into investment through debt (i.e., bonds). The proportional level of these flows into equity and into debt will depend on their relative attractiveness both to the saver and to the actual employer of capital—the real investor. A large part of savings does not originate with individual savers. Ploughed back corporate earnings are savings that may be short-circuited directly into investment. A final source of investment is socially determined savings in the form of taxes that are invested by government. In both of these latter cases, individual decisions to save are not involved. In a sense the latter two classes of savings are forced and semiautomatic.

Economic Evaluation of Investment and Financing Investment

An important distinction should be recognized between the economic evaluation of the investment in a project and the financing of that project. Failure to recognize this fact may lead to considerable confusion. Many studies that are represented as economic studies have been little more than cost estimates coupled with financing plans. This observation is not to imply that the economic evaluation of the investment decision is independent of financial feasibility. There is an important interrelationship. However, the economic evaluation is for the purpose of determining whether the long-run benefit will represent a satisfactory return over the long-run cost. The financing problem is one of establishing the means for flowing savings into investment, or in other words, it is concerned with adjusting the differences between the revenue stream and the expenditure stream. What constitutes a satisfactory return may be constrained both by investor attitudes and by the available mechanisms for directing the saving stream into investment flows. With these preliminary thoughts in mind then, what are the investment characteristics of large-scale systems that warrant special consideration?

Scale of Required Financing

Many of the social systems to which we must address our attention in the next ten to fifteen years represent enormous undertakings that may well dwarf the space and defense programs of the past twenty years. The investments in space and defense were made largely through compulsory savings hidden within taxes. It is possible that the new future civil programs could be financed this way also. However, the new programs are not likely to be substitutions but rather additions to an already large public investment program. We should clearly recognize that, as in the past, this approach could mean an increased involvement by government. If we presume that we wish to avoid inducing further relative growth of government, it would follow that the financing of new social programs should come more from private savings and from automatic corporate savings. Under these circumstances, the magnitude of the financing of individual systems conceivably might be so large that they would create major disturbances in the money markets.

The disturbances created by very large private financing could be manifested in a number of ways. Normally, any single new corporate financing is sufficiently small that the market rate of interest will not be significantly affected by it. In other words, the decision to make the investment can be made with reasonable assurance that the cost of financing will be independent of the decision. This might not be true for financing a truly large system over a short period of time. Second, a social decision to move very rapidly into a whole series of large new private investments might require a marked shift of capital flows into these programs at the expense of capital needs for the normal consumer goods sector. This might induce serious inflation in consumer prices. Third, the market mechanism might fail as a device for setting priorities for the various large programs. Some other more deliberate method might be needed for the capital budgeting of such programs. Finally, the traditional way of financing transportation systems, water resources, and the like has been through debt. If a major trend towards development of such systems occurs and the traditional debt financing approach is employed, it could well result in unbalancing the ratio of debt to equity capital in our economy. This would have an attendant affect of changing the risk distribution over various classes of investors.

The System Approach

The significant contribution of the methodology of systems engineering has been to force the engineer to design the system from a point of view that considers the objectives of the system as a whole rather than considering each component independently. The consideration of a component by itself rather than as part of a system tends to keep one from recognizing its full influence on the system and its interactions with other components of the system.

Every system is a component or a subsystem of some larger and more complex system. To do anything at all, one must always isolate pieces of systems and treat them as independent components. Hopefully, one selects the system that he wishes to consider as independent in such a way as to minimize interactions. However, ability to deal with large and complex systems depends on the ability to cope with ever larger and more complex components to establish boundaries for which interactions can be safely ignored. The interactions tend to become static constraints on the system. The necessity of isolating the system at points where the interfaces are static constraints, applies for investment decisions at least as much as for technical and design decisions.

An example will make the point clear. An airplane may be designed as a system. The total system dictates certain requirements for a wing structure system. Once these requirements are set, we may proceed, at least to a great extent, with the design for the wing as if it were independent of the fuselage, tail, and such. The final design of the wing may involve little more than an analysis and testing of the airplane to ensure that the wing meets the requirements established by the specification of the airplane system as a whole. Now consider the investment in the wing subsystem. One might have a difficult time making an independent investment decision to buy a wing as a separate component of the airplane. If one wanted to consider the unlikely decision of the wing investment alone, the pay-off on the wing could be estimated, by a prorated investment of the total investment in the airplane. If the scope is expanded, it may be possible to consider the investment in the whole airplane based on the revenue that it is expected to earn. However, is this really correct either? Actually, the decision to buy an airplane is one of adding a component to an airline system. The single airplane purchase must be investigated on the basis of its marginal effects on the investment in the airline system as a whole. The decision to buy the extra airplane may be determined in such a way that the analysis could proceed by considering the details of the increment investment much as was done for the technical design of the wing component.

Now, extending the problem to another level of complexity, the airline corporate system may be viewed as only one component of the airline transportation system of the country. At this point the problem of organizational subdivision is introduced. The airline management can consider the investment decision to buy one airplane as part of the system designed to maximize a corporate objective, say profits. The concern of company management is not one of the profitability of the entire air transport system nor of the even larger system of national transportation. However, decisions relating to these systems are necessarily dependent on the smaller decisions being made in such a way that they contribute to the results of the social system objectives. Ideally, the constraints on the investment decisions for the corporate subsystem should be such that some social objective function will be optimized. The philosophy in the economic system of the western world is that the constraints on corporate managements should be minimal and the market mechanism should serve a sufficient regulatory function. In general, where market forces come into play, the constraints provided by the market work pretty well. However, the market mechanism does not work where we must build single large systems. These may have to be designed to satisfy such needs by optimizing the system in terms of some explicitly defined social objective function. This requirement may enlarge the scale of the system which can properly be separated for purposes of making independent investment decisions.

Now it also must be realized that many investments for components of the total economic system are dependent on the existence of other subsystems. Although a large subsystem may be designed to meet some explicit social objective, it also creates the necessary preconditions for independent investment decisions for dependent components.

A further example may clarify this point. A water resource development may be a necessary precondition for the development of certain types of manufacturing firms within the region. The system comprises both the water development and the independent firms that it serves. However, the decisions to invest in a particular manufacturing enterprise will be made on the basis of what only appear to be independent criteria. In reality, the performance of the complete system is that of the combined effect of the water system and the manufacturing industry. The benefits that derive from the total investments are attributable both to the water system and to the supposed independent component manufacturing enterprise. The question that arises is how is the return to be allocated between them. It is not unlike the wing on the airplane. What is needed is that the constraints imposed on the separate independent decisions be such that the objective function to be optimized for the independent investments result in the optimum total system performance.

The problem is complicated by the fact that the major subsystem (in this example, the water supply system) is in the nature of a public or social economic good whereas the goods produced by the components are individual goods. The first one depends on governmental investment decisions; the second on private investment decisions.

Pricing

Development of economic theory over the ages has been characterized by concern over establishing relative values. The ideal model has always been the perfect market. Without going into any discussion of this question, with all of its idealizations and limitations, let us accept the fact that, where a market exists, it does represent an efficient means of determining relative prices. However, it also must be recognized that as our systems become larger and more complex, the less the market mechanism will tend to work; relatively more of our purchases will be for public as opposed to private goods. Furthermore, the market is always an instantaneous representation of collective attitudes of individuals in competition for a limited supply of goods relative to the costs incurred in supplying them. As time goes on, two things must change. The first is the relative desirability of the mix of goods demanded. In other words, demand curves will change in shape relative to one another. Second, the resources expended to meet these demands will also change. Certain resources that tend to be used up, such as wasting natural resources, will become relatively more expensive. At the same time, the extent to which the effectiveness of labor by use of energy can be amplified will be reflected in a relatively reduced cost of energy. Therefore, whether the market acts to establish prices or economists learn better to impute prices that reflect social desires, the price structure, valid at the time of planning a new system, will change over the long range life of the system.

As an example consider the problem of an engineer in designing a multi-purpose power and desalted-water plant. The selling price of water may increase over time relative to that of power. Thus the optimal technical characteristics of the plant, based on present prices, will be different in the future. Such trend changes are normally ignored in present-day design practice.

Present-day methods employed by engineers for evaluating proposed projects virtually ignore pricing questions. Prices often are hypothesized to provide a cash flow that will cover expenditures plus arbitrarily allocated capital costs. This present price is based on some estimate of a need-induced demand that usually is estimated without regard to price. The result may be that demand elasticities for the service result in significantly different demands from those expected. When demand falls below the required level the immediate reaction of administrative agencies to produce the needed revenue may be to raise the price. The result may well be a further reduction in demand to the extent that in turn revenues are reduced.

However, that is not the only aspect of pricing considerations in the investment evaluation of a large-scale system. The above is merely a commentary on the supply-demand functions for the product of a particular system, given that prices of everything else are held constant. The large-scale system may induce changes in the price equilibrium in the economic system itself by changing the allocation of the consumer's income as well as his preferences.

Inflation Effects

One of the problems that has plagued the engineer in analyzing the desirability of his project is that prices will have escalated by the time the project is built, usually some years after his report has been issued. There are two factors that cause this. The first is that the building of the project disturbs the supply-demand relationship within the construction industry. The very fact that the decision is made to invest in the project will induce a rise in the cost of the project. This implies that it is not legitimate to assume that the price structure at the time of the study will be that for the time of construction. The effect is invariably to underestimate what projects will cost.

The other factor is the persistent rise of the general price level, simply inflation. If this effect is separated from the first one, then it is seen that relative prices should remain the same. Accordingly, all estimates of revenues and costs properly are calculated in terms of a reference or base year price index, that is, in constant dollars.

In the case of a steady-state inflation rate, which, except for a few periods, has been true of the United States for a very long time, this inflation rate will be reflected in the interest rate on a one-to-one relationship. In other words, a 3% inflation rate would be added to a basic $2\frac{1}{2}\%$ interest rate, that might be valid in the absence of inflation to give a $5\frac{1}{2}\%$ interest rate in the steadily inflating economy. This might strongly suggest that to be consistent, the discounting of future revenue/cost streams should also be made at the noninflationary interest rate.

The problem is confused by the effect of transients. It is observed and has been explained by Patinkin (1965) that a change in the rate of inflation induces a disproportionate increase in interest rates. Once the new inflation rate is established as a norm, the interest rate may be expected to return to its normal relationship with the inflation rate. For example, if the 3% inflation rate increases suddenly to 4%, interest rates might go to 8% and then gradually decline back to the basic interest plus steady-state inflation rate, that is $4\% + 2\frac{1}{2}\%$ or $6\frac{1}{2}\%$. While such effects are bound to introduce serious financing constraints, the long-range economic effect is probably very little affected. If we may consider that the transient effects of fluctuating interest rates will be attenuated over the long run, then it is indicated that a new project should be evaluated at constant prices, *discounted at the interest rate corresponding to a zero inflation rate*.

METHODS OF PROJECT EVALUATION

To provide perspective for some new ideas to be developed later, it is well to review the fundamental concepts underlying the accepted approaches of engineering economics. The three following methods have been used for comparing alternative investments in engineering projects.

1. The present worth or discounted cash-flow.
2. Equivalent annual cost.
3. The internal rate-of-return (IROR).

The assumptions underlying the PW approach are that:

1. The alternatives are all considered for the same time period or horizon time. Beyond the horizon time any cost or benefit is not considered.
2. The discounting of both benefit and cost streams is accomplished at a rate corresponding to the cost-of-capital to the enterprise. This cost-of-capital is the traditional weighted rate-of-return on both debt and equity capital. Since the total capital that produces the return is contributed from both sources, the weighted average return on equity capital and interest on debt is appropriately taken as the cost-of-capital. This rate-of-return may also be regarded as the minimal acceptable rate-of-return and corresponds to the *opportunity cost-of-capital.*
3. Reinvestment of cash flow is not a problem because on the average there will always be some opportunity available to reinvest at the opportunity cost-of-capital.

In the equivalent-annual-cost approach the same assumptions are made as for the present worth except for the need to specify a horizon time. Different lives of alternatives may be accommodated by the implicit assumption of reinvestment at the end of life of each project alternative. Since the reinvestment is assumed to take place at the same opportunity rate-of-return, it does not matter whether the reinvestment is thought of as a replication, or as some other replacement alternative. For this reason, expected life appears to drop out of the evaluation.

Expressing the discounted cash flow in equation form

$$\text{PW} = \int_0^H x(t)e^{-rt}\, dt \tag{1}$$

where $x(t)$ is the cash flow function (including capital investment), H, the horizon time, and e^{-rt}, the discount function.*

In comparing alternatives, the project with the highest present worth (PW) is selected.

For the equivalent annual cost method (or perhaps more accurately called the equivalent-constant-cash-flow method) let

$$\text{PW} = \int_0^H Re^{-rt}\, dt = \int_0^H x(t)e^{-rt}\, dt \tag{2}$$

Solving the equivalent constant cash flow is

$$R = \frac{\int_0^H x(t)e^{-rt}\, dt}{1 - e^{-rH}} \tag{3}$$

* The use of continuous functions is employed throughout this chapter. The functional nature of the relationships may be more intuitively appealing in continuous form even where practical computational techniques may dictate use of discrete representations. The discrete discount function corresponding to e^{-rt} is $1/(1 + r)^n$, where i is the discrete interest rate.

Thus it is seen that R is an arbitrary parameter* derived from a mathematical manipulation. Comparing R's for alternatives gives the same result as comparing PW's.

The third approach, that of computing the internal rate-of-return, is equivalent to the evaluation of r in (2) for which PW $= 0$. This is usually identified as the internal rate of return (IROR). The implicit assumption here is that reinvestment may be made at the IROR. This is not a reasonable assumption. Alchian (1959) has pointed out the error that may be introduced by use of the method. The inconsistent results that can occur may be seen by referring to Figure 1.

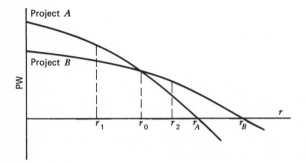

Fig. 1   Present worth versus discount rate.

The PW's of two projects are shown as a function of r. If r_1 is the opportunity cost of capital, project A is preferred. If r_2 is the correct value for r, then B is preferred. The IROR's show $r_B > r_A$ and B is preferred. In other words, the results are consistent and correct only if the opportunity ROR for reinvestment as well as initial investment is higher than r_0 corresponding to the intersection of the two curves.

Benefit/Cost Analysis

Discounted cash flow may be taken as the accepted method for evaluating the worth of a project investment. In principle, if the present worth of the benefit stream discounted at an acceptable rate exceeds that of the investment, the investment may be considered to be sound. The ratio of these two numbers, the benefit/cost ratio, is used to compare the relative attractive-

* It should be noted that $r/(1 - e^{-rH}) = re^{rH}/(e^{rH} - 1)$ which is equivalent to the discrete function $[i(1 + i)^n]/[(1 + i)^n - 1]$ and may be recognized as the capital recovery factor.

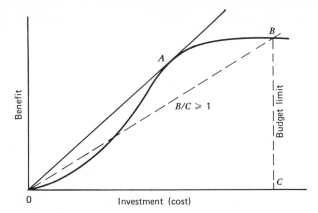

Fig. 2 Benefit-cost ratio.

ness of alternatives where the size of the investments may not be equal. If the value of the benefit/cost (B/C) ratio exceeds unity, the project is worth doing; the larger its value the more attractive the investment. Thus a benefit cost ratio of 3 for an investment of $1.00 is by definition a better project than one with a B/C ratio of 1.5 for an investment of $100. Is it?

The benefit/cost ratio often is used to rank projects. However, in spite of its widespread acceptance and use for this purpose, fundamentally, it is subject to error. In the project ranking problem, the objective is to maximize the return on the total capital budget. This requires a consideration of the return on the marginal capital investment. A simple ranking by benefit/cost ratios does not assure that marginal returns on the projects with the higher B/C ratios will be favorable. Consider Figure 2. The curve $0AB$ may represent the opportunity for investment up to a budget limit of C. Any straight line through the origin represents a B/C ratio. The maximum B/C ratio is that which is tangent to the opportunity curve, $0AB$, at A. However, the $0B$ line, which is a lower B/C ratio, represents a positive benefit over cost and may be preferred as long as the marginal benefit on the marginal cost exceeds one.

The Discount Function

What discount function should be employed in discounting future cash flow streams? The decision to invest in a large-scale system will change the future state of the world forever. Thus by replacing H by ∞ we can express the problem in its most general form as:

$$\text{PW} = \int_0^\infty [x(t)f_1(t) - y(t)f_2(t)]\, dt \geq 0 \tag{4}$$

where x and y are the benefits and costs, respectively, and $f_1(t)$ and $f_2(t)$ are discount functions.

It will be observed that no assumption is made as to the nature of the discount functions or as to costs being discounted in the same way as benefits. This is in contrast to the universally accepted way of discounting both costs and benefits by the function:

$$f(t) = e^{-rt} \tag{5}$$

where r is the acceptable rate of return and is a constant.

The practice has been to place the limits of integration at some arbitrary horizon time. This is done on the rationale that one cannot predict the remote future with any certainty and therefore it is better to ignore it. Furthermore, the value of the discounted cash flow for the remote future is small. This philosophy completely overlooks the problem of investments that are basically long range in nature.

Capital and the Discount Function

To establish what the discount function(s) should be, it is necessary to see how any single investment relates to the total economic system investment. A complete economy may be modeled by using the black box concept, with inputs and outputs (Figure 3).

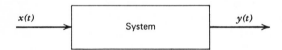

Fig. 3   Idealized economic system.

The total economy may be characterized as a system designed to transform a stream of values from one form to another. Physical goods and labor flow into the production system and come out transformed into a more desirable stream of products and services. This is represented by a stream of money representing these values and flowing in the opposite direction. The physical process necessitates a lag; work is done before products can be consumed. The equivalent money flow representation will correspondingly be represented by a leading output. In either case, there must be storage in the system.

$$y(t) = Tx(t) \tag{6}$$

In the most general case, the transfer function T may be nonlinear and the inputs, $x(t)$ (sales) and the outputs, $y(t)$ (expenditures) may be stochastic. However, for purposes of conceptualizing the process, we will hypothesize that the process is represented by a constant lead of deterministic time dependent functions—simply money flows. The storage will be

$$K = \int [x(t) - y(t)] \, dt \qquad (7)$$

$$= \int y(t)\left(\frac{1}{T} - 1\right) dt \qquad (8)$$

In the model all types of expenditures including those for products, materials, and labor are aggregated. No distinction is made between those that are reflected rapidly into sales and those that are normally considered as capital goods. In terms of money, the identity of separate product flows is lost. All that matters is the averaged effect of the time difference between input and output. In a most general sense, the storage in the system is *capital*. This storage includes both *working capital* and *fixed capital* in the more conventional definition. *It will be observed that capital, rather than being a fundamental variable of production, as was considered by classical economists, is a derived quantity and that the fundamental independent variable is time.*

Now let us further hypothesize an economy that will ensure a steady growth rate, a. For illustration, we will take this to be for an indefinite future. Thus

$$\begin{aligned} y(t) &= y_0 e^{at} \\ x(t) &= x_0 e^{at} \end{aligned} \qquad (9)$$

and the transfer function T corresponding to a simple lag, λ, is

$$T = e^{a\lambda} \qquad (10)$$

Substituting into (5)

$$K = \int_0^t y_0 e^{a\tau}(e^{-a\lambda} - 1) \, d\tau \qquad (11)$$

If we assume that the process has been going on for a sufficiently long time so that the initial conditions that started it may be ignored, then

$$K = \frac{y_0}{a} e^{at}(e^{-a\lambda} - 1) \qquad (12)$$

This is depicted in Figure 4.

Consider now what the societal return on total investment is. The growth may be considered to be the result of capital investment, which is observed to be growing at the same rate as both sales and expenditures. Of course, it is necessary that technology and innovation be such that the system can accept the investment feedback to produce the growth.

The inference of this statement is that all growth derives from capital investment and that a return to labor is zero. Whether this is true is not

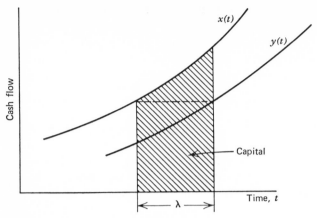

Fig. 4 Capital—Integrated cash flow.

important for purposes of this discussion. However, it may be explained by recognizing that increased labor productivity and innovative ability is a result of education and experience and as such is a consequence of an investment in human capital.

The process of investment may be considered as a feedback, Figure 5. In the usual engineering feedback system, the objective is to achieve a negative feedback and a stabilization of the system. In an economy, the objective is to achieve the opposite effect. A positive feedback is what produces an exponential growth. This by definition represents an unstable system. When one speaks of stabilization of an economic system he is really concerned with stabilizing short-period oscillations about a long-term unstable trend. Some day economists may be concerned with a long-term stabilization, but at least for the foreseeable future the objective is perceived to be one of growth.

The feedback could produce growth without increased storage, but this must be accompanied by a change in the transfer function. Undoubtedly, this occurs in the real world to account for short-range fluctuations between input and output functions. Also, it occurs over the long run as the technical

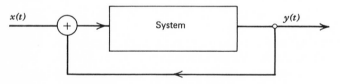

Fig. 5 Idealized economic system with feedback.

characteristic of the technology change. Conversely, the system growth could not be forced beyond its technical capacity. The change of the technical characteristics of the system would produce a nonlinear transfer function which has been excluded from our present concern.

Profit will be the revenue minus expenditure

$$x(t) - y(t) = y_0 e^{at}(a^{-a\lambda} - 1) \tag{13}$$

Thus the rate of return on capital is

$$r = \frac{\text{profit}}{K} = a \tag{14}$$

In other words, the *rate of growth* is the *rate of return* on the capital invested by society.

The assumption that the time lag is constant may not be unreasonable if, in whatever way the system is changing, it is slow relative to the time scale of current interest. Now how does the conclusion above square with the Fisherian principle (Fisher, 1930) that the value of any capital asset is the discounted value of the cash flow that it generates? Remembering that the process requires a continuous regeneration of capital, it follows that a capital expenditure rate of $y(t)$ induces a cash flow at $t + \lambda$. Discounting this cash flow at an arbitrary interest or discount rate, r, gives a;

$$\text{present worth} = [y(t)e^a](e^{-r}) = y(t) \tag{15}$$

The only way in which this condition is satisfied is that $r = a$. In other words, the social rate of discount is equal to the economic growth rate of the economy. It will only differ in practice to the extent of the changing technical characteristics of the transfer function. For practical purposes this may be negligible. Also note that capital book value from the historical point of view is the same as capital value of the discounted cash-flow.

While the argument above establishes a measure of the true rate-of-return for all investments in society, it does little to provide a guide for the individual investment decision. If the investment is made for a project undertaken in the public sector, it might be argued that the social rate of discount should apply in the evaluation of such projects. However, does this argument apply for the case of private investment?

Investment in the Private Sector

Aside from the question of the risk associated with private investment, the question arises as to whether individual decisions to invest would in fact be made at all if the only return perceived by the investor were the social rate of return. Indeed, it is quite obvious that the perceived rate of return would have to be considerably higher than the social rate of return. How then can public investments be made at a rate of return corresponding to the economic growth rate and have private investments at a multiple of the growth rate, without resulting in an average rate on total investment being in excess of the growth rate? Of course, the answer is that the private rate of return in effect cannot be higher than the growth rate unless the private sector is growing faster than the public, which it obviously is not doing. *The private rate of return can only seem to be higher.* What I appear to be saying is that somehow the business investor is fooled into thinking he is getting a higher return than he really is getting. However, this is not quite the case, and indeed it is not obvious that this might be so. As far as an individual business is concerned, the returns that are realized and are in excess of the social rate of return are largely investment flows into reinvestment in other expanding segments of the economy. All segments of industry are not growing at the same rate. New technologies grow rapidly while most of the established industries are essentially static. Correspondingly, capital needs in the new industries are relatively much higher than for the average. To a very great extent, profits do not flow into consumption but are reinvested. However, to the extent that they do represent consumption, they are truly not a return on capital but rather should be regarded as a *wage* paid for entrepreneurship. Thus the rate of return, as perceived to exist, must include this wage increment. Second, the effect of taxes reduces the real return. Even where a corporation may view the desirability of an investment from an after-tax rate of return, as soon as this is reflected into personal incomes, taxes come into play again in many revealed as well as hidden ways. All of these effects combined, amount to ways in which implicit costs may occur. However, it must be recognized that the basis for considering such unperceived costs is that of a proportionality of the capital investment. In short, part of the perceived rate of return is cost in the social framework. In other words, the rate of return, insofar as the corporate owners are concerned, is their return but part of this is an exchange internal to the economy and so is not a net return to the society. One might only then wish to question whether such costs that are thus concealed within the perceived rate of return should appropriately be estimated on the basis of a straight proportionality to capital invested.

Different Discount Rates

The foregoing argument now sets the stage for a consideration of the possibility of discounting the cost stream at a different rate from that of the benefit stream. While some economists have suggested that long-range projects may be justified by use of two interest rates (Ekstein, 1961), their arguments have been largely unconvincing. Mobasheri (1967) argues persuasively for a discount rate at the social rate of return on the benefit side and contends that the cost side should be discounted at the opportunity cost-of-capital. This amounts to the same thing as a recognition that the costs include some components that are a straight percentage of the capital invested in the project. In a public investment, these costs do not reappear as benefits and so the social discount rate is appropriate for discounting the benefits.

Now what about the private investment decision? The point of view of the investor is to maximize his profit that he measures in proportion to his investment. The costs that are included in the discount function on the cost stream side becomes a benefit on the revenue side. Thus for the private investment decision, it would seem that it is quite correct to use the same discount rate for both costs and revenue streams. Again, the only question that needs to be asked is whether such costs and benefits are properly assessed as being proportional to the capital invested.

Risk

Risk may be measured in terms of the variance associated with the expected outcome of the investment. Since for the total social investment the outcome may be reflected in a growth rate of the economy that is essentially deterministic, risk is essentially eliminated. However, it is a consideration for each component investment. Actually, it is a true cost for the individual investor and should be assessed explicitly. The common practice of adjusting the discount rate upward to allow for risk is not rationally justifiable. Because the variance of both costs and benefits is a function of the futurity of the estimates, the risk is an increasing function of futurity. This justifies a discount rate, $r = r(t)$ (English, 1961, 1965). It might also be observed that the risks associated with the costs that occur first as investments are much less than those associated with the estimates of the subsequent benefit stream.

Financing

For many projects the so-called economic studies are analyses of the required cash flow to pay off an interest and principal schedule according to some arbitrary rule. They are not economic evaluations. The cost of borrowed capital is a true cost as is the cost of risk that is associated with a variance in the costs being different from expectations. Thus these costs must be factored into the weighted cost-of-capital for the project. This weighted cost-of-capital is the appropriate discount rate on the cost side. However, this discount rate is not the interest rate on the financing. Financing constraints might dictate a need for a certain constant revenue stream to retire the loan in N years at $r\%$ interest, but the project may not be designed nor may it necessarily operate in an economic environment that will permit the generation of cash flow in such an arbitrary way as to match a particular repayment schedule. In fact, when the growing nature of the demand is considered along with a changing price trend, the cash flow in a perfectly sound economic venture could be deficient for many years. This might necessitate a means of financing a deficit for the interim period. However, such a deficit is not a measure for nonjustification of the project. If sound long-range investment decisions for large-scale systems are to be made, such restrictions of the analyses to consideration of financial feasibility according to outdated conventions must be discontinued and instead true economic evaluations must be instituted. This idea may be so alien to the thinking of investment bankers that its acceptance is not likely to come about easily.

MEASUREMENT OF INVESTMENT PROFITABILITY

While discounted cash flow is the approach by which a project is economically justified, it provides no indication of how well the project may be progressing at any point in time. The accountant is interested in this question from year to year. To state a profit over any given time period, such as a year, he must make some allocation of the capital cost over time. The cash flow less this allocated cost (depreciation) is a *stated* profit. How well it represents a reasonable measure of a true profit estimate depends on two things:

1. The realized cash flow relative to the projected cash flow.
2. The method of allocation.

Conventional accounting methods may not be too unrealistic when the cash flows are the averaged result of many investments and the allocation by any depreciation method represents also an averaged allocation. However, the problem for a single large system is not the same thing as for a manufacturing industry where the averaging effect is more or less operative.

The conventional approach to the measurement of profitability may be one of the inhibitions that makes it difficult to obtain a suitable financing plan. Consider a project in which the expected revenue is generated according to a function $x(t)$ (Figure 6) for some life, H.

A conventional allocation scheme is straight line depreciation, δ_0, which may be represented by AB. Thus the stated profit rate will be

$$P = x(t) - \delta_0 \tag{14}$$

Expressed as a rate of return

$$r = \frac{P}{K(t)} \tag{15}$$

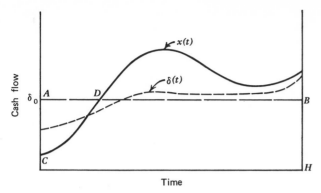

Fig. 6 Transformed depreciation function, $\delta(t)$.

If $x(t)$ is the expected cash flow and it materializes as expected, then the fluctuating profit rate, year-to-year, should be quite acceptable. Nevertheless, investors most likely would still be unhappy during loss periods and over-elated during periods of high stated profit. Actually, if $x(t)$ turns out to be above the projected level at the outset (represented by CD), the investor should be satisfied.

How then might this difficulty be overcome? An allocation (depreciation) function $\delta(t)$ may be defined in such a way as to make expected rate of return on book value a constant. Then if the rate of return turns out to be above its expected level it truly will be a measure of better-than-expected profit. To do this let

$$\frac{x(t) - \delta(t)}{K(t)} = r = \text{constant} \tag{16}$$

The value of capital at any time, t, is the discounted cash flow for the remaining life, $H - t$,

$$K(t) = \int_t^H x(t)e^{-r\tau} \, d\tau \tag{17}$$

Combining (16) and (17)

$$\delta(t) = x(t) - r \int_t^H x(t)e^{-r\tau} \, d\tau \tag{18}$$

Two Example Cases
I. Consider the case where demand may be expected to grow over the life of the project to produce

$$x(t) = x_0 e^{bt} \tag{19}$$

Then

$$\delta(t) = x_0\left\{e^{bt} + r\frac{e^{(b-r)t} - e^{(b-r)H}}{b - r}\right\} \tag{20}$$

II. The case where $x(t) = R = $ constant

$$\delta(t) = R(1 + e^{-rH} - e^{-rt}) \tag{21}$$

This may be shown to be the sinking fund depreciation formula.

LONG-RANGE INVESTMENT

There are many situations for which an investment may require a very long time to pay off. As the economy grows and the scale of many new systems grows much larger and more complex, the need both in the public and private sectors for making long-range commitments becomes ever more evident. At the same time the methodology which has been used to justify the related investments leaves a great deal to be desired.

In the first place, a long-range investment requires a long-range prediction. As the futurity of any prediction is extended, the uncertainty of the outcome expands. This tendency leads one to the argument that it is only valid to estimate costs and benefits for a relatively short-run horizon. Second, the present worth of long-term revenue (benefit) streams, when discounted at what are considered to be attractive or even marginally acceptable discount rates, is so low that the decision is not likely to be altered by ignoring cash flows that may occur in the remote future. On the other hand, there are some who argue for support of certain long-range projects based solely on judgment and a political wisdom that transcends *rational* economic analysis; and indeed many economical large-scale systems in operation today could never have been started if the initial decision had been made on the basis of a conventional present-day economic analysis.

In fact, very strong intuitive feeling about the efficacy of certain undertakings might lead one to a conclusion that many accepted engineering economic studies may be in fact completely wrong. In this section a few rather basic errors in current methodology are pointed out and a new approach that may overcome this difficulty is suggested.

Three Types of Long-Range Investment

For purpose of differentiation long-range investments may be classified into three categories.

Induced Investments Required for Expansion of Capacity or Extension of a Service. The technology in such cases has been well established and the prior pattern of revenues and costs is readily predictable from long-established experience. This category of investment may be readily evaluated by currently accepted economy studies and so is not of concern here. See, for example, Morris (1967).

Development of a New Technology. In this second category there is a fundamental uncertainty about the way in which technology will advance. However, in addition, the investment will require public acceptance of a new product or service. The scale of the final development cannot be known nor can the pattern of costs and prices be readily predicted for far into the future. Indeed the program may appear to offer promise for a considerable period of time before finally being abandoned. Inevitably the initial commitments will have to be small. An example of this would be nuclear power or water desalting systems.

New or Changed Concept of a Need That Depends on Established Technology. This type would have been the same as for type 1 if a trend had developed in the first place so that the new investment decision required only an extension of an existing system. However, sometimes another alternative that appeared more economical at one time during an early stage of development may have expanded beyond its economic limits. Only when such a development reaches some limit that may not have been visualized during its early stages, may it be necessary to resort to a completely different system concept to satisfy the need at the new expanded scale. However, the economics of the changed system may only be justified on a scale comparable with the one to be replaced. Such might be the case for rapid transit systems today. At one point the exploitation of automobile transport, although initially accepted as superior, may not have appeared markedly so relative to other ways of meeting transportation needs at the time when automobile transit started to grow at the expense of public systems. Rapid transit systems may only have been marginally unattractive at the outset. The difficulty today in justifying new rapid transit systems, that possibly may now be more economical than the automobile, may result from the scale of the investment required for an economical system and one that could be expected to affect significantly present transportation modes. The immensity of the required investment may of itself restrict thinking to such a small scale that any proposed new system will inevitably fall below an economical size.

Three Economic Principles Underlying Long-Range Investment

There are three economic principles that often are overlooked or treated incorrectly in economy studies. The error that is introduced comes about by ignoring them in context of the long range and by assuming that the future will be essentially the same as the present.

In the first place the introduction of a new system will change relative prices in the future. Consumer desires partly influenced by an increasing living standard will be different; relative costs will change. Since no effective market exists for futures, particularly long-range ones, the market forces that determine or influence current prices do not afford a guide for future prices. Studies are made on the assumption that relative prices will remain the same.

Second, inflation is a fact of life. The long trend of inflation is reflected in what have come to be accepted interest rates, probably the exaggeration of the interest rate is equal to the steady-state inflation rate. The practice of using projected costs and benefits in constant dollars is justified but only if the interest rate used in discounting is adjusted downward by the amount of the long-term-trend rate of inflation. Of course short-term changes in inflation rates may be shown to perturb interest rates disproportionately, Patinkin (1965). However, such effects are in the nature of transients. These may need to be taken into account but care should be exercised not to assume that a transient high interest rate is valid for the life of the project.

Third, there is an important distinction between the economic evaluation of a project and a financial feasibility analysis. The latter may be an important constraint on the optimal solution of the economic study. Unfortunately it is often looked upon as the economic analysis. Thus interest rates on loans, the amortization time, and the method of repayment are taken as fundamental variables in the economic analysis while, in reality, they have nothing to do with it except to constrain the investment decision. In effect one might determine the optimal investment without any financing constraint and then compare that solution with a financially constrained solution. The difference represents the cost of imposing the financing constraint.

The Time-Horizon Concept

The time horizon is taken as the planning period beyond which the uncertainties of the future are such that any costs or benefits arising from a project are so unpredictable that they are deemed to be better ignored. In general the futurities of many predictions are necessarily short and therefore the horizon time may be much shorter than the long-range effects of the investment decision. Such a view of the horizon may be too limiting in its concept. It certainly does not utilize the full analogy to the physical horizon.

A man may set out on a journey on the earth with an objective of reaching some port a long way beyond the horizon. The navigational decisions that he will be required to make beyond the horizon will be unknowable in detail, but the traveler will start the journey with every confidence that the proper decisions can be made as the problems arise. His immediate problems are first, the decision to start the journey at all, and second, the detailed decisions associated with the prehorizon conditions that are perceived and can be planned.

The planning horizon concept may be used in much the same way for the investment decision. One must be able to weigh the *posthorizon goals* against unknown costs that may occur over the horizon. The detailed initial investment decisions must be made within the horizon time in context with this posthorizon goal. The goal must be defined with a high degree of confidence that it will be achieved; the detailed decisions must depend on the economic environment as it develops. At the same time careful and detailed planning is needed for the prehorizon investments even though the go-ahead on the decision to invest at all should not and really cannot be based on prehorizon considerations. Present methods in effect are predicated on a violation of this principle and so lead to error.

Predictability and Aspiration

Essentially all prediction is an extrapolation of past experience into the future. If one considers a level of confidence attached to the prediction, the region of a given confidence interval will expand with futurity, Figure 7. This region is a prediction interval that is a function of the regression coefficients of the data used in the prediction (Mood, 1950). Thus a meaningful

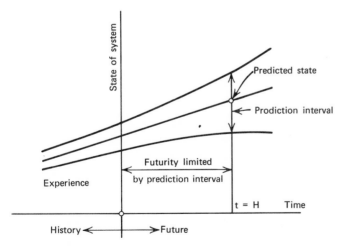

Fig. 7 Diverged system state with futurity.

prediction is valid, within some defined prediction interval, only for the future time required to reach that interval. Obviously some things may be predicted for much longer futurities than others. Often a long-range prediction may apply for the economic environment within which a proposed new system will operate, while it will not be valid for the system. Thus the goals of the system expressed in the economic environmental context may not be too difficult to predict but the exact form it will assume may be. The goal may be achieved by reason of adaptive changes that are made as time goes by.

In dealing with the costs and benefits (revenues) that arise in the pre-horizon, one should take account of the increasing risk attendant on this expanding prediction interval. There is a number of ways in which this may be done (English, 1965, 1966). It was concern for this problem that led the author to search for a way out of the dilemma that arises from effectively discounting the more remote future cash flows to values that approach zero. In principle the prehorizon cash flows are subject to the divergent effect of the prediction interval but the posthorizon goal predictions or aspirations are not. This is depicted in Figure 8. In effect the prediction interval expands

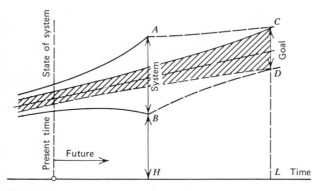

Fig. 8 System state converged toward goal.

to AB for the state of the system because no intervention is assumed between $t = 0$ and $t = H$. The same might be true for the state of the environment CD. However beyond H the state of the system will converge to CD because of the adaptive decisions that will be made in the posthorizon period.

Furthermore, such goal predictions often assume the characteristics of self-fulfilling predictions. Once a program has been initiated, the interested individuals can be counted on to strive to achieve the result. The more hindrances that arise, the harder will the committed individuals work to prove that they were right in the first place. In other words, the goal becomes an aspiration that is not subject to the expanding confidence interval of a prediction.

The hypothesis on which the argument in this chapter is based is predicated on just this distinction between the *divergent nature of a prediction and the convergent nature of an aspiration*. The prediction is valid for detailed estimates of costs and benefits up to a horizon time that is limited by a desired level of confidence. This cannot be very long—say five or at most ten years. On the other hand the aspiration, which is based in part on a broader prediction of the constraining environment, is a goal that lies a long way beyond the horizon.

Bifurcation of the Pay-off

The fact that there is an aspiration cannot in itself justify a long-range investment decision. Many programs, started with high aspirations of ultimate success have ultimately failed to achieve an economically viable condition. Often failure occurs as a result of competing concepts. Ultimately one will dominate. Many examples exist of just such situations: the electric versus the internal-combustion-engine automobile, the lighter-than-aircraft versus the heavier-than-aircraft to cite only two very well remembered cases. In each case there were many die-hards that fought vigorously for the viability of the concept to which they were committed. The end result is always the same for all but one of the competing concepts. At some point it becomes evident that a system will not prove viable and it dies, or it is viable and grows to some mature state, the level of which is almost never visualized at the outset.

Since the bifurcation of the path of development cannot be perceived in the beginning, it always occurs at a posthorizon time. In the prehorizon time it can only be assumed that the system will be viable and will grow exponentially. This is not to say that at the outset one should not recognize some probability that the system will be unsuccessful. As a matter of fact, it is important to assess some probability to this result even though such an assigned probability can only be made with a high degree of subjectivity.

In the long-range investment, the pay-off will not occur in the prehorizon time. It will only occur if the aspiration is reached at some indeterminate posthorizon time. Given that the system proves viable in the long run, it will grow at a rate that will be limited by ability to organize and expand the system to meet a demand that generally may be expected to outpace growth of capacity. The problem then becomes one of predicting the rate of growth,* given

---

* It is of interest to note that new technologies or newly created demands often grow at a rate in the order of 20% per year. This may be explained by the natural social adjustment to innovation coupled with the inertia of development of expertise to build, maintain and operate the resulting systems. This may be a human limitation that constrains the growth to some such rate.

that the system is viable. In effect it is postulated that a growth rate, that will be evident at the horizon time, will then persist. In principle this is a point prediction of the derivative of the cost/benefit function and may be more realistic than any prediction of a posthorizon total cost/benefit function.

The typical course of the investment project may now be depicted as in Figure 9.

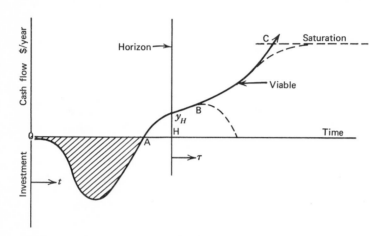

Fig. 9   Cash flow to horizon and beyond.

The investment, including the costs for various studies, engineering and development, construction, and testing, may extend over a period, $0A$, that is significantly long relative to any realistic horizon H. Given that the projected cash flow, y_H (the difference between benefits or revenues and direct costs) at the horizon time is achieved, and that the system proves viable, then the return may be expected to grow at rate, g, in the posthorizon environment. In other words, the investment decision is to introduce a system including its adaptive properties and all of its components irrespective of the time at which they may be needed. The return should be based on a recognition of the complementarity of those elements that will come into being with those that are already initiated.

In the foregoing, development of the cash flow was assumed to be generated by the initial or prehorizon planned investment. If subsequent investment is made the total cash flow function must be attributable to both the initial investment and the follow-on investment, including the reinvestment for replacement of worn or obsolete components of the system. The question then arises as to how one can make a reasonable assessment of this. If the discount rate is, r, then the present worth at H of the posthorizon cash flow will be

$$P_H = \int_0^c y_H e^{g\tau} e^{-r\tau}\, d\tau$$

$$= y_H \frac{e^{(g-r)c} - 1}{g - r} \tag{22}$$

If we cannot make any reasonable estimate for the time of saturation of demand, it may be reasonable to assume that c approaches infinity. Thus

$$\underset{c \to \infty}{P_H} = \frac{y_H}{g - r} \tag{23}$$

The estimate of y_H may be conservative to allow for risk.

If now we assign a probability, π, that the system will prove viable and ignore any pay-off if it does not, then at $t = 0$

$$P = P_0 + \pi \frac{y_H}{g - r} e^{-rH} \tag{24}$$

where P_0 is the present worth of both the investment and cash-return-flows from $t = 0$ to $t = H$. If $P \geq 0$ the decision should be made to invest in the project.

It will be observed that the solution will be very sensitive to the difference between g and r. This sensitivity merely emphasizes the basic difficulty in the long-range investment decision. While it is difficult to estimate g, it may nevertheless be easier and more realistic than to make detailed estimates of cost and revenue streams in the posthorizon region.

The value of P has no meaning other than to define the decision point. Therefore it may be better to set $P = 0$ and rearrange eq. 24 to solve for the minimum growth rate that would justify a positive decision. Thus

$$g_{\min} = r - \pi \frac{y_H}{P_0} e^{-rH} \tag{25}$$

It should be observed that if $P_0 \geq 0$ the project is justified entirely on the basis of the prehorizon conditions without regard to posthorizon pay-offs. Therefore for the posthorizon case in (24), $g_{\min}$ will be greater than r. (Note that P_0 is negative.)

The problem of the decision-maker is then one of judging whether a rate of growth, at least as great as $g_{\min}$, is feasible.

The important concept implied here is that the life of the project is too far into the future to be estimated readily. The decision really hinges on the estimation of the trend beyond the horizon. The probability distribution function of the trend as expressed by a growth rate will be bimodal; it tends either to reach a viable growth rate that will carry the effects beyond any predictable state or the system dies out quite quickly.

Continuing Investment

In the present approach to investment in which the posthorizon is neglected, the scale of the investment is usually limited to the forecast demand at the horizon. Whereas economies of scale might dictate a capacity level that could anticipate demand well into the posthorizon time. There is no assurance that the optimal capacity life of the initial development should not extend into the posthorizon time. It has been shown that not only is this optimum capacity a consideration but that the subsequent investment when taken in conjunction with the initial investment can give an entirely different assessment of the economy of the initial investment (English and El-Ramly, 1967).

As a rule the investment in some new system will require separate consideration for the scale of each subsystem or component. Certain components can be added to the system as demand grows while others may have to be scaled for an overall systems optimum. If it could be known in advance what the detailed requirements of the ultimate development will be, the schedule of investments could be worked out to provide the optimum ultimate system. In this hypothetical system the overall return on investment would have to be proportionately attributable to *all* components of the capital investment. Included in this is both the initial investment and all subsequent posthorizon additions. Since a first step must always be taken before any second step is possible, the initial investment contributes to the return for the whole of the indeterminate long life. In other words the investment decision is to introduce a system including all of its components irrespective of time. The return should be based on a recognition of the complementarity of those elements that will come to be with those that are already initiated.

In the foregoing development, cash flow was assumed to be generated by the initial or prehorizon planned investment. If subsequent investment is made, the total cash flow function must be attributable to both the initial investment and the follow-on investment, including the reinvestment for replacement of worn or obsolete components of the system. The question then arises as to how one can make a reasonable assessment of this.

Now the posthorizon investment decisions cannot be known in detail. Therefore any posthorizon capital expenditures, that must be made to expand capacity to satisfy the growing demand, will be committed at indeterminate times and distributed over time. Perhaps the best assumption that will approximate the true situation is that the capital requirement may be represented by a smoothed capital flow as a fraction of the growing demand. It may be that the capital needs will reflect economies of scale with the increasing size of the systems. However, as a reasonable conservatism we might assume that by the time it is known that the system is viable the capital is growing in proportion to demand. This means that of the total cash flow generated in the system only a part of it is attributable to the initial investment that made the subsequent investment possible. The remainder must be sufficient to cover depreciation and profit at the acceptable rate, r, on the new capital.

By the horizon time, a rate of investment that will be needed to meet the growth in demand will have been established. This can be predicted at $t = 0$. Also the plant additions will have some finite lives and thus will have to be replaced periodically. Again since the details of this cannot be known at the outset, all that is reasonable is to assume an average replacement life. From this one can postulate a capitalized investment rate, I_H, to take care of infinite replication and thereby eliminate the need for considering depreciation explicitly. This means that of the total cash flow at any time $t > H$, the product of the rate of return desired on the continuing investment capital and I_H is allocatable to the continuing investment.

Finally then it must be decided what this rate of return should be. Since the system viability has by then been established, the acceptable discount rate r is indicated as being appropriate. The remainder of the cash flow must therefore be attributable to the initial investment.

In other words, let the cash flow with continuing investment and reinvestment at H be y'_H. Then

$$y_H = y'_H - rI_H \tag{26}$$

It is y'_H that can be estimated directly.

Now substituting into (25), the rate of growth required as a minimum rate to justify the initial investment decision will be

$$g \geq r - \frac{e^{-rH}}{P_0} (y'_H - rI_H) \tag{27}$$

In summary, the foregoing development is a prescriptive methodology for evaluating long-range investment decisions. It must be recognized that any estimates of revenues or costs in the remote future are precarious. Precision is not possible. Therefore what is needed is a realistic rule for a go/no-go decision. This must be greatly influenced by judgment and so the estimates should be of those things for which judgment is most reliable.

In keeping with this point of view, it is contended that detailed cost and revenue estimates are only useful for a relatively short horizon. The main conceptual contribution is the means for doing something about the situation that must occur in a posthorizon time. The best way to do this is to estimate a probability of the system being viable and to couple this with the growth that will occur if it is viable.

SUMMARY

1. A number of questions has been raised. No conclusive answers for most of them have been offered but some new avenues for thinking have been opened. These questions are summarized as follows:

   a. How can a proposed system be isolated for investment decision-making and still take interactions into account?
   b. Long-range planning is essential for development of large complex systems of the future. However, are the methods of forecasting and evaluating long-range economic benefits adequate?
   c. How can future prices be predicted and taken into account in evaluation of economic feasibility of new systems?
   d. A method of evaluating projects by using two rates of discount is advocated; however, what should these rates be?
   e. Are there costs hidden in the rate of return and not properly considered as proportional to capital?
   f. How may risk be considered on a more rational basis than at present?
   g. What should be the method of allocation of capital costs over time?
   h. Should financing constraints be permitted to prohibit investment in otherwise economically justifiable projects?

2. In addition to these questions, a number of new concepts has been introduced. These may afford one an opportunity to view the problem of investment from a distinctly new perspective and may eventually lead to better project evaluation. These concepts are as follows:

   a. The notion of capital as a quantity derived from the difference between value inputs and outputs integrated over time. Thus capital is not a fundamental production variable. Time is the *independent* variable.
   b. The rate of discount should not necessarily be a constant.
   c. The true rate of discount for social benefits is equal to the rate of growth of the economy.
   d. The allocation of capital costs over time should be such as to reflect a better measure of current profit such as would be obtained by using a constant expected rate of return over the project life.

3. A theoretical methodology that incorporates the foregoing concepts was developed. It must be recognized that some of these ideas are sufficiently different from past practice that it will take a long time for people to get used to them and actually employ them in investment decisions. However, it may be useful to use them to compare these conclusions with those obtained by using generally accepted present-day investment criteria. At least when a

conclusion that is reached through traditional methods of analysis is the same as with the new method, there will be greater confidence that it is a correct one. On the other hand, opposite conclusions may be worthy of a more penetrating analysis.

4. One of the most significant problems is that of large-scale investments needed for development of an improved environment. These developments require long-range commitments and present methodology is inadequate for evaluating long-range investment. An entirely new approach for solutions of this problem is developed.

REFERENCES

ALCHIAN, A. A. (1955), "The Rate of Interest, Fisher's Rate of Return Over Cost, and Keynes Internal Rate of Return," *American Economic Review*. Also see Izra Solomon (1959), *The Management of Corporate Capital*, The Free Press, New York, pp. 67–71.

EKSTEIN, OTTO (1961), *Water-Resource Development: The Economics of Project Evaluation*, Cambridge, Mass.

ENGLISH, J. M. (1961), "New Approach to Economic Comparison for Engineering Projects," *Journal of Industrial Engineering*. November–December.

ENGLISH, J. M. (1965), "Discount Function for Comparing Economic Alternatives," *Industrial Engineering*. March–April.

ENGLISH, J. M. (1965), "Economic Comparison of Projects Incorporating a Utility Criterion in the Rate of Return," *Engineering Economist*. December.

ENGLISH, J. M. (1965), "The Rate of Return and Assessment of Risk," *Engineering Economist*. May.

ENGLISH, J. M. (1968), *Cost Effectiveness: The Economic Evaluation of Engineering Projects*, Wiley, New York.

ENGLISH, J. M., and N. EL-RAMLY (1967), *Economic Evaluation of Desalting Sub-System as a Part of the Total Water System*, Desalination.

FISHER, IRVING (1930), *The Theory of Interest*, Macmillan, New York.

GRANT, E. L., and GRANT IRESON (1970), *Engineering Economy*, Ronald Press, New York, N.Y.

MOBASHERI, F (1967), "Economic Evaluation of a Water Resources Development Project in a Developing Nation," Ph.D. dissertation, University of California, Berkeley.

MOOD, ALEXANDER M. (1950), *Introduction to the Theory of Statistics*, McGraw-Hill, New York.

MORRIS, WILLIAM T. (1967), *The Capacity Decision Problem*, Irwin.

PATINKIN, DON (1965), *Money, Interest and Prices*, Harper & Row, New York.

V A Physical Analogy of the Walrasian Model: Ole Immanuel Franksen

INTRODUCTION

The increasing size and complexity of integrated engineering-economic systems, the urgency to control and adapt such systems to a steadily more dynamic environment, the rapidly growing rate at which knowledge is being developed, and the expanding possibilities of utilizing electronic digital computers necessitates a reorganization of the theoretical knowledge for engineers and economists into a unified set of new basic patterns. In particular, such a unification should aim at maximum practical coverage through computational efficiency while conceptually it should concentrate on the development of the most useful generalization.

Economics deals with the interdependence between consumption and production, and its aim is to enable people to influence economic activity. Engineering, just as with economics, is concerned with the allocation of a number of limited resources, and its purpose is to enable people to produce, mostly physical systems and processes. To forecast the results of a planned economic activity or the properties of a proposed engineering product, both disciplines base their analysis on the theories of their primary pure sciences, psychology and sociology, and physics and chemistry, respectively.

The difference between the pure sciences, on the one hand, and economics and engineering, on the other, is primarily one of function or attitude in relation to society rather than one of method, means, or depth of training. Thus to a large degree economists and engineers must acquire the same understanding of behavioral or natural phenomena as the scientists; but, whereas scientific research is aimed entirely towards a fuller understanding of these phenomena, economic and engineering research is directed towards organization of knowledge for use in their ultimate function. In engineering as well as in economics this basic function is "design," by which is meant the procedure of selecting and combining distinct elements to create, in an optimum way, complete systems which will perform in a prespecified manner.

In spite of the fact that engineering and economics are completely interrelated and dependent upon each other, there seems to be a barrier of historical traditions or conventions which emphasizes the differences between the two disciplines and prevents the similarities or common patterns from being crystallized into a unified set of generalized concepts. Probably, the removal of this barrier can best be furthered by comparison of the conceptions formulated in either discipline, and by finding for the conceptions in one of these disciplines the corresponding conceptions in the other. Discovery of analogies between different disciplines or reformulating of theory to emphasize aspects of duality have spurred some of the most significant advances in the history of science. Therefore, the aim of this chapter is the pursuit of those fundamental resemblances which, as a foundation for the establishment of engineering models of economic systems, are most likely to produce new insight and understanding.

Mathematicians and, in particular, electrical engineers, have often endeavored to formulate electrical network models of econometric problems. P. O. Pedersen's model of a production function from 1935 is a typical attempt. Other examples are Koopmans and Reiter (Koopmans, 1951), Enke (1951), Tustin (1957), and Dennis (1959). A common characteristic to all these cases is the fact that the electric network analogies are established by inspection of the equations of the individual econometric models. The purpose of this chapter is (1) to set up an analogy between the basic laws of physics and economics and (2) to use this fundamental correspondence to establish an electric network analogue of an ideal economic system developed by the great French economist Léon Walras in the early 1870s (Walras, 1954). In this connection it should be appreciated that *mathematical programming*, in its original form as an economic discipline under the name *activity analysis*, was developed as a quantitative generalization of the Walrasian equation system of econometrics (see, for example, Dorfman et al., 1958, or Baumol, 1965).

THE FUNDAMENTAL LAWS OF PHYSICS

In physics, from a macroscopic point of view and satisfying a set of statistical assumptions originating in the physics of microscopic phenomena, the basic theoretical structure underlying classical mechanics, electric network theory, and thermodynamics (or, more correctly, thermostatics) is best revealed by concentrating on the latter discipline. Here, the whole of the theory is developed from two basic laws which in general can be designated:

First law: The principle of conservation.
Second law: The statistical principle of flow orientation.

Through the history of physics the two most discussed and most critical of the underlying microscopic assumptions of statistical physics have been those pertaining, respectively, to *isolation* and to *relaxation-time versus process duration*. A perusal of economic literature will show that, indirectly, these two topics underlie much discussed in this chapter, too. Therefore, it will pay off to discuss briefly these two statistical assumptions in relation to the two laws above.

The idea that, in an isolated universe, there must be an invariant entity, changeable in form but indestructable, was first recognized in 1693 by Leibnitz in the study of simple mass points in a terrestrial gravitational field. Mathematically, the invariant entity was depicted as an additive, scalar quantity, the so-called energy. As additional physical types of systems were considered, the established form of the conservation principle repeatedly failed. In each case, however, it was found possible to revive it by the addition of a new mathematical term. This "new kind of energy" was perceived as the contribution of the remaining and, up till then, unknown part of the isolated universe.

Since measurements cannot be performed between systems of different physical kinds (i.e., electrical and mechanical), the principle of conservation is the only manner in which we can describe the interaction between such systems. Thus the mathematical statement of this principle should be considered as *an equation of constraint among systems.*

To be more specific, it should be remembered that energy is a potential for mechanical work. Basically, any energy term can be written as a product of two quantities such as force and displacement. The interaction between an arbitrary system and its disjoint environment, together making up an isolated universe, is determined by first taking the differential of the equation of conservation which, with due consideration for signs, consists of a sum of two factor products. From this differential we pick a subsum of only those terms that contain the differentials of the selected set of independent parameters, suitably chosen to represent the system and the independent influences or sources of the environment. Now, if the selected subsum turns out to be an exact differential of a certain function, we have found a state-function.

In physics a *state-function* is defined as a single-valued function, derivable from a principle of conservation, the value of which, at a given instant of time, depends solely upon the state of the system, and not on past history.

It is a well-known fact that an energy term in a state-function can *depend implicitly on time*. Thus, for example, kinetic energy is a function of velocity, that is, the time-derivative of displacement. Much discussion, however, in classical mechanics centered around the possibility that the total energy was *explicitly dependent on time*. Clearly, in these cases, energy was not conserved. Therefore, it was normally assumed that the change of energy in time was known so that by suitable transformations, involving adding the time t to the mechanical variables, a new equation of conservation, and thereby a new state-function, could be defined.

In electric network theory the conversion of energy in sources and by dissipation depends explicitly on time. For this reason, the principle of conservation for electric networks since Maxwell (Maxwell, 1891) has been stated in terms of *power*, that is, the time derivative of energy. Power, it should be noted, is basically defined as the product of two time derivatives (e.g., electric current and voltage). Later (Millar, 1951) it was discovered that the Maxwellian formulation was valid only in linear cases with the result that two new state-functions, related to power and analogous to the ones used in classical mechanics, were introduced instead. These two power state-functions, *content* and *cocontent*, are defined and used later in this chapter. Here, it suffices to say that a large majority of the powerful, but physically often rather incomprehensible, modern network methods can find a simple interpretation in terms of these two power functions (Franksen, 1968).

Closely related to the discussion above of the principle of conservation in terms of, on the one hand, energy and its dependence on time, and, on the other, the assumption of isolation, is the question of using the state-functions, originating in this principle, for the determination of the equilibrium state. The variables, making up a state-function, are all macroscopical variables. These variables and the corresponding state-functions, however, are only defined if the system is microscopically homogeneous. That is, it changes continuously from one microscopic equilibrium state to another. In each microscopic equilibrium state the external influences of the system will cancel, the result of which is that also macroscopically the system will be in equilibrium. Altogether, therefore, a description of a statistical system in terms of macroscopic state-functions will take place in terms of a succession of equilibrium states. Whether it is possible thus to describe a statistical system by a macroscopic, dynamic theory in terms of equilibrium states depends on the effectiveness of the transition mechanism at the microscopic or atomistic level. The earlier mentioned relaxation time is the characteristic, transitional property of interest in relation to the present discussion.

Basically, the relaxation time is a measure of the time it takes for the system to go from one state of equilibrium to another to adjust to a change in the environment. The relaxation time, actually, is a time-constant, in the exponential dependence sense, for the propagation at the microscopic level. Thus, for a given system with a given relaxation time, only changes that occur in periods much longer than the relaxation time can be described by macroscopic measurements as a succession of equilibrium states. On the other hand, changes that occur in periods shorter than the relaxation time correspond to a succession of microscopic, nonequilibrium states for which no meaningful, macroscopic measurement can be made.

In thermodynamics the relaxation times have such a long duration that the changes must proceed with "infinite slowness" to be defined macroscopically in terms of equilibrium states. This implies that the system is, at every moment, in a quiescent equilibrium state. That is, thermodynamics is actually thermostatics in which all the changes considered are quasistatic in the sense that they are described as an ordered succession of static equilibrium states, neither of which involve considerations of rates, velocities, or time.

In electrical network theory, on the other hand, the relaxation time is in the order of speed of light. Therefore, in many applications, we can adopt the lumped parameter representation with infinite propagation speed in the formulation of the problem in question. The state-functions involved are all related to power (i.e., the rate of change of energy) which for the lumped parameter network, perceived as an isolated universe, sum to zero. That is, at every moment the network is in equilibrium, the conditions of which can be stated in terms of Kirchhoff's laws. It should be noted, however, that the equilibrium states are not static, but dynamic, stationary states. Actually, by using power instead of energy in the formulation of the problem we have reduced dynamics to statics in a manner which completely corresponds to the use of d'Alembert's principle in classical mechanics. This does not mean, of course, that we can actually solve the dynamical problem by statical methods. Rather, we have merely deduced or formulated the dynamical equations, expressing the instantaneous, macroscopic state of the system, by statical equilibrium considerations. Note that this formulation in terms of instantaneous, stationary states does not imply anything about the stability of the system in time.

Turning now to the second law, the statistical principle of flow orientation, it should first of all be emphasized that this law is not absolutely certain, but only highly probable. In thermodynamics, where it originates in the basic experiments of Joule, it was found for an isolated system that, if two states are specified, it is always possible to join them by a mechanical set of changes, but that it might not be possible to define changes leading either way. This experimentally found asymmetry or irreversibility, which is known as the second law of thermodynamics, has been given several formulations. The one most frequently used, probably, is that the entropy of an isolated system tends to a maximum. Here, however, we will rather use the formulation of Clausius, being more applicable from an interdisciplinary point of view. In general terms the second law can be stated: *a flow will occur only from a higher to a lower potential.*

As an example of this qualitative but unique law of orientation we can consider the frictional process involved in a displacement of a mechanical system. During the displacement, due to the friction, energy is dissipated. That is, it is converted from a form included in the system analysis to a form (heat) not considered. Changing sign on the direction of the displacement will not change the direction of dissipative energy conversion. Ideal sources are the duals to dissipations, since here energy is converted from a form not included in the analysis to a form that can be handled in the analysis. Together, dissipations and sources are examples of the unique, "causal" orientation stated more generally by the second law.

MEASUREMENTS AND RELATED CONCEPTS

Basically, economic measurements are oriented towards a description of the time-dependent biological phenomena of psychology and sociology. Utility analysis and similar topics of economic theory, however, are considered outside the present field of interest. That is, we confine ourselves exclusively to the engineering-economic problem of controlling a production.

Pertinent to the latter problem field we can distinguish between two fundamental kinds of measurements, prices, and flows of quantities. Both originate in the economic theory of demand and supply where, as we shall discuss it later, their internal relationships, as influences on a production, are given in terms of demand and supply curves. For the present purpose it suffices to say that they are determined as instantaneous values.

Measurements constitute the only link between the observations of reality and the corresponding theoretical model. Thus the theoretical concepts which can be related to one another by the abstract rules of mathematics originate in measurements. In physics, *meaning* in relation to reality is given to the theoretical model by interpreting the basic concepts, representing the measurements, in either of two ways. Both are dependent on time and position, but differ by being oriented respectively toward the qualitative and the quantitative characteristics of the observations. The two viewpoints are described here as that of operationalism and that of symbolism.

The viewpoint of *operationalism* is characterized by the fact that meaning is given to the concepts of measurement by relating them to a well-defined activity on the part of the observer. That is, the measurements are qualitatively classified by interpretation of the set of operations making up the procedure for the measurement in question. Basically, depending on the manner in which, at least conceptually, the measuring device is used, we can distinguish between two different classes of measurements. A *transvariable* (or across-variable) is measured by simultaneously attaching the instrument to two actual connection points of the system without cutting the interconnections in the latter. Examples of transvariables are voltage, displacement, rotation, and temperature. Note that the one connection point can be a fixed point of reference such as is exemplified in the measurements of nodal voltages, displacement of masses in a gravitational field, and, in economics, prices.

An *intervariable* (or through-variable), on the other hand, is measured by cutting the system at an actual connection point and inserting the instrument at the point of cut. Examples of intervariables are electric current, mechanical force, torque, and heat transfer. In economics, flows of resources and commodities must be characterized as intervariables.

From a mathematical point of view, operationally defined measurements of an arbitrary, observable property are conceivable as elements of the same mathematical set. To classify as measurements, the elements must satisfy, at least, a binary relation of equivalence. If the measurements satisfy only this relation, we say that they are measured on a *nominal scale*. If, in addition to the binary relation of equivalence, the elements satisfy a binary order relation, we say that they are measured on an *ordinal scale*. Note that the resulting arrangement of a set of measurements in a quasiserial order presumes a topological orientation of time and space. Operationally defined measurements do not satisfy a binary operation, such as a rule of additivity. However, they might indicate conclusive evidence as to the possibility of postulating the existence of such an operation.

Psychophysics and the ordinal theory of utility are scientific areas in which theoretical models are established from operationally defined measurements (Samuelson, 1938; Stevens, 1959; and Baumol, 1965). The theory of generalized files, underlying the design of integrated data processing systems, is another area which is based upon operationally defined measurements (Orchard-Hayes, 1959; Franksen and Rømer, 1963).

The viewpoint of *symbolism* is characterized by the fact that the theoretical concepts are given meaning by being derived from certain postulates, the satisfaction of which cannot be proven, but which experience indicates are in agreement with observations. A set of postulates which can be used to identify, in a quantitative manner, theoretical concepts with observable properties are the following three.

The first postulate concerns the question whether the theoretical model should be based upon *causality* or *randomness*. Basically, a macroscopic measurement can be perceived to represent a *deterministic* as well as a *probabilistic* observable property. The choice depends on the overall consistency of the resulting theory with experience (Papoulis, 1964).

The second postulate is introduced to permit the establishment of unified concepts that express the *sameness* of operationally different observables (Bridgman, 1927, 1936). The viewpoint of symbolism does not recognize that, as the physical range increases, the fundamental observables cease to exist and therefore must be replaced by other observables which are operationally quite different. An example of the point in question is the concept of length which is used to describe astronomic length, engineering length, as well as atomic length.

The third postulate concerns the introduction of *continuity* or, at least, piecewise continuity. Continuity is a mathematical idealization the invocation of which by its very nature measurements cannot verify. The justification for introducing continuity lies in the operational discovery of conclusive evidence as to the possibility of postulating the existence of a *binary operation of addition*. Thus it is possible to represent the theoretical concepts by metrical, symbolic entities which, at least within certain ranges, submit to the applicability of calculus.

Siding together with the assumption of continuity is that of *differentiability*. Related to the latter are the concepts of *extensive* and *intensive* variables. These concepts originate in thermodynamics. There, extensive variables are directly proportional to the amount of matter or size of the system, whereas the intensive variables are not. In economics, by analogy, we consider *the amounts of a commodity or a resource as extensive variables*, and *time-derivatives as prices or flows of commodities and resources, as intensive variables.*

Evaluation of the operationally defined measurements, transvariables and intervariables, from the mathematical point of view of their interpretation as metrical entities yields the following results. Dependent on whether the metrical scale of measurement implies a knowledge of an absolute zero point, we distinguish between a *ratio scale* and an *interval scale* (Stevens, 1959). The ratio scale is characterized by having an absolute zero so that it is invariant to transformations of the type: $x' = ax$. The interval scale, on the other hand, is characterized by having no absolute zero point. That is, the interval scale is invariant to transformations of the type: $x' = ax + b$. Experience indicates that direct measurement of an intervariable, for example, an amount or a flow of a commodity, is always based on a ratio scale. On the other hand, direct measurement of a transvariable is normally related to the use of an interval scale. Thus the zero or reference point in measuring electric nodal voltages or economic prices is a matter of convention or convenience. Note, however, that differences on interval scales are measured on ratio scales. For example, the voltage drop over an electric element, determined as the difference between two nodal voltages, or the increase in economic value along a production activity, determined as the difference between two prices, are transvariables measured on ratio scales. In physics, transvariables measured on an interval scale are generally conceived as scalar potentials, whereas intervariables, being measured on ratio scales, are apprehended as vectors. The arbitrary reference of orientation, assigned to an intervariable parameter, is an operationally defined orientation between the two connection points used in the determination of the corresponding transvariable parameter.

After thus operationally having defined the basic measurements as well as symbolically having formulated their corresponding, conceptual abstractions, it is now possible to establish the fundamental relationships or laws. Obviously, the theoretical formulation of basic laws is based on the discovery of structural properties that are invariant under certain well-defined changes. Mathematically, to bring out this invariancy of structure or form we aim at the largest possible amount of *symmetry* in the theoretical formulation, completely disregarding the fundamental role played in experimental practice by the direct measurements making up the basis of the individual unit systems. Examples of such applications of the concept of symmetry as a theoretical tool of formulation, are Maxwell's use of symbol-symmetrical equations in his formulation of the basic laws of electromagnetism (Campbell, 1921) and the use of more advanced group-theoretical concepts in modern quantum mechanics.

As a suitable starting point in the formulation, by the concept of symmetry, of the economic theory of production we will here use the organization in Table 1 of the basic measurements of economics. The explanation of the

Table 1   Basic Measurements in Economics

	Extensive	Intensive
Transvariables	—	Price, p
Intervariables	Amount of resource or commodity in physical units, q	Flow of physical quantities, $i = dq/dt$

variables in this table follows directly from the discussion above of the basic measurements. Note, however, that in economics the extensive transvariable, which is the time-integral of a price, is only defined if we believe in the existence of a *cardinal* measure of aggregated *satisfaction* or *utility* per unit time.

One of the most surprising facts of physics and economics is that the fundamental relationships or laws are all derived from mere direct or inverse proportionalities between a transvariable parameter and an intervariable parameter.

Under linearity or *ceteris paribus* assumptions, physical examples of *direct proportionality* between a transvariable and an intervariable are natural laws such as Ohm's law, which is a proportionality between intensive variables. The corresponding constant of proportionality is known as the impedance. Zero or infinite values of the impedance are considered limiting cases and are used in connection with a specification of one of the variables as an ideal source. In practice the linearity assumption will seldom hold. Instead, therefore, one often considers only differential changes from a given working point.

In economics this type of relationship is exemplified in demand and supply curves which are single-valued relationships between intensive variables, the latter of which are further required to be nonnegative. By tradition, supply and demand curves are defined and determined from the total curves as average curves. Similarly, in physics, all natural laws such as Ohm's law are average curves. The supply and demand curves are assumed linear in both quadratic and linear programming applications, the latter case distinguished by exhibiting curves parallel to either the price axis (perfectly inelastic supply) or to the flow axis (perfectly elastic demand). By analogy to the limiting cases of Ohm's law, perfectly inelastic supply and perfectly elastic demand can be considered respectively as an ideal intervariable or flow source and as an ideal transvariable or price source.

In physics the *inverse proportionality relationships* are always a two-factor product between a transvariable and an intervariable which results in an additive scalar. The resulting scalar is *energy* or *power*, that is, the rate of change of energy. The formulation of the earlier mentioned first law for an isolated system is based exclusively on scalars of this origin. From thermodynamics and modern engineering researches into the theory of electromechanical systems it is realized that energy is a function of a set of independent, extensive parameters. Furthermore, the previously-mentioned research has revealed that *energy should be defined as the integral of an intensive parameter with respect to an extensive parameter* (Cherry, 1951; Franksen, 1965). This definition, of course, is in agreement with the consequences of thermodynamics where the intensive parameters are defined as the partial derivatives of the internal energy with respect to the independent extensive parameters (Callen, 1960). Emphasizing the symmetry in the theoretical formulation of electromechanical problems it turned out to be convenient also to introduce the dual of energy, the so-called coenergy, which *is defined as the integral of an extensive parameter with respect to an intensive parameter*. The different energy state-functions of thermodynamics are composed of energy and coenergy terms. Basically, energy and coenergy are expressions of the potential of a system to do mechanical work. The latter is defined as the mechanical force multiplied by the displacement in the direction of the force, that is, an intensive intervariable multiplied by an extensive transvariable.

A further development, introduced by Maxwell in his celebrated "heat theorem" (Maxwell, 1891), is the use of power as a state-function. Power is defined as the product of an intensive transvariable and an intensive intervariable. To include nonlinear systems, it was later found feasible to introduce instead of power two related functions, content and cocontent (Millar, 1951).

Both functions were defined in complete analogy with the definitions of energy and coenergy. *Thus content is defined as the integral of an intensive transvariable with respect to an intensive intervariable, while cocontent is defined as the integral of an intensive intervariable with respect to an intensive transvariable.*

In economics the corresponding inverse proportionality relationships or two-factor products originate in the conventional determination of cost and profit. However, to use these concepts in the definition of economic state-functions such as has been attempted by Samuelson (Samuelson, 1952, 1960), we discuss the economic analogies to the physical concepts introduced above.

Economic energy and *coenergy* can be introduced in terms of prices p in money units and amounts q in physical units of resources or products. Specifically, we have that energy U and coenergy U' are defined as:

$$U = \int_0^q p \, dq \tag{1}$$

and

$$U' = \int_0^p q \, dp \tag{2}$$

Of these two functions, the energy U seems to be the more useful in economics since it represents *inventory*. Its analogy in electric network theory, as pointed out by the Danish engineer P. O. Pedersen as early as 1935, is the electric energy stored in a capacitor (Pedersen, 1935). If we believe in cardinal utility, coenergy U' can be interpreted as a measure of money satisfaction.

Economic content and *cocontent*, on the other hand, are of primary importance since by means of these two concepts we can formulate economic state-functions completely analogous in all respects to those of physics. In terms of prices p in money units and flows i of physical units we define, with the flow i as independent parameter, the content K as

$$K = \int_0^i p \, di \tag{3}$$

and, with the price p as independent parameter, the cocontent K' as

$$K' = \int_0^p i \, dp \tag{4}$$

Mathematical programming as a tool of economics is based exclusively on content and cocontent state-functions derived from considerations of supply curves and demand curves. In the linear programming case, involving perfectly inelastic supply and perfectly elastic demand, the cocontent state-function will express the total variable cost of the production factors, whereas the content state-function will represent the total revenue.

EQUILIBRIUM CONDITIONS

In the terminology of physics all the measurements described above, physical as well as economical, are macroscopic averages of microscopic, statistical phenomena. The main purpose of the earlier-mentioned statistical assumptions of microscopic physics is to secure the validity of the macroscopic measurements in the sense of uniquely representing these statistical averages. Microscopic states, satisfying these assumptions are designated microscopic equilibrium states. Basically, under the statistical assumptions the system in question will change continuously from one microscopic equilibrium state to another. At each of these microstates, however, the external influences will cancel each other if a homogeneous distribution is upheld. Thus a macrostate can be defined only to represent microscopic equilibrium states. An important result of this observation is that it is possible to establish, directly from the basic properties of the involved, macroscopic measurements, a set of necessary and sufficient conditions for equilibrium in the macroscopic sense.

The *necessary condition of equilibrium* originates in classical mechanics. Here, a statical system is said to be in equilibrium if it is in rest. For a statical system in equilibrium the vector sum of all external and internal forces is zero. This condition, however, is only necessary since it is also satisfied by a nonaccelerated, mechanical system in translation. By postulating for a system in motion, that *the constraint forces constitute a force system in static equilibrium*, d'Alembert extended the applicability of the static condition of equilibrium to dynamics. Basically, forces are intensive intervariables, as are electric currents. The analogous necessary condition in electric network theory, therefore, is Kirchhoff's node law which says that electric currents sum to zero at a node. Thus, in general, the necessary condition of equilibrium for a dynamic system can be stated to say that *intensive intervariables, measured on a ratio scale, sum to zero at a node* (the node law).

In economic theory of dynamic systems it is a well-known fact that the flows involved satisfy this necessary condition (Zeuthen, 1955). The interesting point, however, is that it is normally interpreted as a condition of static equilibrium. Yet, d'Alembert's principle turns the *formulation* of a dynamic problem into a static one, but this does not mean that the dynamic system becomes static or that we can actually *solve* a dynamic problem by statical methods. Only Samuelson in his correspondence principle, which is a complete analogue of d'Alembert's principle, seems to have realized that dynamics can be reduced to statics from the point of view of formulation (Samuelson, 1947). Thus the general economic problem of *comparative statics*, as Samuelson has designated the approach theoretically originating in his correspondence principle, is not a problem of statics. On the contrary, since all variables are intensive variables and the corresponding state-functions are all related to power it is a *dynamic* problem, but it is formulated by the methods of statics. The fact that the underlying microscopic phenomena are statistical, forces the macroscopic model to be in an instantaneous equilibrium. However, this only implies that, at every moment, the economic system is in a stationary state. The problem of *comparative dynamics* (Samuelson, 1947) is to investigate whether the system is *stable in time* in the sense that the original set of assumptions will hold as the external influences change in time.

The condition, which together with the necessary one mentioned above appears as a corresponding *sufficient condition of equilibrium*, originates in electric network theory where it is known as Kirchhoff's mesh law. The law states that electric voltages sum to zero around a closed mesh. Trent later pointed out (Trent, 1955) that this law had an analogue in mechanics which up to then had been overlooked, namely, that proper summation of displacements vanishes around closed loops. In both cases the formulation of the condition can be said to be based on the fact that it concerns transvariables, measured on a ratio scale but derivable from measurements on an interval scale. In general terms, the additional, sufficient condition of equilibrium for a dynamic system is that *transvariables, measured on a ratio scale, sum to zero around a closed loop* (the mesh law).

The economic analogue to this condition is that prices, suitably transformed to changes in value (price differences), sum to zero around a closed mesh or loop.

In economics as well as in electric network theory these two conditions, the node law and the mesh law, will hold at every instant of time, provided, of course, that the earlier-mentioned set of statistical assumptions are fulfilled so that meaningful macroscopic measurements can be defined. Production is a time-consuming process. The most critical of the statistical assumptions, therefore, is the earlier-stated requirement for a sufficiently small relaxation time.

The economists' conception of time in terms of *short run* and *long run*, has enjoyed a long tradition in the history of economics. The latter is flexibly tied up with the period over which the present policies, possessions, and commitments of the firm extend, while the former refers to a period much shorter in relation to this. In comparison with the definition in physical theory of time as one of the basic, independent variables, this economic conception of time is seen to aim at a temporal description where, in the considered time interval, we can assume that, for the subsystem in question, the relaxation time is much smaller.

Basically, the practical procedure must be first to determine the variation in time of all prices and physical amounts in the total economic system. Second, by analogy to Vagn Madsen's principle of variability in cost accounting (Madsen, 1963), prices and flows are grouped according to their variations as a function of definite, physical time intervals (in weeks, months, or years). Thus an economic subsystem, corresponding to a given physical time interval and defined by the pertinent variable prices and amounts, can be considered to have infinitely fast relaxation or mobility, if the total values over the time interval are used to represent the "instantaneous" prices and flows. That is, *we conceive the physical time interval as one unit of economic time.* In this manner we are able to use the dynamic theory of economics, in the form of mathematical programming, in the description of each of the economic subsystems, defined by the principle of variability.

The description of a thus-determined, economic subsystem is the topic of interest here. The Walrasian model, and thereby the methods of linear and quadratic programming, are only valid for such subsystems. Therefore, the analogous electric network to be formulated below is a model of only such systems. In practice, of course, *a total economic system must be described by a whole set of such models or networks each on a different level* defined by the different lengths of the time interval. Note, however, that the relation between two networks at adjacent time levels is such that activities, at the level with the longest time interval, will appear as production factors at the level with the shortest time interval, if the two levels are directly interrelated in the production process.

THE FUNDAMENTAL LAWS OF ECONOMICS

Basically, in economics, the formulation of the Walrasian system of equations for a so-called perfectly competitive commodity market is the description of an atomistic or microscopic isolated system by a dynamical macroscopic theory (Henderson and Quandt, 1958). By satisfying the microscopic assumptions of perfect competition it is secured that the macroscopic, dynamical theory is meaningful. We therefore attempt here to formulate the two basic laws, analogous to those of physics, on which the Walrasian model, in the sense of a dynamic theory, is based.

Before we begin to state and discuss these two laws, however, it should be noted that they and the corresponding dynamic theory do not necessarily have to be based upon a set of statistical assumptions. Classical mechanics might be considered as an analogous physical example where the direction of a gravitational field was perceived as a deterministic edition of the earlier stated second law (Lindsay and Margenau, 1936). Thus a dynamic theory based on the two laws might be useful also in the description of a production where the number of basic elements is so small that no statistical system can be defined.

By considering a closed economy in the form of a perfectly competitive market, earlier economic theorists discovered an important identity which since has come to be called Walras' law (Dorfman et al., 1958; Baumol, 1965). Any person who demands a commodity is by definition prepared to supply in exchange an amount of money or other commodities of equal value. Similarly, anyone who supplies some amount of goods on the market demands in exchange its value equivalent in money or other commodities. Thus each person's demands and supplies are subject to a budget constraint which says that outlays on goods equal income from factor services. Since this is true for each individual separately, it is true for the aggregate. In words, therefore, Walras' law can be stated to say that, *for a closed economy, the total money value of all items supplied must equal the total money value of all items demanded.* According to Baumol (1965), this relationship, which is "little more than an accounting relationship," must hold independently of the state of the system —"whether it is in equilibrium or disequilibrium."

In economic theory, assuming constant returns to scale, Walras' law is often deduced as an equilibrium condition from the Walrasian system of equations, applied to a perfectly competitive market in equilibrium. The point of view taken here is that *Walras' law expresses a principle of conservation for a closed economy.* In the words of Baumol: "It is difficult to imagine an economy in which this law does not hold." Hence we will consider *Walras' law as the first law of economics.* The mathematical statement of the law will be postponed until the formulation of the Walrasian system of equations.

Again, in establishing the second law of economics, we have to draw on analogies from physics. The so-called neoclassical theory of perfect competition on a commodity market and, even more so, of economic production is based on the notion of rational behavior. At the microscopic level rational behavior is tantamount to homogeneity. That is, it is assumed that all firms seek to maximize profits while all consumers endeavor to maximize utility. At the macroscopic level, on the other hand, rational behavior must be formulated in terms of macroscopic measurements, that is, flows and prices. The macroscopic conception of rational behavior, therefore, will differ from the microscopic one.

The general experience, resulting from macroscopic observations of closed economic systems under well-defined influences, is that all changes which occur have a very definite direction. Thus, in an industrial production process, it is impossible to reverse the direction of the physical flow. From the economic point of view, the flows will always occur in the direction from the resources or production factors and to the demands. The use of the designations, input and output, illustrates the point. However, more can be said. The fundamental problem in economics is the best allocation of limited means toward desired ends. The latter are demands as function of prices. From a macroscopic point of view, in a closed economy, it will not make sense to attempt a production if the corresponding flow of activity has a higher price, and thereby value, at the resources than at the demand.

Earlier we showed that prices, in complete analogy with electric nodal voltages, were intensive transvariables measured on an interval scale. Accordingly, we can consider the prices as economic potentials. The *conception of rational behavior*, formulated as a statistical principle of macroscopic flow orientation, is therefore seen to be analogous to the statistical principle of flow orientation in physics. In words, the *second law of economics* can be stated: *a flow will occur only from a lower to a higher price*.

Comparison of the two basic laws of economy:

First law: Walras' law,
Second law: The flow orientation of rational behavior,

with the corresponding two laws of physics shows that they are completely analogous except for a change of sign in the second law. In the terminology of electric network theory, the change of sign in the direction of economic flows can be interpreted by saying that, in economics, we focus the interest on the flows "inside a voltage source" (Enke, 1951).

THE BASIC POSTULATES FORMALIZED

On the basis of the previous discussion we are now able to state in mathematical terms the two fundamental laws or postulates of economics and the state-functions that can be derived from considerations of the first law.

In an isolated economic system let us assume that we have *n limitational resources* or *production factors* available. Being all intensive intervariables measured on a ratio scale we conceive them as flows. In matrix notation (with superscript t indicating transposition) they are written:

$$Y^t = \{y_1, y_2, \ldots, y_n\} \tag{5}$$

The corresponding *n production factor prices* which are intensive transvariables measured on an interval scale are similarly written:

$$V^t = \{v_1, v_2, \ldots, v_n\} \tag{6}$$

Furthermore, let us assume that *m demanded products*, conceived as flows, are produced in the quantities:

$$X^t = \{x_1, x_2, \ldots, x_m\} \tag{7}$$

with the *m market prices*:

$$P^t = \{p_1, p_2, \ldots, p_m\} \tag{8}$$

Among these demanded commodities we have also included money as a standard of value. That is, money is assigned the price "1".

Since the economy is closed, Walras' law (i.e., the total economic power of the system) can be stated:

$$X^t P - Y^t V = 0 \tag{9}$$

At this point it will be advantageous briefly to discuss how, from this mathematical expression of the principle of economic conservation, it is possible to derive *economic state-functions* that are valid also in the nonlinear case of decreasing returns.

First, it should be noted that a differential change in the total power is zero. That is, by virtue of (9), we find

$$d(X^t P - Y^t V) = 0 \tag{10}$$

which by means of (5)–(8) can be rewritten:

$$\sum_{i=1}^{m} x_i \, dp_i + \sum_{i=1}^{m} p_i \, dx_i - \sum_{j=1}^{n} y_j \, dv_j - \sum_{j=1}^{n} v_j \, dy_j = 0 \tag{11}$$

Second, it should be remembered that the two terms in the difference of (9) express the interaction between two independent influences, supply and demand, in the economic system. A proposed state-function, combined of terms from (11), therefore, must contain a term for each of these influences. One way of obtaining such a subdivision is to rewrite (11) as

$$\left(\sum_{i=1}^{m} p_i \, dx_i - \sum_{j=1}^{n} v_j \, dy_j \right) + \left(-\sum_{j=1}^{n} y_j \, dv_j + \sum_{i=1}^{m} x_i \, dp_i \right) = 0 \tag{12}$$

where in the first bracket, the independent variables x_i and y_j are all flows (i.e., intensive intervariables) while, in the second bracket, the independent variables v_j and p_i are all prices (i.e., intensive transvariables). Recalling the definitions of content in (3) and cocontent in (4) it is therefore now possible to propose either a *content state-function* with the flows as independent variables:

$$dK = \sum_{i=1}^{m} p_i \, dx_i - \sum_{j=1}^{n} v_j \, dy_j \tag{13}$$

or a *cocontent state-function* with the prices as independent variables:

$$dK' = -\sum_{j=1}^{n} y_j \, dv_j + \sum_{i=1}^{m} x_i \, dp_i \tag{14}$$

The advantage of these two proposed state-functions is that, in the so-called linear programming case, all market demand curves are, as economists express it, *perfectly elastic* demands of the type facing the individual seller under perfect competition (i.e., all p_i are constants), while all market supply curves are *perfectly inelastic* supplies (i.e., all y_j are constants). Thus, in this case, we will have for each of the demands:

$$x_i \, dp_i = 0 \qquad (15)$$

and for each of the supplies:

$$v_j \, dy_j = 0 \qquad (16)$$

with the result that we can write the content state-function as

$$dK = \sum_{i=1}^{m} p_i \, dx_i \qquad (17)$$

and the cocontent state-function as

$$dK' = -\sum_{j=1}^{n} y_j \, dv_j \qquad (18)$$

In this case of "ideal" demands and supplies, therefore, the proposed two state-functions can be given intuitively appealing, economic interpretations. If we use the content state-function, dK, the system state is characterized by the total market demand of economic power. Thus, for a single firm, K is the total revenue. On the other hand, if we use the cocontent state-function dK', the system state is specified by the total factor supply of economic power.

At present, we shall emphasize that these functions are proposed state-functions. The question, whether they really *are* state-functions, must be decided from considerations of the type of problem that they represent. Mathematically, the selected functions are *state-functions* if they contain terms representing each independent influence (and storage), and if, with respect to the selected independent variables, they are perfect differentials. Thus the state-functions are dependent only on the state of the system and not on past history, that is, the manner in which the state was attained.

The fact that a state-function is independent of past history does not imply that the system itself has no "memory." Actually, most of the systems considered in classical mechanics and electric network theory contain storage elements (for example, mechanical springs or electrical capacitances) that do have "memory." It is a peculiar characteristic of the economic system, as characterized by the formulation in (9) of Walras' law that it does not contain any kind of storage terms. Just as an electrical resistor does not have any "memory" the economic system has not either. With a loan from the theory of random processes, and in analogy with irreversible thermodynamics we call systems, such as the economic, *Markovian* (Callen, 1960). This line of thought will not be developed any further here, but it is of interest in connection with a statistical formulation of economic phenomena.

The manner in which the second law, concerning the flow orientation, conventionally is introduced in economic writings is the following.

Implicitly, to begin with, it is assumed that flows, representing production factor services, are oriented positively *into* the production process, and that flows, representing product demands, are oriented positively *out of* the production. From this orientation in terms of input and output, it can be concluded that all flows in the production are oriented positively in the direction from production factors and into demands. Finally, on the basis of the thus selected positive directions of orientation, the physical irreversibility of the production process is secured by explicitly assuming that all flows are nonnegative:

$$y_j \geq 0 \qquad \text{for} \quad j = 1, 2, \ldots, n \tag{19}$$

$$x_i \geq 0 \qquad \text{for} \quad i = 1, 2, \ldots, m \tag{20}$$

After having stated in this way the positive orientations of the flows, the next step is to relate this orientation to the prices. Basically, the latter are measured on an interval scale. The zero point of the prices, therefore, is quite arbitrary. This, in turn, implies that prices can be assigned arbitrary signs. Thus, in modern economic literature, a commodity is said to be *scarce, free,* or *noxious* depending on whether the price is positive, null, or negative (Debreu, 1959). The designation "noxious" refers to a costly disposal of, for example, some industrial waste product that may be a nuisance. The fact that the signs of the prices in a closed economy are dependent solely on the choice of reference price within that economy is readily demonstrated by a little numerical experimentation with, for example, a simple transportation model (e.g., Dorfman et al., 1958) using, one at a time, the prices of different origins or destinations as references.

In neoclassical economics, however, it is always assumed that the factor prices as well as market prices are all nonnegative:

$$v_j \geq 0 \qquad \text{for} \quad j = 1, 2, \ldots, n \tag{21}$$

$$p_i \geq 0 \qquad \text{for} \quad i = 1, 2, \ldots, m \tag{22}$$

Seemingly, we have here some kind of contradiction. Consequently it is of interest to see how these two viewpoints can be united.

Returning to the orientations of the flows, it should be observed that the flows of factor services into and flows of demanded products out from the production process represent the environmental influences on the latter.

That is, the production process is our system which in discrete localities, depicted as nodes or terminals, interacts with the environment, made up by the supplies and demands. In electric network terminology these nodal influences can be considered either as specified, equivalent nodal current sources or as specified nodal potentials. However, to include the latter possibility of specifying the prices at the nodes or terminals of the production process, it is necessary to choose as reference a price outside the production system. Thus in the isolated economic universe consisting of the production system and the environmental supply and demand influences, we select the reference price in the environment. Furthermore, if we follow the usual practice of setting the price of money equal to "1" and use as reference zero price the environmental node, corresponding to what might be called the empty set of goods, then (21) and (22) apply.

Now, assuming a rational behavior, the explanations above of (21) and (22) actually amount to an implicit statement of the second law of economics. The reasons for this are twofold. First, we have made sure that flows can occur only in the direction from supply to demand. Second, by making all prices nonnegative by a suitable choice of reference price, the rational behavior will be to produce only if the market demand price exceeds the price of the resource. The discussion in later sections, in particular in connection with the formulation of the analogue electric network where prices are interpreted as electric potentials, will further clarify and support this viewpoint that a simple way of introducing rational behavior, conforming to the second law of economics, is to assume nonnegativity of all prices.

THE WALRASIAN SYSTEM OF EQUATIONS

In spite of the fact that the Walras equation system forms the basis of modern, normative economics (e.g., Samuelson, 1953–1954; Zeuthen, 1955; Dorfman et al., 1958; and Baumol, 1965) it was relatively unknown until the period between the two world wars. In economic literature, the Walrasian system is usually described as a macroscopic, dynamical theory of microscopic, statistical phenomena in a closed economy. Thus in economics the attention is primarily on the two types of markets, supply and demand, with the result that the two kinds of markets together are considered as a system interacting with an environmental production system. That is, the economic viewpoint is completely analogous to the situation in thermodynamics where a system of microscopic elements (e.g., molecules) is submitted to macroscopic influences (e.g., changes in pressure or volume).

The manner in which we consider the Walrasian system here is the converse of the viewpoint adopted in economics and thermodynamics. In other words, we focus attention on the deterministic production system and regard the markets of supply and demand as specified influences representing its environment. Thus the concept of perfect competition is but a specified set of statistical assumptions, the fulfillment of which permits us to represent the stochastic phenomena in the environment as a macroscopic set of independent and deterministic influences on our system. It should be noted that this converse viewpoint of a deterministic system submitted to statistical influences is the general structure underlying most computer simulation programs.

Adopting the latter converse viewpoint, the purpose of the following is to derive the Walrasian equations from the two basic laws in such a manner as to show that these equations are the fundamental equilibrium properties of the production system in terms of the involved macroscopic measurements.

If we begin by considering the available n limitational production factors of (5), it is quite obvious that, in an arbitrary production, there will be some unemployed remainders due to the fact that the services are not all consumed. In matrix notation let us designate the *consumed* part of the n *factor services*:

$$(Y')^t = \{y'_1, y'_2, \ldots, y'_n\} \tag{23}$$

and the corresponding n *unemployed remainders*:

$$R^t = \{r_1, r_2, \ldots, r_n\} \tag{24}$$

Both sets are nonnegative, intensive intervariables or flows. Depicting the region of interaction between the production factor and the production system as a node, the flows Y, Y', and R will satisfy the earlier-stated *node law*:

$$Y = Y' + R \tag{25}$$

in equilibrium.

The problem of establishing the dual mesh law of equilibrium for the prices is a bit more tricky. Corresponding to the m market prices P (8) of the m flows of demanded products, there will be a set of nonnegative m *production prices*:

$$(P') = \{p'_1, p'_2, \ldots, p'_m\} \tag{26}$$

which tells us about the cost of production by being a function of the production factor prices V of (6).

Obviously, the market prices p_i and the production prices p'_i need not agree. Now, prices are economic potentials. Recalling that the environmental influences of demand and supply are given as average curves, let us therefore consider the loss or cost per unit output flow results which from the difference:

$$l_i = p'_1 - p_i \tag{27}$$

In general, two kinds of cost are used to characterize a production process. Both kinds involve a determination in monetary terms of the resources consumed by the production; and still they differ basically. The accountant, on the one hand, usually determines the *aquisition cost* of these resources, in the sense of the amount of money paid when the resources initially were acquired. The economist, on the other hand, introduces the *opportunity cost* of the resources. The opportunity cost of devoting a resource to a particular use is the return that the resource could earn in its best alternative use.

Considering, for all flows of demanded products, the difference:

$$L = P' - P \tag{28}$$

as the mesh law of equilibrium, it is immediately seen (Baumol, 1965) that each element l_i of:

$$L^t = \{l_1, l_2, \ldots, l_m\} \tag{29}$$

is the opportunity cost involved in changing the output product flow x_i one unit from its equilibrium value.

For decision-making purposes, the economist's concept of opportunity cost is the relevant one, since a rational decision must involve the comparison of alternative courses of action with respect to a well-defined reference, common to all the possibilities. Under the assumption of linearity our best choice would be to use the equilibrium state as reference which again implies that the opportunity costs l_i are all nonnegative.

Comparison of the equations above of equilibrium with the analogous equations of physics yields the interesting difference that in economics we have the additional requirement that *all the variables involved are nonnegative.* We shall discuss later how this constraint is brought about in the physical analogue.

By means of the two conditions of equilibrium, the node and the mesh laws (25) and (28), let us now rewrite Walras' law (9). Considering the term of demand we find

$$X^t P = X^t (P' - L) = X^t P' - X^t L \tag{30}$$

while the term of supply yields

$$Y^t V = (Y' + R)^t V = (Y')^t V + R^t V \tag{31}$$

That is, in equilibrium Walras' law can also be stated

$$X^t P' - X^t L - (Y')^t V - R^t V = 0 \tag{32}$$

In the latter equation of equilibrium two of the terms, $X^t L$ and $R^t V$, are of special interest in that they give rise to a set of supplementary conditions of economic equilibrium.

An important purpose of the Walrasian system is to permit one to determine from the given data which productive services are *free* (i.e., have a zero price) and which are *scarce* (i.e., command a positive price) in the equilibrium state (Zeuthen, 1955). Obviously, if we have a positive remainder the service will be free. On the other hand, if we have a zero remainder this will indicate a scarce service. For a productive service, therefore, the product of its price and its remainder will be identically zero:

$$r_j v_j = 0 \qquad \text{for} \quad j = 1, 2, \ldots, n \qquad (33)$$

That is, the *supplementary condition of equilibrium for the productive services* can be written:

$$R^t V = 0 \qquad (34)$$

In spite of the fact that this condition was pointed out by Zeuthen as early as in 1932, it was only much later, in connection with the formulation of linear programming models, that it was realized that a dual supplementary condition of equilibrium must exist for the production activities.

From the economic point of view this equilibrium condition is one of rational behavior in that it determines whether a given activity should be used to produce an amount of products. Evidently, if we have a positive opportunity cost for producing one unit of the product it will not be rational to use that activity. Alternatively, if we have a zero opportunity cost it will be rational to use the activity:

$$x_i l_i = 0 \qquad \text{for} \quad i = 1, 2, \ldots, m \qquad (35)$$

Thus we find that the *supplementary condition of equilibrium for the production activities* can be stated

$$X^t L = 0 \qquad (36)$$

Introducing the set of supplementary conditions in the equilibrium formulation of Walras' law (32) yields that the latter can be rewritten

$$X^t P' - (Y')^t V = 0 \qquad (37)$$

From the point of view of establishing the relation between the prices of the services and those of the production activities, this formulation turns out to be the feasible one.

Basically, the process of production is a transformation of production factors into consumption goods. The input side of the production system comprises all the productive services and may typically be given in terms of availabilities or capacities. On the output side of the production system we have the production activities, one for each consumer commodity. Typically, these activities may be described in terms of the words *making* or *moving*.

Usually, the same commodity may be produced in several ways, that is, by different combinations of productive services. By a *given-technique* we will understand the production of a commodity by a unique combination of productive services.

For a given technique the relationship between the amount produced by a certain activity, and the corresponding amount of a certain productive service that is used is given by the so-called *technical coefficient*. For physical reasons, a technical coefficient must be perceived as a kind of saturation curve which easily could be introduced in our analogous electric network. In practice, however, such curves are normally not known. Thus in the following we will assume linearity and *define* the technical coefficient t_{ji} as the fixed or constant ratio equal to the amount of flow of the jth factor service used to produce one unit of flow of the ith product.

Using a zero-valued technical coefficient to indicate that there is no physical relationship between the service and activity in question, we can state the set of technical coefficients in a given technique as a $(n \times m)$ matrix T, defined by

$$Y' = TX \qquad (38)$$

Introducing this equation in the equilibrium formulation of Walras' law (37) yields

$$X^t P' - (Y')^t V = X^t P' - (TX)^t V = 0 \qquad (39)$$

or

$$X^t(T^t V - P') = 0 \qquad (40)$$

Since the latter equation is valid for arbitrary, but nonnegative x_i for all $i = 1, 2, \ldots, m$ it can be concluded that, in equilibrium, we have

$$T^t V - P' = 0 \qquad (41)$$

or

$$P' = T^t V \qquad (42)$$

The next step in the formulation of the Walrasian equilibrium system is to introduce the technical transformations (38) and (42) in the node and mesh laws (25) and (28). That is, we relate, on the one hand, the factor service flows to the product flows of the activities and, on the other, the factor prices to the market product prices.

First, from (25) and (38), we find that the *flow equilibrium* can be written:

$$Y = TX + R \qquad (43)$$

Premultiplying, in this equation, R with a $(n \times n)$ unit matrix δ_n, we can write instead:

$$Y = \{T, \delta_n\} \left\{ \begin{matrix} X \\ R \end{matrix} \right\} \qquad (44)$$

Second, from (28) and (42), we find that the *price equilibrium* can be written

$$P = T^t V - L \qquad (45)$$

Premultiplying, in the latter equation, L with a $(m \times m)$ unit matrix δ_m, it can be rewritten:

$$P = \{T^t, -\delta_m\} \left\{ \begin{matrix} V \\ L \end{matrix} \right\} \qquad (46)$$

Basically, it might be said that the core of the Walrasian system is the *equilibrium equations*, (44) and (46), together with the *nonnegativity conditions*, (19)–(22). The manner in which these equations have been derived clearly shows that, from the viewpoint of physical theory, they are constraints or auxiliary conditions. Thus by virtue of the relation of equality or inequality, we would in physics characterize the two equilibrium conditions as *bilateral* constraints and the four nonnegativity conditions as *unilateral* constraints (Lanczos, 1949). In electric network theory the bilateral equilibrium constraints are but expressions of Kirchhoff's two laws.

Alternatively, we might also compare the Walrasian set of economic constraints with the theory of mathematical programming. In this theory the flow equilibrium (44) together with the nonnegativity flow conditions of (19) and (20), are classified as the *primal* side-conditions or constraints augmented with the *slack variables R*. Similarly, the price equilibrium (46) together with the nonnegativity price conditions of (21) and (22) are characterized as the *dual* side-conditions or constraints augmented with the *slack variables L* (Dorfman et al., 1958; Baumol, 1965). Of course, since the dual of the dual problem is the original linear programming problem it is entirely arbitrary which of the equilibrium conditions is referred to as the primal and which as the dual.

The difference between the Walrasian formulation and the mathematical programming approach, however, is significant from a conceptual point of view. In economics, and in physics too, the total set of constraints is derived simultaneously from the dual set of measurements which characterize the model, whether or not all of the equations are used in the final analysis. In mathematical programming, on the other hand, only the primal set of constraints, usually in terms of the flows, are derived to begin with. The dual set of constraints are found in a manner as if a "mischievous gremlin" produces the converse of everything in the set of primal constraints (Baumol, 1965). Since this approach is based exclusively on the mathematical form of the primal constraints, it results in requiring us, again and again, to use all our ingenuity to reinterpret the dual variables as prices, notwithstanding the fact that the underlying economic model was established on basic measurements including these prices.

From the viewpoint of neoclassical economics the flow equilibrium conditions are usually conceived as a *production function*, since together they state the *physical* relationship between the inputs of resources to the closed economy and its outputs of commodities per unit of time (Danø, 1963). Clearly, since the technical coefficients are constants, we have a linear relationship between inputs and outputs. That is, if *all* inputs are increased by some factor, then, in equilibrium, all outputs will be increased proportionately. In economics this fact is described by saying that we have *constant returns to scale*. Also, this might be described by saying that the production function is *linearly homogenous* or that it is *homogenous of degree one* (Baumol, 1965; Bilas, 1967).

The last step, which should be added to the primal and dual sets of constraint equations to complete the formulation of the Walrasian system, is to establish the functional relationships between flows and demands. These relationships originate in the concepts of demand and supply that we introduced earlier. Basically, it may be recalled, a supply (demand) curve is an expression for the transformation of economic power from (to) one form, the market, which is not included in the analysis, to (from) another form, the production process, which is included in the analysis. Both demand and supply are instantaneous "direct proportionalities" between an intensive intervariable (flow) and an intensive transvariable (price).

In practice, the *demand curve* is generally assumed to have a negative slope if it is depicted with the nonnegative price p_i as ordinate and the nonnegative flow x_i as abcissa. Specifically, to permit the use of either the content or the cocontent state-functions (13) and (14), we will *here assume* either that it is a single-valued function of x_i and cuts the p_i-axis, or, that it is a single-valued function of p_i and cuts the x_i-axis.

The economic interpretation of these assumptions is mainly centered around the problem that the demand curve is supposed to cut at least one of the two axes. If the curve cuts the price axis, the point of cut corresponds to a finite price so great that the demand drops to zero. On the other hand, if the curve cuts the flow axis this corresponds to the fact that consumption will remain finite even when the product gets a zero price, that is, becomes a free good.

A complete analogous argument can be carried out for the supply, with the result that we end up with a *supply curve* complying with the requirements of single-valuedness and the cutting of at least one axis. Furthermore, it will be assumed that the supply curves are positively sloped in the coordinate system used for the description of the demand curves.

In economic literature, the Walrasian system is usually given as the set of equations made up of the primal and dual constraints together with the pertinent demand and supply curves, whereas Walras' law is relegated the unimportant position of a later-discovered superfluous equation (Zeuthen, 1955). The viewpoint taken here, substantiated by the analogy to physics (and also to mathematical programming), is that Walras' law is an essential ingredient of the Walrasian system, since it forms one of the basic laws. As a matter of fact, the state-functions by means of which we determine whether the economic model is in equilibrium, can be derived only from Walras' law. The so-called Walrasian system is but the set of constraints imposed upon the variation of these state-functions.

A NUMERICAL EXAMPLE

In engineering design one of the most important means for thought and creativity is making drawings. The latter can range from architectural sketches supplemented with detailed blueprints drawn to scale of mechanical parts to abstract, functional diagrams of electrical systems, but at all levels of details the logic and the consistency of the design is always visualized and communicated by means of drawings.

Obviously, in the design of an economic system it is only possible to use abstract diagrams. Such a use was anticipated by the Danish engineer Ivar Jantzen, although he described his visualization of a production system solely in words (Jantzen, 1924; 1939; 1954; Brems, 1952a, b).

Considering a *joint production* of a given technique where, by technical necessity, the services of a given production factor are used simultaneously in the manufacture of a set of different products, Jantzen perceived the services of each production factor, the so-called *stage*, to occur *in parallel*. Next, with a finished unit of a demanded product as origin, the concept of a *plant* was crystallized by tracking backwards all through the production to each of the individual factor services used in manufacturing the product in question. A plant or, in a more modern terminology, an *activity* was perceived as the *series-connection* of all those factor services, and thereby stages, pertaining to the act of producing a specific demanded product. It should be noted that the conception of a production factor stage combined with the concept of an activity being served by that factor implies that the activity is uniquely related to only one of the parallel services of the stage. The exact identity of this unique relationship was later revealed (Brems, 1952a) to be that of the technical coefficient (38).

   Thus Jantzen actually gave us a complete diagrammatic description of the Walrasian system of equations. Furthermore, as we shall see in the following, Jantzen's description is a perfectly valid picture of the electric network analogue. Of particular interest in the latter connection is the fact that Jantzen, by his parallel and series description, endows the economic system with topological properties in addition to those of power transformation by means of the technical coefficients. Thus Jantzen was the first to realize explicitly that the concept of a *technology*, or a *given technique* as he called it, must comprise at least two different kinds of properties, the topology (or lay-out) and the technical coefficients, to uniquely describe the combination of services in a production system. That is, the term "a given technique" refers to a unique combination of productive services in the sense of a *precise description of the total set of system constraints*. As will be clear from the formulation of the constraint equations of the analogous electric network, however, it does not refer to the proportions of the production factors. From an economic viewpoint this independence of a technique from the sizes of the limitational production factors can be explained best by briefly reconsidering the concept of a production function.

   Previously, we used the so-called technological definition of a production function when we identified it with the flow equilibrium conditions (44). Actually, most economists assume in their definition of a production function that, given the cost outlay of the firm, it depicts only the "technically most efficient" ways of producing (Schmidt, 1939; Bilas, 1967). In other words, they use not a technological, but an economic definition. Thus assuming a given technique [in essence described by the flow equilibrium conditions of (44)], a *production function* is so defined that to each set of specified values of the limitational production factors there corresponds only that set of activity or output flows, which results in the instantaneous equilibrium of the system with these factors. Mathematically, the determination of a production function can be identified with a parametric programming problem in which the unspecified parameters are the factor values.

   A single point of the thus defined production function is determined as the equilibrium state of a Walrasian system of equations, the constraints of which are defined by the given technique. The purpose of the following is to establish an electric network analogous to the Walrasian system. The solution of this network will be a point of the production function. Possibly, the most expedient way of introducing such a network is by means of an example. To permit comparison with the conventional approach of mathematical programming we will adopt for this purpose a simple, but well documented example from the current literature.

   A significant feature of mathematical programming is the fact that the demand and supply curves are linear or at least piecewise linear. In the discussion of (15) it was explained that under perfect competition the individual firm faced a *perfectly elastic* (horizontal) demand curve. The fact that price is determined solely by demand might in practice be interpreted as a very short-run production situation. Clearly, in a very short time period a firm cannot change its output. Thus the supply faced by each firm is *perfectly inelastic*. In other words, the situation is described by a vertical supply curve like those discussed in connection with (16). Under perfect competition, therefore, a single firm faces demands of the ideal transvariable type and supplies of the ideal intervariable type.

Theoretically, the markets of supply and demand belong to the environment of the closed economic universe described by the Walrasian system. Usually, in economics the production in the Walrasian system is considered on the macroeconomic level as a national sector. Clearly, in a closed universe it is completely arbitrary what we prefer to call our system. Since, under perfect competition, any plant or aggregation is just as efficient as any other regardless of size (Liebhafsky, 1963), we shall in the following use the Walrasian model to determine the equilibrium state of a single firm. What we really do by such an approach, of course, is simply that we lump all other firms into the environment and concentrate solely on the demands and supplies facing the selected firm. The selected example of such a firm can be described in the following manner (Dorfman et al., 1958).

A hypothetical chemical firm manufactures and sells three chemical products. We assume that the firm has available two separate activities, a productive activity and a selling activity, for each of the three chemicals. Let us further assume that we consider these six activities in a physical time interval of one month considered as part of a longer period of continuous production. In this physical time interval the volume of each of the three chemicals produced and sold is so large that the relaxation time can be considered negligible. That is, economically we can perceive the monthly total volumes of the three chemicals as instantaneous flows in a closed production system with perfect mobility. In the following we shall use as per unit value for each of these flows \$100 worth of production or sale per month.

For the joint production of the three chemicals the firm used four types of chemical equipment which we shall call E_1, E_2, E_3, and E_4. Each of these four types is conceived as the stage of a limitational production factor the service of which is use of its capacity. If the maximum available capacity of each factor is taken to be 100%, we can depict the corresponding supply function as a vertical curve determined by a fixed flow of the value of 100% capacity. That is, each production factor will exhibit a perfectly inelastic supply.

Designating the three productive activities C_1, C_2, and C_3, the technical coefficients relating the use of the capacities of the four production factors to the flow of chemicals in these three productive activities are determined on a monthly basis as follows:

1. An output of $100 worth of C_1 requires 10% of the available capacity of E_1 and 5% of the available capacity of E_2.
2. An output of $100 worth of C_2 requires 4% of the available capacity of E_2 and 5% of the available capacity of E_3.
3. An output of $100 worth of C_3 requires 2% of the available capacity of E_2 and 10% of the available capacity of E_4.

A direct cost is associated with each of the three productive activities. In relation to the activity flows measured in terms of $100 worth of output per month these direct costs are $70 for C_1, $50 for C_2, and $15 for C_3. A direct cost, however, may be represented as an equivalent negative net revenue. That is, we can consider each of the direct costs as a demand function for the corresponding productive activity. These demands are all perfectly elastic since each of them corresponds to a horizontal demand curve through the fixed price or net revenue:

1. $-$70 for C_1.
2. $-$50 for C_2.
3. $-$15 for C_3.

Note that, in contradistinction to market demand curves, these imputed demands are all negative.

As a special technological characteristic we shall endow our example with the property that the production of one chemical may require the input of the other chemicals into the productive activity. Thus a given chemical may appear both as a final product and as an intermediate product in which latter role it is used as a factor in the productive activity of another chemical. Specifically, we will assume for the three productive activities that on a monthly basis:

1. An output of $100 worth of C_1 does not require any input of the other chemicals.
2. An output of $100 worth of C_2 requires an input of $30 worth of C_1.
3. An output of $100 worth of C_3 requires an input of $10 worth of C_1 and an input of $50 worth of C_2.

After thus having specified the production opportunities open to the firm we turn to a specification on a monthly basis of its three selling activities C_4, C_5, and C_6:

1. Activity C_4 is the sale of $100 worth of C_1. This consumes $100 worth of C_1 and produces a gross revenue of $100.

2. Activity C_5 is the sale of $100 worth of C_2. This consumes $100 worth of C_2 and produces a gross revenue of $100.
3. Activity C_6 is the sale of $100 worth of C_3. This consumes $100 worth of C_3 and produces a gross revenue of $100.

In the same manner as each of the four types of chemical equipment E_1, E_2, E_3, and E_4 forms a stage in the sense of Jantzen, it should be realized that each of the inventories of the three chemicals C_1, C_2, and C_3 are also stages. By virtue of the instantaneous nature of the Walrasian system our mathematical model of each of these three inventory stages is characterized by the fact that the net inventory of the corresponding chemical must be zero. That is, the whole gross output of each chemical must be absorbed either as input to another productive activity or as input to its corresponding selling activity.

The description above of our chemical firm is summarized in Table 2 in terms of Jantzen's stages (horizontally) and activities (vertically). In the discussion of the Walrasian system we defined a technical coefficient t_{ij} as a positive constant equal the amount used of the ith factor to produce one unit commodity in the jth activity. Thus the negative technical coefficient of -100 in each of the inventory stages indicates not use, but production (in the sense of a source in the model) of the corresponding chemical. The bottom row of the table depicts the net revenues (or direct costs if they have a negative sign) in the sense of demands of each of the six activities.

Table 2   Stages and Activities in the Chemical Firm

Stages		Activities					
		Productive			Selling		
		C_1	C_2	C_3	C_4	C_5	C_6
Net inventories ($)	C_1	-100	30	10	100	—	—
	C_2	—	-100	50	—	100	—
	C_3	—	—	-100	—	—	100
Equipment capacity (%)	E_1	10	—	—	—	—	—
	E_2	5	4	2	—	—	—
	E_3	—	5	—	—	—	—
	E_4	—	—	10	—	—	—
Net revenue (or direct cost) ($)		-70	-50	-15	100	100	100

THE ELECTRIC NETWORK ANALOGUE

Earlier, in connection with our discussion of economic measurements, it was pointed out that the flows in a production are intensive intervariables, measured on a ratio scale, and that the prices are intensive transvariables, measured on an interval scale. In an analogous electric network, therefore, the corresponding variables will be electric currents and nodal voltages. Yet, prices and nodal voltages are not completely analogous if we take into consideration the natural direction of flows in the two kinds of systems.

In electric networks, according to the second law of physics, a flow will occur only from a higher to a lower nodal voltage. In economics, on the other hand, the second law states that a flow will occur only from a lower to a higher price. Thus to establish a complete analogy, we must, for example, change signs of the potentials in either the physical or the economic system. Arbitrarily, we here adopt the convention of transforming all prices into negative prices, which we shall call *negprices*, before we establish the analogous electric network. That is, *in the analogous electric network the nonnegative, economic prices will appear as nonpositive nodal voltages.* An intuitively satisfactory result of establishing the analogy by changing signs of the potentials is the fact that *nonnegative flows in an economic system will be represented by nonnegative currents in the analogous electric network.*

Speaking of nonnegative economic flows, it should be recalled from the discussion leading up to this requirement (19) and (20) that, here, nonnegativity is defined in relation to an arbitrarily fixed, positive orientation of the flows in the production. Specifically, the factor service flows are oriented positively into and the demand flows positively out from the production process. In the electric analogue, therefore, we must also introduce a similar orientation of the corresponding electric currents. However, before we consider the complete electric analogue of the Walrasian system, let us first establish the analogous electric subnetworks corresponding, respectively, to a perfectly inelastic supply curve and a perfectly elastic demand curve.

Basically, if the supply of the jth factor is perfectly inelastic it is depicted by a vertical curve. The consumed part y_j' of the services is a nonnegative flow less than or equal to the total available capacity y_j. The flow y_j' is oriented positively into the production of the factor terminal, which we shall call Γ. If, in equilibrium, the flow y_j' is less than the flow y_j we have a positive remainder r_j. That is, the factor is a free good and the factor price v_j is zero. If, on the other hand, the consumed flow y_j' is equal to the total capacity y_j the factor becomes scarce in the sense that its price changes from zero to a positive value. Clearly, this implies that the supply curve consists of, not only the characteristic vertical curve through y_j, but also that part of the abscissa axis which is situated between origin and y_j.

Introducing negprices is tantamount to the turning upside down of this supply curve in the manner indicated in Figure 1. This figure also shows a diagram of an analogous electric subnetwork which exhibits the same characteristic as measured from its two terminals. Actually, this subnetwork is but a single network arc oriented positively into a node Γ, representing the input terminal of the production process, from a reference node W, depicting

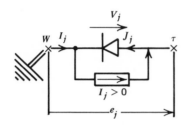

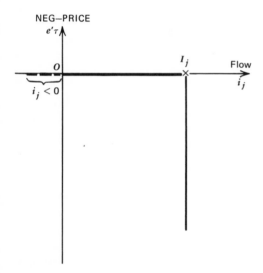

NEG–PRICE

Fig. 1. Perfectly inelastic factor supply and its electric analogue.

the arbitrarily selected, environmental zero point of all prices in the closed economic system.

In this analogous electric network arc, the arc current i_j, oriented positively into the node Γ from the reference node W, represents the consumed part y'_j of the services. Similarly, the ideal current source I_j, depicted by the rectangular box with an arrow for the positive direction of flow, is analogous to the total capacity y_j of the factor. The arrowlike symbol with the vertical slash indicates a rectifier, for example, a diode. The properties of a rectifier are that it has a nonnegative current J_j and a nonnegative counter voltage V_j combined in the following equilibrium characteristic:

$$
\begin{array}{lll}
J_j > 0 & \text{and} & V_j = 0 \\
J_j = 0 & \text{and} & V_j = 0 \\
J_j = 0 & \text{and} & V_j > 0
\end{array}
\tag{47}
$$

Letting the rectifier current J_j represent the positive remainder r_j we see that Kirchhoff's node law yields

$$
I_j = i_j + J_j \tag{48}
$$

which is in complete agreement with the economic node law (25). The break point of the rectifier, given by the condition:

$$
\{J_j, V_j\} = \{0, 0\}
$$

of (47), is known in economics as the economic margin of the limitational factor i_j (Zeuthen, 1955).

The nodal voltage e'_Γ is analogous to the negprice $(-v_j)$. Electrically, since the arc is oriented from node W to node Γ, the voltage drop e_j along the oriented arc is related, by the convention adopted earlier, to the nodal voltages e'_Γ and e'_W in the following way:

$$
e_j = e'_W - e'_\Gamma = -e'_\Gamma \tag{49}
$$

since, for the reference node W, we have

$$
e'_W = 0 \tag{50}
$$

Also, since the counter voltage V_j over the rectifier is equal to the voltage drop e_j along the oriented arc, we find

$$
V_j = e_j = -e'_\Gamma \tag{51}
$$

Thus, in this case, the nonnegative factor price v_j is directly represented in the network by the nonnegative counter voltage V_j over the rectifier. Furthermore, we have here that the supplementary condition of equilibrium for the productive services (33) can be derived from (47) as an equilibrium condition of zero economic power $(J_j V_j = 0)$ in the rectifier.

The approach by means of which we establish an electric subnetwork, analogous to a demand curve, is quite similar. Here, since the demand for the ith product is perfectly elastic, we have a horizontal demand curve corresponding to a fixed price p_i. Just as the supply curve was combined with the idea of an unemployed remainder, we will here in a dual manner combine the demand curve with the concept of a marginal opportunity cost l_i. Thus in equilibrium, a positive activity flow x_i can occur only if the corresponding opportunity cost l_i is zero. On the other hand, if we have a positive opportunity cost l_i (i.e., the cost of production p_i' is higher than the demanded price p_i), then there will be no flow x_i of products out from the production system at the terminal Γ.

With negprices introduced, this situation is depicted in Figure 2, which also shows a diagram of an electric network arc exhibiting the same charac-

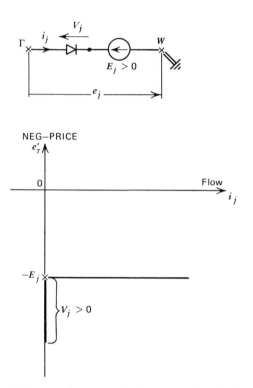

Fig. 2.   Perfectly elastic demand and its electric analogue.

teristic. In this analogous subnetwork the arc current i_j, oriented positively out of the node Γ and into the reference node W, represents the flow x_i of the production activity. The ideal voltage source E_j, depicted by the circled arrow, yields, at the internal node of the arc, a nodal voltage which is equal to the negprice $(-p_i)$ corresponding to the fixed revenue (or direct cost) per unit activity flow. Note that the arrow in an ideal voltage source indicates the direction of the voltage drop. Thus in this case, the nodal voltage of the internal node is E_j lower than the reference nodal voltage. (We have here assumed, of course, that E_j is positive. In the case where the source depicts direct costs, E_j will be negative and thus force the voltage of the internal node to be higher than the reference nodal voltage). The current inside the voltage source, however, will not follow the usual convention in that we here have the exception that it is oriented positively against the arrow. The reason for this, of course, lies in the fact that inside an ideal voltage source the current, by definition, counteracts the tendency expressed by the second law. The counter voltage V_j over the rectifier is analogous to the opportunity cost l_i per unit flow. The rectifier has the same kind of ideal characteristic in equilibrium as given for the production factor remainder (47):

$$i_j > 0 \quad \text{and} \quad V_j = 0$$
$$i_j = 0 \quad \text{and} \quad V_j = 0 \qquad (52)$$
$$i_j = 0 \quad \text{and} \quad V_j > 0$$

The voltage drop e_j over the arc from the node Γ to the reference node W, by virtue of (50), can be written:

$$e_j = e'_\Gamma - e'_W = e'_\Gamma \qquad (53)$$

Or, if we introduce the counter voltage V_j and the ideal voltage source E_j,

$$e'_\Gamma = e_j = -V_j - E_j \qquad (54)$$

Clearly, since e'_Γ is the nodal voltage of Γ with respect to W, the left-hand side of (54) can be interpreted as the voltage drop through the remaining part of the network (not shown in Figure 2) back to reference node W. Thus (51) is in fact Kirchhoff's mesh law of equilibrium.

The nodal voltage e'_Γ is analogous to the production negprice $(-p'_i)$. Thus we have established the following relationships for the variables of (54):

$$e'_\Gamma = -p'_i$$
$$E_j = p_i \qquad (55)$$
$$V_j = l_i$$

which shows that (54) is in complete agreement with the economic mesh law (27).

Finally, for the rectifier, we have in equilibrium that its economic power $(i_j V_j)$ is identically zero, corresponding to the supplementary condition of equilibrium for the production activities (35).

The complete electric network analogue of the economic model of our hypothetical chemical firm is given in Figure 3. To facilitate the discussion of this network model we have for comparison given a lay-out of its basic structure in Figure 4. That is, we shall organize the following detailed description of the network model in Figure 3 in terms of the structural regions of Figure 4.

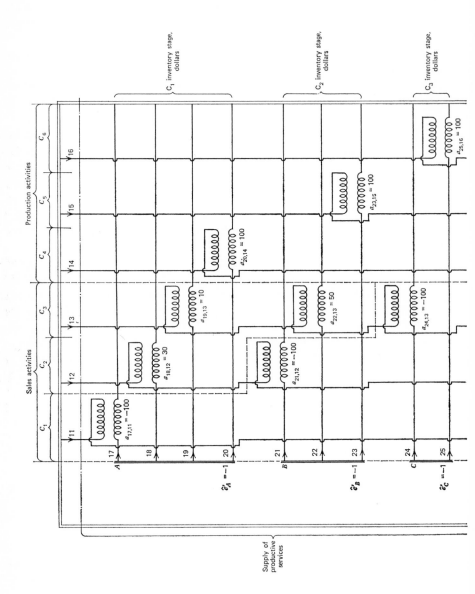

130

130

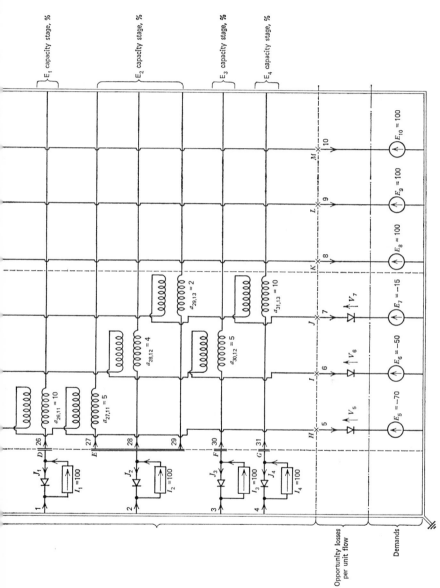

Fig. 3

131

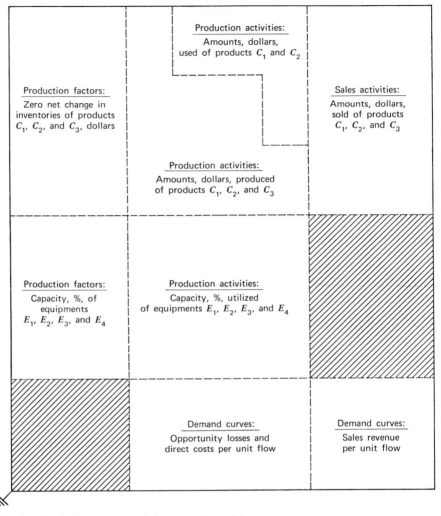

Fig. 4.   The basic structure of the network model.

In the left side of the network model in Figure 3 we have all the production factors. Thus arcs 1–4 depict the four types of equipment E_1, E_2, E_3, and E_4. Each of the four limitational production factors I_j and its corresponding unemployed remainder J_j are measured in per cent capacity. These supply influences energize the production system through the nodes D–G, the corresponding nodal voltages of this are the factor negprices. Since we have zero net change in inventories of the three chemicals C_1, C_2, and C_3 the corresponding limitational production factors I_j are also zero. Electrically, therefore, we have an open circuit (i.e., no network arcs) for each of the three inventory factors. The result of this is that these three factors are depicted solely by the nodes A–C. Now, these inventories were measured in dollars worth of flow. But earlier we assigned money (or dollars) a unit price. Thus nodes A–C in the network model must each be assigned a fixed voltage potential $\hat{e}'_j = -1$ corresponding to a negprice of minus one.

At the bottom of the network model in Figure 3 we have all the demands. The three left arcs 5–7 depict by means of the negative voltage sources the direct costs of the production activities as imputed negative demands in series with the rectifiers representing the opportunity costs per unit flow. The voltage sources in the three right arcs 8–10 depict the net revenues from the selling activities as positive demands. Note that in these three arcs we have no rectifiers. That is, we are not confining the flows in the three selling activities to be nonnegative. The implication of permitting the flows i_8, i_9, and i_{10} to be negative is that we also permit *purchase* for use in the production of the chemicals C_1, C_2, and C_3 at the going market price. From the viewpoint of mathematical programming, network-states with negative flows of i_8, i_9, or i_{10} correspond to feasible solutions that are nonoptimal. Since production of C_2, for example, necessitates by the requirement of zero net inventories that we have available a positive amount of C_1, this approach in terms of a possible purchase of C_1 simplifies the formulation of the network model considerably.

Comparison of the remaining part of the network in Figure 3 with Table 2 reveals the validity of Jantzen's description. To the right of each of the factor nodes A–G we have the sets of *parallel* service flows, each of which forms one of Jantzen's stages. Thus, for example, the parallel combination of arcs 17–20 forms the inventory stage of the chemical C_1, while the parallel combination of arcs 27–29 forms the capacity stage of equipment E_2. Vertically arcs 11–13 are the productive activities while arcs 14–16 are the selling activities. It is immediately seen that each of these activities connects *in series* the services of the different stages involved in that activity. The technical coefficients in Table 2 are represented in the network in Figure 3 by corresponding transformation ratios of ideal (linear and loss-less) transformers which convert economic power from the services to the activities. Thus the production system in Table 2 (apart from the last row) is depicted in the network in Figure 3 by the upper right rectangle of transformer arcs bounded by nodes A–M. Note that all arrows in the network indicate simultaneous, positive orientation of flows and voltage drops (decrease in negprice) corresponding to the second law of physics. The "square box" around the total network is the common environmental reference node W discussed in connection with the problem of obtaining nonnegative prices (21 and 22). Besides securing that the voltage drop over each arc can be expressed as a nodal voltage (negprice), this special way of introducing the reference node also guarantees that the network is isolated in exactly the same manner as the original economic system.

In the introduction it was emphasized that the Walrasian model depicts a closed economy as the interaction, in terms of prices and physical flows, between a deterministic production system and a set of specified environmental influences portraying supply and demand on perfectly competitive and independent markets. The description above of the network analogue in Figure 3 reveals that it is indeed a pictorial representation of a Walrasian model in the form of a diagram in which each element represents, from an economic viewpoint, a fundamental partial interdependence. Thus if we are willing to forget the electrical origin of the established network image it may be considered, in its own right as a theoretical concept, as an *economic network*.

THE ELECTRIC NETWORK CONSTRAINTS

In the previous section an analogous electric network was established for a Walrasian model from considerations of a scalar formulation of the individual equations in the Walrasian system. That is, in the terminology of economics, we have assumed ceteris paribus in order to formulate a total economic theory by combination of partial analysis results in which the supply of each factor and the demand for each commodity has been determined *in isolation* (Zeuthen, 1955). The purpose of this section is to go the opposite way and show how the Walrasian system of equations can be established directly from the network analogue as its total set of constraints.

Basically, the electric network analogue contains three different kinds of constraints: the graph, the transformers, and the unilateral constraints of the rectifiers. If we apply the modern methods of electric network theory to these three types of constraints, the resulting constraints can be established in a completely automatic manner which could be performed just as well by a digital computer (Franksen, 1967). To save space, however, we shall here adopt a more intuitive approach.

By virtue of the fact that the equilibrium conditions of the network analogue are expressed in terms of two complementary sets of variables: electric currents corresponding to flows of commodities and nodal voltages corresponding to negprices, the constraint equations of the network will comprise one set of equations in terms of currents and another set of equations in terms of nodal voltages.

To begin with let us confine ourselves to the formulation of the current constraints. From this point of view the graph constraints are simply statements of Kirchhoff's node law for each node in the network.

Node A:	$i_{17} + i_{18} + i_{19} + i_{20} = 0$	
Node B:	$i_{21} + i_{22} + i_{23} = 0$	
Node C:	$i_{24} + i_{25} = 0$	
Node D:	$i_{26} - i_1 = 0$	
Node E:	$i_{27} + i_{28} + i_{29} - i_2 = 0$	
Node F:	$i_{30} - i_3 = 0$	
Node G:	$i_{31} - i_4 = 0$	(56)
Node H:	$-i_{11} + i_5 = 0$	
Node I:	$-i_{12} + i_6 = 0$	
Node J:	$-i_{13} + i_7 = 0$	
Node K:	$-i_{14} + i_8 = 0$	
Node L:	$-i_{15} + i_9 = 0$	
Node M:	$-i_{16} + i_{10} = 0$	

The other set of constraints, inherent in the electric network analogue in Figure 3, is the representation of the technical coefficients by means of transformation ratios of *ideal transformers* which convert economic power from the services to the activities. The number of transformers to be used depends upon the number of activities involved. In the present example with six activities in arcs 11–16, namely three productive and three selling activities, six transformers are needed.

Physically, these transformers are duals to the transformers normally used in electrical engineering, in the sense that the windings of each transformer must be perceived placed on the spokes of a wheel making up the corresponding magnetic frame. On an analogue computer, of course, the transformers must be represented by electronic amplifiers since they are of the dc type. From a conceptual point of view, however, this is of no interest.

In each of the ideal transformers the activity in, for example, arc 13 makes up the primary winding, while services in, correspondingly, arcs 19, 22, 24, 29, and 31 make up the corresponding sets of secondary windings. Assigning the primary winding a unit number of turns and the secondary windings a number of turns $a_{j,i}$ equal to the corresponding technical coefficients $t_{j,i}$, it is now possible to establish the equilibrium constraint equations of the technical coefficients corresponding to (34) of the economic system.

Basically, the equilibrium constraints of economic power transformation between the secondary and the primary flows through the windings of the two ideal transformers can be determined by Ampére's law which, applied to the closed magnetic meshes through the spokes, yields the fifteen constraint equations.

Activity C_1: $\dfrac{i_{11}}{l} = \dfrac{i_{17}}{a_{17,11}} = \dfrac{i_{26}}{a_{26,11}} = \dfrac{i_{27}}{a_{27,11}}$

Activity C_2: $\dfrac{i_{12}}{l} = \dfrac{i_{18}}{a_{18,12}} = \dfrac{i_{21}}{a_{21,12}} = \dfrac{i_{28}}{a_{28,12}} = \dfrac{i_{30}}{a_{30,12}}$

Activity C_3: $\dfrac{i_{13}}{l} = \dfrac{i_{19}}{a_{19,13}} = \dfrac{i_{22}}{a_{22,13}} = \dfrac{i_{24}}{a_{24,13}} = \dfrac{i_{29}}{a_{29,13}} = \dfrac{i_{31}}{a_{31,13}}$

Activity C_4: $\dfrac{i_{14}}{l} = \dfrac{i_{20}}{a_{20,14}}$

Activity C_5: $\dfrac{i_{15}}{l} = \dfrac{i_{23}}{a_{23,15}}$

Activity C_6: $\dfrac{i_{16}}{l} = \dfrac{i_{25}}{a_{25,16}}$

$$(57)$$

Combining the graph constraints of (56) with the transformer constraints of (57) it seems intuitively most advantageous to express the combined constraints in terms of the currents in arcs 1–10:

$$
\begin{aligned}
a_{17,11}i_5 + a_{18,12}i_6 + a_{19,13}i_7 + a_{20,14}i_8 & = 0 \\
a_{21,12}i_6 + a_{22,13}i_7 \quad\quad + a_{23,15}i_9 & = 0 \\
a_{24,13}i_7 \quad\quad\quad\quad + a_{25,16}i_{10} & = 0 \\
a_{26,11}i_5 \quad\quad\quad\quad\quad\quad - i_1 & = 0 \quad (58) \\
a_{27,11}i_5 + a_{28,12}i_6 + a_{29,13}i_7 \quad\quad - i_2 & = 0 \\
a_{30,12}i_6 \quad\quad\quad\quad\quad\quad - i_3 & = 0 \\
a_{31,13}i_7 \quad\quad\quad\quad\quad\quad - i_4 & = 0
\end{aligned}
$$

Introducing in this latter equation the numerical values of the technical coefficients from Figure 3 and the results of (48) for the four production factor arcs 1–4, the combined bilateral current constraints (corresponding to the Walrasian from equilibrium condition of 43) can be written

$$
\begin{aligned}
-100i_5 + 30i_6 + 10i_7 + 100i_8 \quad\quad\quad\quad\quad\quad & = 0 \\
-100i_6 + 50i_7 \quad\quad + 100i_9 \quad\quad\quad\quad & = 0 \\
-100i_7 \quad\quad\quad\quad + 100i_{10} \quad\quad & = 0 \\
10i_5 \quad\quad\quad\quad\quad\quad\quad\quad + J_1 & = 100 \quad (59) \\
5i_5 + 4i_6 + 2i_7 \quad\quad\quad\quad\quad\quad + J_2 & = 100 \\
5i_6 \quad\quad\quad\quad\quad\quad\quad + J_3 & = 100 \\
10i_7 \quad\quad\quad\quad\quad\quad + J_4 & = 100
\end{aligned}
$$

The corresponding unilateral current constraints originate in the rectifier characteristics of (47) and (52) and can be written

$$\{i_5,\, i_6,\, i_7,\, J_1,\, J_2,\, J_3,\, J_4\} \geq \{0,\, 0,\, 0,\, 0,\, 0,\, 0,\, 0\} \quad (60)$$

After thus having determined the current constraints of the network analogue we turn to the formulation of the voltage constraints. Here, the graph constraints are simply statements of Kirchhoff's mesh law for a set of independent meshes in the network. Whereas Kirchhoff formulated his node law as a postulate analogous to d'Alembert's principle, he derived his mesh law as a logical consequence of the fact that nodal voltages are electric potentials measured on an interval scale. The nodal voltages of an electric network with respect to a given reference voltage are completely analogous to measures of heights in a mountainous terrain with respect to, say, sea level. If we sum differences in heights (with appropriate signs) from an arbitrary starting point around a closed path back to this point, we will find that this sum of differences is zero. The situation is, of course, an exact analogy if we sum differences between nodal voltages around a closed mesh in the electric network.

Considering the inventory stages for the three chemicals C_1, C_2, and C_3 (arcs 17–25% in Figure 3) even the mesh law will appear superfluous since each of the arcs involved is oriented from a node with a potential of -1 to the reference node W. Thus the voltage drops across these arcs can be determined directly

Stage C_1: $e_{17} = e_{18} = e_{19} = e_{20} = -1$

Stage C_2: $e_{21} = e_{22} = e_{23} = -1$ (61)

Stage C_3: $e_{24} = e_{25} = -1$

If in the remaining part of the network we pick arcs 1–4 and 11–16 as tree-branches it is seen, at least intuitively, that each of the remaining links (i.e., arcs 5–10 and 26–31) forms an independent mesh together with these ten tree-branches. To facilitate the later use of these mesh equations we shall divide them somewhat arbitrarily into two groups of mesh equations as follows.

Stage E_1: $e_1 + e_{26} = 0$

Stage E_2: $e_2 + e_{27} = 0$; $e_2 + e_{28} = 0$; $e_2 + e_{29} = 0$

Stage E_3: $e_3 + e_{30} = 0$

Stage E_4: $e_4 + e_{31} = 0$ (62)

Activity C_1: $e_5 + e_{11} = 0$

Activity C_2: $e_6 + e_{12} = 0$

Activity C_3: $e_7 + e_{13} = 0$

and

Activity C_4: $e_8 + e_{14} = 0$

Activity C_5: $e_9 + e_{15} = 0$ (63)

Activity C_6: $e_{10} + e_{16} = 0$

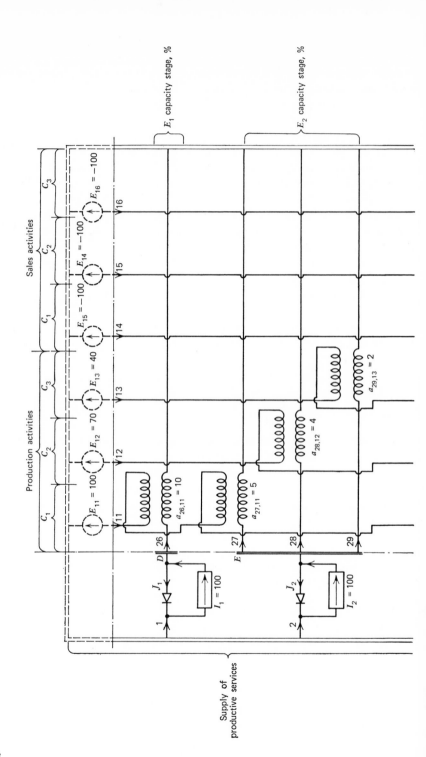

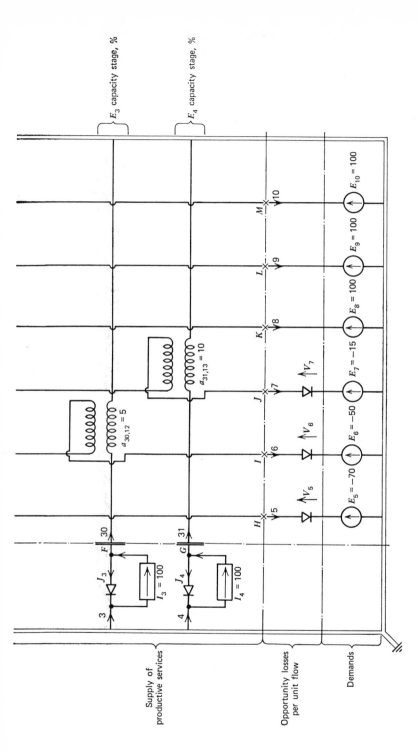

Fig. 5. Intermediate step in the dual formulation.

The equilibrium constraints of economic power transformation between the secondary and the primary voltage drops across the windings of the six ideal transformers can be derived, by means of Faraday's law, from the node equations for the magnetic fluxes to the hub of each transformer as the six constraint equations:

Activity C_1: $le_{11} + a_{17,11}e_{17} + a_{26,11}e_{26} + a_{27,11}e_{27} = 0$

Activity C_2: $le_{12} + a_{18,12}e_{18} + a_{21,12}e_{21} + a_{28,12}e_{28} + a_{30,12}e_{30} = 0$

Activity C_3: $le_{13} + a_{19,13}e_{19} + a_{22,13}e_{22} + a_{24,13}e_{24} + a_{29,13}e_{29}$
$$+ a_{31,13}e_{31} = 0 \quad (64)$$

Activity C_4: $le_{14} + a_{20,14}e_{20} = 0$

Activity C_5: $le_{15} + a_{23,15}e_{23} = 0$

Activity C_6: $le_{16} + a_{25,16}e_{25} = 0$

Introducing the numerical values of the technical coefficients from Figure 3 together with the results of (61) into the transformer constraints of (64) yield that the latter can be rewritten:

$$\begin{aligned}
100 + e_{11} + 10e_{26} + 5e_{27} &= 0 \\
70 + e_{12} + 4e_{28} + 5e_{30} &= 0 \\
40 + e_{13} + 2e_{29} + 10e_{31} &= 0
\end{aligned} \quad (65a)$$

and

$$\begin{aligned}
-100 + e_{14} &= 0 \\
-100 + e_{15} &= 0 \\
-100 + e_{16} &= 0
\end{aligned} \quad (65b)$$

Physically, (65) might be interpreted as a revision of the electric network analogue in Figure 3 into the equivalent network shown in Figure 5.

Visual inspection of Figure 5 immediately reveals that the equivalent voltage sources in arcs 14–16 will cancel the voltage sources in arcs 8–10 with the result that these six arcs can be deleted from the network. Of course, this result can also be obtained by combining (63) and (65b). Thus we are left with only two sets of equations, namely (62) and (65a). Combining the latter two equations we find in terms of the voltage drops across the factor arcs 1–4 and the demand arcs 5–7, after having reversed all signs, that we end up with the following expression:

$$\begin{aligned}
10e_1 + 5e_2 \qquad\qquad + e_5 &= 100 \\
4e_2 + 5e_3 \qquad + e_6 &= 70 \\
2e_2 \qquad + 10e_4 + e_7 &= 40
\end{aligned} \quad (66)$$

Further inspection of the equivalent network in Figure 5 shows us that the equivalent voltage sources in arcs 11–13 can be combined with the voltage sources in arcs 5–7. That is, introducing into (66) the characteristics of the demand arcs 5–7 from (54):

$$e_5 = -V_5 - (-70)$$
$$e_6 = -V_6 - (-50) \qquad (67)$$
$$e_7 = -V_7 - (-15)$$

we find that the combined set of bilateral voltage constraints corresponding to the Walrasian price equilibrium (45) can be written

$$
\begin{aligned}
10e_1 + 5e_2 & & - V_5 &= 30 \\
4e_2 + 5e_3 & & - V_6 &= 20 \qquad (68) \\
2e_2 & + 10e_4 & - V_7 &= 25
\end{aligned}
$$

to which must be added the unilateral constraints originating in the non-negativity of the counter voltages across the rectifiers (47 and 52):

$$\{e_1, e_2, e_3, e_4, V_5, V_6, V_7\} \geq \{0, 0, 0, 0, 0, 0, 0\} \qquad (69)$$

where by virtue of (49) the voltage drop e_j represents the factor price v_j. The physical interpretation of (68) and (69) is a further revision of the network analogue into the equivalent network shown in Figure 6.

In linear programming terminology, (59) and (60) make up the constraints of the *primal* formulation while (68) and (69) make up the constraints of the corresponding *dual* formulation as can be seen by comparison with the original formulation of the economic example discussed here (Dorfman et al., 1958). The basic difference between the conventional formulation of the economic system constraints and the one adopted here in terms of a procedure of constraint-partitioning rests on the fact that application of the latter approach permits a much closer relationship between theory and engineering practice. Thus determination of the graph is closely related to the topological arrangement or lay-out of the production factors, while the technical co-efficients are constraint properties of the individual stages. Furthermore, as we have emphasized earlier, the network will yield us all the constraints at once and not only the primal or only the dual.

THE ELECTRIC NETWORK STATE FUNCTIONS

In connection with the establishment of the electric network analogue it was pointed out that, in equilibrium, the power of each of the rectifiers in the production factor arcs 1–4 and the market demand arcs 5–7 was identically equal to zero. Furthermore, since the transformers representing the technical coefficients are ideal, we know from electric network theory that, in equilibrium, the sum of the power input to the transformers from the production

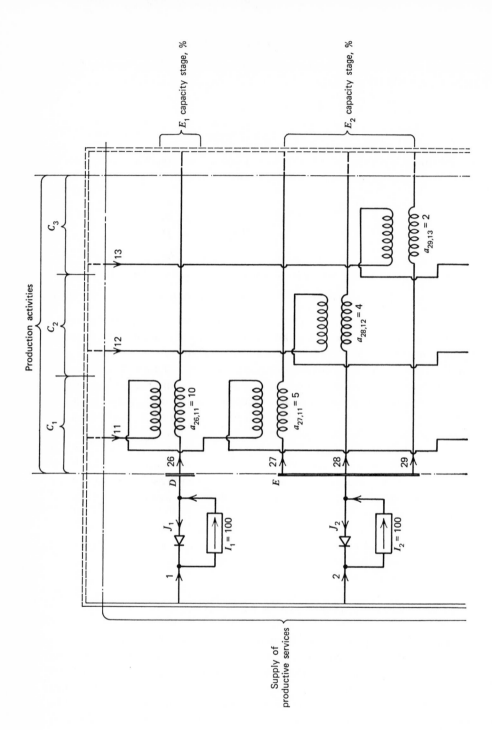

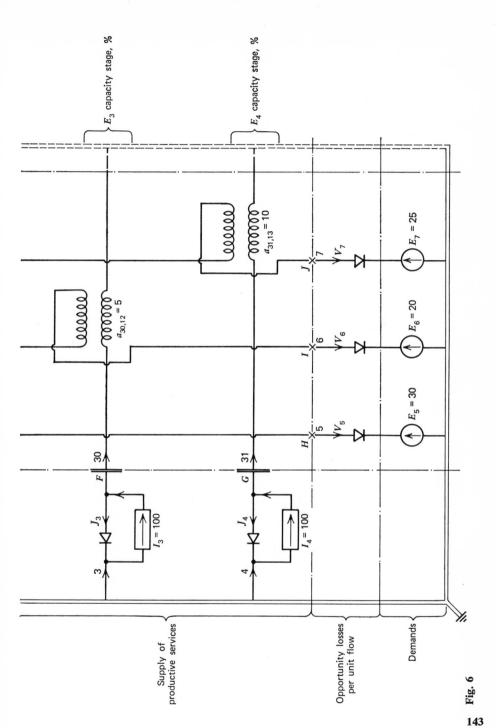

Fig. 6

factor arcs equals the sum of power output from the transformers into the market demand arcs. That is, each of the transformers satisfies a zero power condition of equilibrium.

Thus a nonzero contribution to the power in equilibrium originates only in each of the production factor arcs 1–4 and the market demand arcs 5–10. With the production factor flow sources I_j (corresponding to the limitational production factors y_j), the production factor arc voltage drops e_j (corresponding to the production factor prices v_j by virtue of 51), and the market demand voltage sources E_j (corresponding to the market prices p_i by 55), it is possible, using the electric network notation of Figure 3, to state the physical principle of power conservation as

$$-\sum_{j=5}^{10} i_j E_j + \sum_{j=1}^{4} I_j e_j = 0 \tag{70}$$

which corresponds to Walras' law of (9) for the closed economic system.

Now, by virtue of (70) we can define for the electric network analogue the *content state-function*:

$$K = \sum_{j=1}^{10} \int_0^{i_j} e_j \, di_j = -\sum_{j=5}^{10} E_j i_j \tag{71}$$

and the *cocontent state-function*:

$$K' = \sum_{j=1}^{10} \int_0^{e_j} i_j \, de_j = \sum_{j=1}^{4} I_j e_j \tag{72}$$

which in the economic system corresponds to (17) and (18). Note in (72) that, by virtue of (49), the nonnegative arc voltage drop e corresponds to the nonnegative production factor price v_j. Incidentally, the fact that the only contribution to the cocontent function comes from arcs 1–4 agrees with the revision of the analogue model into the equivalent network in Figure 6. That is, no virtual variations can be performed for the voltage drops across the network arcs incident on nodes A, B, and C since by (61) they are all assigned a fixed value of minus one.

Introducing from Figure 3 the numerical values of the ideal sources in (71) and (72), yields that these equations can be rewritten:

$$K = 70i_5 + 50i_6 + 15i_7 - 100i_8 - 100i_9 - 100i_{10} \tag{73}$$

and

$$K' = 100e_1 + 100e_2 + 100e_3 + 100e_4 \tag{74}$$

which, except for the changing of signs in (73) due to the reversed flow orientation, agrees with the original formulation of the economic example (Dorfman et al., 1958).

The *linear programming* problem now corresponds to determining the equilibrium or extremum state of either of the two power state-functions, (71) and (72), under the constraints between the variables used in describing the state-functions. More specifically, we might say that the *primal* problem is to determine the extremum state for the content state-function of (73) under the constraints of (59) and (60), while the *dual* problem is to determine the extremum state of the cocontent state-function of (74) under the constraints of (68) and (69).

In accordance with economic practice in the formulation of Walras' law, (9), a minus sign was introduced in front of the term representing the power contribution of the production factors. The economic reasoning that led to this difference in sign between the term representing the market demand of economic power, and the term describing the production factor supply for economic power was based upon a conception of market demand as output from the system and factor supply as input to the system. The thus-conceived economic orientation, however, pertains only to the physical flows of the economic system. Actually, application of this orientation to the direction of power flows leads to a violation of the second law. As was pointed out earlier, the latter law is based upon the irreversible conversion of power in the direction from input from the ideal sources to output in the form of dissipation. Since, in the linear programming case, both production-factor supply and market demand are represented solely as ideal sources the two terms in Walras' law should be assigned identical signs. Therefore, as is implied by (12), it is only possible to be logically consistent by including the negative sign of the production-factor supply in that term and determining the total economic power as an additive scalar which is composed of the sum of the content and the cocontent state-functions of (13) and (14).

From economics it is known that the extremum state of the Walrasian system is characterized by the fact that total revenue [i.e., the economic content state-function of (17)] is maximized while total cost [i.e., the negative value of the economic cocontent state-function of (18)] is minimized. Since both types of variables in the latter state-function are nonnegative, the last-mentioned extremum characteristic can be restated to say that the cocontent state-function of (18) (i.e., the negative of the total cost) is also maximized. Introducing the difference in orientation between the second law of economics and the second law of physics which makes negprices correspond to nodal voltages, we find that the extremum characteristics of the electric network analogue will be exactly the opposite of the characteristics of the Walrasian system. Thus for the electric network analogue the extremum state is determined *by minimizing the content state-function* of (73) or *minimizing the cocontent state-function* of (74).

THE ECONOMIC PROBLEM OF PRODUCTION

In physics, as can be exemplified by considering electric network theory or classical mechanics, it is a well-known fact that we characterize the structure of a system by its types of constraints. The economic network is a pictorial way of representing the constraints of the Walrasian conception of a production system. The purpose of the following discussion is to consider this model in a broader framework of the economic and technological decisions of a firm or of an aggregation of firms into an industry.

With Jantzen we defined a given technique as a production system in which the graph as well as the technical coefficients are fixed. From an economic viewpoint this is clearly a short-run situation characterized by the lack of possibilities for varying the production method. With limitational production factors the management problem here is to determine the optimum output. Analytically, this problem of finding *the optimal production with a given technique* amounts to determining the extremum state of the corresponding economic network.

Clearly, if we have indivisibilities the economic network is not a convenient model. Still it is interesting to note that the structure depicted by the network is preserved also for this case. Basically, the characteristics of the solution of this problem, which today is known as the *integer programming problem*, were formulated by Jantzen in his celebrated *law of harmony* (Jantzen, 1924). In more modern terminology this law can be stated:

If an activity in a production scheme is based upon the use of different, indivisible factor services, then the most harmonious co-ordination (i.e., the greatest possible degree of utilization for all the different kinds of services involved) is obtained in only those cases where the number of units of the product resulting from an activity is a common multiple of the available capacities of the services, each divided by the corresponding fixed technical coefficient.

It should be added that Brems, in his exposition of Jantzen's law of harmony (Brems, 1952a, b), anticipated the integer programming approach in the use of diagrams depicting integer lattice points (i.e., points the coordinates of which are integers). The validity of this law can be verified by inspection, if we consider in Figure 3 the manner in which a given activity flow is composed of transformed factor services.

In the short run it is often possible to increase the services of certain factors such as purchase of raw materials or intermediate products. That is, limitational factors such as fixed machines or workshops will cooperate with variable factors in the production system. Basically, we have here a *parametric programming problem* which in the economic network of Figure 3 can be depicted by making some of the current sources in the factor arcs variable. In addition to these variations which earlier have been used to define the production function, it is, of course, also possible to consider variations in the voltage sources representing the demands.

From the economic point of view one of the most severe criticisms of the mathematical programming model of the Walrasian system is the fact that, apart from the possibility of variations of the technical coefficients (by parametric programming), it does not preserve the feature of substitutability. Thus in economics the *long-run* managerial decision of substituting one production factor for another is usually introduced in the Walrasian model by making each technical coefficient a function of all the factor prices (Zeuthen, 1955):

$$t_{ji} = t_{ji}(v_1, v_2, \ldots, v_j \ldots, v_n) \tag{75}$$

However, as pointed out by Ivar Jantzen in his pioneering paper of 1924 (see also, Jantzen, 1939; 1954; and Brems, 1952a, b), it is much more realistic and in much closer relation to engineering practice to substitute instead one completely specified system configuration or technique for another. After all, substitution of factors implies changes in *both* the transformer constraints and in the graph.

Thus the conventional long-run/short-run economic analysis of a firm can be conceived as a two-step approach. The first step, *design of a technique*, is the heuristic problem of setting up the causal logicophysical and temporal relationships which, for the production in question, specify the interconnections between the production factors and the activities, the technical coefficients, the supply curves of the productive services, and the demand curves. Clearly, this is an open-ended problem for which no optimal solution can be defined. Since change in the system configuration is perceived as a new technique, the problem of determining a technique is closely related to the design approach undertaken in computer simulation. The second step, *optimal production with a given technique*, then, is the analytical problem of determining the extremum state of an economic network. Thus for a given technique, we have no possibility of substitution, but only that of producing more or less by each of the different, fixed kinds of activities.

CONCLUSION

The purpose of this chapter has been to establish a correspondence between a fundamental subset of economic theory and its counterpart in physics and, then, to use this correspondence to formulate an electric network analogue of the Walrasian system and, thereby, of the mathematical programming problem.

In the education of engineers as well as economists we tend to neglect bridging the gap to the other discipline. Thus while engineering is intimately interrelated with physics in our engineering schools, economics tends to become an esoteric discipline that conceptually is completely separated from engineering. It was another purpose of this chapter to show a way in which it is possible to present an interdisciplinary account of engineering-economic problems. Let it be remarked, though, that the crossing of boundaries between scientific disciplines brings with it, by the insight which it furnishes, disillusionment as well as elucidation. We become disillusioned to the extent that we recognize facts already known, although our new recognition is more distinct and more definite. On the other hand, we also find elucidation in that we now see throughout the most complicated relations in the different disciplines the same simple structures of scientific thinking.

REFERENCES

BAUMOL, W. J. (1965), *Economic Theory and Operations Analysis*, 2nd ed., Prentice-Hall, Englewood Cliff., N.J.

BILAS, R. A. (1967), *Microeconomic Theory—A Graphical Analysis*, McGraw-Hill, New York.

BREMS, H. (1952a), "En sammenligning mellem den gængse og den Jantzen'ske omkostningsteori" (A comparison between the conventional and the Jantzen theories of cost), *Nationaløkonomisk Tidsskrift*, Vol. 90, pp. 193–211.

BREMS, H. (1952b), "A Discontinuous Cost Function," *The American Economic Review*, Vol. 42, No. 4, pp. 577–586.

BRIDGMAN, P. W. (1927), *The Logic of Modern Physics*, reprinted by MacMillan, New York, 1960.

BRIDGMAN, P. W. (1936), *The Nature of Physical Theory*, reprinted by Dover, New York.

CALLEN, H. B. (1960), *Thermodynamics—An Introduction to the Physical Theories of Equilibrium Thermostatics and Irreversible Thermodynamics*, Wiley, New York.

CAMPBELL, N. (1921), *What is Science*, reprinted by Dover, New York, 1952.

CHERRY, C. (1951), "Some General Theorems for Non-Linear Systems Possessing Reactance," *Philosophy Magazine*, Series 7, Vol. 42, No. 333, October, pp. 1161–1177.

DANØ, S. (1963), *Linear Programming in Industry—Theory and Applications*, Springer Verlag, Wien.

DEBREU, G. (1959), *Theory of Value—An Axiomatic Analysis of Economic Equilibrium*, Wiley, New York.

DENNIS, J. (1959), *Mathematical Programming and Electrical Networks*, M.I.T. Press, and Wiley, New York.

DORFMAN, R., P. SAMUELSON, and R. SOLOW (1958), *Linear Programming and Economic Analysis*, McGraw-Hill, New York.

ENKE, S. (1951), "Equilibrium Among Spatially Separated Markets: Solution by Electric Analogue," *Econometrica*, Vol. 19, January, pp. 40–47.

FRANKSEN, O. I. and M. D. RØMER (1963), "Information og cifferregnemaskiner (Information and Digital Computers)," *Ingeniøren.*, No. 7, April 1, pp. 243–260.

FRANKSEN, O. I. (1965), "Kron's Method of Tearing," presented at the Fourth Power Industry Computer Application Conf., Clearwater, Fla., May.

FRANKSEN, O. I. (1967), "Mathematical Programming in Economics by Physical Analogies," presented at the International Symposium on Mathematical Programming, Princeton University, N. J., August.

FRANKSEN, O. I. (1968), "A Search for a Universal Engineering Language," *Journal of The Franklin Institute*, Vol. 286, No. 6, December, (special issue).

FRANKSEN, O. I. (1969), Mathematical Programming in Economics by Physical Analogies, Simulation Councils Inc., San Diego, Calif.

HENDERSON, J. M., and A. E. QUANDT (1958), *Microeconomic Theory. A Mathematical Approach*, McGraw-Hill, New York.

JANTZEN, I. (1924), "Voksende udbytte i industrien" (Increasing return in industrial production), *Nationaløkonomisk Tidsskrift.*, Vol. 62, pp. 1–78.

JANTZEN, I. (1939), *Basic Principles of Business Economics and National Calculation*, Gad's Forlag, Copenhagen.

JANTZEN, I. (1954), "Stage Unit Cost—Study of a Simplified Model," presented at the 16th European Meeting of the Econometric Society, Uppsala, Sweden, August.

KOOPMANS, C., Ed. (1951), *Activity Analysis of Production and Allocation*, Wiley, New York.

LANCZOS, C. (1949), *The Variational Principles of Mechanics*, University of Toronto Press, Toronto.

LIEBHAFSKY, H. H. (1963), *The Nature of Price Theory*, Dorsey, Homewood, Ill.

LINDSAY, R. B., and H. MARGENAU (1936), *Foundations of Physics*, reprinted by Dover, New York, 1957.

MADSEN, V. (1963), "Regnskabsvæsenets opgaver og problemer—I ny belysning". (The Tasks and Problems of Accounting—In a New Light), 2nd ed., Gyldendal, Copenhagen.

MAXWELL, J. C. (1891), *A Treatise on Electricity and Magnetism*, Vol. I and II, 3rd ed., reprinted in 1954 by Dover, New York.

MILLAR, W. (1951), "Some General Theorems for Non-Linear Systems Possessing Resistance," *Phil. Mag.*, Ser. 7, Vol. 42, October, pp. 1150–1160.

ORCHARD-HAYES, W. (1959), "General Data Files and Processing Operations," *SHARE Committee on Theory of Information Handling*, Report TIH-1, reprinted in *General Information Manual*, E 20-8040, IBM, New York.

PAPOULIS, P. (1964), "The Meaning of Probability," *IEEE Transactions on Education*, Vol. E-7, No. 2 and 3, June–September, pp. 45–51.

PEDERSON, P. O. (1935), "Et produktionsdynamisk problem" (A dynamic problem of production), *Nordisk Tidsskrift for Teknisk Økonomi*, Serial No. 1, September, pp. 28–48.

SAMUELSON, P. A. (1938), "The Numerical Representation of Ordered Classification and the Concept of Utility," *The Review of Economic Studies*, Vol. VI, No. 1, October, pp. 65–70.

SAMUELSON, P. A. (1947), "Foundations of Economic Analysis," *Harvard Economic Studies*, Vol. LXXX, Harvard University Press, Cambridge, Mass.

SAMUELSON, P. A. (1952), "Spatial Price Equilibrium and Linear Programming," *The American Economic Review*, Vol. XLII, No. 3, June, pp. 283–303.

SAMUELSON, P. A. (1953–1954), "Price of Factors and Goods in General Equilibrium," *The Review of Economic Studies*, Vol. XXI (1), No. 54, pp. 1–20.

SAMUELSON, P. A. (1960), "Structure of a Minimum Equilibrium System," in *Essays in Economics and Econometrics: A Volume in Honor of Harold Hotelling*, Ralph W. Pfouts, Ed., University of North Carolina Press, Chapel Hill, pp. 1–33.

SCHMIDT, E. (1939), "Økonomisk definerede Produktionsfunktioner" (Economically defined production functions), *Nordisk Tidsskrift for Teknisk Økonomi*, October, pp. 275–296.

STEVENS, S. S. (1959), "Measurement, Psychophysics, and Utility," in *Measurement: Definitions and Theories*, C. West Churchman, and P. Ratoosh, Eds., Wiley, New York, pp. 18–63.

TRENT, H. M. (1955), "Isomorphisms between Oriented Linear Graphs and Lumped Physical Systems," *Journal of the Acoustical Society of America*, Vol. 27, No. 3, May, pp. 500–527.

TUSTIN, A. (1957), *The Mechanism of Economic Systems*, 2nd ed., W. Heinemann, London.

WALRAS, L. (1954), *Elements of Pure Economics*, Jaffé translation, George Allen and Unwin, London.

ZEUTHEN, F. (1955), *Economic Theory and Method*, Longmans, Green and Co., London.

VI
Econometrics and Economic Forecasting: Michael D. Intriligator

ECONOMETRICS

Econometrics is the branch of economics that combines economic theory, economic data, and statistical theory to measure and test economic relationships.* The econometric approach is outlined in Figure 1. Economic theory is expressed in terms of an econometric model; sample data are refined into usable data; and statistical techniques are suitably modified into econometric techniques. The model is then estimated with econometric techniques on the basis of the usable data. The estimated model, which is a quantitative inference about economic phenomena, can then be used, as shown in Figure 1, for structural analysis and for economic forecasting. *Structural analysis* is the quantitative measurement of economic relationships, and economic forecasting is the quantitative prediction of the values of certain economic variables. Structural analysis and economic forecasting can be used to test theories and to evaluate policy alternatives.

In combining economic theory with economic facts, econometrics avoids the extreme approaches of "theory without facts," on the one hand, which treats economics as a purely deductive science, and "facts without theory," on the other hand, which treats economics as a purely observational science. Econometrics utilizes the theories of the former and the data of the latter and combines them, using statistical techniques, to give empirical content to *a priori* economic reasoning.

THE ECONOMETRIC MODEL

To use the econometric approach, economic theory, or, more generally, any *a priori* reasoning in economics, must be expressed in the form of an econometric model.

* The basic references for econometrics are Johnston (1963), Goldberger (1964), Christ (1966), and Malinvaud (1966).

151

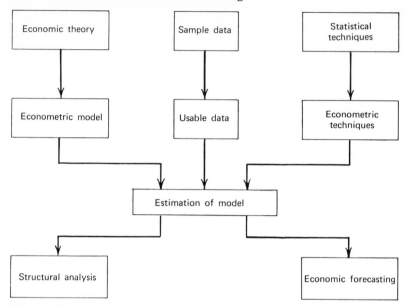

Fig. 1.   The econometric approach.

An *econometric model* is a representation of economic phenomena by a set of equations. The model explains one set of variables, the *endogenous variables*, in terms of another set of variables, the *predetermined variables*. The predetermined variables, which influence the model but are not in turn influenced by it, include lagged endogenous variables, determined by the model at an earlier point in time and *exogenous variables*, determined at the same point in time but by a mechanism not explained within the model.

The economic model can be expressed in three generally different forms, each of which consists of a set of interdependent equations. In the first, the *structural form*, each of the equations is suggested by economic theory, where the equations can be in the form of either identities that hold exactly, or behavioral, technical, or institutional equations that are approximate representations of real phenomena. Secondly, the structural form is used to obtain the *reduced form*, in which each of the endogenous variables is expressed as a function of only predetermined variables. Thirdly, the reduced form can then be used to obtain the *final form* in which each of the endogenous variables is expressed as a function of current and lagged exogenous variables, the lagged endogenous variables having been eliminated from the model. Typically the equations in all three forms are linear.

The nature of an econometric model and the three forms it can take can be illustrated using a very simple model of national income determination which, in addition to exemplifying an econometric model, can be considered a prototype of the large scale econometric models to be discussed in the section on econometric models of the United States economy, p. 159. In this *prototype national income model* there are three endogenous variables:

Y_t = gross national product (GNP) at time t
C_t = consumption expenditure at time t
I_t = investment expenditure at time t

and two predetermined variables:

Y_{t-1} = GNP at time $t - 1$; that is, GNP of the previous year
G_t = government expenditure

where Y_{t-1} is a lagged endogenous variable, and G_t is an exogenous variable. The first equation of the model is the national income accounting identity:

$$Y_t = C_t + I_t + G_t \tag{1}$$

stating that total expenditures by consumers, investors, and governments add up to total GNP. The second equation is the behavioral equation:

$$C_t = \alpha + \beta Y_t \tag{2}$$

stating that consumption is a linear function of GNP, where α and β are constant parameters and β is the marginal propensity to consume (MPC). The third equation is the behavioral equation:

$$I_t = \gamma + \delta Y_{t-1} \tag{3}$$

stating that investment is a linear function of lagged GNP, where α and δ are constant parameters. While (1) is an identity; (2) and (3) are approximate representations of behavior; and, as such, need not hold exactly. For example, many variables other than income influence consumption even on the individual family level, such as previous consumption and assets. In addition, the relationship between the included variables in (2), consumption and income, need not be linear. The econometric approach takes into account both missing variables and the incorrect specification of the relationship between included variables by adding a *stochastic disturbance term* to all equations other than identities. Thus (2) and (3) become

$$C_t = \alpha + \beta Y_t + u_{1t} \tag{4}$$

$$I_t = \gamma + \delta Y_{t-1} + u_{2t} \tag{5}$$

where u_{1t} and u_{2t} are stochastic disturbance terms, that is, random variables. Thus according to (4), consumption expenditure at time t is obtained by adding the parameter α to the product of β and GNP at time t, and then adding to this sum a number obtained by a single drawing from some underlying probability distribution. The number may be positive, negative, or zero, and, to the extent that the stochastic disturbance terms represent many independent missing variables, by the central limit theorem of statistics, the probability distribution is approximately normal (Gaussian).

The structural equations of this prototype national income model are then:

$$Y = C + I + G$$
$$C = \alpha + \beta Y + u_1 \tag{6}$$
$$I = \gamma + \delta Y_{-1} + u_2$$

where time subscripts are understood. The model can be conveniently expressed in matrix notation as:

$$\begin{pmatrix} 1 & -1 & -1 \\ -\beta & 1 & 0 \\ 0 & 0 & 1 \end{pmatrix} \begin{pmatrix} Y \\ C \\ I \end{pmatrix} + \begin{pmatrix} 0 & -1 & 0 \\ 0 & 0 & -\alpha \\ -\delta & 0 & -\gamma \end{pmatrix} \begin{pmatrix} Y_{-1} \\ G \\ 1 \end{pmatrix} = \begin{pmatrix} 0 \\ u_1 \\ u_2 \end{pmatrix} \tag{7}$$

where $(YCI)'$ is a column vector of endogenous variables, and $(Y_{-1}G1)'$ is a column vector of predetermined variables. For the general econometric model the structural equations are of the form:

$$B\mathbf{y} + \Gamma\mathbf{z} = \mathbf{u} \tag{8}$$

where $\mathbf{y}$ is a column vector of G endogenous variables, $\mathbf{z}$ is a column vector of K predetermined variables, B is a $G \times G$ matrix, Γ is a $G \times K$ matrix, and $\mathbf{u}$ is a column vector of stochastic disturbance terms.* Thus the structural equations are a set of G linear equations in G endogenous and K predetermined variables.

The reduced form equations are derived from the structural equations by solving for the endogenous variables in terms of the predetermined variables. In the prototype national income model (6), the consumption and investment equations can be substituted in the income equation and solved for GNP to obtain:

$$Y = \frac{\alpha + \gamma}{1 - \beta} + \frac{\delta}{1 - \beta} Y_{-1} + \frac{1}{1 - \beta} G + \frac{1}{1 - \beta} (u_1 + u_2) \tag{9}$$

Inserting this value of Y into the consumption equation yields

$$C = \frac{\alpha + \beta\gamma}{1 - \beta} + \frac{\beta\delta}{1 - \beta} Y_{-1} + \frac{\beta}{1 - \beta} G + \frac{1}{1 - \beta} (u_1 + \beta u_2) \tag{10}$$

Since the investment equation determines investment as a function of pre-

---

* Do not confuse G, the number of endogenous variables in an econometric model, with $G = G_t$, government spending in the prototype national income model.

determined variables only, in this case the structural equation for investment is also a reduced form equation. Thus the reduced form equations are (9), (10), and (5). In the general case, where the structural form is (8) and B is assumed nonsingular, the reduced form is

$$y = \pi z + w \qquad (11)$$

where

$$\pi = -B^{-1}\Gamma, \qquad w = B^{-1}u \qquad (12)$$

The final form is derived from the reduced form equations by eliminating lagged endogenous variables. By (9) for Y_t and the corresponding equation for Y_{t-1}:

$$Y_t = \frac{\alpha + \gamma}{1 - \beta} + \frac{\delta}{1 - \beta}\left[\frac{\alpha + \gamma}{1 - \beta} + \frac{\delta}{1 - \beta}Y_{t-2} + \frac{1}{1 - \beta}G_{t-1}\right.$$

$$\left. + \frac{1}{1 - \beta}(u_{1t-1} + u_{2t-1})\right] + \frac{1}{1 - \beta}G_t + \frac{1}{1 - \beta}$$

$$\times (u_{1t} + u_{2t}) \qquad (13)$$

Continuing in this way and collecting terms:

$$Y_t = \frac{\delta}{1 - \beta}{}^tY_0 + \left(\frac{1}{1 - \beta}G_t + \frac{\alpha + \gamma}{1 - \beta}\right) + \left(\frac{\delta}{1 - \beta}\right)\left(\frac{1}{1 - \beta}G_{t-1} + \frac{\alpha + \gamma}{1 - \beta}\right)$$

$$+ \left(\frac{\delta}{1 - \beta}\right)^2\left(\frac{1}{1 - \beta}G_{t-2} + \frac{\alpha + \gamma}{1 - \beta}\right) + \cdots$$

$$+ \left(\frac{\delta}{1 - \beta}\right)^t\left(\frac{1}{1 - \beta}G_0 + \frac{\alpha + \beta}{1 - \beta}\right) + \cdots \qquad (14)$$

where the missing terms are those involving the stochastic disturbance terms. Thus each final form equation expresses an endogenous variable as a function of initial values of the endogenous variables and the current and lagged values of the exogenous variables. In the general case, if the reduced form (11) can be written:

$$y_t = \pi_1 y_{t-1} + \pi_2 z_2 + w_t \qquad (15)$$

where only one period lags are considered and no lagged exogenous variables appear in the model, then

$$y_t = \pi_1(\pi_1 y_{t-2} + \pi_2 z_{t-1} + w_{t-1}) + \pi_2 z_t + w_t \qquad (16)$$

and, in general,

$$y_t = \pi_1{}^t y_0 + (\pi_2 z_t + \pi_1\pi_2 z_{t-1} + \pi_1{}^2\pi_2 z_{t-2} + \cdots + \pi_1{}^t\pi_2 z_0) + \cdots \qquad (17)$$

where the missing terms involve the stochastic disturbance terms. All three forms, the structural, reduced, and final forms, are thus systems of equations which are generally linear (in parameters), stochastic (including stochastic disturbance terms), and dynamic (involving time lags).

An important use of the reduced form and final form is that of determining the *comparative statics* of the model; that is, the effect on an endogenous variable of an autonomous change in an exogenous variable or a parameter. For example, in the national income prototype model, from the reduced form (9):

$$\Delta Y = \frac{1}{1 - \beta} \Delta G \qquad (18)$$

that is, an autonomous change in government spending ΔG will generate a change in GNP of $1/(1 - \beta) \Delta G$, where the factor $1/(1 - \beta)$ is called the *multiplier*. If, for example, β were 0.75, so every extra dollar of income results in 75¢ added consumption expenditure, then the multiplier is four; thus every extra dollar of government spending increases GNP by \$4.

Equation 18 gives the change in GNP due to a contemporaneous change in G and the corresponding multiplier $1/(1 - \beta)$ is called a *short-term multiplier*. A change in government spending over several periods leads to a *long-term multiplier*, and from the final form (14):

$$\Delta Y_t = \frac{1}{1 - \beta} \left(\Delta G_t + \frac{\delta}{1 - \beta} \Delta G_{t-1} + \left(\frac{\delta}{1 - \beta} \right)^2 \Delta G_{t-2} + \cdots \right.$$

$$\left. + \left(\frac{\delta}{1 - \beta} \right)_t \Delta G_0 \right) \qquad (19)$$

In particular, if $\Delta G_t = \Delta G_{t-1} = \cdots = \Delta G_0$, then:

$$\Delta Y_t = \left(\frac{1 - [\delta/(1 - \beta)]^{t+1}}{1 - \beta - \delta} \right) \Delta G_t \qquad (20)$$

where $1 - [\delta/(1 - \beta)]^{t+1}/(1 - \beta - \delta)$ is the long-term multiplier, which, assuming $\delta < 1 - \beta$, asymptotically approaches $1/(1 - \beta - \delta)$.

USABLE DATA

The data used to estimate an econometric model consist of observed values, over time, of all variables, endogenous and predetermined, of the model. For the prototype national income model the data would be observed values of Y, C, I, and G, for example, annual observations of each of these variables.*

* The basic data referred to here are *time series data*, defined over time. Another type of data used in the estimation of econometric models are *cross-section data*, defined over economic units. An example would be data on income and expenditure for a sample of households at a point in time.

Economic data are typically nonexperimental in that they refer to observations of the "real world" in which underlying conditions are not controlled and cannot be repeated. As a result there are several problems with the data which may be referred to, using the terminology of astronomy, which faces somewhat similar problems, as the problems of "bad seeing." Among the more important problems are that there is simply not enough data (*the degrees of freedom problem*); that the data tend to be bunched together (*the multicollinearity problem*); that because changes occur slowly over time, the data from time periods close together tend to be very similar (*the serial correlation problem*); that there may be a discontinuous change in the real world so that the data refer to different populations (*the structural change problem*); and that there are many inaccuracies and biases in measuring economic variables (*the errors of measurement problem*).

Because of these problems the data are usually refined in several ways. Most refinements which help overcome one of the problems, however, do so only at the cost of aggravating one of the other problems. For example, replacing annual data by quarterly data increases the number of data points but tends to aggravate both the multicollinearity and the serial correlation problems; eliminating data points referring to unusual periods, such as during war years, overcomes the structural change problems but aggravates both the degrees of freedom and the multicollinearity problems; and replacing variables by their first differences overcomes the serial correlation problem but aggravates the errors of measurement problem. Clearly, judicious choices must be made in obtaining usable data from a sample of raw data.

ECONOMETRIC TECHNIQUES

Econometric techniques are simply extensions of statistical techniques, primarily those of regression theory, to allow for the special features of econometric models.

One of the most widely used techniques of regression theory is *least squares estimation*, according to which the parameters of an equation are estimated by minimizing the sum of squared error terms. For example, the least squares estimators of the parameters of the equation

$$y = a + bx + u \tag{21}$$

are obtained from the sample data $[(x_1, y_1), (x_2, y_2), \ldots, (x_T, y_T)]$ by minimizing:

$$S = \sum_{t=1}^{T} e_t{}^2 = \sum_{t=1}^{T} [y_t - (a + bx_t)]^2 \tag{22}$$

by choice of the parameters a and b. The resulting estimators are the least squares estimators a and b.

A fundamental result in statistical theory is the Gauss-Markov theorem, according to which least squares estimation yields estimators with desirable properties if applied to a model having certain characteristics. The desirable properties are that the estimators are *linear* transformations of the sample data; that they are *unbiased* in that the expected values of the least squares estimators are the true population parameters; and that they are *best* in the technical sense—of all linear unbiased estimators, the least squares provide estimators with minimum variance. The assumptions required for this theorem are that the model be linear, that the explanatory variables be linearly independent and uncorrelated with the error term (the latter being a statistical definition of what constitutes an exogenous variable), and that the stochastic terms exhibit zero means and finite covariances and be distributed independently and identically at all periods. Under these conditions least squares estimators are BLUE, that is, best, linear, unbiased estimators.

The structural form (8) clearly does *not* satisfy these assumptions since the explanatory variables include endogenous variables which are statistically dependent on the error terms. For example, in the national income prototype model, consumption expenditure is explained by GNP, which, according to the national income identity, (eq. 1), has as one component consumption expenditure. Thus GNP in the consumption equation, (4) is not independent of the stochastic disturbance term of that equation, u_1. The conditions of the Gauss-Markov theorem are not satisfied.

The reduced form (11) can, however, satisfy the Gauss-Markov theorem if the stochastic disturbance terms W_t satisfy the assumptions above. Under these conditions, least squares estimation can be applied to each equation of the reduced form to obtain BLUE estimators of the reduced form coefficients, π. These estimators are useful *per se*, but for structural analysis it is important to estimate the structural coefficients, the matrices B and Γ in (8). From (12) it is known that $\pi = -B^{-1}\Gamma$ so the problem of structural estimation involves disentangling $\hat{B}^{-1}$ from $\hat{\Gamma}$, given the product $\hat{\pi} = -\hat{B}^{-1}\hat{\Gamma}$, a problem known as *the identification problem*.* The way these two structural coefficient matrices are obtained from the estimated reduced form coefficient matrix is to add certain *a priori* restrictions to the problem, restrictions that typically take the form of specifying that certain structural coefficients are zero, that is, that the certain variables have no direct effect on an endogenous variable. In the prototype national income model, for example, the eight zeroes in the two matrices of (7) represent such *a priori* restrictions. With sufficient information

---

* See Fisher (1966).

in the form of such restrictions it is possible to estimate the structural coefficients from the estimated reduced form coefficients.

In fact, most econometric models are so rich in *a priori* information that there are several ways of estimating structural coefficients from reduced form coefficients, in which case the model is *overidentified*. In such a case there are two possible approaches to estimating structural coefficients: *limited information approach*, in which the coefficients of each equation of the structural form are estimated, neglecting information available about the rest of the system of equations; and the *full information approach*, in which all structural coefficients are estimated simultaneously using all the *a priori* information available. An example of the limited information approach is *two stage least squares* in which the reduced form coefficients, π, are estimated by least squares in the first stage, and the structural form coefficients, B and Γ, are estimated by least squares in the second stage. In this second stage all explanatory endogenous variables are replaced by the values estimated in the first stage, that is, by linear combinations of predetermined variables, to obtain estimators with desirable properties.

SOME ECONOMETRIC MODELS OF THE UNITED STATES ECONOMY

Some econometric models of the United States economy are summarized in Table 1.

These models can be considered extensions of the prototype national income model (6). For example, the estimated structural equations for the Klein Interwar Model are

$$
\begin{aligned}
C &= 16.8 + 0.02\pi + 0.23\pi_{-1} + 0.80(W_P + W_G) \\
I &= 17.8 + 0.23\pi + 0.55\pi_{-1} - 0.15K_{-1} \\
W_P &= 1.6 + 0.42Y + 0.16Y_{-1} + 0.13t \\
Y &= C + I + G \\
\pi &= Y - W_P - T \\
K &= K_{-1} + I
\end{aligned}
\tag{23}
$$

where the variables are defined in Table 1, and the coefficients in the first three behavioral equations were estimated using 1921–1941 United States data. Comparing this model to the national income prototype model, it is evident that the basic structure is the same, the only difference being somewhat more detailed disaggregation in the Klein interwar model. Thus the explanatory variable for consumption, income, has been disaggregated in the Klein interwar model into wage income ($W_P + W_G$) and profit income (π), and lagged profit income (π_{-1}) has been added as an explanatory variable.

Similarly the explanatory variable for investment has been disaggregated in (23).

Comparing the three models in Table 1, the more recent models involve a greater degree of disaggregation than the earlier models. For example, the 1950 Klein interwar model, like the prototype national income model, involved only a single aggregate measure of consumption expenditure, whereas the 1967 Wharton-EFU model involves five different categories of consumption expenditure. The most ambitious model to date as far as the

Table 1   Three Econometric Models of the United States Economy

Klein Interwar

Description	Endogenous Variables	Exogenous Variables
Annual	Output $= Y$	Government spending $= G$
1921–1941	Consumption $= C$	Public wages $= W_G$
(21 observations)	Investment $= I$	Business taxes $= T$
6 equations	Private wages $= W_p$	Year $= t$
(3 stochastic;	Profits $= \pi$	
3 identities)	Capital stock $= K$	
10 variables		
(6 endogenous;		
4 exogenous)		

Klein-Goldberger

Description	Endogenous Variables		Exogenous Variables
Annual	5	Income	Government expenditure
1929–1941; 1946–1952		Consumption	4 Direct tax
(20 observations)		Fixed investment	Indirect tax
20 equations		Depreciation	5 Population and labor force
(15 stochastic;		Imports	Weekly hours
5 identities)		Corporate savings	Excess reserves
		Corporate surplus	Import prices
34 variables		Capital stock	
(20 endogenous;	2	Liquid assets	
14 exogenous)	3	Prices	
	2	Interest rates	
		Private employees	

[a] For the Klein interwar model see Klein (1950); for the Klein-Goldberger model see Klein and Goldberger (1955); and for the Wharton-EFU model see Evans and Klein (1967).

Table 1 (*Continued*)

Wharton-EFU

Description	Endogenous Variables		Exogenous Variables	
Quarterly	5	Output	2	Output
1948 I–1964 IV	2	Sales		Income
(68 observations)	4	Income		Consumption anticipations
	5	Consumption		Farm fixed investment
76 equations	5	Fixed investment	8	Distributed lag weights
(47 stochastic;	4	Depreciation	2	Investment anticipations
29 identities)		Exports		Depreciation
	3	Imports	2	Government purchases
126 variables	2	Corporate profits		Interest payments
(76 endogenous;		Dividends	2	Social security contributions
50 exogenous)	2	Retained earnings		Housing starts
		Cash flow		Population
		Inventory valuation adjustment	5	Labor force
		Rent and interest payments	2	Wage bill
	3	Taxes		Farm inventories
		Transfer payments		Net free reserves
	4	Labor force	7	Prices
	2	Hours worked		Discount rate
	2	Wage bill		Time
	2	Unemployment rate	6	Dummy variables
	6	Capital stocks		Productivity trend
	3	Inventories		Index of world trade
		Unfilled orders		Statistical discrepancy
		Index of capacity utilization		
	10	Prices		
	2	Wage rates		
	2	Interest rates		

degree of disaggregation is concerned, however, is the Brookings-SSRC model of the United States economy, a quarterly model covering the period 1949 to 1960 with more than 175 equations.* The development of such large-scale disaggregated models has been greatly facilitated by the increased availability of economic data and the decreased cost of computation, using high-speed computers.

* See Duesenberry et al., Eds. (1965).

ECONOMIC FORECASTING

One of the major objectives of econometrics is *economic forecasting* by which is meant a prediction of values of certain variables outside the available sample of data. It will generally be assumed that the forecast is quantitative, explicit, unambiguous, hence refutable.

Assuming a single variable, y, to be forecast, the problem of economic forecasting is that of predicting y at time $T + h$, given the T observations $y_1, y_2, \ldots, y_T$ and, possibly, observations of certain other variables. The time T is taken to be the present and the positive time interval h is called the *forecast horizon*. A point forecast is the single number:

$$y_{T+h} \qquad (24)$$

which is a prediction of the value of y at time $T + h$. To the extent that the true value of the variable at this time, y_{T+h}, is determined according to a probability distribution, the point forecast, (24), is generally taken to be the expected value (mean) of the distribution of y_{T+h} as estimated at time T from the data $y_1, y_2, \ldots, y_T$. This expected value can be bracketed by the *forecast interval*, for example, the 95% confidence interval

$$[\bar{y}_{T+h}, \bar{\bar{y}}_{T+h}]_{0.95}$$

defined by:

$$\text{probability } (\bar{y}_{T+h} \leq y_{T+h} \leq \bar{\bar{y}}_{T+h}) = 0.95 \qquad (25)$$

This forecast interval is illustrated in Figure 2, where, because of the greater uncertainty in the more distant future, the forecast "fans out" over time. The rate at which the interval fans out determines what constitutes a "short-term" forecast as opposed to a "long-term" forecast. Thus a short-term economic forecast might involve a forecast horizon of 18 months, whereas a short-term weather forecast might involve a forecast horizon of up to 3 days ahead. The time scale for economic forecasts is much longer than that for weather forecasts since the confidence interval for weather forecasts fans out much more rapidly than that for economic forecasts.

The econometric approach to economic forecasting is based on the reduced form equation (11). Assuming the variable(s) of interest are the endogenous variables, and given that the reduced form coefficients are estimated as $\hat{\pi}$ the point forecast of y_{T+h} is

$$\hat{y}_{T+h} = \hat{\pi}\hat{z}_{T+h} \qquad (26)$$

where the $\hat{z}_{T+h}$ are the predicted future values of the predetermined variables,

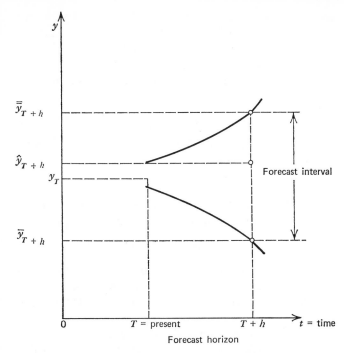

Fig. 2.   The point forecast and the interval forecast.

which are predicted on the basis of considerations other than those of the model.

Several currently used methods of economic forecasting can be considered special cases of the econometric approach. For example, perhaps the most widely used method of forecasting is *persistence forecasting*, based on the assumption that the future will exactly replicate the present. The simplest example is the *status quo* forecast, that the present value of the variable will continue through time:

$$\hat{y}_{T+h} = y_T \tag{27}$$

This forecast can be considered an econometric forecast for which the reduced form states that

$$y_t = y_{t-1} + u_t \tag{28}$$

so that first differences $(y_t - y_{t-1})$ are random.

By iteration,

$$y_{T+h} = y_T + u_{T+1} + u_{T+2} + \cdots + u_{T+h} \tag{29}$$

so, by (26), the forecasted value is the current value. This *status quo* forecast works quite well for certain systems which are influenced by a multitude of random causal factors, such as the Brownian motion of small particles suspended in a gas or the motion of prices in the stock market.*

Another type of persistence forecast is that of a linear time trend, for which the econometric model is

$$y_t = \pi t + u_t \tag{30}$$

where the single explanatory variable is calendar time. By (26), the point forecast is

$$\hat{y}_{T+h} = \hat{\pi}(T + h) \tag{31}$$

Assuming the random variables are distributed independently and normally with zero means and finite and equal variances, the variance of $\hat{y}_{T+h}$ is

$$\text{var}\,(\hat{y}_{T+h}) = (T + h)^2\,\text{var}\,(\hat{\pi})(T + h)^2\sigma^2 \tag{32}$$

where σ^2 is the common variance of the random variables. This result can be used to construct interval forecasts, where the dependence on $(T + h)^2$ shows explicitly how the confidence interval "fans out" as the forecast horizon, h, increases.

A wholly different approach to economic forecasting is that of *leading indicators*, in which certain variables "lead" other variables over time in that they turn upward or downward before these other variables. From the viewpoint of an econometric model the explanatory variables are lagged variables:

$$y_t = \pi_{x_{t-1}} + u_t \tag{33}$$

where the x's, which may be endogenous or exogenous, lead y. The method is used primarily to forecast turning points. For example, if all the x variables turn down at time T then it would be predicted that y will turn down at time $T + 1$ since, from (26) and (33):

$$\hat{y}_{T+1} - y_T = \hat{\pi}(z_T - z_{T-1}) \tag{34}$$

assuming $\pi > 0$:

$$z_T < z_{T-1} \quad \text{implies} \quad \hat{y}_{T+1} < y_T \tag{35}$$

An example of this approach is the forecast of a downturn in the rate of growth of GNP 9 to 12 months after a downturn in the rate of growth of the money supply.† A set of leading indicators, which lead general economic

---

* For a discussion of Brownian motion in the stock market see Cootner, Ed. (1964).
† See Friedman (1958, 1960).

activity by 6 to 9 months has been developed by the National Bureau of Economic Research and includes such variables as new orders, business incorporations, wholesale prices, and hours worked per week.* The main difficulty with this approach, however, is that any single leading indicator moves erratically and, given a set of leading indicators, at any time, some will be rising and others falling. Thus it is hard to discriminate true signals from false ones.

Yet another approach is the *conditional forecast*, which is conditional upon predictions of certain contemporaneous variables. In terms of the econometric model:

$$y_t = \pi x_t + u_t \tag{36}$$

thus

$$\hat{y}_{T+h} = \hat{\pi}\hat{x}_{T+h} \tag{37}$$

where the x's now contain current exogenous variables only. The forecast is conditional on $\hat{x}_{T+h}$, which must be obtained elsewhere.

The full-fledged *econometric forecast*:

$$\hat{y}_{T+h} = \hat{\pi}\hat{z}_{T+h} \tag{38}$$

contains elements of all three approaches discussed above. Thus one of the exogenous variables can be calendar time, some of the predetermined variables can be lagged, and the forecast is also typically conditional on the contemporaneous values of certain exogenous variables. The absolute error of the econometric point forecast (38) is

$$\begin{aligned} y_{T+h} - \hat{y}_{T+h} &= (\pi z_{T+h} + w_{T+h}) - \hat{\pi}\hat{z}_{T+h} \\ &= \pi z_{T+h} - \hat{\pi}\hat{z}_{T+h} + w_{T+h} \end{aligned} \tag{39}$$

showing explicitly how the error is based on incorrect estimation of the coefficients ($\pi \neq \hat{\pi}$), incorrect prediction of future values of predetermined variables ($z_{T+h} = \hat{z}_{T+h}$) and neglect of the stochastic term ($w_{T+h} \neq 0$).

The expected error is

$$E(y_{T+h} - \hat{y}_{T+h}) = \pi(z_{T+h} - \hat{z}_{T+h}) \tag{40}$$

since the expected value of the stochastic disturbance term is zero

$$[E(w_{T+h}) = 0]$$

and the estimators of π are unbiased [$E(\hat{\pi}) = \pi$]. Thus, on the average, the error in the econometric forecast is due to incorrect assumptions or predictions concerning the predetermined variables.

* See Moore, Ed. (1961).

In terms of percentage change, the forecasted percent change is

$$F = \frac{\hat{y}_{T+h} - y_T}{y_T} = \frac{\hat{\pi}\hat{z}_{T+h} - y_T}{y_T} \tag{41}$$

while the actual percent change is

$$A = \frac{y_{T+h} - y_T}{y_T} = \frac{\pi z_{T+h} + w_{T+h} - y_T}{y_T} \tag{42}$$

The accuracy of economic forecasts is often analyzed by relating the actual percentage change A, to the forecasted percentage change F, in a diagram, as shown in Figure 3.* In this figure the 45 degree line is the *line of perfect forecasts*, for which the actual and forecasted percentage changes are equal. The first quadrant contains points for which an increase was forecasted and for which the increase actually occurred, and the third quadrant contains points for which a decrease was forecasted and for which the decrease actually occurred. The second and fourth quadrants contain the *turning point errors*: in the second quadrant a decrease was forecasted but the variable actually

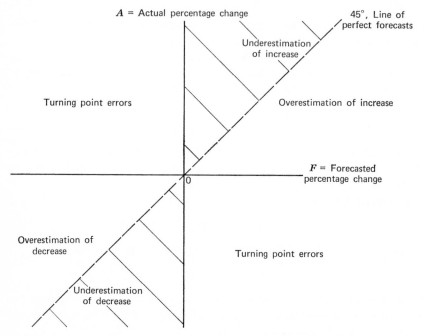

Fig. 3. Actual percentage change versus forecasted percentage change.

* See Theil (1961, 1964).

increased in value, and in the fourth quadrant an increase was forecasted but the variable actually decreased in value.

Economic forecasts of different variables in different countries and over different periods tend to fall, in terms of Figure 3, in the shaded cone between the line of perfect forecasts and the actual percentage change axis, that is, economic forecasts tend to exhibit a systematic underestimation of change. For example, a forecast of 3% increase might typically, in certain economic forecasts, involve an actual increase of 5%. In terms of the definitions above of F and A (41) and (42), typically $A > F$, or

$$\pi z_{T+h} - \hat{\pi}\hat{z}_{T+h} + w_{T+h} > 0 \tag{43}$$

so, since on the average w_{T+h} vanishes and $\hat{\pi}$ is π, assuming $\pi > 0$:

$$z_{T+h} > \hat{z}_{T+h} \tag{44}$$

Thus there is a tendency to underestimate the future values of the predetermined variables. One possible explanation of this systematic underestimation of both y's and z's is that all forecasting methods are based on some explicit or implicit model, and all models involve, in their simplification of reality, an assumption that certain variables do not change in value—the *ceteris paribus* assumption. To the extent that these variables actually do change and to the extent that they all positively affect the forecasted variable, the result of the *ceteris paribus* assumption is the observed systematic underestimation of change. This explanation is a basis for the use of the full-fledged econometric approach as opposed to the simpler persistence and leading indicator approaches. Since the full-fledged econometric approach involves fewer *ceteris paribus* assumptions it should involve less systematic underestimation of change than simpler approaches.

REFERENCES

CHRIST, C. F. (1966), *Econometric Models and Methods*, Wiley, New York.

COOTNER, P., Ed. (1964), *The Random Character of Stock Market Prices*, M.I.T. Press, Cambridge, Mass.

DUESENBERRY, J. S., G. FROMM, L. R. KLEIN, and E. KUH, Eds. (1965), *The Brookings Quarterly Econometric Model of the United States*, Rand-McNally & Co., Chicago; North-Holland Publishing Co., Amsterdam.

EVANS, M. K. and L. R. KLEIN (1967), *The Wharton Econometric Forecasting Model*, Department of Economics, Wharton School, University of Pennsylvania.

FISHER, F. (1966), *The Identification Problem in Econometrics*, McGraw-Hill, New York.

FRIEDMAN, M. (1958), "The Supply of Money and Changes in Price and Output," in *The Relationship of Prices to Economic Stability and Growth*, compendium of papers submitted to the Joint Economic Committee, U.S. Government Printing Office, Washington, D.C.

168   Econometrics and Economic Forecasting

FRIEDMAN, M. (1960), *A Program for Monetary Stability*, Fordham University Press, New York.

GOLDBERGER, A. S. (1964), *Econometric Theory*, Wiley, New York.

JOHNSTON, J. (1963), *Econometric Methods*, McGraw-Hill, New York.

KLEIN, L. R. (1950), *Economic Fluctuations in the U.S., 1921–1941*, Cowles Commission Monograph 11, Wiley, New York.

KLEIN, L. R. and A. S. GOLDBERGER (1955), *An Econometric Model of the United States, 1929–1952*, North-Holland Publishing Co., Amsterdam.

MALINVAUD, E. (1966), *Statistical Methods of Econometrics*, transl., North-Holland Publishing Co., Amsterdam.

MOORE, G., Ed. (1961), *Business Cycle Indicators*, National Bureau of Economic Research, Princeton University Press, Princeton.

THEIL, H. (1961), *Economic Forecasts and Policy*, 2nd ed., North-Holland Publishing Co., Amsterdam.

THEIL, H. (1964), *Applied Economic Forecasting*, North-Holland Publishing Co., Amsterdam.

VII Capital Budgeting and Project Selection: Raoul J. Freeman

INTRODUCTION

"Capital investment" is concerned with the present use of capital resources to reap benefits from them in the future. "Capital budgeting" denotes that there are limited amounts of resources, and that they have to be allocated. "Project selection" has to do with picking the specific items to which the capital resources are to be allocated. This chapter makes some general remarks about capital budgeting and project selection and develops an integer linear programming approach to the subject. The latter is a formulation that has practical relevance to many industrial situations.

AN INTEGER PROGRAMMING FORMULATION

It seems appropriate to view the capital budgeting and project selection question as a constrained optimization problem (Weingartner, 1963). In other words, some function is to be maximized (or minimized) subject to certain side conditions. For example, the present value of future earnings could be maximized, subject to not exceeding certain expenditure levels. Furthermore, it seems appropriate to consider the candidate projects for capital support (e.g., the building of a new plant of given capacity) as discrete entities. That is to say, projects are concretely defined with specific estimated costs, revenues, investment requirements, and such. The question that must be answered is whether a specific project will be supported at a present level of required funding. There is no concern with establishing the level of funding to be awarded to a project other than the "yes-no" decision on the preset amount mentioned above. This is a more realistic formulation in terms of obtaining the necessary data regarding various projects, as only specific numbers are required as opposed to functional relationships between costs, revenues, and capacities which would be required in the nonpresent case. Probabilistic aspects of the problem are ignored in the formulation to be developed in this chapter. The nonstochastic model has major advantages in terms of understandability in the typical industrial environment, data input requirements, and computational requirements. Stochastic models may be considered a desirable future extension of the approach described herein (Hillier, 1967).

If realism is desired, the model should allow the candidate projects to be initiated at various points in time and to take on several levels of scale (each of which is well defined in terms of present requirements). By simultaneous consideration of all possible starting times and scales for all projects, the model should be able to select the appropriate starting time and scale for each individual project. The integer programming formulation is capable of accomplishing this.

The investment decision of *today* influences the return, thus the investment decision, of *tomorrow* and the *day after* and so on. For example, projects supported this year may produce cash next year, which can then be invested in projects, which in turn produce cash the following year and so forth. In developing a capital budgeting model, it is essential to consider this dynamic interaction. It is possible to do this by means of a temporal, integer programming formulation using certain recursive relationships which typify the capital budgeting process.

Once a constrained optimization with discrete entities is postulated, then an integer programming model becomes the appropriate mathematical technique to consider. A simple illustration of an integer programming formulation will show what is involved in a model of this kind. If there are two projects, A and B, which are candidates for funding, then there are four basic choices available:

1. Do A and do B.
2. Do A and not B.
3. Do B and not A.
4. Do neither A nor B.

Constraints on resources can rule out some of the choices above. For example, assume that the cost of A is 1, the cost of B is 1, and that the total available for all projects is 1. Then, clearly, choice 1 is no longer feasible, and the *best* of 2, 3, and 4 must be selected. The latter can be done by comparing the "benefits" of projects A and B. Let us suppose the benefit of A is 3 and the benefit of B is 2. Then the optimal choice with a budget constraint of 1, is choice 2, do A and not B. With a budget constraint of 2, choice 1, do A and do B, is best.

A mathematical representation of the option of doing or not doing a project can be made by means of auxiliary variables whose values are restricted to 0 or 1. Thus X_A could be the auxiliary variable for project A and X_B the auxiliary variable for project B. The various basic choices could then be represented by the following sets of values of (X_A, X_B):

1. (1, 1)
2. (1, 0)
3. (0, 1)
4. (0, 0)

If we let

$$V_A = \text{benefit of } A$$
$$V_B = \text{benefit of } B$$
$$C_A = \text{cost of } A$$
$$C_B = \text{cost of } B$$

then a budget constraint can be written as

$$C_A X_A + C_B X_B \leq \text{budget} \tag{1}$$

The objective of the problem can be to make that choice which yields the greatest total benefit or that choice which maximizes

$$V_A X_A + V_B X_B \tag{2}$$

Thus the decision-making problem is to maximize (2) subject to (1) and to the restriction that the variables be 0 or 1. This is a linear integer programming problem and can be solved by various computerized mathematical routines (Balas, 1965; Driebeck, 1966; Freeman, 1966; Geoffrion, 1965; Graves and Whinston, 1968; Lawler and Bell, 1968; Petersen, 1967).

The general problem of capital budgeting and project selection will have the same basic structure as the simple example outlined above. However, in practice, there will be large numbers of projects (perhaps a hundred or more) and large numbers of constraints (e.g., return on investment over time, cash flow over time, and earnings over time) which are simultaneously considered. The number of basic allowable choices of which projects to support with two projects was four; with three projects it is eight; and with twenty projects it is more than a million. Thus the computational burden in a real-world situation can be anything but trivial in developing the array of possible solutions and selecting the best ones from such an array. However, the essence of the solution process is the same as in the numerical example. First, feasible solutions (i.e., those satisfying the constraints) are calculated, and then the best of these in terms of the objectives of the company (i.e., that solution giving the highest value to the objective function) is determined. The mathematical process of achieving the above is accomplished via the internal workings of the algorithm chosen to solve the problem. If the formulation of the problem fits the linear integer programming format, then various mathematical techniques can be applied to the particular data of a firm to derive a solution (Balas, 1965; Driebeck, 1966; Freeman, 1966; Geoffrion, 1965; Graves and Whinston, 1968; Lawler and Bell, 1968; Petersen, 1967).

SOME GENERAL ASPECTS OF CAPITAL BUDGETING AND PROJECT SELECTION

The general capital investment problem can be stated as, "How much should be invested at various points in time, and to which projects should the investment be allocated?" The two parts of this question should be answered simultaneously. Given that an allocation technique (e.g., an integer linear programming model) is available and using a given budget level, an optimal allocation can be made. In other words, an appropriate set of projects can be selected for support out of all the projects which are candidates for support. The total benefit of this selection is assessed from the specific value of the objective function which it engenders. The same allocation procedure can be utilized with a different setting for the budget. Again, the best selection would yield a specific total benefit. This procedure can be repeated a number of times and a relationship between total benefit values and associated budget values can be ascertained. For example, if we have three projects, A, B, and C, whose individual benefits are 5, 4, and 6, respectively; and whose costs are 3, 2, and 5, respectively; and there is a budget of 5; then the best selection consists of projects A and B and the total benefit of this optimal selection is 9. Repeating the allocation process with different budget settings, we generate the total benefits and optimal projects sets indicated below:

Budget	Total Benefit	Optimal Project Set
5	9	A, B
6	9	A, B
7	10	B, C
8	11	A, C
9	11	A, C
10	15	A, B, C

Management, by means of marginal analysis (i.e., by comparing the incremental benefits with the incremental costs), can decide which point(s) on the "budget-total benefit" relationship above is best. Although in the numerical example it looks very attractive to spend the extra unit between 9 and 10 due to the fact that benefits rise from 11 to 15, it may be extremely "painful" for the company to expend that extra unit. This could possibly violate some loan agreements, or cast the asset/liability ratio into an unacceptable arena, and so on. Thus the "bigger picture" may indicate that a budget of 9 may be the best. If management is given the budget-benefit relationship, it can proceed in a rational manner to weigh the pros and cons of various expenditure levels. Once an optimal point(s) is selected, the size of the actual budget has been determined. The optimal allocation of this budget to competing projects is then also available, since it was necessary to develop this information in order to establish the "budget-total benefit" relationship in the first place (Freeman, 1960).

The element of "time" is very important in the capital budgeting context. Most investments are not just instantaneous inputs of resources *today* and instantaneous outputs of returns *tomorrow*. They usually consist of some stream of inputs over time and some stream of outputs over time. The evaluation or comparison of the "value" of various streams of future returns can be done by use of the concept of discounting or taking the present value of different income streams.

Since the capital budgeting and project selection problem is a dynamic one, the solution thereof will constitute a menu for action of which only a part will be implemented immediately (i.e., the support of those projects which the model indicates should be supported *now*). Some projects will be indicated for support next year and some for the year after. Obviously, a reevaluation will be done of these projects before resources are committed in the future. Thus the capital budgeting process by its very nature sets up some immediate action and also plans for future action. The latter can then be reevaluated for a variety of reasons including new information that may become available, revised needs of projects in process, and changes in management objectives.

SOME SPECIFIC ASPECTS OF A CAPITAL BUDGETING AND PROJECT SELECTION MODEL

Among the considerations of any capital budgeting and project selection model that still need to be specified after the general form of the model (e.g., linear integer programming) has been chosen are the inputs, the factors to be included, and the outputs of the model.

Inputs

The inputs to the model have to be specified. Thought on two levels is required: first, the purely organizational aspects which set up forms, deadlines, places to deliver the forms, and such; second, an analysis of the nature of the data to be requested and how they are to be processed.

Data regarding individual projects involve the prediction over time of various attributes of projects, for example, sales, investment, cost, and depreciation. A project may be defined as building of a new plant, improvement of an existing process, acquisition of a new firm, and such. Obviously the originators or planners of a project are a prime source for such data about a project. However, other independent sources can be called on as well. For example, suppose the project in question is construction of a new plant to produce a certain product. The most likely market price for that product is better arrived at by the market analysis people than by the plant planners. It is precisely that market price which is an essential input to the determination of net revenue for the entire project.

Estimates or forecasts should not be accepted without close scrutiny. The latter can consist of more than just arbitrary modifications made by the management chain. For example, there is a computerized method (Freeman, 1971) which takes (1) internal estimates of company sales made by personnel in the company and (2) economy or size of market estimates made by independent sources external to the company, and changes both sets of estimates so as to make sure that they are reasonable in light of each other. Market share, which is defined as the ratio of company sales in a market to the size of that market, relates these two sets of estimates. Obviously, "size of market" *times* "market share" *equals* "company sales" (in that market). If the estimates of the three components noted above come from independent sources (e.g., managers of the company may make its sales forecasts, economists may make forecasts of the size of various markets, and a mathematical model or extrapolation may be used to estimate market share), then there is nothing to guarantee that these quantities so derived will be in the required *balance* to achieve the equality noted above. The computerized method changes the estimates so as to force "consistency" or "balance" between internal and external estimates while accounting for the credibility of estimates as established by past record. What comes out of this procedure are *revised* estimates about the projects. These revised estimates can then be utilized as inputs to a capital budgeting and project selection model.

It is also necessary to obtain statements of objectives and constraints from top-level management. Certain minimum expectations as to cash flow, earnings, growth in earnings, return on investment, return on sales, and such must be obtained. Furthermore, management views about trade-offs between now and later (e.g., earnings next year versus earnings five years out) and also trade-offs between various criteria [e.g., earnings and return on investment (ROI)] need to be ascertained. This will enable consideration of an appropriate range of discount rates and relevant combinations of earnings and ROI requirements for sensitivity analysis runs of the model. If it is obvious, for example, that management is willing to give up quite a bit in terms of ROI to achieve a small gain in earnings, then a different range of alternatives (i.e., computer runs with certain values of parameters) has to be considered than if the case were reversed. Thus the expression of management desires will allow for a relevant determination of the make-up of the sensitivity analyses which the capital budgeting model will be called on to produce. Sensitivity analysis is illustrated in the numerical example which follows.

Factors to be Included

The following are important in most capital budgeting contexts and also can be represented within a linear integer programming format:

Earnings requirements over time.
Cash requirements over time.
Return on investment requirements over time.
Return on sales requirements over time.

The above are examples of "primary" constraints, and minimum management expectations on these quantities will have to be ascertained. The elements which play a role in the constraints above must be specified. For example, the following are relevant:

Taxes (including investment credits, if any).
Interest (both paid for loans and received for deposits).
Depreciation.
Dividends.
Loan repayment periods.

Further aspects that can be built into the constraint structure include the following.

Limitations on the maximum amount the firm may borrow.
Minimum acceptable values on various criteria for admitting a project into the "candidate for support" set.
Forcing continuations of certain portions of the business or guaranteeing inclusion of certain projects.
Allowing various admissible starting dates for projects.

An objective function needs to be formulated. For example, "maximization of the present value of an earnings stream" is a likely candidate. The latter can be adjusted by the appropriate discount rates to reflect management preferences for maximization over near term or long term.

Outputs

The precise outputs of the model must also be decided on. Basically, what is wanted is a capital allocation or project selection plan for the next so many years, the conditions under which such a plan is desirable, and the relative expected costs and benefits to be derived from such a plan. The plan is an indication whether and when certain members of a set of candidate projects should be supported. The model should also indicate if significant variation in the projects selected or value of the objective function(s) is to be expected as a result of certain changes in the constraints or the input data. The sensitivity of the solution to certain changes in project data, business parameters, or management requirements should be easily calculated and displayed.

A NUMERICAL ILLUSTRATION

We now consider in outline form an example based on the linear integer programming model. The objective, primary restrictions, other considerations, parameter values, and data are stated below.

Objective: Maximize present value of earnings through 1972.

Primary restrictions: Cash of at least 6 million, 6 million, and 6 million (1969–1971).

Pretax earnings of at least 13 million, 22 million, and 35 million (1969–1971). Pretax return on investment $\geq 20\%$ pretax (1969–1971).

Other considerations: Maximum amount to be borrowed ≤ 0.7 investment -1.5 outstanding loans. Allowable starting dates for projects (Table 1).

Table 1

Date	69	70	71
Project 1	a	a	a
2	a		
3		a	a
4	a		a
5		a	a
⋮			
10	a		

a It is feasible to start a given project in a specified year.

Parameters. Tax rate $= 50\%$
Investment credit $= 7\%$
Loan repayment period $= 10$ years (equal installments)
Interest rate $= 8\%$
Depreciation rate $= 10\%$
Discount rate for future earnings $= 10\%$

Data. Initial cash position = $40 million
Initial loans = $60 million
Initial investment = $200 million
Number of shares = $10 million
Dividends = $0.50/share annually
Estimates on individual projects (Table 2)

Table 2

	1969	1970		1972
Project 1				
Sales	36,000	42,000	· · ·	49,000
Cost of sales	25,000	29,000		32,000
Depreciation	3,000	5,000		6,000
Net revenue[a]	8,000	8,000		11,000
Investment	30,000	20,000		0
Project 2				
Sales	25,000	25,000	· · ·	25,000
Cost of sales	11,000	11,000		11,000
Depreciation	7,000	7,000		7,000
Net revenue[a]	7,000	7,000		7,000
Investment	70,000	0		0
⋮				
Project 10				
Sales	15,000	18,000	· · ·	25,000
Cost of sales	10,000	11,000		12,000
Depreciation	4,000	5,000		7,000
Net revenue[a]	0	2,000		6,000
Investment	40,000	10,000		10,000

[a] Pretax.

If some of the projects represent the same physical entity but at different capacities, then constraints must be included to assure that only one of these representations appears in any optimal solution. This can be done by constraints such as

$$X_i + X_j \leq 1$$

where project i represents a potential plant at one capacity and where project j represents the same potential plant at a different capacity. All X's are binary variables limited to values of 0 or 1.

To accommodate the various possible starting dates indicated in Table 1, it is necessary to describe every possible project which has more than one possible starting date by means of more than one variable (the number of variables used is equal to the number of possible starting dates for the project). Thus project 1 (see Table 1) would have three variables (call then X_{1A}, X_{1B}, X_{1C}), and a constraint would have to be included to allow at most one of these to assume the value of 1 in any solution. This can be done by means of the following:

$$X_{1A} + X_{1B} + X_{1C} \leq 1$$

The values of the coefficients in the objective function are calculated from the data of Table 2. The net revenue numbers from Table 2 for each project for each year (call them r_{it} for project i in year t) are divided by $(1 + p)^t$ (where p is the discount rate), respectively, and all the terms so derived for each project are added. Thus the coefficient, s_i, for project i in the objective function turns out to be

$$s_i = \sum_t \frac{r_{it}}{(1 + p)^t}$$

where $t = 0$ for 1969, $t = 1$ for 1970, and so on.

The objective function, in its entirety, becomes

$$\sum_i s_i X_i$$

The first primary constraint of the example states that the amount of cash that has to be available in 1969 is to be at least 6 million. To formulate this mathematically, all the terms which contribute to the amount of cash available and all those which subtract from it must be assembled. In general, we have the following.

End available cash$_t$ = beginning available cash$_t$ + amount borrowed$_t$
+ post tax net project revenue$_t$ + post tax interest income$_t$
− past tax interest expense$_t$ + depreciation$_t$
+ investment credit$_t$ − investment$_t$
− loan repayment$_t$ − dividends$_t$ + $\cdots$
≥ req. amount

Some of the terms above in the "end available cash" expression are easy to formulate and some are not.

Some of the simpler ones include:

$$\text{depreciation}_t = \sum_i d_{it} X_i$$

where the d_{it} are the depreciation numbers for the individual projects for year t as given in Table 2,

$$\text{investment}_t = \sum_i I_{it} X_i$$

where the I_{it} are the investment numbers for the individual projects for year t as given in Table 2, and

$$\text{investment credit}_t = 0.07 \sum_i I_{it} X_i$$

Beginning cash available$_t$ for the year 1969 is given as 40 million. However, in the formulation of the cash constraint for the year 1970 (which must be done for the 1969 calculation because of the dynamic interaction property), beginning cash available$_t$ (which is equivalent to end cash available$_{t-1}$) will be a complex function of various coefficients and the X_i. It is precisely the value of the left-hand side of the 1969 cash inequality. The 1971 cash constraint situation is even more complicated. However, due to some interesting recursive properties, all these constraints can be written as linear functions of the X_i. The solution maximizes the objective function and satisfies the constraints. In essence, it considers all possible funding combinations in year $t + 1$ based on all possible combinations in year t and finds that set of combined possibilities over the period in question which maximizes the objective function.

In total, three cash constraints (1969–1971) need to be formulated for this example. Similarly, three earnings and three return on investment constraints need to be formulated. Other constraints that need to be included are those that will prevent the same physical entities at different capacity levels or at different starting times to be included in the same optimal solution, and those that make sure that the maximum loan limitations on the firm are observed.

Once all of the above are appropriately formulated and the data are preprocessed so as to be ready for computer input, then an appropriate computer program has to be selected to solve the problem. The immediate output from such a program is an indication of which projects should be supported and when they should be started (as shown in Table 3).

This, then, is the set of projects which observes all the constraints and also produces the greatest present value of earnings through 1972. Other outputs of interest include the value of the objective function of the solution and the amount of slack in the constraint values engendered by the optimal solution. By slack is meant the difference between present requirements and actual performance (e.g., cash of 6 million required in 1970 and 7 million actually generated by the optimal set of projects).

It is now of interest to vary some of the conditions under which the problem

Table 3

Project Number	Year of Start
1	69
2	69
3	70
4	71
5	70
⋮	⋮
9	Not to be done
10	69

was run to determine the sensitivity of the solution to such changes. Examples of three types of such variations are listed below:

1. Use of a different objective function by means of the following.

   a. Various discount rates.
   b. Different time horizons over which to optimize.
   c. Use of criteria other than discounted earnings (e.g., ROI).

2. Use of different management requirements in the following constraints.

   a. Various cash requirements.
   b. Various earnings requirements.
   c. Various return on investment requirements.

3. Changes in operating conditions.

   a. Use of different borrowing limitations.
   b. Elimination of the investment credit.

An output similar to that developed in Table 3, together with associated objective function and constraint slack values, can be generated for these various cases and then intercompared. Each of the changes in types 1, 2, and 3 could be tried in combination with each other to form a larger number of interesting possibilities from which to derive facts to call to management's attention.

CONCLUSION

This chapter has discussed a quantitative approach to capital budgeting and project selection. No attempt has been made to completely cover the field and to handle such factors as project interdependencies, risk aversion, stochastic elements, unreliability of data, and such (Graves and Whinston, 1968; Hanssman, 1968; Mao and Wallingford, 1968; Weingartner, 1966). However, even the integer programming model described here is far ahead of what many firms are using today. The theory of capital budgeting is far ahead of actual practice, and the next big step forward in this field is the sustained application of already existing models.

Among the advantages to be gained from the installation of a quantitatively based capital budgeting system are the following.

1. Systematic accumulation of data about capital projects in a form which makes them comparable and relevant to management objectives.
2. Introduction of a method of thought and discipline regarding capital allocation which is more "scientific" (i.e., more closely aligned to economic and mathematical theory) than "intuitive" approaches.
3. Development of an entity which can be viewed as a building block towards a comprehensive management information and control system for the complete financial management of the firm.

REFERENCES

BALAS, E. (1965), "An Additive Algorithm for Solving Linear Programs with Zero-One Variables," *Operations Research*, Vol. 13, pp. 517–546.

DRIEBECK, N. J. (1966), "An Algorithm for the Solution of Mixed Integer Programming Problems," *Management Science*, Vol. 12, No. 7, March.

FREEMAN, R. J. (1960), "A Stochastic Model for Determination and Allocation of Research Budgets," *IRE Transactions on Engineering Management*, Vol. EM-7, No. 1, March.

FREEMAN, R. J. (1966), "Computational Experience With a 'Balasian' Integer Programming Algorithm," *Operations Research*, Vol. 14, No. 5, September–October.

FREEMAN, R. J. (1971), "A Company-Economy Interactive Approach to Sales Forecasting," submitted for publication to the Proceedings of the International Federation for Information Processing Congress 71 held in Yugoslavia, in September 1971.

GEOFFRION, A. (1965), "A Reformulation of Balas' Algorithm for Integer Linear Programming," *The RAND Corporation*, RM-4783-PR, September.

GRAVES, G. and A. WHINSTON (1968), "A New Approach to Discrete Mathematical Programming," *Management Science*, Vol. 15, No. 3, November.

HANSSMAN, F. (1968), *Operations Research Techniques for Capital Investment*, Wiley, New York.

HILLIER, F. S. (1967), "Chance Constrained Programming with 0–1 or Bounded Continuous Decision Variables," *Management Science*, Vol. 14, No. 1, September.

LAWLER, E. L. and M. D. BELL (1968), "A Method for Solving Discrete Optimization Problems," *Operations Research*, Vol. 14, November–December.

MAO, J. C. T., and B. A. WALLINGFORD (1968), "An Extension of Lawler and Bill's Method of Discrete Optimization with Examples from Capital Budgeting," *Management Science*, Vol. 15, No. 2, October.

PETERSEN, C. C. (1967), "Computational Experience with Variants of the Balas Algorithm Applied to Selection of R&D Projects," *Management Science*, Vol. 13, No. 9, May.

WEINGARTNER, H. M. (1966), "Capital Budgeting of Interrelated Projects: Survey and Synthesis," *Management Science*, Vol. 12, No. 7, March.

WEINGARTNER, H. M. (1963), *Mathematical Programming and the Analysis of Capital Budgeting Problems*, Prentice-Hall, Englewood Cliffs, N.J.

VIII

Systems Problems in Economic Development: David A. Kendrick

INTRODUCTION

In this chapter a description and analysis of experimentation in the use of simulation and optimization models for national economic planning is given. The simulation model discussed is of the dynamic multisectoral "consistency" type in that final demands are projected exogenously, and consistent sectoral levels of production and investment are then determined by the model. The optimization models discussed differ by levels of temporal and sectoral disaggregation. Those which are highly disaggregated in the sectoral sense tend to be single period models, while the multisectoral models tend to have only a few sectors. The use of both mathematical programming and control theory methods in solving various of these optimization models is discussed. Also, special attention is given to the economic assumptions that are implicit in the use of each type of model.

The chapter is written for scientists and engineers who are at home with simulation and optimization techniques but relatively innocent of economics.

In recent years economists have begun to experiment in the construction of computable models for development planning in underdeveloped countries. While these models suffer from the inherent social science difficulties of dearth of data and complexity of technological and behavioral relations, they have the appealing property of being able to capture much of the interdependent nature of economic systems.

Although the area of systems problems and economic development is by no means confined to the use of experimental models for national economic planning, this chapter is restricted to a discussion of these models. For example, there are a large class of models for sectoral planning in heavy industry, agriculture, transportation, and education, but these models are undoubtedly similar to those discussed in the other chapters. Also, this chapter is restricted to a discussion of computable models, that is, models that are solved numerically on digital computers. There is a large group of

I am grateful to Peter Dixon for his comments on this material.

theoretical models for analyzing economic growth.* These models have been applied to both developed and underdeveloped economies. However, they are usually highly aggregative with the entire output of the economy considered to be coming from one or two sectors. The computable models are in general more disaggregated and richer in detail and structure.

The best introduction to the subject of economic planning models can perhaps be made through a description of the interdependent nature of economic systems and some of the trade-offs that economic planners face. Consider a relatively small and not very heavily industrialized country that exports raw materials and/or agricultural crops, and imports machinery and consumer durable goods such as automobiles and refrigerators. Assume that the planners are able to control the amount and type of new investment in all major sectors of the economy either through incentive schemes or through direct controls on imported machinery and equipment.

The planners are assumed to be able to decide at each point in time (1) how much of output of each sector will be used for consumption purposes; (2) how much of output will be used for investment purposes and how it will be allocated among sectors; (3) what proportion of foreign exchange earnings will be used for importing investment goods for the various sectors and for importing consumption goods to meet consumer demands; and (4) how much of the available labor force will be used in each sector. The planners are charged with the task of informing the policy-makers about the effects of various allocational plans over a 30-year planning period.

They may decide to allocate a large share of output and foreign exchange for the creation of additional production capacity in the heavy industry sectors in the early years of the plan. This strategy would result in fewer consumption goods in the short run and more in the long run, since more machinery would be available to produce the output of future years. However, this approach may run into difficulty from a shortage of foreign exchange, since large investment in heavy industry will require the importation of considerable numbers of expensive machines. Alternatively, the planners may decide to allocate investment heavily in the early years of the plan to agriculture to increase exports and thereby the availability of foreign exchange for investment in heavy industry in later years.

Simultaneously with these policies, the planners may be making decisions about how much of the labor force and output of the society should be devoted to increasing the education and skill of future members of the labor force. Up to some levels the greater the education of these people, the greater will be their future contribution to output; however, this increased future output can be obtained only by the sacrifice of present consumption in the society.

* See, for example, the models in Shell (1967).

The point of this description is to provide a glimpse of the kinds of trade-offs and the web of interdependencies that must be captured in economic planning models. The trade-offs are present in all economies, no matter what mix of incentives, and direct controls are used to modify the direction of flow of the economy. The use of models to study an economic system does not assume that the controls are direct or indirect but rather attempts to yield insight into the underlying structure, direction of movement, and trade-offs implicitly or explicitly being made in the economy.

The trade-offs in the models come from three sets of constraints which represent availability of output, foreign exchange, and labor force. Output may provide more consumption now or more machines provide more consumption later. Also it may furnish more foreign exchange earnings now and/or at some future point in time. Like output, foreign exchange may give present consumption or machines for future consumption and/or it may provide imports to exporting industries that will yield more foreign exchange in the future. Labor may be used in industries that produce consumption goods or investment goods and/or sent into the schools to train others or to receive additional training.

In the allocation of each type of scarce resource, the effects throughout the rest of the economy may be important. For example, the decision to invest more in heavy industries may require increased flows of imports at present for machinery and in the future for imported raw materials for those industries. Also, heavy industry will require inputs from light industry and agriculture that must be produced domestically or imported, and it may require highly educated labor that must be trained domestically or sent abroad for training. As is apparent, the timing of these interdependent actions is usually of importance.

We now turn to a discussion of a set of economic planning models that have been and are being developed to analyze the trade-offs discussed above within the comprehensive framework of computable models. We begin by setting up a classification of the existing models.

For our purposes here it is most convenient to classify the existing national economic planning models into two groups according to the method of solution used in the model.* The groups are simulation and optimization models. This method of classification has the virtue of clarifying the relationship between the economic assumptions made and the solution method

---

* We are excluding from this classification the set of econometric models whose focus is on short-range fiscal and monetary and exchange rate policy, namely, Duesenberry, Klein, and Kuh (1965). Also, this chapter contains no discussion of models with multiple regions. For two examples of multiregion models, see Lefeber (1958) and MacEwan (1968).

employed. It has the shortcoming that in some cases the models may be shifted from one group to another with relatively minor modifications.

The *simulation models* are mostly of the input-output variety in that they are built around the use of linear technology in the form of the Leontief input-output matrix.* The level of final demand† for goods and services which is used in the model is projected exogenously (i.e., outside of or independently from the model), and the model is used to compute production and investment levels for each sector which will be consistent with the levels of final demand.

In the *optimization models* final demand is not set exogenously but rather a measure of consumption similar to final demand and/or a measure of production is maximized subject to the constraints which represent the production and use of output in the economy. Within the set of optimization models, we discuss four types:

1. Terminal year.
2. Projection.
3. Dynamic linear.
4. Dynamic nonlinear models.

Models within the first three groups have commonly employed linear programming techniques, while models in the last group have used nonlinear programming or control theory methods.

Terminal year models are single period models that describe the structure of the economy in detail for the terminal year of the planning period (usually a year which is 5 or 10 years from the present). The objective in these models is to maximize the change in consumption between the current and target years or the level of consumption in the terminal year. These one-period models are usually much more highly disaggregated than the dynamic models and may include variables for production levels in from 30 to 150 sectors. The dynamic models, on the other hand, commonly include from two to ten sectors and from 5 to 30 time periods.

Projection models are the simplest of the dynamic models, usually containing only two sectors but having 20 to 30 time periods. This class of models is also commonly called two-gap models, since they focus on the gaps between (a) savings and investment and (b) exports and imports.

Dynamic linear models are disaggregated to about ten sectors but include

---

* See Leontief (1951).

† The demand for goods and services may be divided into "final" and "intermediate" demand. Final demand is most easily thought of as the demand of consumers for goods and services, for example, automobiles. Intermediate demand is the demand for raw and processed materials which is generated by the final demand, for example, steel for the production of automobiles.

fewer time periods than the projection models. As with the target year and projection models to be discussed in this chapter, the dynamic linear models have linear (linearized) welfare and production relationships and thus are solved with linear programming techniques.

The *nonlinear dynamic models* are commonly disaggregated to two to four sectors and have ten to 30 time periods. Also, they permit specification of the criteria functions and production functions in nonlinear form.

SIMULATION MODELS*

The input-output simulation model described here is basic to most economy-wide planning models. Here we see the structure in the form of an inter-industry simulation model; later we see the same structure in the context of linear and nonlinear optimizing models.

The analysts using this type of model frequently pose the following types of questions to be studied in the exercise. Given present levels of production and exogenous projections of private consumption, government consumption, exports, and other uses of output, how much should be produced in each sector in each year of the plan, and how much should be invested to increase the capital stock in each sector in each year? This type of model has been used in South Korea† with some success. The simulation was run with a variety of exogenous projections of final demand with close attention paid to the sectoral investment levels over time implied by different plans. These sectoral investment levels were then compared to planned investment, and efforts were made to shift the sectoral composition of investment. One result of the analysis was to discover that investment was too low in a number of light industries such as food processing, finished textiles, leather products, and printing and publishing.‡

Planning of this sort is sometimes referred to as consistency planning, since output and investment levels which are consistent with exogenously estimated final demand are computed. We continue to use the term simulation models rather than consistency models, since we want to emphasize the fact that simulation and optimization models are very closely related. We do so by showing later how the model described here is converted to an optimization model.§

* I am grateful to Allan Samansky for his comments on this section.
† The development here draws on the work of Adelman, Cole, Norton, and Jung (1968) as applied to the Korean economy. It might alternatively have been developed from the study of Bergsman and Manne (1966). For a different approach to simulation models see Holland and Gillespie (1963).
‡ Cole (1966), p. 18.
§ A note on notation: lowercase italic letters are used for vectors, uppercase italic letters for matrices, and lowercase Greek letters are used for scalar quantities.

The basic input-output model for a closed economy (in which exports and imports are not considered) may be written:

$$q_t = Aq_t + h_t + d_t \qquad (1)$$

where q_t = a vector of production levels at time t

A = the Leontieff matrix for intermediate inputs
h_t = vector of inputs for investment
d_t = a vector of final demands

This expression implies that all of the output q_t at any point in time is used up as intermediate inputs, inputs to investment, or as final demand.

For a closed economy model the final demand vector might be the sum of consumer and government requirements for domestic products, and the inputs to inventory accumulation, namely,

$$d_t = c_t + g_t + s_t \qquad (2)$$

For an open economy model, we add imports to the total goods available to be used and exports to the total uses of these goods. Adding these components and using (2) in (1), we obtain:

$$q_t + m_t = Aq_t + h_t + c_t + g_t + s_t + e_t \qquad (3)$$

where q_t = output
m_t = imports*
h_t = investment
c_t = private consumption
g_t = government consumption
s_t = inventory investment
e_t = exports

This is the distribution relationship that is common to almost all economy-wide input-output models. It implies that the total output produced and imported must equal the uses of that output for intermediate goods, investment, private consumption, government consumption, inventory investment, and exports.

The *capital accumulation relationships* are also central to this class of models. They are of the form:

$$k_{t+1} = k_t + z_t - Dk_t \qquad (4)$$

---

* These are untied imports. Later in the chapter we discuss the role of imports which are tied to production levels as intermediate inputs and to investment levels. Consistent with this treatment of imports the A matrix (and later the B matrix) does not include imported inputs.

where k_t = vector of sectoral capital stocks
   z_t = new capital stock created in period t through investment
   D = diagonal matrix whose elements represent the percentage depreci-
      ation of the capital stock in each sector during each time period
      covered by the model.

Thus (4) states that next period's capital stock in each sector equals this period's capital stock plus new investment less depreciation.

Production functions are frequently not stated explicitly in such models though a fixed coefficient production function of the form:

$$q_t = Gk_t \tag{5}$$

is usually implied. Here G is a diagonal matrix of output-capital ratios. Note that the use of (5) implies the assumption of fully utilized capital. This assumption can be modified in a rather arbitrary way by premultiplying the left-hand side of (5) by a diagonal matrix of capacity utilization coefficients. The relationship also embodies the assumptions of (a) constant returns to scale, (6) absence of technical change, and (c) no substitution between inputs.

Substituting (5) into (4), we obtain

$$G^{-1}q_{t+1} = G^{-1}q_t + z_t - DG^{-1}q_t \tag{6}$$

and premultiplying by G yields

$$q_{t+1} = q_t + Gz_t - Dq_t \tag{7}$$

(Note that since D and G are diagonal matrices of the same dimension, $GDG^{-1} = D$.)

Since z_t is a vector of additions to capital and G is a diagonal matrix, we can define:

$$u_t = Gz_t \tag{8}$$

as the increase in capacity (defined in output terms) which results from the increase z_t in the capital stocks. Using (8) in (7) and collecting terms, we obtain

$$q_{t+1} = (I - D)q_t + u_t \tag{9}$$

and then solving for u_t yields

$$u_t = q_{t+1} - (I - D)q_t \tag{10}$$

This expression states that the increase in capacity in each time period must equal the increase in output without loss of capacity due to depreciation plus that loss.

Now let us look back for a minute over the ground we have covered. We have discussed the distribution relationship:

$$q_t + m_t = Aq_t + h_t + c_t + g_t + s_t + e_t \tag{3}$$

the capital accumulation relationship:

$$k_{t+1} = k_t + z_t - Dk_t \tag{4}$$

the production function:

$$q_t = Gk_t \tag{5}$$

and what might be called a *capacity accumulation relationship*:

$$q_{t+1} = q_t + Gz_t - Dq_t \tag{7}$$

with

$$u_t = Gz_t \tag{8}$$

defined as the increase in capacity due to new investment.

Now we need to tie together the capacity accumulation relationships with the input to investment, h_t, that is, we need to establish the relationship between inputs to investment and increases in capacity. This is usually done with a matrix which is commonly referred to as "the B matrix" and with a relationship of the form:

$$h_t = Bz_t \tag{11}$$

where the elements of $B = (b_{ij})$ represent the amount of inputs from the ith sector required per unit of capital stock creation in the jth sector.* Relatively few sectors contribute to capital stock creation (i.e., usually only the construction, heavy and light machinery, electrical equipment, and similar sectors). Thus all but a few of the rows of B consist entirely of zeroes, causing B to be singular and therefore noninvertible. This fact causes some difficulty in solving the model in the Appendix.

To demonstrate a simple method for performing the calculations in this class of models, it is necessary to reorder the rows of the B matrix so that the rows with nonzero elements are the first n rows of the matrix. The matrix may then be partitioned as

$$B = \begin{bmatrix} B_{11} & \vdots & B_{12} \\ \cdots & & \cdots \\ B_{21} & \vdots & B_{22} \end{bmatrix} = \begin{bmatrix} B_{11} & \vdots & B_{12} \\ \cdots & & \cdots \\ 0 & \vdots & 0 \end{bmatrix} \tag{12}$$

---

* The elements of the B matrix exclude imported inputs for investment. See the footnote following (3).

All other vectors and matrices in the model are then reordered and partitioned to conform to this partitioning. Thus q_t^1 represents the first n_1 elements of q_t and q_t^2 represents the last $n - n_1$ elements.

With this partitioning it is possible to derive the following sets of difference equations for q_t^1 and q_t^2:

$$q_{t+1}^1 = Wq_t^1 + R_1 r_{t+1}^2 + R_2 r_t^2 + R_3 r_t^1 \qquad \text{for} \quad t = 1, \ldots, \tau - 1 \quad (13)$$

$$q_{t+1}^2 = Uq_t^1 + Vr_t^2 \qquad \text{for} \quad t = 1, \ldots, \tau - 1 \tag{14}$$

$$r_a = S_1 + C_1 + q_1 + C_t - m_t \tag{14a}$$

where $W = Z^{-1}Q_1$
$\qquad R_1 = -Z^{-1}Q_2$
$\qquad R_2 = -Z^{-1}Q_3$
$\qquad R_3 = -Z^{-1}Q_4$
$\qquad U = [I - A_{22}]^{-1}A_{21}$
$\qquad V = [I - A_{22}]^{-1}$

with $Z = B_{11}G_{11}{}^{-1} + B_{12}G_{22}{}^{-1}[I - A_{22}]^{-1}A_{21}$
$\qquad Q_1 = I - A_{11} + [B_{12}G_{22}{}^{-1}(I - D_{22}) - A_{12}][I - A_{22}]^{-1}A_{21}$
$\qquad\qquad + B_{11}G_{11}{}^{-1}[I - D_{11}]$
$\qquad Q_2 = B_{12}G_{22}{}^{-1}[I - A_{22}]^{-1}A_{21}$
$\qquad Q_3 = -[A_{12} + B_{12}G_{22}{}^{-1}(I - D_{22})][I - A_{22}]^{-1}$
$\qquad Q_4 = I$

Since the final demand vector r_t is computed exogenously to the model, the components of this vector are given for all time periods. Also, the initial level of output for all sectors, that is, q_1, is assumed known. Using this information, the difference equation, (13), can be integrated forward to obtain the path of q_t^1. This information is then used in (14) to compute the path of q_t^2. Thus the difference equations, (13) and (14), enable us to compute output levels for all time periods which are consistent with the exogenously given levels of final demand.

Once the production levels for all time periods have been computed from (13) and (14), then the investment levels may be computed by using the following relationship which is obtained from (7):

$$z_t = G^{-1}[q_{t+1} - (I - D)q_t] \tag{15}$$

rather handily on a small computer and might even be done by hand calculations. The major part of the work will be in computing the matrices W, R_1, R_2, R_3, U, and V, but once those are obtained, the rest of the calculations can be done quickly.

Because of the relative simplicity of the calculations, this method of consistency planning can be accomplished at rather detailed levels of disaggregation without large computer systems. However, let us review the price (in terms of restrictive assumptions) that must be paid for this simplicity in calculation.

Most confining is the assumption that all components of net final demand can be projected apart from the results of the "consistent" output and investment levels. Since projections of the components of net final demand, that is, exports, imports, and inventory investment, are usually made on the basis of expected output and investment paths, it is useful in most cases to iterate between the projections and the consistency calculations.

Second, the use of consistency or simulation methods instead of optimization methods precludes the operation in the model of allocation measures that are important to the efficient operation of any economic system. The amounts produced, invested, imported, and exported are in no sense optimal but rather only consistent with assumed (or in some cases empirically estimated) relationships. Labor and capital are not allocated to those sectors where they will yield the greatest return in terms of some kind of a performance measure but rather only in a way that is consistent with the posited relationships.

In a later section of this chapter, a nonlinear optimizing model which takes consistent paths as nominal or starting paths and attempts to find other consistent paths which are more efficient is described. The performance measure used in that optimizing model is a function of consumption levels. Though the original (or nominal) consistent paths were chosen in what seemed to be a reasonable manner, the optimizing procedure usually resulted in significant improvements in performance measures.

While such optimizing procedures are still in their infancy in terms of their use in economic planning problems, there are already some indications that consistency planning (which is much less expensive to do) may yield results that are significantly inferior to those which can be obtained with optimizing methods.

OPTIMIZING MODELS

The same basic economic structure is used in the optimizing models as in the simulation models. The principal differences between the two methods is that a criterion function is added to the simulation models to convert them to optimizing models and that final demand is not treated as exogenous but rather is used as an argument in the criterion function.

As indicated earlier, terminal-year models are discussed first. Then projection, dynamic linear, and dynamic nonlinear models are described and analyzed.

Terminal Year Models

The first type of optimizing model we discuss is the terminal-year model. The name is derived from the fact that the objective specified in the model is to maximize some measure of production or consumption in the terminal year of the plan.

The questions addressed with this class of models are similar to those addressed with the simulation models, that is, the focus is on output and investment levels and on exports and imports. The major difference from the simulation models is precisely in the difference between optimization and simulation. With simulation, the objective is to find feasible or consistent paths, while here it is to find the best set of sectoral allocations. "Best" is defined by that feasible set of allocations which maximizes a criterion function of some kind defined over production or consumption levels.

The terminal-year models are not as complete in their dynamics as the input-output simulation models. The solution is dependent upon base-year output levels and capital stocks, but the time paths of variables are not made explicit; rather, production and investment levels are explicitly computed only for the terminal year. Thus the closest optimization model analog to the input-output simulation models is not the target-year model but rather the dynamic models that are discussed in the next section.*

The terminal-year models are usually specified in the form of linear programming models. From this fact we know immediately that the performance function will be linear in consumption and the production function will be linear in capital stocks. This in turn implies that assumptions of constant marginal utility of consumption and constant marginal product of capital in production have been made. Though this situation generally holds true, the effects of the linearity can be and frequently are modified somewhat through the use of piecewise linear approximations in the objective function or the constraints. This is done more commonly for the objective function than for the constraints.†

The *criterion function* for the terminal-year model can be written:‡

$$\max \xi = \omega = 1'c \tag{19}$$

* The closest simulation model analog to the terminal-year targets is that of Bergsman and Manne (1966).
† The conditions under which this is possible and the methods of specification employed are discussed in Hadley (1964), Chap. 4. Examples of applications are in Carter (1967), Barr and Manne (1967), and Adelman and Sparrow (1966).
‡ The development in this section draws on many important aspects of the work of Bruno (1966). Alternatively, it might have been developed from the models of Manne (1966) or Weisskopf (1966).

where ξ = the criterion index
ω = total consumption
c = consumption vector

Note that the criterion function is linear in the consumption of goods for each sector. Also, we drop the time subscripts for this model, since all variables represent levels in the target year.

The *distribution relationship* of this model is almost the same as that for the simulation model, namely:

$$q + m \geq Aq + h + c + g + s + e \qquad (20)$$

where q = output levels
m = untied imports—exogenously specified*
A = Leontief matrix
h = investment inputs
c = private consumption
g = government consumption—exogenously specified
s = inventory investment
e = exports

Note that (20) is an inequality relationship while the distribution relationships, (3), of the input-output model are equalities. Here a property of linear programming models is used to permit less restrictive assumptions in an economic model. In the simulation model the equality relationship imposed full utilization of all production. Here (20) requires only that production plus imports must *equal* or *exceed* the uses of commodities as intermediate inputs, investment inputs, consumption, government, inventory investment, and exports.

The reader will recall that the basic structure of a linear programming model is

$$\max \xi = c'x \qquad (21)$$

subject to

$$Ax \geq b \qquad (22)$$

The right-hand side, b, is fixed exogenously. To write the economic planning model in the same form, it would be necessary to place all the exogenous elements on the right-hand side of the inequality and the endogenous elements on the left-hand side. Thus if exports, imports, inventory investment,

---

* The distribution relationship includes only untied imports because the imports which are tied to production and investment are excluded from the A and B matrices, respectively, and therefore do not enter the distribution relationships on either the supply or demand side.

and government consumption were exogenously estimated, the relationship (20) would be written in the form:

$$(I - A)q + h + c \geq g + s + e - m \tag{23}$$

and in the x vector of (22) could be written in partitioned form as

$$x = \begin{bmatrix} q \\ h \\ c \end{bmatrix} \tag{24}$$

and the right-hand side b as the sum of other vectors, that is,

$$b = g + s + e - m \tag{25}$$

In general, we follow the rule of specifying which variables are exogenous and which are endogenous rather than letting the side of the inequality be determinant, that is, we do not reshuffle relationships in the form (20) into the form (23), since doing so would add to the length of the exposition without increasing its clarity proportionately.

The *production relationships* are not always written out explicitly in this class of models. When they are, they are in the form:

$$q = Gk \tag{26}$$

where G = a diagonal matrix of output-capital ratios
k = capital stocks*

As in the simulation models, output is assumed to be a linear function of the capital stocks. No substitution of capital for labor is permitted in the production of goods and services. If one could know what the relative prices of capital and labor would be in the terminal year and could know the true production functions for that year, this assumption would be accurate. However, since the model solution yields information on the shadow prices of production factors, these prices cannot be fully known in advance. Thus the degree of inaccuracy of the assumption may be decreased by employing an iterative procedure of solving the model, obtaining the shadow prices, using them to determine a new output-capital matrix, and solving the model again. Such a procedure might converge.

Exogenous technical change can be incorporated into this class of models by choosing a G matrix for the terminal year based on expectation about the rate and direction of technical change.

---

* Bruno uses a slightly different form of production function. Here the capital stocks are capital stocks by *sector of use*; that is, the total amount of buildings, machines, and vehicles that make up the capital stock of each sector. In Bruno's model, the capital stocks are disaggregated by *sector of origin*, that is, by the sector from which that part of the capital stock came, namely construction, machinery, vehicles, and such.

The *investment relationships* ensure that enough resources are put into investment to permit the continued growth of capacity at exogenously specified levels, namely:

$$h \geq BRG^{-1}q \qquad (27)$$

where B = a matrix whose elements b_{ij} represent the amount of inputs from the ith sector required per unit of capital stock creation in the jth sector

R = a diagonal matrix whose elements represent the required growth rate of the capital stock in each sector.

Since $G^{-1}q$ is the vector of capital stocks, the vector $RG^{-1}q$ is the gross amount by which the capital stock in each sector is required to grow. The B matrix then maps this capital stock increase into requirements for inputs from the various sectors.

This inequality assumes that capacity is created in a linear way from inputs, that is, the marginal product of investment inputs in creating new capacity is constant. This assumption is of questionable validity if the range of the function is large. Therefore, it is important to check the solution to be certain that the posited relationships are likely to hold in the neighborhood of the solution. In some linear programming models this is ensured by placing upper and lower bounds on the capital stocks (or in this case on production levels, since the capital stocks may not explicitly enter the problem). However, this is a somewhat arbitrary way of including the economic phenomena of the increasing marginal resource costs which are associated with changes in capital stocks within any single time period. The most direct way of modeling this phenomena would be to include a nonlinear (and diminishing returns) mapping from inputs to capacity increases. A less direct way would be to include a nonlinear absorptive capacity function which places upper bounds on the rate of increase of the capital stock in each sector. This approach is used in the dynamic nonlinear models discussed later in this chapter. For the moment, though, we are discussing linear models and must be content with using less direct means of modeling the phenomena.

Inventory investment is required to be in a fixed relationship to output, namely:

$$s = Hq \qquad (28)$$

where H = a diagonal matrix whose elements are inventory investment-output level ratios.

The sectoral components of *consumption* are related to total consumption in a manner which is labeled "the fixed market basket," that is:

$$\omega\bar{c} = c \qquad (28a)$$

where $\bar{c}$ = an exogenously fixed vector whose elements represent the percentage of total consumption which originates in each sector, thus $\sum_i \bar{c}_i = 1$. With this formulation the proportion of all commodities in consumption remains the same no matter what the income level, that is, the income elasticity of demand is one for all commodities. Therefore, when this formulation is employed, it is important to ascertain that the income level on which the calculation of the elements of $\bar{c}$ were based is near the income level implied in the solution of the model. If sensitivity testing is done which significantly alters the income level from one run to the next, it is important in each case to use an appropriate $\bar{c}$ vector.*

Imports are divided into three parts: imports tied to domestic production, imports tied to capital formation, and untied imports, namely:

$$\mu = 1'(Mq + Nh + m) \tag{29}$$

where μ = total imports

M = a diagonal matrix whose elements are import-production ratios for each sector

N = a diagonal matrix whose elements are import-investment input ratios for each sector

m = untied imports—exogenously specified

Upper and lower bounds are placed on *exports* for each sector, that is:

$$e \le e_u \tag{30}$$

$$e \ge e_l \tag{31}$$

where e_u = a vector of upper bounds on export levels

e_l = a vector of lower bounds on export levels

In most economy-wide planning models some components of imports and exports are set exogenously and others are determined endogenously. The reason for this is that many of the determinants of exports and imports are outside of the national economy. The usual procedure is to tie some imports to domestic production and investment levels to take account of the fact that certain raw materials and types of machinery and equipment will not be produced domestically within the time period covered by the plan. Other imports are then left free or untied and act something like slack variables in the model. Since export levels are strongly affected by economic conditions outside of the domestic economy, by the climate and raw material base of the country, and by deliberate government decision to develop certain lines

* An alternative approach is to explicitly write income elasticities into the constraints. This has been done by Bruno (1966). This procedure is discussed in connection with dynamic models where its use is more important than for target year models.

of exports, the determination of exports is frequently assumed to be entirely outside of the model. However, as in this model, sectoral levels of exports may vary within certain bounds, or they may be specified with decreasing marginal revenues through piecewise linear segments, as is suggested by Bruno (1966).

With exports and imports calculated as above, the *foreign exchange constraint* may be written:

$$\rho\mu - p'e \le \phi \tag{32}$$

where ρ = hard currency price of imports
p = vector of hard currency price coefficients for exports
ϕ = foreign capital inflow

Note here that this constraint is in terms of hard currency while the units of the rest of the model are domestic currency.

An upper bound on the marginal propensity to save may be written into the model in the form:

$$\frac{(\eta - \omega - \gamma) - (\eta_0 - \omega_0 - \gamma_0)}{\eta - \eta_0} \le \sigma \tag{33}$$

where η = total gross national product
$\omega = 1'c$ = total consumption
$\gamma = 1'g$ = total government consumption of domestically produced goods
$\eta_0, \omega_0, \gamma_0$ = base year levels of the corresponding variables above
σ = upper bound on marginal propensity to save
and

$$\eta = 1'(c + h + e + g) - \mu \tag{34}$$

The constraint (33) requires that the increase in total domestic savings from base period savings of $\eta_0 - \omega_0 - \gamma_0$ to terminal year savings of $\eta - \omega - \gamma$ divided by the increase in gross national product be less than a certain fixed percentage. This constraint is a behavioral relationship and assumes that individuals, businesses, and government will not be willing to save more than a certain proportion of their income or profits. This type of behavioral relationship plays an important role in linear economy-wide planning models. It models the behavior of individuals which might be represented in a nonlinear model with a welfare or utility function with declining marginal utility. In the linear models, marginal utility is assumed to be constant unless piecewise linear segments are used in the criterion function. In the nonlinear models, declining marginal utility of consumption within any one time period assures that the consumer will want to spread his consumption out over many periods and therefore that he will want to save in some period and dissave in others.

Finally, a labor force constraint may be included in the form:

$$Lq \leq l \qquad (35)$$

where L = matrix of labor input-output coefficients
l = a vector of labor force availability by different classes of labor.

The labor force constraint is frequently not included in national economy models, particularly when the models are constructed for countries in which there is assumed to be excess labor. However, the absence of the labor force constraints can lead to erroneous results. Where possible, it would be useful to include not only a labor force constraint but also educational or training activities which transform laborers in one education class into another class. Even this kind of specification may run afoul of the fact that laborers in different educational classes may be substituted for one another. Some recent empirical work has lent support to the hypothesis that different types of labor are highly substitutability for one another, namely, Bowles (1969). If this is true, then the production relationships should be modeled with non-linear production functions that permit substitution of inputs. However, this requires linearization or the use of nonlinear programming methods.

In summary, the model is

$$\max \omega = 1'c \qquad (19)$$

subject to *distribution relationships:*

$$q + m \geq Aq + h + s + \omega c + g + e \qquad (20)$$

and *production relationships* (may not be included):

$$q = Gk \qquad (26)$$

investment relationships:

$$h \geq BRG^{-1}q \qquad (27)$$

$$s = Hq \qquad (28)$$

import and export relationships:

$$\mu = 1'(Mq + Nh + m) \qquad (29)$$

$$e \leq e_{u'} \qquad (30)$$

$$e \geq e_{l'} \qquad (31)$$

foreign exchange constraint:

$$\rho\mu - p'e \leq \phi \qquad (32)$$

savings constraint:

$$\frac{\eta - \omega - \gamma - (\eta_0 - \omega_0 - \gamma_0)}{\eta - \eta_0} \leq \sigma \tag{33}$$

$$\eta = 1'(c + h + e + g) - \mu \tag{34}$$

and *labor constraint:*

$$Lq \leq l \tag{35}$$

To put the model in the usual linear programming format, we substitute (29) into (34) and the resulting expression into (33), and use the definitions of ω and γ to obtain

$$(1 - \sigma)1'\left[\left(\frac{\sigma}{\sigma - 1}\right)c + (I - N)h + e - Mq\right]$$

$$\leq (1 - \sigma)\eta_0 - \omega_0 - \gamma_0 + \sigma1'g + (1 - \sigma)1'm \tag{35a}$$

Also we substitute (29) into (32), and (28) into (20). The model in linear programming format with all exogenous variables on the right-hand side of the inequalities may be written:

$$\max \omega = 1'c \tag{19}$$

Equation	Number of constraints	Subject to
$(I - A - H)q - h - \omega c - e \geq q - m$	n	(36)
$h - BRG^{-1}q \geq 0$	n	(27)
$e \leq e_u$	n	(30)
$e \geq e_l$	n	(31)
$\rho1'Mq + \rho1'Nh - p'e \leq \phi - \rho1'm$	1	(37)
$(1 - \sigma)1'\left[\left(\dfrac{\sigma}{1 - \sigma}\right)c + (I - N)h + e - Mq\right]$ $\leq (1 - \sigma)\eta_0 - \omega_0 - \gamma_0 + \sigma1'g + (1 - \sigma)1'm$	1	(35a)
$Lq \leq l$	r	(35)

Some insight into the operation of the model may be gained by examining the model in this linear programming format. Assume for the moment that the upper and lower bounds on exports, (30) and (31), are dropped and that the distribution relationships (36) and investment relationships (27) are written as equalities. Use (27) to substitute out the investment inputs, h, and (36) to substitute out consumption levels, c. Then the model may be written to maximize a linear function of production and export levels subject to three sets of constraints. These constraints are the foreign exchange constraint (37), the savings constraint (35a), and the labor force constraint (35). Constraints of this type play an important role in almost all national economies. The savings constraint is a behavioral constraint that government may attempt to affect principally through taxation decisions, but they do so only at some risk of being removed from office. The foreign exchange constraint may be eased by borrowing, by permitting foreign investment to come into the country, and by receipt of foreign aid. All of these methods are pursued in varying degrees by most less developed and many rather highly developed economies. Third, the labor force constraint plays a major role in constraining the permissible levels of economic activity. Finally, it is worthwhile to note that the availability of capital does not explicitly constrain the solution because capital is itself a produced good.

From a computational point of view the model has $4n + r + 2$ constraints where n is the number of sectors. Assuming a 30-sector level of disaggregation, the model becomes a linear programming problem with about 120 constraints. Since models like this are frequently solved on computers of the size of the IBM 7094 in between 5 and 10 minutes, the cost of solution is not too high. Thus it is possible on a model of this size to do rather extensive sensitivity testing and thereby to learn how the model functions. In general, model builders have learned that it is more fruitful to employ a level of disaggregation that permits repeated solution of the model. The temptation is usually to build as large a model as can possibly be solved to incorporate all the desired detail. Experience has taught that this is usually a nonoptimal strategy, since the model is so costly to solve that sensitivity analysis cannot be carried out. This usually results in the model being left with a number of specification errors that could have been found with sensitivity testing.

Though there are many different types of problems that may be analyzed with models of this class, the following are some of the more obvious:

1. Defining total consumption in the target year as ω and foreign capital inflow in that year as ϕ, a function $\omega(\phi)$ can be traced out by solving the model for various values of ϕ in the constraint (37). This kind of calculation provides the analyst with a rough function from which he can determine the marginal value (in terms of total consumption) of foreign capital inflow. Also, such an analysis could give him an idea of how low consumption might have to go if foreign capital inflow decreased or was halted altogether.

As we see in some of the dynamic models discussed later, the time path of foreign capital inflow is very important; thus this kind of static analysis may provide misleading results in situations where the amount of foreign capital inflow can be changed sharply from year to year, and/or when the economy is faced with some large indivisible investments that require high level of imports during the years of their construction.

2. A rough measure of the value of transforming (educating) labor of one class into labor of another class can be obtained by solving the model for various values of the components of l in constraint (35). If, in the original solution, the shadow price on one class of labor is much higher than on other classes, it is likely that such a transformation would result in increased value of total consumption in the target year.

Projection Models

This class of models is also called "two-gap" models from the notion that either the foreign exchange availability-usage gap and/or the savings-investment gap can inhibit economic growth at any point in time.* The original two-gap model developed by Chenery and Strout (1966) was in the form of a simulation model. The development here parallels that of a linear programming variant of the two-gap model as developed by Chenery and MacEwan (1966). This model is used here to introduce a range of issues that arises with dynamic optimization models, namely, treatment of consumption and investment and of terminal conditions.

These models are highly disaggregated in the time dimension but at very low levels of disaggregation in the number of sectors treated. The models cover periods of 20 to 30 years with annual time periods but employ only one or two sectors. The model discussed here has two aggregated sectors, the first of which contains everything except a few "trade improvement" sectors. These trade improvement sectors are the sectors of the economy which are most subject to import substitution measures.

The model differs from those discussed earlier in that production is included in value-added terms instead of in terms of activity levels. Thus all intermediate inputs are netted out and never appear explicitly in the model. These changes make the model much closer to econometric models as used for short-run policy.

The performance index is a discounted sum of total consumption in each period, that is:

$$\max \xi = \sum_{t=1}^{\tau} \frac{1}{(1 + \rho)^t} \omega_t + \zeta \eta^\tau \qquad (38)$$

* These two-gaps correspond to two of the three effective constraints discussed for the simplified version of the terminal year model. Labor constraints are not included in the two-gap models so the third type of constraint is not present.

where ω_t = total consumption in period t
   ρ = social discount rate
   ζ = a terminal condition constant
   η_τ = gross national product in the terminal year τ

Since the discount factor is a constant, we see that consumption enters linearly into the performance function, that is, the marginal value of consumption in each time period is constant. The terminal condition constant is discussed later. Here it is sufficient to remark that this term is used in an attempt to include in the model the effects of events which occur after the period covered by the model.

The distribution relationship for this class of models is in the form of a GNP identity, that is:

$$\eta_t = \omega_t + \psi_t + \gamma_t - (\mu_t - \eta_t{}^2) \tag{39}$$

where η_t = gross national product
   ω_t = total consumption
   ψ_t = investment
   γ_t = exports
   μ_t = imports
   $\eta_t{}^2$ = gross national product originating in the "trade improvement" sector

The relationship (39) is the familiar national income identity except for the $\eta_t{}^2$ term. This term illustrates the way that the trade improvement sector is used in this type of model. It plays the role of reducing imports through the process of import substitution.*

The *production relationships* are linear on the margin, as is dictated by the use of a linear programming model, that is:

$$\eta_t{}^1 = \eta_0{}^1 + \frac{1}{\kappa_1} \sum_{\varepsilon=1}^{t-1} \psi_\varepsilon{}^1 \tag{40}$$

$$\eta_t{}^2 = \eta_0{}^2 + \frac{1}{\kappa_2} \sum_{\varepsilon=1}^{t-1} \psi_\varepsilon{}^2 \tag{41}$$

$$\eta_t = \eta_t{}^1 + \eta_t{}^2 \tag{42}$$

* Import substitution investment was not considered explicitly in the terminal year model. This type of investment is used to build plants that produce imported goods and thereby to reduce the amount of imports required to sustain a certain level of economic activity.

where η_t^1 = GNP for the main sector

η_t^2 = GNP for the trade improvement sector

η_t = total GNP

κ_i = marginal capital output ratio for the ith sector, $i = 1$ for main sector, and $i = 2$ for trade improvement sector

ψ_ε^i = investment in the ith sector in the εth period

η_0^i = GNP in the ith sector in the base year

Aside from the assumption of constant marginal products, these production functions assume away depreciation; that is, it is implicitly assumed that the capital stock in each sector in each time period is equal to the capital that was necessary to produce the initial GNP in the base year plus all the investment that has occurred since the base year. Note also that assumption of full utilization of capacity is implicit as is the assumption that output is produced by machines (capital) only without the benefit of any assistance from labor. The latter assumption is based on the notion that for many economies labor is available in excess supply. Finally, it is assumed that there is no technical change in the production relationships. However, exogenous technical change could be incorporated by making the κ_i coefficients a function of time.

The investment relationships are as follows:

$$\psi_t = \psi_t^1 + \psi_t^2 \tag{43}$$

$$\psi_t \le (1 + \beta)\psi_{t-1} \tag{44}$$

$$\psi_t \ge \psi_{t-1} \tag{45}$$

where ψ_t = total investment

ψ_t^i = investment in the ith sector

β = upper limit on the rate of growth of investment in percentage terms

Relationships such as (44) and (45) appear repeatedly in optimizing economy-wide models. The first of these is called an absorptive capacity constraint and requires that investment in any year cannot increase more than a certain percentage over investment in the previous year. It is justified on the grounds that most economies do not have enough administrative people and highly trained manpower to efficiently absorb large increases in investment within short periods of time. The relationship (45) requires that investment be monotonically increasing. It can be justified on the ground that society might prefer to have everything nicely increasing (with no dips) even when such a policy results in a suboptimal investment program.

Aside from the economic or other arguments as to why relationships of the type (44) and (45) should be included, they are also included because their exclusion often yields "strange" results. These results are usually in the form of very high investment levels in the early or late years of the plan period. In a linear model (and to a lesser extent in some nonlinear models) investment and consumption demonstrate these bang-bang effects, that is, all investment bangs to the earlier (or late years) and then with some changes in parameters bangs to the late years (or early years) in the period covered by the model.

These results are caused by the fact that in a linear model, all marginal rates are constant. Since all output is used in each time period for consumption, investment, or exports, one can talk about the marginal value—in terms of the units of the performance index—of the use of output in each of these ways. The constancy of these marginal values in any time period implies that if the marginal value of the use of output for investment purposes is greater than in its marginal value in consumption or exports, all output in that period will be used for investment purposes. The discount rate on consumption results in different marginal values for consumption from one time period to the next. If the marginal value for consumption exceeds that for investment in the first few time periods, all output will go into consumption; then, due to the discount factor, the marginal value of consumption will suddenly go just below the marginal value of investment, and all output will suddenly bang into investment.

Along with constraints such as (44) and (45), there may be monotonicity constraints on consumption of the form:

$$\omega_t \geq (1 + \pi)\omega_{t-1} \tag{46}$$

where π = lower bound on rate of growth of consumption. Also constraints on the marginal savings rate of the form (33) as discussed in the target year model may be included. The role of all these constraints can be justified in institutional terms, but they can also be viewed as simply a mathematical device which is used to prevent "unrealistic" results in the model.

Of course, as was discussed earlier, a more satisfactory solution to the bang-bang problem is to introduce nonlinearities into the model in the performance function and in the constraints. Then the marginal value of the use of output for consumption in any particular period will not be constant but will be declining if the performance function exhibits declining marginal value to consumption. Similarly, the use of nonlinear production functions will result in nonconstant marginal value attributed to the output used in investment.

All of this is familiar to the beginning student of economics who is drilled on the notion that equilibrium is attained at a point at which the marginal value of the use of inputs in all production processes is the same. Mathematically this may be described as obtaining solutions at interior points as opposed to obtaining solutions on a boundary. In linear models all solutions are on the boundaries while in nonlinear models the solutions may be on boundaries. Smoothly working economic systems where some resources can be transformed into others by various production processes and in which goods can be substituted for one another in production and consumption can be thought of as systems with interior solutions. Systems in which there are rigidities, lack of substitution, and absolute limits on various resources are analogous to mathematical problems with boundary or corner solutions.

Imports in this class of models are tied to changes in GNP and investment over the base year levels, that is:

$$\mu_t = \mu_0 + \nu_1(\eta_t - \eta_0) + \nu_2(\psi_t - \psi_0) \tag{47}$$

where μ_t = imports in year t
μ_0 = base year imports
ν_1 = marginal import rate on GNP
ν_2 = marginal import rate on investment

Exports are projected exogenously as

$$\gamma_t = \gamma_0(1 + \lambda)^t \tag{48}$$

where γ_t = exports in year t
γ_0 = base year exports
λ = rate of growth of exports

The *balance of payments* constraint may be written as a limit on the total amount of foreign borrowing over the period covered by the model, that is

$$\sum_{t=1}^{\tau} \frac{\phi_t}{(1 + \rho)^t} \leq \phi^* \tag{49}$$

where ϕ_t = net foreign capital inflow in period t
ρ = social discount rate
ϕ^* = upper limit on total discounted foreign capital inflow that would be available over the period covered by the model where

$$\phi_t = \mu_t - \eta_t{}^2 - \gamma_t \tag{50}$$

Notice that value added in the trade improvement sector, $\eta_t{}^2$, is subtracted from imports here as in the distribution relation (39) to take account of import substitution effects.

This formulation of the foreign exchange constraint can be written in the alternative form of a *foreign debt accumulation equation*, that is:

$$\delta_{t+1} = \delta_t + \mu_t - \eta_t{}^2 - \gamma_t \tag{51}$$

where δ_t = total foreign debt in period t. Then a term which is linear in δ_t

can be subtracted from the objective function in each period to represent interest payments on foreign debt.

The *savings-investment constraints* are written:

$$\theta_t \leq \theta_0 + \alpha(\eta_t - \eta_0) \tag{52}$$

$$\psi_t = \phi_t + \theta_t \tag{53}$$

where θ_t = domestic savings in period t
θ_0 = base year domestic savings
α = marginal savings rate

The constraint (53) requires that investment must equal foreign capital inflow plus domestic savings.

We delay until later in the paper a full discussion of *terminal conditions*. Here we discuss one formulation of these conditions. Since the model covers a finite and rather short period of time, it is important to include in the model some measure of the effects of the program within the period on the welfare of the society after the period covered by the model. In models where the performance measure is a function of consumption levels, this is particularly important because in the absence of some kinds of terminal conditions, there will always be a tendency to cease investment in the later periods of the model and to use all output for consumption purposes.

The most obvious way to prevent this is to require that certain target levels of capital stocks be attained at the terminal year, thereby forcing the generation covered by the model to leave a certain amount of capital stock to the next generation. Another method is to add a term to the performance function which reflects the postterminal consumption possibilities of the economy. We do this by assuming that consumption—as based on terminal year consumption—will grow at a constant rate in the postterminal years. The discounted value of this infinite consumption stream may be written as

$$\zeta\eta_\tau = (1 - \alpha)\eta_\tau \sum_{\varepsilon=1}^{\infty} \frac{(1 + \chi)^\varepsilon}{(1 + \rho)^{\varepsilon+\tau}} \tag{54}$$

where ζ = the weight assigned to terminal GNP to account for postterminal consumption levels
χ = required postterminal rate of growth of consumption

Since the term $(1 - \alpha)\eta_\tau$ represents terminal year consumption, we can write the consumption level in each postterminal year as

$$(1 + \chi)^\varepsilon(1 - \alpha)\eta_\tau \tag{55}$$

Without carrying out a detailed substitution in the model, one can see that this class of models involves 10 to 15 constraints per time period. Therefore a model with 20 time periods of one year each would include from 200 to 300 constraints and be relatively expensive to compute.*

In summary, the two-gap models provide very detailed temporal disaggregation but sectoral disaggregation of only one or two sectors. They are perhaps best suited for studying long-run growth in which little or no attention to sectoral detail is required, but in which foreign capital inflows, export levels, and domestic savings constraints are expected to play an important role.

For cases in which sectoral disaggregation is important, the linear dynamic multisectional models to be discussed next are more useful.

Dynamic Linear Models

In the terminal year models, we have seen a method of analysis well-suited for detailed sectoral disaggregation in a static framework. In the projection models, we found a method of analysis for two sectors and many time periods. Now we turn to models with intermediate levels of time and sectoral disaggregation. Our development here will parallel that used in the models of Eckaus and Parikh (1968), Chakravarty and Lefeber (1965), and Westphal (1970). All of these models are basically linear models (although Westphal's is unique in that it treats problems of planning under economies of scale and includes some integer variables). In the latter part of this section, we discuss some alternative specifications of various parts of dynamic multisectional models, several of which result in nonlinear formulation of the models.

We assume here that the reader is familiar enough with the general structure of multisectoral models so that detailed exposition is merited only when new concepts are introduced.

The *criterion function* may be written:

$$\max \zeta = \sum_{t=1}^{\tau} \frac{\omega_t}{(1 + \rho)^t} \tag{56}$$

where ρ = social discount rate
ω_t = total consumption in period t

The usual assumption of constant marginal value of consumption in any time period is implied by this specification of the criterion function.

The distribution relationships are

$$q_t + m_t \geq Aq_t + h_t + c_t + g_t + e_t \tag{57}$$

* The Chenery-MacEwan model included roughly 165 constraints and required about 10 minutes on an IBM 7094 with CEIR's LP 90 code, without a good starting basis.

where q = output levels
  m = imports*
  A = Leontief matrix
  h = investment
  c = private consumption
  g = government consumption
  e = exports

Note that we have dropped the inventory investment expressions. Though they are empirically important, their inclusion with a lag structure parallel to the lag structure that is used for investment in fixed assets complicates the present exposition more than was deemed desirable.

The *production relationships* are linear in the capital stocks, that is:

$$q_t \leq Gk_t \tag{58}$$

where G = a diagonal matrix of output capital ratios
  k_t = vector of sectoral capital stocks

Exogenous technical change or exogenous factor substitution can be incorporated into the model via the device of using different G matrices in different time periods.

The *consumption relationships* can be specified without allowance for income elasticities as

$$c_t = \omega_t \bar{c} \tag{59}$$

where $\bar{c}$ = an exogenously fixed vector whose elements represent the percentage of total consumption which originates in each sector, thus $\sum_i \bar{c}_i = 1$. As was mentioned earlier, if this formation is used in a dynamic model, it is important to use different $\bar{c}$ vectors for different time periods in a manner that is roughly consistent with the expenditure levels achieved in each period and with the observed expenditure elasticities of demand for the products of each sector.

An alternative formulation of the consumption relationship which has been used by Bruno (1966) and by Eckaus and Parikh (1968) employs a function of the form:

$$c_{it} = a_{it} + b_i \omega_t \tag{60}$$

where a_i, b_i = parameters which are functions of (a) ε_i, the expenditure elasticity of demand for the ith product, (b) c_{i0}, the consumption level of the ith product in some base period, and (c) ω_0, total consumption expenditure in the base period
  c_{it} = consumption of the ith product in year t

---

* Here imports include both tied and untied imports, and the A and B matrices include imported inputs.

The relationship is derived from the definition for a linear approximation to the income elasticity as defined for some base year, that is:

$$\varepsilon_i = \frac{[(c_{it}/\pi_t) - (c_{i0}/\pi_0)]/(c_{i0}/\pi_0)}{[(\omega_t/\pi_t) - (\omega_0/\pi_0)]/(\omega_0/\pi_0)} \tag{61}$$

where π_0 = base year population

π_t = population in year t (exogenous estimates of π_t are made separately)

The expenditure elasticity of demand is defined locally in (61) as the percentage change in per capita income of the ith product divided by the percentage change in total consumption.

Solving (61) for c_{it}, we obtain

$$c_{it} = \frac{\pi_t}{\pi_0}(1 - \varepsilon_i)c_{i0} + \frac{\varepsilon_i c_{i0}}{\omega_0}\omega_t \tag{62}$$

which is in the form of (60).

Government use of domestic resources is obtained from exogenous projections and is therefore fixed, that is:

$$g_t = \bar{g}_t \tag{63}$$

where an upper bar on a variable means that it is fixed exogenously to the model.

The *investment relationships* separate investment into creation of new fixed capital and restoration of depreciated fixed capital. Another component of investment, inventory accumulation, has been dropped from the exposition here. Investment h_t is then defined:

$$h_t = v_t + r_t \tag{64b}$$

where v_t = deliveries of investment goods for new fixed capital creation

r_t = deliveries of investment goods for restoring depreciated fixed capital

Since the time lag between the input of resources for new capacity creation and the availability of the new capacity for production varies from industry to industry as well as by components of the investment, a lag structure of the following sort is introduced:

$$v_t = B_1 z_{t+1} + B_2 z_{t+2} + B_3 z_{t+3} \tag{64c}$$

with

$$B = B_1 + B_2 + B_3 \tag{64d}$$

where B = a matrix whose elements represent the total input from sector i required per unit of fixed capital creation in sector j

B_i = that part of the input which results in the capacity being available in the ith period after the resource input occurs

z_t = units of new capacity which begin operation in period t

The particular lag structure shown here is for three time periods. When each time period is of a one-year duration, a three- or four-period lag structure is expected to capture almost all of the investment. As the length of each time period is increased to two or three years, the number of lagged steps can be decreased.

The expression (64c) involves the assumption of a linear relationship between capacity increases by sector, and investment input by sector. That is, a fixed factor proportions transformation of inputs into capacity is assumed. If exogenous projections are made for the input coefficients, the elements of the B matrix will be different from time period to time period rather than identical over all time periods. Thus the model, as formulated, rules out endogenous substitution of factor inputs in capacity creation but permits the specification of exogenous substitution through the mechanism of different B_{it} matrices for different time periods.

The other principal component of investment in this model is investment to restore or replace depreciated capital goods. Depreciation may be calculated in the rather detailed manner suggested by Eckaus and Parikh (1968, Chap. 2). Here we assume that the amount of capacity which requires replacement or restoration in each time period is given exogenously, that is:

$$d_t = \bar{d}_t \tag{64e}$$

where d_t = the amount of capacity that requires replacement or restoration in period t. Confusion between accounting concepts of depreciation and actual restoration or replacement requirements should be avoided. In many countries depreciation procedures are heavily involved with corporate taxation and may have a close relationship to the actual wearing-out of plant and equipment. The model should reflect real changes in resource availabilities rather than accounting relationships.

With the definition (64e), we restrict the amount of restoration investment by

$$w_t \leq d_t \tag{64f}$$

where w_t = amount of capacity restored in period t; that is, the amount of capacity restored in any time period must not exceed the capacity that has depreciated. With these relationships we then compute the resource input for capacity restoration as

$$r_t = Q_1 w_{t+1} + Q_2 w_{t+2} + Q_3 w_{t+3} \tag{65}$$

where Q_i = a matrix whose elements represent the input from sector i required per unit of capacity creation in sector j with a time lag of i periods. The matrices Q_i will be closely related to the matrices B_i, though not necessarily identical. In (65) we have a lag structure for capacity restoration which is similar to the lag structure for new capacity creation.

One of the reasons for using a lag structure on replacement investment is the rather great difference between the useful life of the different components of capacity, even within a single industry. For example, buildings usually have considerably longer life than most machinery. Likewise equipment in some industries has much shorter time to obsolescence than in other industries.

With investment determined as above, the *capital accumulation relationships* can be written:

$$k_{t+1} \leq k_t + z_{t+1} + w_{t+1} - d_{t+1} \tag{66}$$

All changes in capacity are assumed to occur at the beginning of each time period; that is, on the first day of any time period new capacity goes into operation, restored capacity goes into operation, and depreciated capacity is shut down. Then there is assumed to be no change in these capacity levels until the beginning of the next time period.

Once the capacity is installed, it is not required by the model to operate at full capacity; that is, output can be less than full capacity because of the inequality in (58), the production function. However, output is assumed to be constant during any single time period. As the length of time periods decreases, this assumption of intraperiod constancy of variables becomes more realistic. However, as the number of time periods in a model is increased, the computational cost rises rapidly.

Imports are the sum of "free" imports and imports tied to production levels, that is:*

$$m_t = Mq_t + s_t \tag{67}$$

where M = matrix of import-production ratios
s_t = "free" imports, that is, imports that are not tied to production or investment

Exports are based on projections made outside of the model and are therefore exogenous, that is:

$$e_t = \bar{e}_t \tag{68}$$

The balance of payments constraint may then be written as

$$1'm_t - 1'e_t \leq \phi_t \tag{69}$$

---

* Note that there are no imports tied to investment levels in this formulation.

where ϕ_t = net foreign capital inflow, that is, the sum of foreign aid, private foreign investment, and changes in reserves.

There is not an explicit *saving rate constraint* in this model. However, there is an implicit constraint of the following sort:

$$\omega_{t+1} \geq (1 + \theta)\omega_t \tag{70}$$

where θ = lower bound on percentage rate of increase of total consumption. This relationship places an upper bound on the savings rate but not a lower bound. Thus it would be possible for investment to go to zero in any time period, but not possible for consumption to go to zero unless consumption had been zero in all previous periods.

The linearity of the model will result in the same bang-bang behavior in this multisectoral model that was discussed in connection with the two-sector projection models. Consumption is constrained as discussed above. The constraints on investment are more subtle and are in the form of terminal conditions.

The model is completed by the specification of the *initial and terminal conditions*. Because there is a three-period lag in the investment process specified in this model, it is necessary to specify not only an initial capital stock but also the amount of new capacity and replacement capacity that is under construction and which will come on line during the first years of the plan period. This should be done by inequality constraints on the new capacity and restored capacity put into operation in the first periods. The amount of capacity coming on line in the first period will be entirely determined by preplan investment; therefore, both z_1 and w_1 are determined exogenously. Since z_2, z_3, w_2, and w_3 are partially determined by investment made during the plan and partially determined by investment made prior to the plan, they should be appropriately constrained. Eckaus and Parikh (1968) suggest the following constraints:

$$k_1 = (I + R_0)G^{-1}q_0 \tag{71}$$

$$z_2 + w_2 \leq R_0(I + R_0)G^{-1}q_0 + d_2 \tag{72}$$

$$z_3 + w_3 \leq R_0(I + R_0)^2 G^{-1}q_0 + d_3 \tag{73}$$

where R_0 = a diagonal matrix of preplan sectoral growth rates. These relationships are derived from the capital accumulation relationships:

$$k_{t+1} \leq k_t + z_{t+1} + w_{t+1} - d_{t+1} \tag{66}$$

Thus

$$z_2 + w_2 \geq k_2 - k_1 + d_2$$

and

$$k_1 \geq (I + R_0)G^{-1}q_0$$
$$k_2 \geq (I + R_0)^2 G^{-1}q_0$$

therefore

$$z_2 + w_2 \geq R_0(I + R)G^{-1}q_0 + d_2$$

In the simplest form the terminal conditions can be tied directly to a target level of output. It is assumed that the government is willing to name: (a) desired levels of output in the terminal year for each sector, and (b) desired levels of postterminal rates of growth for the capital stock in each sector. Then the terminal conditions may be written*

$$k_{\tau+1} \geq (I + R_\tau)G^{-1}q_\tau$$
$$k_{\tau+2} \geq (I + R_\tau)^2 G^{-1}q_\tau \qquad (74)$$
$$k_{\tau+3} \geq (I + R_\tau)^3 G^{-1}q_\tau$$

where q_τ = an exogenously fixed production target for the terminal year
  R_τ = a diagonal matrix with elements which are equal to the desired postterminal growth rate

A number of other specifications of the terminal conditions have been suggested. See, for example, Eckaus and Parikh (1968, pp. 34–36), Sen (1967), and Chakravarty and Eckaus (1968).

In summary, the complete model is as follows: *performance function:*

$$\max \xi = \sum_{t=1}^{\tau} \frac{\omega_t}{(1 + \rho)^t} \qquad (56)$$

subject to *distribution relationships:*

$$q_t + m_t \geq Aq_t + h_t + c_t + q_t + e_t \qquad (57)$$

production relationships:

$$q_t \leq Gk_t \qquad (58)$$

consumption:

$$c_t = \omega_t \bar{c} \qquad (59)$$

government:

$$g_t = \bar{g}_t \qquad (64a)$$

---

* These terminal conditions correspond to those used in Eckaus and Parikh's "target" model.

investment:

$$h_t = v_t + r_t \tag{64b}$$

$$v_t = B_1 z_{t+1} + B_2 z_{t+2} + B_3 z_{t+3} \tag{64c}$$

$$d_t = \bar{d}_t \tag{64e}$$

$$w_t \le d_t \tag{64f}$$

$$r_t = Q_1 w_{t+1} + Q_2 w_{t+2} + Q_3 w_{t+3} \tag{65}$$

capital accumulation relationships:

$$k_{t+1} \le k_t + z_{t+1} + w_{t+1} - d_{t+1} \tag{66}$$

imports, exports, and balance of payments:

$$m_t = Mq_t + s_t \tag{67}$$

$$e_t = \bar{e}_t \tag{68}$$

$$1'm_t - 1'e_t \le \phi_t \tag{69}$$

savings constraint:

$$\omega_{t+1} \ge (1 + \theta)\omega_t \tag{70}$$

initial conditions:

$$k_1 = (I + R_0)G^{-1}q_0 \tag{71}$$

$$z_2 + w_2 \le R_0(I + R_0)G^{-1}q_0 + d_2 \tag{72}$$

$$z_3 + w_3 \le R_0(I + R_0)^2 G^{-1}q_0 + d_2 \tag{73}$$

and *terminal conditions:*

$$\begin{aligned} k_{\tau+1} &\ge (I + R_\tau)G^{-1}q_\tau \\ k_{\tau+2} &\ge (I + R_\tau)^2 G^{-1}q_\tau \\ k_{\tau+3} &\ge (I + R_\tau)^3 G^{-1}q_\tau \end{aligned} \tag{74}$$

In rough terms, a model of this type includes about $6n$ constraints per time period, where n is the number of sectors.* Thus a model with ten sectors and five time periods would include about 300 constraints. Computational experience with models of this size suggest that the first solution (without a good starting basis) requires about 25 minutes on an IBM 7094 computer and subsequent solutions (with a good basis) require an average of 2 to 5 minutes each. While computation time may vary greatly from one model to the next, these data provide a rough idea of the expense of solving large economic planning models.

* A method of reducing the number of constraints by specifying some of the inequalities as equalities and then substituting them out of the model is described in Bruno, Frankel, and Doughterty (1968).

Since sensitivity analysis is an extremely important part of any model-building exercise, it is important to construct models which are small enough to permit repeated solution with the available computational facilities. For example, instead of building a model with five time periods of one year each, it may be preferable to construct a model with three time periods of two years duration each.

Now, what does all this machinery give you? If everything worked the way the planner envisioned it when construction of the model began, the model could be used to answer many interesting questions about the economy. However, the first runs of the model inevitably produce many results that the planner did not expect. Some are due to mistakes, but many may be due to misspecifications of the model. These misspecifications may frequently be traced to linearity assumptions for processes in the economy that are not linear. The investment savings process is one area in which these kinds of results frequently occur because of the bang-bang problems discussed earlier. Also, they may occur in exports or imports if appropriate bounds are not placed on these variables. Slowly but surely, then, additional nonlinearities (via piecewise segments) and additional direct constraints are built into the model so that the solutions represent a closer approximation to the economy under analysis. This part of the model-building exercise is more of an art than a science. The process may result in the model-builder learning something about the economic system, or it may result in his so constraining the model that the results reflect nothing more than his original ideas about how the economy should function.

Assuming that these difficulties are mastered, then what kinds of questions can this particular class of models be used to answer? First, the most important question is the sectoral allocation of investment over time. The basic question posed by the model is how investment should be divided among sectors in the face of the given initial capital stocks, a changing mix of consumption preferences, foreign exchange availabilities, and export and import possibilities in particular products. If foreign exchange earnings are high at present but expected to decline over time as some exportable resources are exhausted, the model solution may suggest heavy investment in the early years in sectors that require a large import component in their investment. If foreign exchange earnings are low in the early years, the model solution may suggest heavy investment in exporting sectors or import substitution investment in importing sectors. In any event, the model should enable the planner to study the effects of the competing demands for investment funds and foreign exchange.

Second, the model may give the economists some idea of the effects of changes in foreign exchange earnings or foreign aid. If for political reasons a country should want to decrease its receipt of foreign aid from some other country, the model could be used to give a rough idea of the impact on the economy of such a policy. Perhaps more importantly, the model should give some idea of the sectors in the economy that will feel the impact most strongly.

Another problem of interest may be to examine the effects of large increases or decreases in military expenditures. For example, the model might be used to determine the sectoral and time-phased impact of sudden increases in resource utilization for defense purposes.

In many of the less-developed countries of the world, there is a number of investment projects which are so large that they would require a substantial portion of the total resources used in investment and/or the available foreign exchange if they were constructed. Examples of such investments are large iron and steel complexes, petrochemical complexes, and certain hydroelectric and industrial complexes. In most cases, the questions asked about such projects are whether they should be constructed, and, if so, when. These questions are crucial to the economy because a decision to undertake such large projects means that so much investment must flow into them that investment in other industries will be sharply reduced. This in turn implies a decreased demand for the products of the complex either as intermediate inputs or as investment inputs to these other industries. Thus the decision to build one of the complexes may so reduce the effective demand for its products as to make it an inefficient investment.

When these kinds of close interdependencies on large indivisible projects arise in an economy, modifications in the planning models discussed earlier must be made. Westphal (1970) has suggested the inclusion of some zero-one variables in the models to represent the yes-no decision on constructing a given complex in a particular time period. He has applied this analysis to a planning problem for the South Korean economy in which the complexes under consideration are an iron and steel project and a petrochemical project.

Consider such a model in which x_i represents the yes-no decision to construct an iron and steel complex in time period i, and y_i represents the same kind of decision for a petrochemical complex. Such a linear programming model with three time periods would then include six zero-one variables and would thereby become a linear mixed integer programming problem. A linear mixed integer programming model with r zero-one integer variables can be solved by solving no more than 2^r linear programming problems by enumeration. Thus a problem with six zero-one integer variables could require the solution of as many as 64 linear programming problems. In practice, Westphal discovered that the algorithm he used permitted the solution of this problem with about one-fourth this number of linear programs.

Thus it is possible and computationally feasible to solve planning problems involving a few indivisible investment projects in dynamic multisectoral linear programming models. What is more, the timing on such projects may be an extremely important factor in the development of an economy, so that solving models in a linear form when they should be in a mixed integer form can give rather misleading results.

Dynamic Nonlinear Models

In moving from medium-range models covering 5- to 10-year periods to long-range models for 20 or 30 years, we shift from models with fixed co-efficients in production and little or no technical change to models with an emphasis on substitution between factor inputs and on technical change in production. Over these long periods of time, technical change and factor substitution play an important role in the development process. While it is frequently assumed in the medium-range models, as applied to less-developed countries, that labor is in such abundant supply as not to be a binding constraint, the longer range models usually include neoclassical production functions with smooth substitution possibilities between capital and labor inputs. Such production functions can be approximated by linear activity analysis models, or they can be incorporated directly into nonlinear programming models.

In addition to interest in substitution possibilities and technical change, the focus of the long-range models is on the savings-consumption decision and on the question of the optimal accumulation of foreign debt. The savings-consumption decision centers on the question of how much of the society's total output should be produced in the form of consumption goods and how much should be produced in the form of capital goods which can be used to produce more output at some future date. Thus the saving-consumption decision is directly tied-in with the question of sectoral allocation of invest-ment, with high investment in the service or light industry sectors, implying lower rates of capital formation than high investment levels in the heavy industry sectors.

The time path of foreign debt also is highly interdependent with the savings-consumption decision. In countries where a large part of the new machinery must be imported, high rates of investment and low levels of consumption in the early years of a plan may result in rapid increases in foreign debt. There are frequently institutional constraints on the level of foreign debt as well as cost constraints which operate through the necessity of paying interest on and ultimately repaying the debt.

A variety of dynamic nonlinear models has been formulated and solved. These can be divided by the method of solution into log-linear models, nonlinear programming models, and control theory models. The log-linear models of Radner (1966) use production and welfare functions of the Cobb Douglas form, namely:

$$q_t = \alpha k_t^{\beta_1} l_t^{\beta_2} \tag{75}$$

where q_t = output
$\quad k_t$ = capital input
$\quad l_t$ = labor input
which are linear in the logs, namely:

$$\log q_t = \log \alpha + \beta_1 \log k_t + \beta_2 \log l_t \tag{76}$$

The welfare function is of the same form with the arguments being sectoral consumption levels instead of inputs.

The nonlinear programming models are not restricted to any particular form of production welfare function except that they should result in convex programming problems if one is to be assured that any local optimum obtained will be a global optimum. In general terms, a planning model will be a convex programming problem if the performance function to be maximized is concave and the feasible set is convex. These conditions in turn require that the welfare function exhibit diminishing marginal welfare and that the production functions have constant or decreasing returns to scale. Examples of nonlinear programming applications to national economic models can be found in the works of Chenery and Kretschmer (1956), Chenery and Uzawa (1958), Johansen and Lindholt (1964), and Mirrlees (1967).

Control theory methods require the same convexity assumptions as nonlinear programming; however, they employ a solution technique that exploits the dynamic property of multiperiod economic models. This property is the fact that any action taken at time t produces effects in only the years after and including time t, that is, a consumption or investment decision at time t affects future but not previous production levels.

Any dynamic model which can be solved as a nonlinear programming model can be solved as a control theory model and vice versa. However, there are some subclasses of models which may be more efficiently solved with the one method than the other.* We return to the question of the comparative advantages of nonlinear programming models after presenting a finite horizon dynamic nonlinear planning model.

This model contains all of the same basic relationships as the medium-range dynamic linear models except that the nonlinear character of the model permits specification with nonlinear functions and the long-run nature dictates interest in substitution between inputs and technical change.†

---

* One of the first applications of numerical techniques for solving economic models with control theory models is given by Dobell and Ho (1967).

† The development here parallels the model of Kendrick and Taylor (1968a). One example of a theoretical model in this same general class is Bardhan (1967).

The *performance function* is written as

$$\max \xi = \sum_{t=1}^{\tau} (1 + \rho)^{-t} \sum_{i=1}^{n} a_i c_{ti}^{b_i} \qquad \begin{matrix} 0 \leq b_i \leq 1 \\ a_i \geq 0 \end{matrix} \qquad (77)$$

where ξ = total discounted welfare
    ρ = social discount rate
    c_{ti} = consumption level for goods from the ith sector in time period t
    a_i, b_i = parameters

This function is discussed in detail in Kendrick and Taylor (1968a). Here it suffices to mention that the restriction of the parameter values to the ranges shown ensures that the function has the properties of positive but diminishing marginal welfare for any good within each time period. This particular functional form is an additive welfare function in which:

$$\frac{\partial \xi}{\partial c_{ti} \, \partial c_{tj}} = 0 \qquad i \neq j \qquad (78)$$

and

$$\frac{\partial \xi}{\partial c_{ti} \, \partial c_{t+\theta,i}} = 0 \qquad \theta \neq 0 \qquad (79)$$

that is, it is assumed that the welfare effects of different goods in the same time period and of the same good in different time periods are independent. This is a rather stringent assumption. It is not required by the mathematical methods of control theory or of nonlinear programming, since either of these methods can be used with nonseparable performance functions.* The separability assumption employed here is not required by the mathematics but may be required by data considerations. Also, this particular form of welfare function has the virtue of permitting inference of the parameters from income elasticity and budget shares data.

The *distribution relationship* is of the same form as in the medium-run models, that is:

$$q_t + Dq_t + m_t = Aq_t + h_t + c_t + g_t + e_t \qquad (80)$$

where q = output
    D = matrix of marginal propensities to import for production
    m = united imports
    A = input-output matrix

---

* Equation 78 implies a commodity-wise separable welfare function, and 79 implies a time-wise separable welfare function. Control theory methods of solution are complicated somewhat by time-wise nonseparability through the necessity of defining additional variables.

h = investment*
d = investment levels
e = exports
c = consumption
g = government

This distribution relationship differs from those we have discussed earlier only in the treatment of tied imports and of investment. The tied imports Dq are included directly, leaving the symbol m_t to represent only the united imports.

The materials inputs to investment are related to increases in capacity in this model in a slightly different way than was done in the linear models, namely:

$$h_t = Br_t \tag{80a}$$

where

$$r_t = g(z_t, k_t) \tag{80b}$$

with B = capital coefficient matrix, that is, the elements of the matrix represent units of domestic resource use from sector i per unit investment level of capacity creation in the jth sector
r_t = vector of investment levels
g = a function that maps increases in capacity into investment levels with the efficiency of this process being dependent upon the capital stock already in place
z_t = vector of gross increments to capacity

Since the function g is discussed in detail below, it suffices here to point out that the nonlinear character of the model permits a more general specification of the relationship between capital formation and the inputs that are required in order to create capital.

Production and investment relationships in this model may be thought of in the following way: the output of each sector is produced, using capital and labor inputs as specified in the production functions described below and using intermediate material inputs as required by the fixed coefficient relationships in the Leontief A matrix. Output may then be used for intermediate inputs, investment, consumption, exports, or government as specified in the distribution relationships. However, if the output is to be used to create capacity, it must undergo an additional transformation which brings together inputs from a number of different industries and transforms them into the capital of the using industry. This process of transforming inputs into

* Since the elements of B are defined for *domestic* resource use (see Eq. 80a), (80) does not include imports which are tied to investment.

capacity may be subject to diminishing returns of some kind. Let us describe this process with a function which we call a "capacity" function to distinguish it from a production function. A capacity function would then establish a relationship between capacity formation and inputs to capacity formation, or in our notation:

$$z = g(h)$$

More frequently we shall use the inverse of the capacity function which we shall call the capacity input function, and write*

$$h = f(z)$$

In the linear model we have written this relationship as

$$h_t = Bz_t$$

and have thereby assumed that the process of aggregating and transforming inputs from various sectors into the capital stock of a using sector is a linear process. With highly aggregated models this assumption may be more realistic than with highly disaggregated models. For example, if the only sectors which provide inputs for capital formation are the construction sector and the machine tools sector, then the process of aggregating and transforming these inputs can be approximated rather well with a linear process. At greater levels of disaggregation it could be desirable to specify these capacity and/or capacity input functions in a nonlinear fashion to incorporate both diminishing returns and substitution possibilities between various kinds of inputs.

The model under discussion here is a halfway house between the linear models and the fully nonlinear models, in that the capacity input function may be written

$$h_t = Bf(z_t)$$

where B is the familiar capital coefficient matrix from the linear models, and f is a nonlinear relationship. Actually, in this model the capacity input function is of the form:

$$h_t = Br_t = Bf(z_t, k_t)$$

and the relationship f does not appear explicitly but rather in the form:

$$z_t = g(r_t, k_t) \tag{81}$$

The function g, which is invertible, is discussed later in this section of the chapter.

* As was discussed earlier, f may not be inevitable.

The *production relationships* embody both technical change and substitution of capital and labor inputs. They are given here in the constant elasticity of substitution (CES) form, though a number of other forms that permit the specification of technical change and factor substitution could be employed.* The function is

$$q_{ti} = \alpha_i(1 + \nu_i)^t[\delta_i k_{ti}^{-\rho_i} + (1 - \delta_i)l_{ti}^{-\rho_i}]^{-\beta/\rho_i} \tag{82}$$

where α = efficiency parameter
ν = rate of technical progress per time period
δ = distribution parameter
k = capital input
l = labor input
$\rho_i = (1/\sigma_i) - 1$, where σ_i is the elasticity of substitution for the ith sector
β = degree of homogeneity or returns to scale

This production function form involves an assumption of disembodied technical change. Technical progress in any given sector is assumed to occur with the passage of time and to be independent of the levels of capital and labor input to the sector. If technical change is embodied in the labor force through new ideas and approaches gained through schooling or if technical change is embodied in new machines and therefore dependent on the rate of investment, a production function of the form indicated above would not be a very accurate representation of reality. A discussion of production functions with embodied technical change is given in Solow (1967). The disembodied form is used here for its simplicity. There is no reason in the mathematics of optimization why an embodied form should not be used.

The production function given above involves the implicit assumption that the entire capital stock in any given sector can be used in substituting for labor inputs in that sector and vice versa. A more appropriate specification of the function has been suggested by Johansen (1959). Capital is assumed to be substitutable for labor at the time of investment but must be used in the resulting fixed proportion thereafter. The institutional arrangements which underlie this kind of assumption is that in designing new machines, the engineers chose an appropriate relationship between capital and labor inputs depending on the technology available and on the relative prices of capital and labor. However, once the machine has been designed and constructed, it requires a certain number of men to operate it, and this number cannot be changed. Thus capital of each vintage can be substituted for labor at the time of investment but must then be operated with fixed proportions thereafter until the time of its retirement. Theoretical models which embody this kind

* A review of empirical work with this functional form is given by Nerlove (1967).

of assumption are called putty-clay models; that is, the capital is soft and malleable at the time of investment but hardens into clay thereafter.

While the notion of using production functions of this form is attractive, the empirical detail that is employed by them can become rather large, and the number of nonlinear constraints in the resulting optimizing model may cause the model to be unwieldy if the number of sectors, time periods, or other types of disaggregation is not decreased.

With regard to returns to scale, the production function (82) is written in a general form with the parameter β left unspecified. For $\beta = 1$, the function will exhibit constant returns to scale; $\beta < 1$ implies diminishing returns; and $\beta > 1$ implies increasing returns to scale. For the cases of constant or diminishing returns to scale, the constraint embodying the production function will produce a convex set. However, when increasing returns to scale occur, the constraints may produce nonconvex sets.* This destroys the convex-programming-problem nature of the economic model, and requires the use of much less efficient programming techniques such as mixed integer linear programming.

However, many production processes which are characterized by economies of scale are for particular parts of the manufacturing process in certain industries. It may be that as these processes and industries are aggregated to form the highly aggregated sectors which are used in economy-wide planning models, the economies of scale in some parts are empirically outweighed by diseconomies of scale in other processes and industries. Thus one may observe that a production function for the rolling operation in a large steel mill was a process that exhibited strong economies of scale, but that a production function estimated for the heavy industry sector in an economy would show constant or diminishing returns to scale. Empirical relations of this sort are the reason that the specification of national planning models as convex programming problems can be done without including assumptions that seem too contradictory to actual economies.

There are no *consumption relationships* in this model. Rather, it is assumed that the nonlinear welfare function permits specification of the model in such a form that the consumption and savings relations imposed in the linear model are not necessary. This formulation presupposes that the observed savings behavior is not a result of institutional limitations but rather of the time preferences of the society, as manifest in the parameters of the welfare function.

In the absence of more sophisticated behavioral relations for the government, it is assumed that government use of resources is fixed exogenously

---

* Some economies of scale may be included in the functions without the constraint sets becoming nonconvex. These processes can be represented with quasiconcave or quasiconvex functions; see Arrow and Enthoven (1961).

and enters only the right-hand side of the distribution relationships, that is:

$$g_t = \bar{g}_t \qquad (82a)$$

The *investment relationships* in this model embody the empirically untested notion of absorptive capacity constraints. The amount of investment that a country can efficiently carry out in any given year is related to the amount of capital stock already in place in each sector. The shortage of technically trained people to implement investment programs is sometimes given as the rationale for such functions. The counterargument is that a country—especially small countries—can hire foreign firms to supervise the investment process and can thereby carry out virtually unlimited amounts of investment in any given year with constant levels of efficiency.

There is also a mathematical reason for incorporating these absorptive capacity relationships when control theory methods are used to solve the model. When a control variable enters a model linearly, as investment does in this model in the absence of the absorptive capacity relationships, the variable may not appear in the first-order conditions. Such a model is said to be singular and exhibits the kind of bang-bang behavior that was discussed earlier in connection with the linear models. Since there are techniques for solving such singular models,* the model-builder should not avoid such formulations; however, he should be aware that different computational procedures are necessary when the controls enter the model linearly.

The absorptive capacity relationships used in this model are of the form:

$$z_{ti} = g_{ti}(r_{ti}, k_{ti}) \qquad (83)$$

where z_{ti} = increment to capacity from investment in the ith sector in period t
r_{ti} = investment input level
k_{ti} = capital stock

with

$$\frac{\partial z_{ti}}{\partial r_{ti}} \geq 0, \qquad \frac{\partial^2 z_{ti}}{\partial r_{ti}^2} \leq 0, \qquad \frac{\partial z_{ti}}{\partial k_{ti}} \geq 0$$

that is, the increment to capacity increases with increases in investment inputs but at a decreasing rate. Also, the increment to capacity increases with increases in the sectoral capital stock, other things being equal. The absorptive capacity relationship is related to the capacity input function as discussed earlier and is the same form as the relationship:

$$z_t = g(r_t, k_t) \qquad (81)$$

---

* See Bryson and Ho (1968) for a discussion of the methods; and Dobell and Ho (1967) for one application of such techniques.

The particular function used is*

$$z_{ti} = \mu_i k_{ti}\left[1 - \left(1 + \frac{\varepsilon_i r_{ti}}{\mu_i k_{ti}}\right)^{-1/\varepsilon_i}\right] \qquad \begin{matrix} \varepsilon_i \geq -1 \\ \mu_i \geq 0 \end{matrix} \qquad (84)$$

The assumption behind this particular specification is that as the increase in capacity, z_{ti}, approaches some function, μ_i, of existing capacity, k_{ti}, then investment, r_{ti}, becomes less and less effective in increasing z_{ti}. This can be seen in the graph of the function given in Figure 1.

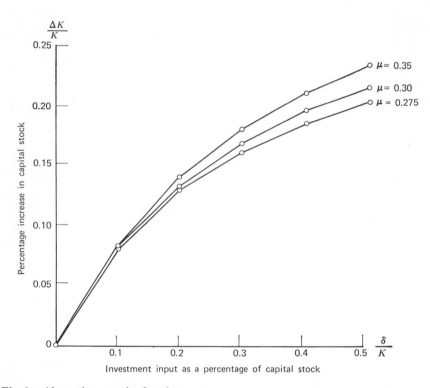

Fig. 1.   Absorptive capacity function.

The parameter ε has been introduced to indicate how rapidly the decrease in investment efficiency takes place. Note that $\varepsilon = -1$ means that $z = r$ so that a linear relationship holds between change in capacity and investment (although there is still an implied upper bound of μ on z/k). For $-1 < \varepsilon < 0$, z/k is a concave and monotonically increasing function of r/k until $z/k = \mu$

* This function was suggested by R. Dorfman for use in a different model.

at which point the function becomes complex-valued. For $\varepsilon = 0$, we have

$$\frac{z}{k} = \mu\left(1 - \exp\frac{\delta}{\mu k}\right) \tag{85}$$

which increases asymptotically to μ. In general, when $\varepsilon \geq 0$, this sort of behavior occurs, so there are both diminishing returns and an absolute upper bound μ on z/k which is approached when $r/k \rightarrow \infty$.

The *capital accumulation* relations are specified as

$$k_{t+1,i} = k_{ti} + z_{ti} - \eta_{ti}k_{ti} \tag{86}$$

where η_{ti} = percentage rate of depreciation of the capital stock in ith sector during time period t. A very simple form of depreciation is used in which exogenous projections are made as to the percentage of the ith sector's capital stock which will retire during the period t.

The labor force constraint for the model is

$$\sum_{i=1}^{n} l_{ti} = l_t \tag{87}$$

where l_{ti} = labor input to the ith sector in time period t

l_t = total available labor force in time period t, set exogenously

An implicit assumption is made here that the size of the labor force is not affected by any of the endogenous economic variables in the model. Sectoral labor forces, l_{ti}, do vary, but the sum must equal the total exogenously fixed labor force. The total labor force projections should take account of the changing age and sex composition of the work force as well as the overall growth in population.

Another important implicit assumption made here is that all labor is homogenous. Labor has not been disaggregated by training or educational levels, neither in the constraint above nor in the production functions. A more disaggregated treatment of the labor force would involve (1) writing separate constraints of the form (87) for each class of labor, (2) estimating production functions for an education and training sector which transforms persons from one education or training level to another, and (3) specifying the production functions (82) with several types of labor inputs. The first two of these three steps are somewhat easier to accomplish than the third. The first step is principally a matter of data collection to determine what part of the labor force at the time of the initiation of the plan belongs to each of the educational groups. This step also involves the specification of the constraint relationships. The second step involves determination of the production functions of the educational sector. Since the key inputs to the educational sector are people of particular age and education levels, specification of the model with disaggregated labor force groups may involve rather elaborate accounting relationships wih parallel in form the capital accumulation relationships. Since human capital in the form of education and training can be accumulated in a society much as physical equipment can be accumulated, this parallel specification is not surprising. The third step involves the specification and estimation of production functions for all sectors of the economy with various types of labor inputs as well as capital inputs. Since different pairs of inputs, that is, capital and highly skilled labor or highly skilled and medium skilled labor, undoubtedly have different degrees of substitutability, one would like to specify the production function in a form that permits this degree of generality.

Disaggregation of the labor force in national planning models usually adds both to the size of the model and the quality of the results. The decision as to the desired degree of disaggregation must be made with respect to the types of questions that the analyst hopes to study with completed model. For example, if highly skilled labor is in extremely short supply and the time required to train such people is long, then it may be desirable to disaggregate the labor force along these lines.

The *foreign trade relationships* in this model are similar to those used in other models in this chapter. *Exports* are specified exogenously by sector and time period, that is:

$$e_{ti} = \bar{e}_{ti} \qquad \text{all} \quad t, i \qquad (88)$$

Imports are divided into three classes: (1) those tied to current production, (2) those tied to investment levels, and (3) those which are free and act more or less as slack variables.

$$\hat{m}_t = Dq_t + \Pi r_t + m_t \qquad (89)$$

where $\hat{m}_t$ = total imports.

These three classes of imports appear in the *foreign debt accumulation constraint*, that is:

$$\gamma_{t+1} = (1 + \theta)\gamma_t + 1'(Dq_t + \Pi r_t + m_t - e_t) \qquad (90)$$

where γ_t = foreign debt
     θ = interest rate on foreign debt
     1 = a vector of ones
     D = diagonal matrix of marginal propensities to input for production
     Π = diagonal matrix of marginal propensities to import for capacity creation
     m_t = united imports
     e_t = exports

This relationship assumes that foreign debt can be paid back only by running an export surplus. Also, it assumes that the country must pay interest on the foreign debt and that these interest payments use up foreign exchange just as imports do. Along with (90), initial foreign debt and a target level of foreign debt are specified, that is:

$$\gamma_1 \quad \text{known} \quad \text{and} \quad \gamma_\tau \quad \text{chosen} \tag{91}$$

This formulation assumes that the level of foreign debt can reach any height during the period covered by the model provided only that it reach the fixed target level at terminal time. The appeal of this formulation is that a country may desire to formulate plans which include repayment of all foreign debt by a certain date or which require reduction of the debt to a certain fixed level at some future time. However, to be complete, this specification should probably include a constraint on the rate at which foreign debt can be incurred or on the relationship between foreign debt and foreign exchange earnings. International banking organizations and foreign aid agencies sometimes operate with such rules. If the country concerned is faced with such a constraint, it is usually of interest to solve the model both with and without the imposition of the constraint to provide a rough idea of the effect of the constraint.

The *initial conditions* for the model include specification of the initial capital stock in each sector and the initial level of foreign debt, that is:

$$k_1 = \bar{k} \tag{92}$$

$$\gamma_1 = \bar{\gamma} \tag{93}$$

Terminal conditions are specified simply as target levels for the capital stock in each sector and for foreign debt, that is:

$$k_\tau = k^* \tag{94}$$

$$\gamma_\tau = \gamma^* \tag{95}$$

In summary, the model may be written

$$\max \xi = \sum_{t=1}^{\tau}(1+\rho)^{-t}\sum_{i=1}^{n} a_i c_{ti}^{b_i} \quad \begin{array}{l} 0 \le b_i \le 1 \\ 0 \le a_i \end{array} \tag{77}$$

subject to *distribution relationships*:

$$q_t + Dq_t + m_t = Ag_t + h_t + e_t + c_t + g_t \tag{80}$$

production relationships:

$$q_{ti} = \alpha_i(1+\nu_i)^t[\delta_i k_{ti}^{-\rho_i} + (1-\delta_i)l_{ti}^{-\rho_i}]^{-\beta/\rho_i} \quad \rho_i = \frac{1}{\sigma_i}-1 \tag{82}$$

government:

$$g_t = \bar{g}_t \tag{82a}$$

capital accumulation:

$$k_{t+1,i} = k_{ti} + z_{ti} - \eta_{ti}k_{ti} \tag{86}$$

investment:

$$h_t = Br_t \tag{80a}$$

$$z_{ti} = \mu_i k_{ti}\left[1 - \left(1 + \frac{\varepsilon_i r_{ti}}{\mu_i k_{ti}}\right)^{-1/\varepsilon_i}\right] \qquad \begin{matrix} \varepsilon_i \geq -1 \\ \mu_i \geq 0 \end{matrix} \tag{84}$$

labor force:

$$\sum_{i=1}^{n} l_{ti} = l_t \qquad l_t \text{ exogenous} \tag{87}$$

foreign trade (exports):

$$e_t = \bar{e}_t \tag{88}$$

(imports):

$$\hat{m}_t = Dq_t + \Pi r_t + m_t \tag{89}$$

(foreign debt accumulation):

$$\gamma_{t+1} = (1 + \theta)\gamma_t + 1'(\hat{m}_t - e_t) \tag{90}$$

end conditions (initial):

$$k_1 = \bar{k} \tag{92}$$

$$\gamma_1 = \bar{\gamma} \tag{93}$$

(terminal):

$$k_\tau = k^* \tag{94}$$

$$\gamma_\tau = \gamma^* \tag{95}$$

In more formal mathematical terms, the problem then is to maximize the performance function (77), subject to the system equations (86) and (90) and the initial and terminal conditions (92)–(95) with the side conditions (80), (82), (82a), (80a), (84), (87), (88), and (89), which, as equality relations, can be substituted out. The substitution results in a problem of $n + 1$ state variables (the n capital stock and the foreign debt variable) and $3n - 1$ control variables ($n - 1$ labor inputs, n investment activity levels, and n untied imports).

Computational experience with this class of models is limited. However, Kendrick and Taylor (1968) report the solution of models with four sectors (i.e., five state variables and nine control variables*) for 30 time periods in about 20 to 30 minutes on an IBM 7094. Furthermore, they speculate that due to the nature of the calculations, computational time in these models will increase in a roughly linear way with the number of sectors.

As was mentioned earlier, this class of models can also be solved with general nonlinear programming techniques rather than with control theory methods. A comparison of the two approaches is given in Kendrick and Taylor (1968b).

CONCLUSION

From the foregoing description and analysis of simulation and optimization models for national economic planning, one can see the relationships between the choice of mathematical method and the economic assumptions implicit in the model.

The simulation model discussed here makes final demand exogenous and seèks patterns of production and investment that will be consistent with that pattern of final demand. No explicit ordering over the set of consistent patterns is made in the model, leaving this task to the policy-makers or to some other group.

The optimization models discussed here embody the assumption that the policy-makers are willing to and capable of specifying the preferences of the society over outcomes defined in terms of sectoral time paths of consumption levels. In the linear models these ordering relationships are restricted to the linear form with the resulting assumption of constant marginal utility within time periods. In the nonlinear models the assumption of declining marginal utility within time periods is permitted.

The linear models specify production relationships in that form and with fixed coefficients while the nonlinear models permit the inclusion of both diminishing returns in production and substitution between factor inputs. Most nonlinear models, however, are of the convex programming problem type, and therefore are restricted to treating problems in which the production relationships exhibit constant or diminishing returns.† To incorporate economies of scale into the analysis, methods of nonconvex programming such as linear mixed-integer programming must be employed.

The conversion of output into capital stocks through capacity functions or

---

* Two of their untied import-type variables were exogenously set to zero.
† With the exceptions discussed in Arrow and Enthoven (1961).

capacity input functions is specified with linear equality or inequality relationships in the linear models, but can be generalized to incorporate nonlinear absorptive capacity or capacity functions in the nonlinear models so long as the assumption of diminishing or constant returns holds in this transformation process.

Finally, the entire class of models discussed in this chapter is of the deterministic variety and therefore embodies the assumption that any uncertainty can be incorporated into the model by taking the mean value of any random variables and then solving the model as certainty equivalence models. Sensitivity testing of the deterministic models is often used as a means of mitigating the effects of, but not of completely relaxing, this assumption. While there has been some experimentation with stochastic economic models, so far there has been little or no work of that type on national economic planning models.

REFERENCES

ADELMAN, IRMA, Ed. (1968), *Practical Approaches to Development Planning; Korea's Second Five Year Plan*, Johns Hopkins University Press, Baltimore, Maryland.

ADELMAN, IRMA, DAVID COLE, ROGER NORTON, and LEE KEE JUNG (1968), "The Korean Sectoral Model," in Adelman (1968).

ADELMAN, IRMA, and FREDERICK T. SPARROW (1966), "Experiments with Linear and Piece-Wise Linear Dynamic Programming Models," in Adelman and Thorbecke (1966), Chap. 11, pp. 291–316.

ADELMAN, IRMA, and ERIK THORBECKE, Eds. (1966), *The Theory and Design of Economic Development*, The Johns Hopkins Press, Baltimore.

ARROW, K. J., and A. C. ENTHOVEN (1961), "Quasi-Concave Programming," *Econometrica*, October, pp. 779–800.

BARR, JAMES L., and ALAN S. MANNE (1967), "Numerical Experiments with a Finite Horizon Planning Model," *Indian Economic Review*, Vol. II, No. 1, April.

BAUMOL, WILLIAM J. (1951), *Economic Dynamics*, 2nd ed., MacMillan, New York.

BERGSMAN, JOEL, and ALAN S. MANNE (1966), "An Almost Intertemporal Model for India's Fourth and Fifth Plans," in Adelman and Thorbecke (1966), pp. 239–256.

BOWLES, SAMUEL (1969), *Planning Educational Systems for Economic Growth*, Harvard University Press, Cambridge, Mass.

BRIOSCHI, F., and S. ROSSI (1967), "The Complementarity of Consumption in the Optimal Savings Problem," *Estratto da Calcolo*, Vol. 4, No. 2, April–June.

BROWN, MURRAY, Ed. (1967), *The Theory and Empirical Analysis of Production; Studies in Income and Wealth*, Vol. 31, Conference on Research in Income and Wealth, National Bureau of Economic Research, distributed by Columbia University Press, New York, 1967.

BRUNO, MICHAEL (1966), "A Programming Model for Israel," in Adelman and Thorbecke (1966), Chap. 12, pp. 327–354.

BRUNO, MICHAEL, MORDECAI FRAENKEL, and CHRISTOPHER DOUGHERTY (1970), "Dynamic Input-Output, Trade and Development," July, in A. Carter and A. Brody (Eds.), *Applications of Input-Output Analysis*, North-Holland Amsterdam.

BRYSON, ARTHUR E., and YU-CHI HO (1968), *Optimization, Estimation, and Control*, Blaisdell Publishing Company, Waltham, Mass.

CHAKRAVARTY, S. (1962), "Optimal Savings With Finite Planning Horizon," *International Economic Review*, September.

CHAKRAVARTY, S. (1967), "Alternate Preference Functions in Problems of Investment Planning on the National Level," in Malinvaud and Bachrach (1967), Chap. 6, pp. 150–169.

CHAKRAVARTY, S., and R. S. ECKAUS (1964), "An Approach to a Multi-Sectoral Intertemporal Planning Model," in Rosenstein-Roden (1964), Chap. 7, pp. 110–126.

CHAKRAVARTY, S., and LOUIS LEFEBER (1965), "An Optimizing Planning Model," *The Economic Weekly*, Annual Number, February.

CHAKRAVARTY, S., and A. S. MANNE (1968), "Optimal Growth When the Instantaneous Utility Function Depends Upon the Rate of Change in Consumption," *American Economic Review*, December.

CHENERY, H. B., and PAUL G. CLARK (1959), *Inter-Industry Economics*, Wiley, New York, 1959.

CHENERY, H. B., and K. KRETSCHMER (1956), "Resource Allocation for Economic Development," *Econometrica*, October.

CHENERY, H. B., and ARTHUR MACEWAN (1966), "Optimal Patterns of Growth and Aid, The Case of Pakistan," *Pakistan Development Review*, Vol. VI, No. 2, Summer, pp. 209–242.

CHENERY, H. B., and A. M. STROUT (1966), "Foreign Assistance and Economic Development," *American Economic Review*, Vol. LVI, No. 4, Part 1, September.

CHENERY, H. B., and H. UZAWA (1958), "Non-Linear Programming in Economic Development," in *Studies in Linear and Non-Linear Programming*, Arrow, Hurwicz, and Uzawa, Eds., Stanford University Press, Stanford, California, pp. 203–229.

COLE, DAVID (1966), "An Interindustry Model for Korea," Economic Development Report No. 49, Project for Quantitative Research in Economic Development, Center for International Affairs, Harvard University, Cambridge, Mass., December.

DOBELL, A. R., and YU-CHI HO (1967), "Optimal Investment Policy: An Example of a Control Problem in Economic Theory," *IEEE Transactions on Automatic Control*, Vol. AC-12, No. 1, February.

DORFMAN, R., P. A. SAMUELSON, and R. M. SOLOW (1958), *Linear Programming and Economic Analysis*, McGraw-Hill, New York, 1958.

DUESENBERRY, J. S., L. R. KLEIN, and ED KUH (1965), *The Brookings Quarterly Econometric Model of the United States*, Rand McNally.

ECKAUS, R. S., and KIRIT PARIKH (1968), *Planning for Growth: Multi-Sectoral Inter-Temporal Models Applied to India*, M.I.T. Press, Cambridge, Mass., 1968.

FISHER, IRVING (1930), *The Theory of Interest*, re-issued 1954, Kelly and Millman, New York, N.Y.

HADLEY, G. (1962), *Nonlinear and Dynamic Programming*, Addison-Wesley, Reading, Mass.

HOLLAND, EDWARD P., and ROBERT W. GILLESPIE (1963), *Experiments on a Simulated Underdeveloped Economy: Development Plans and Balance of Payments Policies*, M.I.T. Press, Cambridge, Mass.

HOUTHAKKER, H. (1965), "A Note on Self Dual Preferences," *Econometrica*, October.

JOHANSEN, LIEF (1959), "Substitution Versus Fixed Production Coefficients in the Theory of Economic Growth: A Synthesis," *Econometrica*.

JOHANSEN, LIEF (1964), *A Multi-Sectoral Study of Economic Growth*, North Holland Publishing Co., Amsterdam, Holland.

KENDRICK, DAVID A., and LANCE J. TAYLOR (1967), "Numerical Methods and Nonlinear Optimization Models for Economic Planning," in H. Chenery, Ed., *Studies in Development Planning*, Harvard University Press, Cambridge, Mass.

KENDRICK, DAVID A., and LANCE J. TAYLOR (1968a), "Numerical Solution of Nonlinear Planning Models," Economic Development Report No. 98, Project for Quantitative Research in Economic Development, Center for International Affairs, Harvard University, May.

KENDRICK, DAVID A., and LANCE J. TAYLOR (1968b), "A Dynamic Nonlinear Planning Model for Korea," forthcoming in Adelman (1968).

KURZ, MORDECAI (1965), "Optimal Paths of Capital Accumulation Under the Minimum Time Objective," *Econometrica*, Vol. 33, No. 1, January, pp. 42–66.

LEONTIEF, WASSILY W. (1951), *The Structure of the American Economy, 1919–1939*, 2nd ed., Oxford University Press, New York, 1951.

MACEWAN, ARTHUR (1968), *Development Alternatives in Pakistan*, Ph.D. dissertation, Department of Economics, Harvard University, Cambridge, Mass.

MANESCHI, A. (1966), "Optimal Savings with Finite Planning Horizon: A Note," *International Economic Review*, Vol. 7, January.

MANNE, ALAN S. (1966), "Key Sectors of the Mexican Economy, 1962–72," in Adelman and Thorbecke (1966), pp. 263–286.

MANNE, ALAN S., and THOMAS E. WEISSKOPF (1967), "A Dynamic Multi-Sectoral Model for India, 1967–75," Memorandum No. 57, Research Center in Economic Growth, Stanford University, Stanford, California.

MERA, KOICHI (1968), "An Empirical Determination of a Dynamic Utility Function," *The Review of Economics and Statistics*, Vol. XLX, No. 1, February.

NERLOVE, MARC (1967), "Recent Empirical Studies of the CES and Related Production Functions," in Murray Brown (1967).

RADNER, ROY (1966), "Optimal Growth in a Linear-Logarithmic Economy," *International Economic Review*, Vol. 7, No. 1, January.

RADNER, ROY, and SANTIAGO FRIEDMAN (1964), "An Algorithm for Dynamic Programming of Economic Growth," Working Paper No. 99, Center for Research in Management Science, University of California, Berkeley, California.

ROSENSTEIN-RODAN, P. N., Ed. (1964), *Capital Formation and Economic Development*, M.I.T. Press, Cambridge, Mass.

SEN, A. K. (1967), "Terminal Capital and Optimal Savings," in *Socialism, Capitalism, and Economic Growth*, C. A. Feinstein, Ed., Cambridge at the the University Press, Cambridge, England, pp. 40–53.

SHELL, KARL (1967), *Essays on the Theory of Optimal Economic Growth*, M.I.T. Press, Cambridge, Mass.

SOLOW, ROBERT M. (1967), "Some Recent Developments in the Theory of Production," in M. Brown (1967).

UZAWA, H. (1958), "Iterative Methods for Concave Programming," in *Studies in Linear and Nonlinear Programming*, Arrow, Hurwics, and Uzawa, Eds., Stanford University Press, pp. 154–165.

WEISSKOPF, THOMAS E. (1966), *A Programming Model for Import Substitution in India*, Ph.D. dissertation, Department of Economics, Massachusetts Institute of Technology, Cambridge, Mass.

WESTPHAL, LARRY E. (1970), "Public Investment with Economics of Scale", North-Holland Amsterdam.

IX Interindustry Economic Models and Regional Water Resources Analyses: E. M. Lofting

INTRODUCTION

Regional investment decisions, if they are to be defensible require some knowledge of the structure of the regional economy, the magnitude and value of commodity imports and exports, and the real value, as opposed to a market or a subsidized value, of the regional resources that may be developed. The so-called terms of trade and national comparative advantage were cornerstones of classical economic thought (Roll, 1956) but the applicability of similar considerations within national boundaries have, for the most part, been neglected.

Historical accident, or the "invisible hand" of the market, may have, in some instances, played a general role in determining a particular pattern of regional specialization. However, in the face of such pressing problems as environmental quality, scarce natural resources, and the depletion of resources at the regional level that can be considered to be renewable only over a planning period of future generations, it is questionable whether national market forces or local inertia will play similar roles in the future.

Since World War II, many important public decisions, including investment decisions, have been based increasingly on planning information generated by the newer techniques of mathematical economics, operations research, and system analysis (Chenery and Clark, 1959). Transportation studies, land use planning, resource availability, model cities programs, and plant site and location studies are much less subject to casual or intuitive judgment for the ultimate implementation of programs in which they may play a crucial role. This is not to say that the newer methods have gained full acceptance (Committee Report of the National Academy of Sciences, 1966), but it might be judged from the main stream of the literature in this area that broader acceptance may be a function of time and the increased availability of basic data whereby the effectiveness of the new techniques may be patently demonstrated. For the specific problem of judging the appropriateness of regional resource development programs, some estimate of the intrinsic value of a natural resource is of crucial importance.

VALUE OF WATER AS A RESOURCE IN THE HISTORY OF ECONOMIC THOUGHT

The value generally imputed to water, notwithstanding the overriding importance that it holds for human existence, has a very long history in economic thought. Plato (427–347 B.C.) noted*:

> That which is scarce is valuable: Water is not valued, altho' the most useful thing in the World.

Pufendorf (1632–1694) quoted Plato and systematically reviewed the matter of price and value as they pertain to the elements and nature (von Pufendorf, 1729):

> Yet it is observable, that some of the most useful things of human Life have no Price set upon them; either because they are and ought to be free from Property or because they are excluded from Commerce.... Thus the Air, the Sky, the Heavenly bodies, and the vast Ocean not being appropriated, can bear no Price, how serviceable soever they may be to human life....
>
> Many things also have no Price, because they are not capable of being possessed separately by themselves, which yet very much enhance the Price of the thing they appertain to; as the want of them takes from it not a little. Thus the lying open to the Sun, a clear and wholesome Air, a pleasant Prospect, the Winds, Shades, and etc., considered separately in themselves, bear no Price, because they cannot be enjoyed without the Land they belong to; but yet of what Moment they are in the Purchase of Lands and Tenements, no Man is ignorant....
>
> ... If Water were difficult to be met with, how much more valuable would it be than the things we most value now? Or, if Gold lay in the Streets as common as Stones, who do you think would value it, or lock it up?...

Adam Smith (1937), generally taken to be the founder of classical economic thought, carried forward the same line of reasoning:

> Nothing is more useful than water: but it will purchase scarce any thing; scarce any thing can be had in exchange for it. A diamond, on the contrary, has scarce any value in use; but a very great quantity of other goods may frequently be had in exchange for it.

David Ricardo (1957), in the opening paragraph of his major work, dealt immediately with the value of water and air:

> Water and air are abundantly useful; they are indeed indispensable to existence, yet, under ordinary circumstances, nothing can be obtained in exchange for them. Gold, on the contrary, though of little use compared with air or water, will exchange for a great quantity of other goods.

* Plato, *Euthydemus*, quoted in von Pufendorf (1729).

Viewing the full effects of the industrial revolution in Britain, Frederick Engels (1939) wrote in his characteristically blunt manner:

The first necessity for the steam engine, and a main requirement of almost all branches of production, is relatively pure water. The factory town, however, transforms all water into ... ditch water .... The present poisoning of the air, water and land can only be put an end to by the fusion of town and country ...

Almost 100 years later, not only the factory town, but also virtually entire regions of most of the industrialized nations face the problem of maintaining the quantity and quality of their water supplies. Those charged with the responsibility of planning and developing new supplies are grappling just as sincerely as their predecessors with the problems of prices and valuations for the output of their projects. The measurement of benefits, costs, and damages in areas that are, in Pufendorf's terminology, "excluded from Commerce," still eludes the engineer, the economist, and the administrator.

INVESTMENT CRITERIA PROBLEMS AND WATER RESOURCES ANALYSES

Fundamentally, the capital investment issues involved in the staging of development projects are those relating to their economic and financial feasibility. The terms are often felt to be interchangeable, but strictly speaking the concept of economic feasibility deals in the broadest way with judging the practicability of a project in relation to the total increase in real goods and services that the project will afford the community. Financial feasibility judgments relate to the community's capacity for repayment of the capital costs and other charges for the project in money terms over a set period of time.

The financial feasibility of the project can be viewed in a number of ways. Basically, there is a dichotomy of thought in financial feasibility analysis. On the one hand, there are specialists who advocate that public projects should be self-liquidating in a commercial manner. There are also those who hold that the prices for the products and services of public projects should be held low, possibly subsidized, so that a demand for the outputs would be stimulated, increased productive activity would be generated in an interdependent way, and with increasing levels of productive activity in the economy the costs of the development project could be recouped by general taxation. In the strictest sense, the revenue from public projects can be thought of as a particular form of taxation (United Nations, 1951).

Without debating the merits of either policy, it is clear that it is necessary to take an overall view of the economy and make as comprehensive an analysis as is possible where major investment decisions are concerned. Unless the important industries and their water demands are seen in relation to available water supplies, policy measures concerning the distribution and utilization of water in the most economically desirable fashion may not be suitably formulated.

The United Nations (1958) panel of experts on river basin development stresses:

It is essential that information relevant to establishing the economic viability of a scheme should be assembled as completely as possible, but it is evident that deficiencies of data will vary considerably in different situations . . . . Each situation must be treated on its own merits. Nevertheless, if all the factors which need to be taken into account are recognized and carefully considered, it will generally be possible to arrive at a reasonably defensible decision . . . .

In general, the economist's ability to analyze the suitability and overall effects of particular investments has been to some extent limited. Business cycle theory has emerged from the fact that a smooth flow of investments in the private sector of an economy is not always maintained over the longer run, and a comprehensive economic theory for calculating the desirability of major autonomous investments in the public sector has not yet been thoroughly established.

In classical and neoclassical thought, the free and unimpeded mechanism of the market forces would lead to a maximum national income. Any normative deliberate, active policy at any level designed to influence the amount and composition of capital investment could not in the longer run raise national income, according to this school (Rosenstein-Rodan, 1955). Under such circumstances the focus of economics tended to fall on certain supply and demand relationships for particular products with *ceteris paribus* (other things being the same) conditions assumed to hold elsewhere in the economy. This type of analysis, usually termed partial equilibrium analysis, tended to become predominant and governed most capital investment decisions.

With these few remarks one can begin to see the types of policy implications that must be grappled with by economists and engineers advising in all types of resource development programs. Is the program fundamentally necessary or will the market mechanism ultimately draw the necessary capital investment into play to make the resources available? Are the prices in the market representative of truly competitive prices and will therefore the resources be allocated efficiently? Should protection or subsidy be given to some sector of the economy to strengthen it in the national (or regional) interest, or would this be inefficient? If the resource development program is deemed in the national interest, what types of investment should be made, where should they be made, and what should be their magnitude? Cases in point can include those relating to the development of railway transportation versus certain barge canal routes in Germany and the United States; the development of hydropower versus thermal power in Japan; and to come closer to our problem, the question of whether irrigation projects should be undertaken in the West or whether fertilizer plants should be expanded in the dry farming areas of the East.

These are clearly capital investment decisions and it is on this score that the liberal classical doctrine and the marginalist theory give us the least guidance at an operational level for efficiently allocating national resources on a large scale.

Within the relatively recent past, attempts have been made to establish a simplified form of general equilibrium analysis which may be more useful in determining the desirability of certain capital investments and their interrelationships with the rest of the economy. These attempts have yielded moderate success and, with improvement of both method and data, there is considerable hope that these latest methods can complement traditional benefit-cost analysis (Subcommittee on Evaluation Standards, 1958) on many points.

The newer methods of analysis, generally known as input-output or interindustry economics, and linear programming have as their basis the study of the technological relations of production. The study of these technological relations attempts to bring a greater measure of empirical analysis and inductive reasoning to economic problems (Leontief, 1951) and to indicate the necessary balance that must be maintained between the respective sectors of the economy and their resource inputs if deliveries to final demand (ultimate consumers) are to be fulfilled in required proportions.

INTERINDUSTRY ECONOMICS

Early Developments and General Background

Most major developments in economic theory have been introduced relatively quickly into the current teaching of economics, even at an elementary level. However, interindustry economics, or input-output analysis as it is more popularly known among specialists, usually receives scant treatment in introductory courses and texts. Although the literature on the subject has grown steadily, most of it is quite technical and is generally accessible only to economists who have specialized in this area of study. Unfortunately, this state of affairs has tended to limit the general understanding of the fact that such a form of analysis is available and can provide broad guidance in many economic issues if research effort is marshalled in this direction (Miernyk, 1957).

From an historical point of view, the first step toward a form of general equilibrium analysis, from which the input-output method stems, is customarily traced to the famous *Tableau Economique* of the French physiocrat Francois Quesnay. Quesnay's table was published in 1758. Later, in 1877, the French economist Leon Walras provided an abstract mathematical model based on the interdependencies of the productive sectors of the economy, but it was not until the mid-1930s that Professor W. Leontief (1936) of Harvard University developed the first applied model of this type on the basis of the empirical data available for the economy of the United States.

Research in input-output economics has grown rapidly since the 1930s and statistical analyses of interindustry relations have now been undertaken for more than fifty national economies to complement the more traditional forms of economic studies (Carter, 1966).

Fundamentally, the prime importance of input-output analysis attaches to its national (or regional) accounting scheme. The input-output method has been used for the preparation of a consistent set of national income accounts since the early 1930s in Denmark (Bjerke, 1955). The merit of such accounting was firmly established in international discourse some time ago (Barna, 1955, Parts II and III) and at the national level for the United States with the revision of the domestic income and product accounts (U.S. Department of Business Economics, 1966) on the basis of the U.S. Department of Commerce, Office of Business Economics (OBE) 1958 interindustry relations study (U.S. Department of Business Economics, 1966a).

Classical and neoclassical political economy has as its basis the idea that certain proportions between the outputs of the various branches of the economy would be maintained automatically in response to consumer demand. As has been noted the theoretical tools of marginal analysis and utility analysis were used to demonstrate the validity of the postulates (Margolis, 1955).

Although the notion of a certain "horizontal" balance in the economy is a crucial one, it is sometimes held that the question of the "vertical" relations governed by the technological conditions of production may provide a much deeper insight into the workings of the economy and offer a more satisfactory basis for policy formulations where investment decisions are concerned. At the present time, while the classical approach still has its adherents, it is generally recognized that more normative policy considerations involving systems analysis in a simplified general equilibrium setting will tend to foster a better economic growth pattern at the regional and national level. Leontief (1941) states the following:

The principal merit of the general equilibrium theory is that it enables us to take account of the highly complex network of interrelationships which transmits the impulses of any local primary change into the remotest corners of the economic system. While in the case of partial analysis, which operates simultaneously with only two or three variables, the interrelation among these few elements can often be perceived directly, such intuitive inference becomes practically impossible as soon as the number of variables increases up to four or five, not to say ten or twenty. A doubtful reader of these lines can ascertain the limitation of his own common-sense intuition by trying to hazard at least an approximate solution of a system of three simple linear equations with three variables; or, after having found the right answers mathematically, by trying to guess out intuitively what effect a change in one of the constants would have on the values of all three unknowns.

No economist would seriously deny the existence of analogous, and even much more complicated, interrelations within the actual economic system he is endeavoring to study. The critics of the theory of general interdependence seldom fail to mention that in its present state and on the basis of existing empirical information, this theory cannot possibly cope with the extreme complexity of actual economic processes. But then, instead of trying to refine the theory or to fortify the shaky base of our factual information, these critics proceed to solve, or at least interpret, the very same complicated problems, relying upon their own common-sense intuition and shopworn partial-equilibrium concepts of 'shifts,' 'elasticities' of substitution 'relations,' etc.

The problem is indeed extremely complex, but if the most powerful theoretical tools applied to the fullest amount of available factual information should prove inadequate for even an approximate solution, it is difficult to see how shrewd common-sense observations backed up by approximate short-cut methods of partial analysis could possibly achieve more significant results.

From the technical viewpoint the basis of the Leontief analytical system is the input-output table. The table is so termed since it shows the manner in which the output of each industry is distributed among other industries as inputs for further processing; it also depicts the output going into final consumption in various forms.

The normal method of preparing an input-output table is from the dollar values of all industry purchases and sales given in census or other survey data. For a particular industry, the basic assumption is that the dollar values can be taken as a quantitative measure of physical purchases in real terms and that long-run relative price changes will not grossly distort the quantitative pattern of purchases per unit of output. A further underpinning for the theoretical system lies in the condition that the technology of an industrial society changes rather gradually so that although the dollar value matrix of transactions is prepared with data from a single year, a similar pattern of transactions can be assumed to have occurred in both preceding and succeeding years. The only major difference noted is that the industry output to final consumption may have been greater or less.

Professional controversy over the theoretical points on which the Leontief system rests has been registered on a number of occasions (*Input-Output Analysis*, 1955), but empirical evidence seems to indicate that the results obtained by the input-output method are at least broadly comparable with results obtained by other less comprehensive methods of aggregate analysis that have been specifically designed for test purposes (Koopmans, 1957).

The preparation of an input-output table for use in empirical work takes place in several stages. Decisions must be made as to the ultimate size of the table and the manner in which producing industries can be "aggregated" or cumulatively added together into representative productive sectors, depending on the uses that the table will serve (Barna, 1955).

The basic business unit in an economy is the firm, and all firms producing similar goods or services are usually thought of as comprising an industry. This is a fairly elastic concept, as is the concept of a sector in which a series of industries are grouped because of certain similarities. The concept of a sector is most useful for analytical purposes and we have input-output tables comprised of aggregates such as the agricultural sector, the manufacturing sector, and the household sector, for example. The term "sector" is also used to include government operations, foreign trade, and capital formation. Frequently, all the groups which purchase products as final purchasers are aggregated together as a so-called final demand sector. Essentially, it must be realized that the practical problem confronting the input-output analyst in the preparation of a table is that of reducing the number of individual industries existing in the economy which may number several thousands, to a more manageable number.

Once the size and sectoral composition of the table is settled, the matrix of interindustry transactions in dollar values is prepared. This transactions matrix is then converted into an input coefficient table showing direct industry purchases per unit of output. The table of direct coefficients is then converted into a special "inverse matrix," known as the "Leontief inverse," which shows direct plus indirect industry purchases necessary for a unit increase in industry output to final purchasing sectors.

The application of the completed table to problems of economic analysis generally falls into three major categories. These are the analysis of the existing economic structure, the formulation of sectoral programs on the basis of present structure, and the prediction of sectoral capacity needs by projecting the requirements of the final purchasing, or demand, sector into the future.

In a review article on regional economics John R. Meyer (1963) noted that input-output techniques are naturally subject to a number of criticisms since they entail so many simplifying assumptions. However, he stresses:

The fact still remains that with all its problems and difficulties input-output does have the great advantage of being an empirically workable model that provides an organizational framework and set of consistency checks that are difficult to achieve with less formal techniques .... Finally, it must be recognized that input-output and economic base analyses, with all their shortcomings and deficiencies, are the tools almost invariably relied upon at the present time when actual empirical work in regional economics must be performed.

The Static, Open, Interindustry Model

The basic theory and underlying assumptions of interindustry analysis need not be dealt with extensively for present purposes. Formal coverage and exhaustive references are given in many of the works previously cited. A rather comprehensive coverage is given in Hadley (1962). To give the current work a self-contained character the general accounting aspects of the method and the formal mathematical model are presented.

The transition from the formal mathematical model to satisfactory empirical results is usually complicated by the so-called open aspects of the model which must be dealt with empirically by means of exogenous sectors. The typical mathematical model normally used for expository purposes tends to focus attention on the productive sectors of the economy and the general solution of the system of equations relating changes in gross output to unit changes in final demand. In this way the empirical difficulties relating to export, import, and value-added vectors are bypassed, but such omission make for a more elegant clear-cut presentation (Gale, 1960).

The basic interindustry accounting system is shown in Table 1. Quadrant I is the final demand (use) quadrant, essentially the net output of the productive system (i.e., the economy). Quadrant II is the interindustry transactions matrix which ultimately describes the technology of the economy under study. Quadrant III shows a row vector of value added (wages, salaries, and profits, etc., including taxes). Frequently the vector may be decomposed into several vectors under each of the foregoing categories. Imports are usually set out as a row vector in this quadrant but this is not mandatory—they may indeed be treated endogenously. Quadrant IV is a continuation of the row vector or vectors of the value added, associated with payments made to these categories in connection with final consumption expenditures and government purchases.

For a given time period, usually one year, the X_i are equal to the X_j. Gross national (or regional) product is simply the sum of the final demand vectors less total imports. The same figure is obtained by summing the entire value-added row vector. Thus alternately, GNP is the sum of Quadrants III and IV, less imports.

Table 1   Basic Interindustry Accounting System

		Purchasing Sectors						
		Intermediate Use	Final Use (Net Output)					Gross Output
			Investment	Consumption	Government	Exports	Total final use	Production
		Sector 1 $\cdots$ j $\cdots$ n						
	1	$X_{11} \cdots X_{1j} \cdots X_{1n}$	I_1	C_1	G_1	E_1	Y_1	X_1
	2	(Quadrant II)		(Quadrant I)				
	$\vdots$	$\vdots$ $\vdots$ $\vdots$					$\vdots$	$\vdots$
Producing sector	i	$X_{i1} \cdots X_{ij} \cdots X_{in}$	I_i	C_i	G_i	E_i	Y_i	X_i
	$\vdots$	$\vdots$ $\vdots$ $\vdots$					$\vdots$	$\vdots$
	n	$X_{n1} \cdots X_{nj} \cdots X_{nn}$	I_n	C_n	G_n	E_n	Y_n	X_n
Primary inputs (value added)		$V_1 \quad V_j \quad V_n$ (Quadrant III)	V_I	V_C	V_G	V_E	(Quadrant IV)	V
Total production		$X_1 \quad X_j \quad X_n$	I	C	G	E	Y	X

Let the matrix of interindustry transactions be represented in standard notation as

$$\begin{bmatrix} x_{11} & \cdots & x_{1j} & \cdots & x_{1n} \\ \vdots & & \vdots & & \vdots \\ x_{i1} & \cdots & x_{ij} & \cdots & x_{in} \\ \vdots & & \vdots & & \vdots \\ x_{n1} & \cdots & x_{nj} & \cdots & x_{nn} \end{bmatrix}$$

Then the direct input coefficients per dollar of output are given by

$$\frac{x_{ij}}{X_j} = a_{ij} \qquad i,j = 1 \cdots n$$

and the matrix of "technical coefficients," as these direct input values are usually termed, is of the form

$$\begin{bmatrix} a_{11}, a_{12}, \ldots, a_{1n} \\ \vdots \quad \vdots \qquad \vdots \\ a_{n1}, a_{n2}, \ldots, a_{nn} \end{bmatrix}$$

Similar coefficients can also be derived for the value-added sectors. This vector is equally important in the final analysis and use of the table, but for the moment is neglected.

The final demand and the total output vectors for the system can be shown as

$$
Y = \begin{bmatrix} y_1 \\ \vdots \\ y_i \\ \vdots \\ y_n \end{bmatrix}
\qquad
X = \begin{bmatrix} x_1 \\ \vdots \\ x_i \\ \vdots \\ x_n \end{bmatrix}
$$

Gross output minus intermediate use equals the net output of the system, or final use. In matrix notation this can be shown as

$$ X - AX = Y $$

To perform the indicated operation matrix algebra requires that the initial vector X in the expression be multiplied by the identity matrix I, defined as

$$
\begin{bmatrix}
1 & 0 & 0 & \cdots & 0 \\
0 & 1 & & & \\
\vdots & \vdots & & & \vdots \\
0 & & \cdots & & 1
\end{bmatrix}
$$

This results in

$$ IX - AX = (I - A)X = Y $$

which can be written

$$
\begin{bmatrix}
1 - a_{11}, & -a_{12}, & \ldots, & -a_{1n} \\
\vdots & \vdots & & \vdots \\
-a_{n1}, & -a_{n2}, & \ldots, & 1 - a_{nn}
\end{bmatrix}
\begin{bmatrix} x_1 \\ \vdots \\ x_i \\ \vdots \\ x_n \end{bmatrix}
=
\begin{bmatrix} y_1 \\ \vdots \\ y_i \\ \vdots \\ y_n \end{bmatrix}
$$

To be most useful we should like, however, to have the inverse of the function, with X expressed explicitly in terms of Y. We can then say, find X, given certain components for Y.

The inverse of any matrix A is defined as that matrix which when multiplied by the original matrix A will yield the identity matrix I. Thus

$$AA^{-1} = I$$

By obtaining the inverse of the matrix $(I - A)$, the general solution of the system can be given as

$$(I - A)^{-1}Y = X$$

where $(I - A)^{-1}$ is known as the "Leontief inverse" and gives the direct plus indirect requirements of each industry per dollar of output to final demand.

This can be written as

$$
\begin{bmatrix} q_{11}, q_{12}, \ldots, q_{1n} \\ \\ q_{21}, q_{22}, \ldots, q_{2n} \\ \vdots \quad \vdots \\ q_{n1}, q_{n2}, \ldots, q_{nn} \end{bmatrix}
\begin{bmatrix} y_1 \\ \vdots \\ y_i \\ \vdots \\ y_n \end{bmatrix}
=
\begin{bmatrix} x_1 \\ \vdots \\ x_i \\ \vdots \\ x_n \end{bmatrix}
$$

and is frequently written in transposed form for convenience of reading tabular data.

The similarities between a general linear programming system and the Leontief system should not be overlooked. In the solution of the "open" input-output model we are seeking a vector x to satisfy

$$(I - A)x = y$$

whereas in the linear programming system we are looking for the vector x subject to

$$Ax = b$$

INTERINDUSTRY MODELS AND REGIONAL RESOURCE ANALYSIS

Unique Aspects of the Interindustry Approach

Interindustry studies as stressed earlier can be valuable in guiding both private and public bodies in investment decisions and other matters related to resource allocation (Chenery and Clark, 1959, p. 301).

The input-output method lends itself well as an aid to the solution of numerous regional problems, and its possible value in dealing with the dynamics of river basin development has been properly emphasized.

In 1954 Professor Ciriacy-Wantrup (1954) pointed to the fact that the input-output system might be useful in promoting the type of regional accounting necessary for analyzing the effects of public investment in water resources projects. Some time later Professor William Folz (1957) noted that although no studies were on record of the interindustry method being applied to a river basin, it seemed probable that such an approach could be the most fruitful of any yet devised for determining the general pattern of growth that might be anticipated in the given region.

At the third international conference on input-output methods, academician V. S. Nemchinov (1963) of the USSR placed special emphasis on the use of interindustry models for regional resources development and allocation with particular reference to water, power, timber, and minerals. Professors Martin and Carter (1962) noted similar possibilities in their work. A. W. Wilson (1964) in a UNESCO publication emphasized further the value of inter-regional input-output analysis in water planning:

> Through an input-output matrix, the dynamic processes of change can thus be isolated, their effect on employment and income spotlighted, and their pressure on water supply determined.

As has been stressed earlier in more general context, the fundamental aspects of the role that input-output analysis can play in water resource economics relates to its accounting scheme. This scheme immediately provides a basic national, or regional, framework within which resource needs can be assessed and compared with their availability.

Having an understanding of the technology of the economy and its structure in some degree of fineness, certain realistic assumptions can be made about the prospective growth (or decline) of final demand, that is, household consumption, government purchases, capital investment, or exports. Since interindustry demands are tied, invariably, through a relatively fixed technology, to final demands, any increase or decrease in final demand governs total output. Indeed, quantitatively, the effect of a unit change in final demand can be traced through the typical interindustry table and the effects on interindustry purchases and gross output can be analyzed for any sector.

Thus as total output levels (interindustry demand plus final demand) can be estimated for any projected level of final demand, the crucial consideration is then whether any given sector or industry can meet the new level of total output that may be required of it with its existing productive facilities (i.e., capacity). The normal definition of industry capacity is the maximum output which can be achieved by an industry with its existing plant and equipment. While such estimates lack precision they are usually sufficiently meaningful for feasibility testing in interindustry models (Goldstein, Crosson, and Sonenblum,

1953). If it cannot be achieved, then the amount of expansion of its productive capacity will be indicated by subtracting its existing plant capacity from the gross output level required of it to satisfy the demands of other industries and final demand for the industry's products. This calculation then gives the capital requirements of the industry to meet the needs of the economy at a certain level of final demand. This procedure carried out successfully for all sectors, or industries, will give the total capital requirements of the economy and in the process will indicate which sectors or industries may have excess capacity and therefore may not need expansion even though an intuitive judgment may, under conditions of a growing economy, indicate that plant expansion may be in order (Leontief, 1964). Likewise, the interindustry method may thus indicate in turn the extent to which public projects should be undertaken to meet the growing demands of industry for inputs such as water and power, and so on. It is at this stage that input-output and benefit-cost analysis can merge (Ciriacy-Wantrup, 1964).

In the first place, if at the level of the national economy, no expansion of the industries that the public project is to serve is indicated for the foreseeable future, then scarce capital should not be allocated to the project at this time. If a moderate expansion of the industries is in order and indivisibilities are not present in the public project, then the staging of the project can better be estimated. If, as may be the case, indivisibilities are present then the decision to undertake this particular project at this time may be weighed against other variants at other locations, or against other technological variants.

If sufficient effective demand for the products of the public project is indicated via the anticipated expansion of the capacity of the dependent industries, then benefits may be estimated on the basis of the estimated demands in both instances. In benefit-cost terminology the direct benefits are those resulting from the immediate output of the proposed project; the secondary benefits are those which are generally conceived of as "stemming from" or "induced by" the public project.*

Within an input-output framework the satisfaction of effective demand by the industries dependent on the public project can be considered a benefit—that is, regional and national welfare are enhanced. More specifically, however, only the net benefit, or value added shown in the typical input-output flow table, can be considered for benefit-cost procedure. In input-output parlance the direct plus indirect income and employment and tax effects (value added) can be considered to be net benefits in benefit-cost terminology. By postulating unit increases in the final demand of any of the industries dependent on the public project, the new income, employment, and tax effects upon the industries directly affected and upon structurally related

* In the benefit-cost analytical framework the question of whether the "induced" effects can genuinely be termed "secondary" benefits has been a matter of open concern.

industries can be determined. These "net" effects represent the income, employment, and such effects accruing from the first and successive rounds of interindustry expenditures made to increase output to final demand by one unit. These effects are shown in a standard input-output table as being made at once in the time period under consideration. However, they usually take place in successive rounds extending over the time period. The additional expenditures made by the recipients of the income (households, etc.) in the form of new consumption expenditures are not shown in the table but can be calculated by assuming or determining in a substudy an appropriate Keynesian type consumption function and applying it to the data obtained from the table.

Essentially, the difference in the "expectations" under uncertainty forms of investment, the benefit-cost method, and input-output methods relate to the frame of reference, the view of the economy, and the assumptions regarding final demand. The benefit-cost approach assumes on a partial equilibrium basis that the output of the project and the output of the dependent industries will be absorbed regardless of other proposed projects and national or regional productive capacity in total. Input-output makes no such assumption and passes judgment on the project from a needed capacity expansion viewpoint. Occasionally, during periods of inflation, major projects which may have high benefit to cost ratios may be held up on the assumption that their undertaking may only bid resources away from other uses and further add to the inflationary conditions. With a comprehensive input-output analysis, however, a resource balance for a region, including labor, can be drawn up and selective controls used to combat inflation rather than proceeding on a broad plane to limit new capital formation in the public sector.

If new capacity is needed then the interindustry methods can determine if there is sufficient slack in the economy in the form of idle resources, labor, and such to build the capacity and use the capacity to operate the dependent industries at new levels of output to satisfy new levels of final demand. If classical full employment, competitive equilibrium conditions are assumed then the need for the input-output analysis is assumed away since no new resources can be drawn into production. Given the prevailing conditions of most advanced industrial economies, the assumption of input-output, that is, underemployment of resources, is somewhat more realistic than that of traditional benefit-cost, which does not recognize explicitly the possibility of excess capacity and lagging effective demand.

In summary, input-output takes a simplified general equilibrium view of the economy with technology and structure taken as empirically given. Interindustry demands and final demands are formally separated and a national or regional accounting procedure is set up with consistency cross-checks in the form of a chessboard-type table. If purchases and sales cannot be made to balance for a specified time period the data are suspect and continue to be suspect until the accounts do balance. Even if the structural coefficients of production as yielded by the input-output accounting procedure were not used for further analysis, the accounting procedure forces the analyst to look at the fine structure of production and allot output in a logical way. Typical benefit-cost analyses, along with most multiequational and correlation types of models, it might be added, do not provide consistency cross-checks on assembled data and tend to obscure the interindustry effects by postulating a lump sum output as satisfying a given effective demand, be it derived (interindustry) or not. Professor H. Chenery (1959) makes the point quite clearly in the following way:

The initial attempts at planning in most countries have started from a consideration of individual projects. This starting point has led to an extensive discussion of investment priorities ... which has been conducted almost exclusively in terms of partial analysis. Where it has been used, input-output analysis has usually been added later as a way of making the projects that had been selected initially by partial analysis consistent with one another.

...The formulation of a development program by starting from a study of individual projects has sometimes been called the "bottom up" approach, in contrast to the "top down" method which starts from aggregate projections and an overall analysis of economic interdependence. Inconsistencies between the two are inevitable because each takes into account some information that is ignored in the other. The final development program must reconcile the specific aspects of project analysis—scale and location of plants, effects of natural resources, etc.—with the requirements of consistency and balance that are inherent in overall programming.

In summary, for the greatest efficiency in investment planning it appears to be necessary to begin with an analysis of the structure of the economy and its expected expansion and work back to the project on an iterative basis rather than begin with the project and let the economy structure itself around it as best it can, largely under impact considerations.

Some Specific Applications

The traditional method of preparing input-output tables, as noted earlier, is by the reduction of census data to a form which can be used to represent the interindustry transactions of the various sectors of the economy and augmenting these with data obtained from substudies on final demands. The most desirable method would be basic surveys of the economy combined with census data designed specifically to meet the requirements of the input-output accounting system (Chenery and Clark, 1959). Such surveys, in many instances, may be prohibitively expensive, particularly at the regional level.

Regional input-output tables may be subject to special difficulties in their preparation, and should reflect, to the extent possible, the particular features of the region under study (Meyer, 1963 and Boudeville, 1967).

The use of national technical coefficients for regional input-output work has been discussed (Arrow and Hirsch, 1965) and while the matter is still unsettled such coefficients probably provide a reasonably good approximation to the actual structure of a regional economy where the product mix does not differ substantially from that of the nation.

After the first major effort in United States input-output work undertaken by the Bureau of Labor Statistics (BLS) with 1947 census data were completed, several regional tables were developed based in varying degrees on the BLS work and other secondary data sources pertaining to the region (Moore and Petersen, 1955).

With the completion of the BLS work and its expansion into the so-called Emergency Model (E-M)* intensive interindustry analysis work at the national level in the United States was largely suspended until the development of the Office of Business Economics study (OBE) for 1958 (see "Transaction Table," 1965). With the release of this work considerable impetus appears to have been given to regional studies as a recent survey has shown (Bourque and Hansen, 1967). A national study by OBE† was released late in 1969 which adds considerably to the detail regarding the structure of individual sectors of the economy.

The most useful concept for regional economic studies is that of defining the programming region for the particular objectives of the study. Frequently, as is the case for river basins, geographic, administrative, and political boundaries may not coincide. The concept requires that practical objectives be defined and jurisdictions be established for carrying forward the necessary policy decisions to reach the desired objectives in the most efficient manner.

As Boudeville (1967, p. 75) has further pointed out:

A prerequisite, however, is the preparation of simple and pragmatic models free from excessive academic refinement, that will appeal to the private business-man and to the public administrator. Such models must clearly show the practical objectives to be reached, the social and economic structure. They must distinguish also between medium-term development (four to five years) and long-term planning of natural resources (twenty years). The models, too, must be based firmly on available statistical data and on existing economic tools, both public and private.

* The Emergency Model, based on the BLS work, was expanded or "dissaggregated" so as to show some 450 sectors of the United States economy and was intended to show the critical areas of the economy which might need additional capacity to meet the needs of a national emergency.

† This study, based on 1963 data, shows some 367 sectors of the national economy. See Input-Output Structure of the U.S. Economy: 1963 a Supplement to the Survey of Current Business, U.S. Dept. of Commerce, Washington, 1969.

Insofar as establishing regional input-output tables is concerned, professional opinion varies from the firm position that an exhaustive field survey of regional production units is necessary to obtain reliable results, to that of being cautiously optimistic that national variables applied to a region may yield sufficiently valid results to be of considerable use in planning policies. Some research remains to be done in this area of endeavor; however, a few studies are on record that show promise (Manne, 1961; Moore and Petersen, 1955; Martin and Carter, 1962; Allen and Watson, 1965).

Boudeville (1965) notes further, in line with the established positions:*

Regional accounting can be achieved through two possible methods. The first is precise, but difficult to coordinate with other regions and with the nation. It is an "upward movement" starting from the accounts of regional firms and family expenditure budgets, and ending with the regional economy as a whole. The second method has the virtue of being more coherent but can be said to be less precise. It is a "downward movement" from the national level to the region. The aggregation and equivalent transformation techniques help to make it a ready-made and useful analytical tool. Technical progress and price disparities can be introduced for a number of sectors through this method.

For some states and regions where it was felt that as high a degree of accuracy as possible might be warranted in the preparation of a regional table, proposals have been made and extensively funded for gathering data as comprehensively as possible from local enterprises. Arrow and Hirsch (1965) have commented specifically on this procedure:

Very few manufacturers of any scale keep accurate accounts in a manner which permits them to summarize readily their annual shipments by geographical destination. In addition, many types of manufacturers cannot know what the destination of their product is. For example, a peach canner who sends his shipment to a warehouse in Los Angeles cannot know whether those peaches will be consumed there, shipped to the east coast, or exported abroad. As a matter of fact, at the time the canner is making his shipment, no decision may have been reached about the final disposition.

...The data used in national tables come from the purchaser of the inputs rather than the shipper. These data are harder to come by but clearly more reliable in that they require no guessing by the respondent.

If indeed the foregoing is in order then regional surveys may not produce, with any degree of certainty, coefficients which can be compared with those derived on the basis of national averages. The entire matter still seems to be an open question and yet one which is being pressed as an aid to the solution of a range of regional problems.

In matters relating to the use of regional structural models for water

* See also Stone, 1962.

resource analyses it is clear that if data on water inputs per dollar of product output for each sector can be assembled, then considerable insight may be gained in respect to efficient patterns of water allocation and use. If water is, or may potentially become, a single scarce factor of production then value added per acre-foot of freshwater input, sector by sector, may be analyzed. Additionally, sectoral interdependencies are clearly revealed by a regional model, and a balanced allocation of available water can be envisioned to meet any feasible final bill of goods (Lofting, 1970).

In arid and semiarid regions, interregional input-output models can be developed to evaluate trade patterns and water "embodied" in product shipments. Again, an incisive view can be afforded with respect to "comparative advantage" and efficiency of water use for the regions under study (Carter and Ireri, 1970).

The examples cited deal with the traditional input-output model augmented by substudies on sectoral water intake. Equally, or in some respects, even more revealing models can be developed if similar substudies on water and waste constituent discharges can be undertaken. In such instances a spectrum of potential analyses is presented for water quality management, along with policy implications for pollution abatement at the source. Value added, net of treatment costs, to maintain effluent discharge standards may readily indicate those sectors which might be more closely scrutinized in regional water quality management programs (Martin, 1968).

In broader perspective, a regional interindustry model emphasizing major waste generating sectors can be set up, and with receiving water quality standards used to develop discharge constraints, a linear programming model can be formulated and solved for "optimal" treatment levels. Alternately, a programming model can be solved in which treatment costs are minimized to meet a given final bill of goods for the region coincident with the maintenance of water quality standards (Bargur, Lofting, and Davis, 1969).

DIRECTIONS OF FUTURE ANALYSES

In matters of waste management and the maintenance of environmental quality it is readily recognized that water analyses cannot be divorced from the total view of the environment in which solid and gaseous wastes are also considered. This was recognized by Isard and Romanoff (1967) who stated the following aims:

The input-output model . . . is being developed . . . to relate the economy of a . . . region to its environment in as complete a manner as possible. The development . . . attempts to achieve a much more complete accounting framework than is now possible. It would enable the evaluation of national and regional policies concerned with the quality of the environment as well as the state of the economy.

Ayres and Kneese make a broad plea on theoretical grounds for the development of similar regional models in which resource inputs and residual wastes will be explicitly recognized (Ayres and Kneese, 1969). Leontief (1970) also, in a path-breaking article noted the clear relationship of the environment to the economic structure. The article ends on the hopeful note that the compilation and organization of the needed quantitative information for the development of regional tables will be accelerated by systematizing the efforts of all groups, now diverse, working in the input-output field. This is necessary, but not sufficient. Particularly in the field of water analyses, as the recent discovery of mercury contamination shows, many exotics are both unknown and unsuspected. A recent editorial stresses urgent need for a national inventory of industrial wastes (Howells, 1970). The framework for undertaking the analyses is well understood and formulated. The crucial issue now is to set up national and regional data banks for meaningful comparison and standardization of water use and water pollution abatement practices.

REFERENCES

ALLEN, R. L., and D. A. WATSON (1965), *The Structure of the Oregon Economy: An Input/Output Study*, Bureau of Business and Econ. Research, Univ. of Oregon, Eugene, Oregon. Unmodified national coefficients were used for all sectors of the Oregon economy.

ARROW, K. J., and W. Z. HIRSCH (1965), *Analysis of Economic and Demographic Models and Their Usefulness for the California State Development Program*, unpublished memorandum, July 15.

AYRES, R. U., and A. V. KNEESE (1969), "Production, Consumption, and Externalities," *The American Economic Review*, Vol. LIX, No. 3, June, pp. 282–297.

BARGUR, J. S., E. M. LOFTING, and H. C. DAVIS (1969), "A Multisectoral Programming Analysis for the Management of the Waste Water Economy of the San Francisco Bay Region," Section II, Final Report, Economic Evaluation of Water Quality, Sanitary Engineering Research Laboratory, University of California, Berkeley.

BARNA, T. (1953), *The Structure and Growth of the Italian Economy*, U.S. Mutual Security Agency, Rome, Chap. 7, p. 17.

BJERKE, KJELD (1955), "Denmark," in Tibor Barna, Ed. *The Structural Interdependence of the Economy*, Wiley, New York, p. 235.

BOUDEVILLE, J. R. (1967), *Problems of Regional Planning*, Edinburgh Univ. Press, also Nourse, Hugh O. (1968), *Regional Economics*, McGraw-Hill, New York.

BOURQUE, P. J., and C. HANSEN (1967), *An Inventory of Regional Input-Output Studies in the United States*, Graduate School of Business Admn., Univ. of Wash., Seattle, Wash., August.

CARTER, ANNE P. (1966), "The Economics of Technological Change," *Scientific American*, Vol. 214, No. 4, April, p. 27. A review of some of this work is given in Tibor Barna, Ed. (1955), *The Structural Interdependence of the Economy*, Wiley, New York; and Hollis B. Chenery and Paul G. Clark (1959), *Interindustry Economics*, Wiley, New York, see also *Problems of Input-Output Tables and Analysis, Studies in Methods*, Series F, No. 14, United Nations, Dept. of Econ. and Social Affairs, New York,

1966; and C. E. Taskier (1961), *Input-Output Bibliography, 1955–1960*, (ST/STAT/7), United Nations, 1961; and *Input-Output Bibliography, 1060–1963*, (ST/STAT/ SER.M/39), United Nations, 1964.

CARTER, H. O., and D. IRERI (1970), "Linkage of California-Arizona Input-Output Models to Analyze Water Transfer Patterns," *Applications of Input-Output Analysis*, Proceedings of the Fourth International Conference on Input-Output Techniques, Geneva, January, 1968, A. P. Carter and A. Brody, Eds., North Holland Publishing Company, Amsterdam, pp. 139–167.

CHENERY, H. B., P. G. CLARK, and VERA CAO PINAIA (1953), *The Structure and Growth of the Italian Economy*, U.S. Mutual Security Agency, Rome.

CHENERY, H. B., and P. G. CLARK (1959), *Interindustry Economics*, Wiley, New York.

CIRIACY-WANTRUP, S. V. (1954), "The Role of Benefit-Cost Analysis in Public Resource Development," *Water Resources and Economic Development of the West, Rept. No. 3, Benefit-Cost Analysis*, Committee on the Econ. of Water Resources Develop. of the Western Agr. Econ. Research Council, Berkeley, Calif., p. 25.

CIRIACY-WANTRUP, S. V., in collaboration with E. M. LOFTING (1964), "Economic Analysis of Secondary Benefits in Public Water Resources Development," *Proceedings Irrigation Economics Conference*, T. W. Manning, Ed., Univ. of Alberta, Edmonton, Alberta, June.

Committee Report of the National Academy of Sciences (1966), "The Gap Between Scientific Knowledge of Optimal Methods and Their Application by Farmers, Manufacturers, and Government Officials Is Large and Widening," *Alternatives in Water Management*, National Academy of Sciences, Washington, D.C.

ENGELS, FREDERICK (1939), *Anti-Deuhring, Herr Deuhring's Revolution in Science*, Martin Lawrence, London, p. 331.

FOLZ, WILLIAM (1957), "The Economic Dynamics of River Basin Development," *Law and Contemporary Problems*, Vol. 22, No. 2, Spring, p. 211.

GALE, DAVID (1960), *The Theory of Linear Economic Models*, McGraw-Hill, New York, p. 301.

GOLDSTEIN, H., P. CROSSON, and S. SONENBLUM (1953), "The normal definition of industry capacity is the maximum output which can be achieved by an industry with its existing plant and equipment. While such estimates lack precision they are usually sufficiently meaningful for feasibility testing in interindustry models" (Goldstein, Crosson, and Sonenblum, 1953). U.S. Bureau of Mines, *Capacity Estimates for 23 E-M Industries*, Interindustry Item No. 36, pp. 4 and 5.

HADLEY, G. (1958), *Linear Programming*, Addison-Wesley, Reading, Mass., 1962 and also in Gass, S. I., *Linear Programming*, McGraw-Hill, New York.

HOWELLS, DAVID H. (1970), "Guest Editorial," *Water Resources Bulletin*, Vol. 6, No. 6, December.

Input-Output Analysis: An Appraisal, Conference on Research in Income and Wealth (1955), Vol. 18 of Studies in Income and Wealth. Princeton University Press, Princeton; see the several papers herein.

ISARD, WALTER, and ELIAHU ROMANOFF (1967), *Water Use and Water Pollution Coefficients*, Preliminary Report, Regional Science Research Institute, Cambridge, Mass.

KOOPMANS, T. J. (1957), *Three Essays on the State of Economic Science*, McGraw-Hill, New York, pp. 107–125. A rather fair appraisal of the input-output method and its possibilities.

LEONTIEF, W. W. (1970), "Environmental Repercussions and the Economic Structure: An Input-Output Approach," *Review of Economics and Statistics*, August.

LEONTIEF, W. W. (1951), "Input-Output Economics," *Scientific American*, October.

LEONTIEF, W. W. (1964), "Proposal for Better Business Forecasting," *Harvard Business Review*, November–December.

LEONTIEF, W. W. (1936), "Quantitative Input-Output Relations in the Economic System of the United States," *Review of Economics and Statistics*, Vol. 18, No. 3, August, pp. 105–125.

LEONTIEF, W. W. (1941), *The Structure of American Economy 1919–1939*, Oxford University Press, New York, pp. 33–34.

LOFTING, E. M. (1970), *An Interindustry Analysis of the California Water Economy*, Engecon Publications, Berkeley (revised).

MANNE, ALAN S. (1961), "Key Sectors of the Mexican Economy, 1960–1970," *Studies in Process Analysis: Economywide Production Capabilities*, A. S. Manne and H. M. Markowitz, Eds., Proceedings of a Conference Sponsored by the Cowles Foundation for Economic Research, Wiley, New York. Professor Manne was cautiously optimistic in applying United States national data to sectors of the Mexican economy for projection purposes

MARGOLIS, JULIUS (1955), *Benefit-Costs Analysis: Efficiency, Financial, and Economic Feasibility, and External Economies*, Water Resources and Econ. Develop. of the West, Report No. 4, Western Agr. Econ. Research Council, Pullman, Washington, June. "In the case of reclamation projects . . . discontinuity prevents the applicability of marginal analysis and of simple pricing mechanisms." In the area of resource development these postulates have been called into question.

MARTIN, W. E. (1968), *The Use and Value of Input-Output Models in the Analysis of Water Pollution Abatement*, Discussion Paper No. 68-5, Harvard Water Program, Harvard University, mimeo.

MARTIN, W. E., and H. O. CARTER (1962), *A California Interindustry Analysis Emphasizing Agriculture*, Giannini Foundation of Agr. Econ., Univ. of Calif., Berkeley, February.

MEYER, JOHN R. (1963), "Regional Economics: A Survey," *American Economic Review*, Vol. 53, No. 1, Part 1, March, pp. 35–36.

MIERNYK, WILLIAM H. (1957), *A Primer of Input-Output Economics*, Business and Econ. Educ. Series No. 2, Northeastern University, Boston. A broader coverage of input-output economics is given in a more recent publication by the same author; W. H. Mierynk (1965), *The Elements of Input-Output Analysis*, Random House, New York.

MOORE, F. T., and J. W. Petersen (1955), "Regional Analysis: An Inter-Industry Model of Utah," *Review Economics and Statistics*, November. Also Moore, F. T., and J. W. Petersen (1955), "Regional Economic Reaction Paths," *American Economic Review*, May.

NEMCHINOV, V. S. (1963), "Statistical and Mathematical Methods in Soviet Planning," *Structural Interdependence and Economic Development*, Proceedings of an International Conference on Input-Output Techniques, T. Barna, Ed., St. Martin's, p. 180.

VON PUFENDORF, SAMUEL (1729), *Of The Law of Nature and Nations*, Wilkin, Bonwicke, Birt, Ward, and Osborn, London, Book 5, Chap. I, Sec. F. pp. 460–62. The last sentence is stated by von Pufendorf to be from Sextus Emiricus, Pyrrhon. *Hypoth.* lib. i.

RICARDO, DAVID (1957), *The Principles of Political Economy and Taxation*, New York, Dutton, p. 5.

ROLL, ERIC (1956), *A History of Economic Thought*, Prentice-Hall, Englewood Cliffs, N.J.

ROSENSTEIN-RODAN, P. N. (1955), "Programming in Theory and in Italian Practice," in *Investment Criteria and Economic Growth*, Massachusetts Institute of Technology, Cambridge.

SMITH, ADAM (1937), *An Inquiry Into the Nature and Causes of the Wealth of Nations*, The Modern Library, Random House, New York, p. 28.

STONE, RICHARD (1962), *A Computable Model of Economic Growth*, Chapman and Hall, Cambridge.

Subcommittee on Evaluation Standards (1958), *Report to the Inter-Agency Committee on Water Resources: Proposed Practices for Economic Analysis of River Basin Projects*, Washington, D.C. (This Publication is generally known as the "Green Book.")

"The Transaction Table of the 1958 Input-Output Study and Revised Direct and Total Requirements Data" (1965), U.S. Department of Commerce, *Survey of Current Business*, Vol. 45, No. 9, September.

United Nations (1951), *Formulation and Economic Appraisal of Development Projects*, vol. 1, UN Dept. Econ. and Social Affairs, New York, p. 94.

United Nations (1958), *Integrated River Basin Development*, Department of Economic and Social Affairs, New York, p. 1.

U.S. Department of Commerce, Office of Business Economics (1966), *The National Income and Product Accounts of the United States, 1929–1965: Statistical Tables* (a supplement to the *Survey of Current Business*), Washington, D.C.

U.S. Department of Commerce, Office of Business Economics (1966a), *Survey of Current Business*, Washington, D.C., November 1964; September 1966.

WILSON, ANDREW W. (1964), "Economic Aspects of Decision-Making on Water Use in Semi-arid and Arid Lands," *Arid Zone Research*, UN Educ. and Sci. Comm., Vol. 26, United Nations, New York, pp. 47–50.

X System Dynamics and Control: Herman E. Koenig

The theoretical concepts in simulation, stability, control, optimization, and other basic concepts of systems science are mathematically based. They depend only on the mathematical form of the model and not the particular identification or meaning associated with the variables in the model. In view of the extensive literature on the analysis, control and optimization of dynamic processes using state-space models, the motivation is very high to structure, if possible, models of organizational, economic, and socioeconomic processes in the state-space form.

In the physical sciences, relatively well-defined procedures have been developed for structuring mathematical models in the state space. Is it possible to identify similar procedures and techniques for structuring state-space models for processes as complex as business firms, educational processes, health care systems, economic development, and other processes associated with or designed to provide for human needs and wants? If so, what are the implications, both conceptually and computationally, of the modern control theory in management and resource allocation problems?

The first part of the subsequent development deals specifically with the problems of structuring models of economic or socioeconomic processes in the state-space form.

The second part deals briefly with the use of state-space concepts in long-range planning and development, resource allocation, and management, the primary objective being to establish a tie between these concepts and the concepts of modern control theory and to show that fundamentally they are one and the same problem.

THE SYSTEM AS A SET OF INPUT-OUTPUT RELATIONS

Perhaps the most abstract concept of a system S_i is a set of input-output relations. For the sake of definiteness and without excessive loss of generality we assume that these relationships are presentable as a set of state equations of the form

$$\dot{\psi}_i = F_i(\psi_i, E_i, t) \tag{1}$$
$$R_i = G_i(\psi_i, E_i, t)$$

where vectors E_i and R_i, each of order n_i, represent, respectively, the independent (input) and dependent (output) variables of the system. The components of the vector ψ_i, of arbitrary order, represent the "internal states" of the system, and F_i and G_i are vector functions of the vectors ψ_i and E_i, and the scalar t (time). Note that there is no loss in generality in taking E_i and R_i of equal order if it is understood that some of the components can be identically zero. Also, in the special case where the order ψ_i is zero the input-output relations reduce to algebraic form.

In concept, the components of the "input" vector E_i and "output" vector R_i are said to "isolate" the system S_i from its environment, that is, all interactions with the environment are said to be reflected through these variables. In general, it is up to the systems analysts to define operationally the components of E_i, R_i, and ψ_i and to establish, through controlled experiment or correlation analysis of historical data taken under uncontrolled conditions, the vector functions F_i and G_i. At this point in the development we place no other restriction whatsoever on the variables included in these vectors. However, in the interest of the subsequent development, it is convenient to subdivide the components of R_i and E_i into at least two arbitrary types, say x and y, so that the $2n_i$ components of the direct sum* of R_i and E_i can be rearranged in the form

$$[R_i, E_i] = [x_1, x_2, \ldots, x_{n_i}, y_1, y_2, \ldots, y_{n_i}]$$

where it is understood that the n_i components of R_i may be any combination of the two types, and similarly for E_i. If the two types of variables identified by the subdivision are voltages and currents, the system S_i is identified as electrical in nature; if they are velocities and forces, the system S_i is mechanical in nature; if they are prices and flow rates of real goods and services the system is economic in nature.

INTERCONNECTED SYSTEMS

If we had to be content with the concept of a system as a set of input-output relations and were forced always to develop these relations from controlled experiments or historical data, then system theory would be very limited

---

* The components of R_i and E_i taken collectively.

indeed. One of the real values of system theory derives from the fact that it is possible to view a system as a set of interconnected subsystems of lesser complexity. Furthermore, if properly selected and structured, the subsystems of one interconnected system can serve as "building blocks" in modelling other systems. It is through this mechanism that modeling efforts are accumulative—the results of one study carry over to the next study.

But what is the nature of this "building block" approach? Does it place restrictions on how the input-output variables of the subsystems are defined? How is the model of the overall system constructed from the models of the building blocks?

To view this problem in its general context, consider a set of N systems S_i, $i = 1, 2, \ldots, N$ each of the form given in (1). Let the direct sum of the models of this set of N systems* be written as

$$\dot{\psi} = F(\psi, E, t)$$

$$R = G(\psi, E, t)$$

where the vectors E and R represent the direct sum of the components in E_i and R_i, $i = 1, 2, \ldots, N$, and each is of order $e = (n_1 + n_2, \ldots, n_N)$. Let their collective components be rearranged to form two vectors X and Y each of order e, that is, let

$$X = [x_1, x_2, \ldots, x_e], \qquad Y = [y_1, y_2, \ldots, y_e]$$

where the vector $[X, Y]$ represents a rearrangement of the vector $[R, E]$.

The analyst must provide e independent constraints on the $2e$ components of the vector $[R, E] \approx [X, Y]$ to establish a model of the interconnected system. These constraints are as much a part of the problem of specifying the system as is the problem of specifying the models of the subsystems. If the components of R and E are really of two types, such as velocity and force, voltage and current, or price and flow rates of goods or services, and if the constraints represent sums and differences among the variables of each of the two types, then the most general form of the e constraints is

$$\begin{matrix} & \overset{e}{} & \overset{e}{} \\ k & \\ e-k & \end{matrix} \begin{bmatrix} A & 0 \\ 0 & B \end{bmatrix} \begin{bmatrix} Y \\ X \end{bmatrix} = 0 \qquad (2)$$

where, in general, A is a matrix of maximum rank and of order kxe, $k \le e$ and B is of maximum rank and order $(e - k)xe$. The analyst now has a choice to work within one of two modeling frameworks: (*a*) he can provide the e constraints indicated in (2) in any way whatsoever that appears to be consistent and correct within the context of his particular application, or (*b*) he

---

* The models of the N subsystems taken collectively.

may require that the variables used to model the subsystem and the e constraints applied to them shall be such that the closed system is conservative in the sense that

$$X^T Y = Y^T X = 0 \qquad (3)$$

When the components of the vectors X and Y represent, respectively, the voltages and currents in an electrical network or the velocities and forces in a mechanical system, the constraints in (3) imply conservation of energy within the entire system—a property fundamental to the physical sciences. When the vectors X and Y represent unit prices and the flow rate of goods and services as in an economic process, the constraints in (3) imply a balance of payments in the system—a property fundamental to economics.

The conservative property in (3) places very specific restrictions on the constraints given in (2). Indeed since A is of rank k, there exists a rearrangement and a partitioning of A such that

$$k[A_1 \quad A_2] \begin{bmatrix} Y_1 \\ Y_2 \end{bmatrix} = 0 \qquad \qquad (4)$$

where the columns are labeled k and $e - k$.

where A_1 is nonsingular and of order k as indicated. From (4) it follows that

$$\begin{bmatrix} Y_1 \\ Y_2 \end{bmatrix} = \begin{bmatrix} -A_1^{-1}A_2 \\ U \end{bmatrix} Y_2 \qquad (5)$$

Likewise, since B is of rank $e - k$, there exists a rearrangement of B such that

$$e - k[B_1 \quad B_2] \begin{bmatrix} X_1 \\ X_2 \end{bmatrix} = 0 \qquad (6)$$

where the columns are labeled k and $e - k$.

where B_2 is nonsingular and of order $(e - k)$ as indicated. From (6) it follows that

$$\begin{bmatrix} X_1 \\ X_2 \end{bmatrix} = \begin{bmatrix} U \\ -B_2^{-1}B_1 \end{bmatrix} \qquad (7)$$

Upon substituting (5) and (7) into (3) it follows that the system is conservative if the coefficient matrices in the constraint equations are such that

$$A_1^{-1}A_2 = -(B_2^{-1}B_1)^T \qquad (8)$$

Thus if the systems analyst can be sure that the constraints he imposes on prices and the constraints he imposes on the flow rate of goods and services satisfy (8), he is assured that the model he develops is at least consistent to the extent that there is a balance of payments.

Network theoretic concepts developed for the analysis and design of electrical networks provide procedures for identifying constraints on the voltages and currents in the system that are consistent with (8) (Seshu and Reid, 1961). Within the past decade formal application of these procedures have been extended to mechanical, hydraulic, and other types of physical processes (Koenig, Tokad, and Kesavan, 1967; Shearer, Murphy, and Richardson, 1967; Martens and Allen, 1969). Can these same concepts be applied effectively in structuring models of economic processes? If so, how are they applied and what are their limitations? The answer to this question is perhaps best answered by considering an illustrative example.

AN ILLUSTRATIVE EXAMPLE

Consider an economy in which each of three industrial sectors produce one good from possibly four raw materials as indicated schematically in Figure 1.

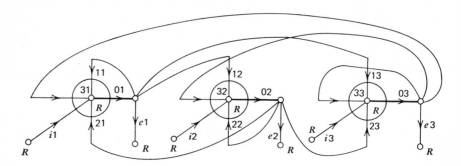

Fig. 1.   A simple three-industry economy.

For a completely general topology, it is assumed that there is a flow rate y_{1j} of goods from the output of industry j to the input of each of the industries as indicated. If a given industry uses none of their own products then, of course, $y_{1j} = 0$ for $j = l$. For complete generality, each industrial output flow is shown to feed into an *external* market $e1$, $e2$, $e3$ as indicated, and each industry is shown to require a flow rate of *imported* raw material y_{ij}.

Industry 1 may be regarded as the aggregate of all nondurable goods industries, industry 2 as the durable goods industry, and industry 3 as the population sector. Other interpretations, of course, are possible, and the indicated structure obviously can be extended to a system of N interconnected industries.

Note that the edges in the system graph are conceptualized as representing the flow of goods between the identified industries (the subsystems of the total system). With each flow identified by the edges in the graph we also associate a price x_{ij}.

Static Model

Consider first, the case where each of the production sectors is modeled in the simple linear form

$$
\begin{bmatrix} y_{1j} \\ y_{2j} \\ y_{3j} \\ y_{ij} \\ \hline x_{0j} \end{bmatrix} = \begin{bmatrix} & & & & k_{1j} \\ & & & & k_{2j} \\ & & & & k_{3j} \\ & & & & k_{ij} \\ \hline -k_{1j} & -k_{2j} & -k_{3j} & -k_{ij} & 0 \end{bmatrix} \begin{bmatrix} x_{1j} \\ x_{2j} \\ x_{3j} \\ x_{ij} \\ \hline y_{0j} \end{bmatrix} \qquad j = 1, 2, 3 \quad (10)
$$

where k_{lj}, $l = 1, 2, 3, i$, are called the production coefficients of industry j. Observe that the "inputed" price of the goods produced x_{0j} is negative if the prices of the raw materials x_{kj}, $k = 1, 2, 3$, are positive. This convention provides an automatic accounting procedure. Indeed, since the coefficient matrix in (10) is shew symmetric, the scale product of the dependent and independent vectors in (10) vanishes, that is,

$$ y_{1j}x_{1j} + y_{2j}x_{2j} + \cdots + x_{0j}y_{0j} = 0 $$

Thus the production model for each sector is structured so that the total expenditure for raw materials is equal to the value of the products produced. Actually, the last expression in (10) is the operational definition for the inputed price of the output.

Edges $e1$, $e2$, and $e3$ in the system graph each correspond to an export market. It is assumed that these sectors have known demands y_{e1}, y_{e2}, and y_{e3}. In a similar manner, edges $i1$, $i2$, and $i3$ correspond to import sectors for which the prices x_{i1}, x_{i2}, and x_{i3} are considered known.

Applying the same postulates and terminology used in the analysis of electrical networks, three independent constraints on the flow rates of goods are identifiable as cut-set equations

$$
\begin{aligned}
y_{01} &= y_{11} + y_{21} + y_{31} + y_{e1} \\
y_{02} &= y_{12} + y_{22} + y_{32} + y_{e2} \\
y_{03} &= y_{13} + y_{23} + y_{33} + y_{e3}
\end{aligned}
\qquad (11)
$$

If the vertices identified as R (reference) are considered as a common vertex, three independent constraints on the prices are identifiable as the circuit equations for the system graph.

$$x_{e1} = -x_{01}, x_{e2} = -x_{02}, x_{e3} = -x_{03} \tag{12}$$

Note that a reference vertex is associated with each of the identified subsystems—the three industries, the three markets, and the three imports.

Substituting the first four expressions in the component models for the three industries given in (10) into (11) gives

$$
\begin{bmatrix} y_{e1} \\ y_{e2} \\ y_{e3} \end{bmatrix} = \begin{bmatrix} 1 - k_{11} & -k_{12} & -k_{13} \\ -k_{21} & 1 - k_{22} & -k_{23} \\ -k_{31} & -k_{32} & 1 - k_{33} \end{bmatrix} \begin{bmatrix} y_{01} \\ y_{02} \\ y_{03} \end{bmatrix} \tag{13}
$$

or symbolically

$$Y_e = (U - K)Y_o \tag{13b}$$

where Y_e and Y_o are the vectors of exports and industrial outputs, respectively; U is the unit matrix and $K = [k_{lj}]$, $l, j = 1, 2, 3$ is the matrix of production coefficients.

Substituting the constraints in (12) into the last expression in the component models in (10) gives

$$
\begin{bmatrix} 1 - k_{11} & -k_{21} & -k_{31} \\ -k_{12} & 1 - k_{22} & -k_{32} \\ -k_{13} & -k_{23} & 1 - k_{33} \end{bmatrix} \begin{bmatrix} x_{e1} \\ x_{e2} \\ x_{e3} \end{bmatrix} = \begin{bmatrix} k_{i1}x_{i1} \\ k_{i2}x_{i2} \\ k_{i3}x_{i3} \end{bmatrix} \tag{14a}
$$

or symbolically

$$(U - K)^T X_e = K_i X_i \tag{14b}$$

where X_i is the vector of import prices; K_i is a diagonal matrix of import production coefficients k_{ij}, $j = 1, 2, 3$.

The flow rate of imports as obtained from the component models in (10) are

$$
Y_i = \begin{bmatrix} y_{i1} \\ y_{i2} \\ y_{i3} \end{bmatrix} = \begin{bmatrix} k_{i1} & 0 & 0 \\ 0 & k_{i2} & 0 \\ 0 & 0 & k_{i3} \end{bmatrix} \begin{bmatrix} y_{01} \\ y_{02} \\ y_{03} \end{bmatrix} \tag{15a}
$$

or symbolically

$$Y_i = K_i Y_o \tag{15b}$$

If $(U - K)$ is nonsingular, then the system has a complete solution.

Industrial output $Y_o = (U - K)^{-1}Y_e \tag{16}$

Export prices $X_e = (U - K^T)^{-1}K_i X_i \tag{17}$

Import flows $Y_i = (U - K)^{-1}Y_e \tag{18}$

Comment: The results above, of course, present nothing new insofar as economic theory is concerned—they are consistent with the foundations for the classical input-output analysis developed by Walras, Leontief, and Allen (1959). Indeed, the production coefficients in the matrices K and K_i are obtained from input-output tables of national accounts. The primary purpose of the example here is to demonstrate the consistency of the network theoretic concepts developed in the physical sciences with classical economic theory.

It should also be pointed out that the structure of the system in this example is very simple in comparison to the structure of most physical systems— simple in the sense that the graph and constraint equations have a repeating pattern that can be easily visualized and described without drawing out the graph explicitly.

It is also evident that there is relatively little difficulty in generating constraints on the prices that are consistent with the conservative property in (2), that is, we do not necessarily need the formalism of the system graph to identify price constraints that are consistent with the flow constraints in the sense of (8).

It is obvious that linear static models in (1) are too simple to represent reality; and this is fully recognized by economists. Except for the very real problems of evaluating the parameters, there is no theoretical reason, of course, why the subsystem models cannot be adjusted to be more realistic. One significant step in this direction is to account for capital investment (in the form of goods and services) required to increase production. For monotonically increasing sector outputs, a linear approximation to this added dimension of the problem is included when the sector models are taken as

$$
\begin{bmatrix} y_{1j} \\ y_{2j} \\ y_{3j} \\ y_{ij} \\ \hline x_{0j} \end{bmatrix} =
\begin{bmatrix} & & & & \vdots & k_{1j} \\ & & & & \vdots & k_{2j} \\ & & & & \vdots & k_{3j} \\ & & & & \vdots & k_{ij} \\ \hline -k_{1j} & -k_{2j} & -k_{3j} & -k_{ij} & \vdots & 0 \end{bmatrix}
\begin{bmatrix} x_{1j} \\ x_{2j} \\ x_{3j} \\ x_{ij} \\ \hline y_{0j} \end{bmatrix}
$$

$$
+ \begin{bmatrix} & & & & s_{1j} \\ & & & & s_{2j} \\ & & & & s_{3j} \\ & & & & s_{ij} \\ -s_{1j} & -s_{2j} & -s_{3j} & -s_{ij} & 0 \end{bmatrix} \frac{d}{dt}
\begin{bmatrix} x_{1j} \\ x_{2j} \\ x_{3j} \\ x_{ij} \\ y_{0j} \end{bmatrix} \qquad j = 1, 2, 3 \quad (19)
$$

The second term in this expression assumes that the rate of flow of goods and services is directly proportional to the rate of expansion and that the imputed price x_{0j} of the product is proportional to the rates of change of the resource prices.

Applying the constraint equations of the graph given in (11) and (12) the state equations of the system are obtained as

$$\frac{d}{dt} Y_o = S^{-1}(U - K)Y_o - S^{-1}Y_e \tag{20}$$

and

$$\frac{d}{dt} X_o = (S^T)^{-1}(U - K^T)X_e + (S^T)^{-1}K_i X_i + (S^T)^{-1}S_i \frac{d}{dt} X_i \tag{21}$$

where the components of the vector Y_o and Y_e represents the sector outputs and exports, respectively, and $S = [s_{lj}]$, $l, j = 1, 2, 3$, is a square matrix representing the capital expansion coefficients in (19). The components of the vectors X_e and X_i represent the imputed export prices and the import prices, respectively, and S_i is a diagonal matrix with entry s_{ij}, $j = 1, 2, 3$. The coefficient matrices K and K_i are as defined in the previous development.

Note that the output flow rates Y_o and output prices X_o represent the states of the system—they determine future values, and all other variables in the system are expressible as a function of them. The "response" variables of particular interest are the import flow rates Y_i and the export prices X_e.

$$Y_i = K_i Y_o + S_i \frac{d}{dt} Y_o$$

$$= [K_i + S_i S^{-1}(U - K) - S_i S^{-1}]Y_o \tag{22}$$

$$X_e = X_o \tag{23}$$

Comment: The system model consisting of the state equations in (20) and (21) and the response equations (22) and (23) are of the standard linear form

$$\dot{\psi} = P\psi + QE$$
$$R = M\psi + NE \tag{24}$$

and, of course, form the basis for any number of analyses of the system.

Note that the states of the system fall into two mutually independent subsets (flow rates Y_o and prices X_e), since the sector models assumed that prices and flows are mutually independent. These two classes of variables become interdependent when in (19) the resource flows y_{1j}, $j, l = 1, 2, 3$, are functions of the prices x_{1j}, $j, l = 1, 2, 3$. The problems, however, of establishing these relationships are another matter!

In this particular example, there is no great difficulty in reducing the constraint equations and component models to state-space form. However, for more complex structures this reduction is by no means trivial. For linear systems, necessary conditions have been established on the structure of the system (its topology and component models) under which a state model of the form given in (24) exists for the interconnected system, given a set of component models of the same general form (Koenig, Tokad, and Kesavan, 1967). Systematic operational procedures are also given for realizing the state model when such a model does, in fact, exist.

The basic concepts demonstrated in the example above have been used effectively to structure a state-space model for management, planning, and resource allocation in institutions of higher education (Koenig, Keeney, and Zemach, 1968; Koenig, 1969). An example of their application in the agricultural industry can be found in Koenig, Hilmerson, and Yuan, 1969.

What then can be said about the applications and value of the modeling theories developed in the physical sciences to socioeconomic processes? If we accept the concept of economics implicit in the opening sentence of Allen's book (1959)—"economics is concerned with quantities of goods or factors and their prices"—then it can be said first of all that economic processes are conservative in the same sense that electrical, mechanical, thermal, and other physical processes are conservative. As such, these interconnected systems fall within the general framework of generalized network theoretic concepts. However, it can also be said that the structures of physical systems and economic systems tend to be complex in quite different respects. Electrical networks, for example, typically contain a very large number of very simple components interconnected in rather arbitrary patterns. These applications therefore give strong motivation to graph theoretic concepts as operational tools for identifying independent constraint equations and for structuring state-space models of interconnected systems. Since the building blocks are relatively simple and since they are taken from a relatively small set of well-defined types, identification theory as such tends to fade into the background.

In contrast, the structure of economic systems typically contains relatively complex subsystems (sectors) connected in relatively simple or regular patterns. Furthermore, few, if any, of the component models can be determined from data taken under controlled conditions. Consequently, identification-theoretic concepts such as correlation analysis, statistical variance, and other concepts of econometrics are of primary concern, while graph theoretic concepts fade into the background. It can be said, therefore, that the theoretical concepts and techniques developed in engineering and in economics are complimentary—they are both concerned with the same basic spectrum of concepts and techniques but each emphasizes a different region of the spectrum.

MANAGEMENT AND LONG-RANGE PLANNING

To show how modern control concepts relate to the problems of management and long-range planning it is convenient to consider the discrete-time model with the variables identified as follows:

$$
\begin{array}{c}
\text{system states} \\
\left|\quad \text{parameters} \right. \\
\left|\quad \left|\quad \text{exogenous variables} \right. \right. \\
\left|\quad \left|\quad \left|\quad \text{control inputs} \right. \right. \right. \\
\left|\quad \left|\quad \left|\quad \left|\right. \right. \right. \right.
\end{array}
$$

$$\psi(t + 1) = F[\psi(t), \alpha(t), \beta(t), E(t)] \tag{25}$$

$$R(t) = G[\psi(t), \alpha(t), \beta(t), E(t)] \tag{26}$$

response
variables

where $\psi(t)$, $R(t)$, $\beta(t)$, $E(t)$, and $\alpha(t)$ are finite vectors; $\psi(t)$ and $\psi(t + 1)$ represent the internal state of the system at times t and $(t + 1)$, respectively; and $R(t)$ represents the output or response of the system to its state, parameters, and inputs. In general the components parameter vector $\alpha(t)$ represents the allocation policies and production coefficient of the sectors identified in the system structure. They are assumed to be variable over some space A.

The components of the exogenous variable vector $\beta(t)$ represent the time-varying uncontrollable inputs or influences of the environment on the system under management or control. They may be stochastic or deterministic in nature.

In the case of the educational system discussed in Koenig, Keeney, and Zemach (1968) and Koenig (1969) the components of the state vector $\psi(t)$ represent the number of students in various areas and levels of education at a particular point in time and the corresponding accumulated cost of education to that point in time. In the case of the poultry production example given in Koenig, Hilmerson, and Yuan (1969) the components of the state vector represent the number of units in the various stages of production at time t and their associated cost of development to that point. Thus the components of the state vector typically have a very significant and direct association with the process.

The solution over time of the state model, for any admissible set of time variations in parameters, exogenous variables, or control inputs, establishes the time variation in the system states and responses. Such solutions are usually carried out on a computing machine and, of course, give the analyst an opportunity to experiment with selected changes in parameters, exogenous variables, and control inputs. Such solutions are referred to as *simulations*.

The system control problem, in its most general context, is for some well-defined goal, determined, within the set of all admissible parameters and control inputs, the time sequence of parameters, and/or controls required to achieve this goal in an optimum manner. The expression showing these required inputs as an explicit function of the state of the system is referred to as a *control strategy* or *control policy*.

Note the significance of the fact that the policy parameters and controls are known as an explicit function of the state of the system. This implies that the optimal set of production policies and controls can be reevaluated periodically by simply observing the current state of the system, that is, the optimal control policy depends on the *present state of the system*. It is fixed only when the system is not changing.

The system in equations (25) and (26) is said to be *state controllable* if there exist vector **E** which will transfer any given state Ψ_1 to a preassigned future state Ψ_2 in a finite number of time intervals. It is said to be *output* controllable if any given output vector $\mathbf{R}_1$ can be transferred to a preassigned future value $\mathbf{R}_2$ in a finite number of time intervals. It is easy to establish that state controllability implies output controllability but not vice versa. Indeed, the output vector may contain fewer components than the state vector.

To demonstrate this important concept more clearly consider a linear time-invariant system.

$$\psi(t) = A\psi(t-1) + BE(t) \tag{27}$$

$$\mathbf{R}(t) = C\psi(t) \tag{28}$$

Applying this equation recursively for k intervals of time beginning at $t = t_1$ gives

$$\psi(t_1 + k) = A_k\psi(t_1) + [A^{k-1}B \cdots AB/B] \begin{bmatrix} E(t_1) \\ E(t_1 + 1) \\ \vdots \\ E(t_1 + k - 1) \end{bmatrix} \tag{29}$$

If the matrix $\phi = [A^{k-1}B \cdots AB/B]$ is square and nonsingular, then for given values of $\psi(t_1 + k)$ and $\psi(t_1)$, (29) has a solution for the control vector

$$\mathbf{E}_k = [E(t_1)/E(t_1 + 1) \cdots E(t_1 + k - 1)]^T \tag{30}$$

If the solution exists, the system is said to be output controllable with the control law or control strategy given as a function of the state vector by

$$\mathbf{R}_k = \phi^{-1}[\psi(t_1 + k) - A^k\psi(t_1)] \tag{31}$$

Note that $A^k\psi(t)$ represents the solution to (27) after k intervals when

$E(t) = 0$. Consequently, the bracketed term in (31) represents the difference between the desired future state and the state that would be obtained in the absence of control, that is, it represents the free system *error* state.

In the special case where $E(t)$ is of order one (B is a column vector) and the vector ψ identifies k internal states, ϕ is a square matrix of order k. The columns of this matrix may be linearly independent, depending on the properties of the matrices $A^j, j = 0, \ldots, k - 1$. However, even if a solution does exist, the resulting scalar inputs $e(t_1), e(t_1 + 1), \ldots, e(t_1 + k - 1)$ required for control may not be feasible. Indeed, some may be negative.

The problem of determining the parameter vector $\alpha(t)$ required to transfer the system from one state to another is somewhat more complex, since the state equations are almost always a nonlinear function of the components of $\alpha(t)$.

In any application of practical interest there are invariably bounds on the values that the components of the control and parameter vectors can assume as imposed by the availability of funds or the admissible production functions.

Within the context of these very real constraints one can only search for the time sequence of parameter $\alpha(t)$ and controls $R(t)$ that will take the system to a prescribed state in a given time period. These control problems fall within a class of optimal control problems realized by first defining a scalar *object* function of the state vector, the control vector and the parameter vector of the general form

$$J = G[R(t_1 + k)] + \sum_{t_i}^{t_1 + k} H[\beta(t), \alpha(t), \beta(t), t] \qquad (32)$$

The optimal control problem can now be stated as: minimize J subject to the constraints that $R(t)$ satisfies (27) and (28) and that $\beta(t)$ and $\alpha(t)$ are within the admissible sets.

Since the components of the output vector $R(t)$ and control vector $E(t)$ span all flow streams in and out of the system and their associated prices, the object function J in (32) can be defined so as to represent the total cost of operation, the total cost of control, or a weighted combination of these cost functions as evaluated over the k time periods of control.

CONCLUSION

This chapter has emphasized the use of state space models in the management and planning for economic and socioeconomic processes. It should be recognized, however, that insofar as pragmatic results are concerned, computer simulations of economic processes, rather than application of control and optimization theory, are likely to be the most productive in the immediate future. This statement has its origin in three major considerations: (*a*) models of many economic processes (Manetsch, 1966, 1967) are very difficult to reduce to state-space form—the form required for formal application of modern control theory; (*b*) even in situations where state-space forms can be realized, the order of the system frequently precludes the application of many of the formal analytical methods; (*c*) the demand that the objective of control or optimization be articulated as an object function unduly restricts the power and utility of models.

This is not to imply, however, that the theoretical concepts involved in structuring state-space models and deriving optimal control policies have no contribution to make. Even though one may not formally structure a state model, the implications that such a model exists and that any given computer simulation program can be reduced to that form contribute in a very real way to conceptual understanding of the problem. Furthermore, it should be evident that an understanding of control theoretic concepts gives clear definition to the management and planning problem even though the numerical computations as such may never be carried out.

REFERENCES

ALLEN, R. G. D. (1959), *Mathematical Economics*, MacMillan, New York.

KOENIG, H. E. (1969), "A Systems Model for Management, Planning and Resource Allocation in Institutions of Higher Education," *Journal for Engineering Education*, March.

KOENIG, H. E., A. M. HILMERSON, and L. YUAN (1969), "System Theory in the Agricultural Industry," *Transactions of The American Society of Agricultural Engineering*.

KOENIG, H. E., M. G. KEENEY, and R. ZEMACH (1968), "A Systems Model for Management, Planning, and Resource Allocation in Institutions of Higher Education," Final Report Project C-518, Division of Engineering Research, Michigan State University.

KOENIG, H. E., Y. TOKAD, and H. K. KESAVAN (1967), *Analysis of Discrete Physical Systems*, McGraw-Hill, New York.

MANETSCH, T. J. (1966), "Transfer Function Representation of a Class of Economic Processes," *IEEE Transactions on Automatic Control*, October.

MANETSCH, T. J. (1967), "The U.S. Plywood Industry—A Systems Study," *IEEE Transactions on Systems Science and Cybernetics*, November.

MARTENS, HENRICH R., and DON R. ALLEN (1969), *Introduction to Systems Theory*, Merrill, Columbus, Ohio.

SESHU, S. and M. B. REID (1961), *Linear Graphs and Electrical Networks*, Addison-Wesley, Reading, Mass.

SHEARER, J. LOWEN, A. T. MURPHY, and H. H. RICHARDSON (1967), *Introduction to System Dynamics*, Addison-Wesley, Reading, Mass.

XI

The Costs of High Speed Ground Transportation: George A. Hoffman

This chapter examines some engineering features and forecasts cost estimates of an interurban high-speed ground transportation system with speeds of travel exceeding 200 miles per hour (mph). The principal parameters are the train propulsion power expended for travel in tunnels, vehicle suspension power, vehicle acquisition costs, the construction costs of the facilities, and other system operating costs.

These factors were summed in a model of the yearly commitments required for providing high-speed surface transportation between Washington, New York, and Boston. The study indicated the most economic travel to be with speeds of 230 to 270 mph and at a cost of 3.5 to 4.5¢/passenger-mile. The model yielded the least-cost enclosure to be about 20 ft in diameter, and the evacuated tunnel was discussed as a desirable innovation in transportation technology.

This analysis of a system engineered for societal betterment is an example of the preliminary technoeconomic definition of complex systems that should precede the planning phase. When conceptualizing a new ground transportation network, the factors to be studied at this preplanning stage must span from consideration of rapidly advancing vehicle technologies to anticipation of the economic impact and social effects from the improved intercity personal mobility.

ALTERNATIVE SYSTEMS

Some alternate technologies of high-speed ground transportation (HSGT), and their costs, as instances of conceptual-stage analytical methods are examined. However, why look at HSGT, rather than, for instance, VTOL systems of comparable intercity capability? The reason is that whenever radically different systems (e.g., air vs. ground transport) for achieving similar socioeconomic tasks are conceived, parametric models of each concept are convenient for deciding between the candidates or for proportioning the mixes of competing system sizes. Thus HSGT models (the one reported here

272

dating back to 1966) have been developed to compare these trains with their competing systems of future air short-haul travel.

The critical trends in these studies are that passenger traffic between cities grows continuously in volume and is handled by the increasing speeds of travel and the demands for reducing delay times. Advancing vehicle technologies (see "Special Issue on Transportation," 1968) in automobile, bus, train, ship, and aircraft travel have shortened the transportation time between population centers throughout the world. This speed-up trend, ongoing now for two centuries, is apparently still beneficial to society, although questions are being raised as to the future point at which its detrimental effects in human disadaptation begin growing at a more rapid rate than the benefits. There are presently also biological adaptation limits on the speed of man-guided vehicles (e.g., motorbikes, automobiles, and buses) and cost/reliability bounds will emerge on the electronic intricacy of external guidance and control of vehicles on automated highways. These limitations seemed to exclude untracked vehicles from above the 200 mph regime in this study. Beyond 200 mph, it was decided to consider *tracked* and speed-unlimited transportation vehicles, coupled to and controlled by fixed guideways, rails, or tubes. The HSGT trains were intended for the short-range closely spaced cities exemplified by the Eastern United States, although at a higher level of planning, tracked vehicles should be viewed as adjuncts to the S/TOLs or V/TOLs (Kirchner, 1967; Pickerell, 1968) that will carry an increasing share of megalopolitan travel.

It is foreseeable that mostly people and little freight will be carried in these HSGT tracked vehicles. The concern of the United States in the first half of this century was manufacturing and product-consumption. This was evident in the GNP being composed of over two-thirds consumable products, and in over two-thirds of our train vehicles then carrying freight and goods. Now our society has changed to a service-consumptive one with emphasis on services; thus it is apparent that HSGT trains will carry mostly passengers. In the following generations of HSGT, we might perhaps even find passengers wanting to bring along their means of individual mobility—their automobile.

A first conclusion about the future movement of passengers in extended urban complexes and corridors was that fast train-like vehicles on fixed guideways were to be the base for a cost model of HSGT. Second, if trains are to remain competitive with aircraft in passenger services, their speeds should be in the 200 to 300 mph regime, that is, twice that of the fastest rail-cars (see *Proceedings of the 1969 Conference on High Speed Ground Transportation, 1969*) in scheduled operation today. Third, high speed and cost implications related thereto will be pacing items in this analysis.

The assumption of greatly increased speed of operation anticipated some characteristics of HSGT requiring parametric cost definition:

1. High propulsion power consumption at high speed. The rate of energy expended to overcome aerodynamic drag is proportional to the cube of the speed.
2. Fast vehicles travel in an enclosure or tunnel along much of the route. Part of this requirement for an enclosed system stems from the high costs of land in urban regions where HSGT is to be routed. In rural or suburban regions the need for a protected guideway comes from the high speed of operation. The enclosure excludes snow, ice, hail, cross-winds, air gusts, and rain that hinder the vehicle's high-speed all-weather operations. In addition, linear induction motors that might propel the trains become inefficient when snow, ice, rain, or moisture fill the primary/secondary air gaps. Furthermore, vehicle drag is increased in rain or snow, while any air cushion device that might be employed is adversely affected in foul weather. The intrusion into the guideway of unwanted objects, either by accident or intentionally, should be prevented by an enclosure. This also seems mandatory for abating the noise (see *Proceedings*, 1969) of the passing vehicles, for reducing the possibilities of arcing and shorting of the high-power electric distribution lines, and for removing hazards of electrocution or buffeting of nearby persons.*
3. On-board power consumption for suspending the vehicles above the track. This supporting power is proportional to the speed and vehicle weight for wheeled trains on rails, and quadratic with speed for a tracked air-cushion vehicle.
4. Light-weight aircraft-type fabrication techniques and high-speed and high-power tracked vehicles, because of suspension dynamics and power requirements, will resemble the fuselages of air transports. Vehicle cost predictions should rely on commercial aircraft manufacturing practices.
5. Twin-tube enclosures. Closely spaced vehicles passing in opposing directions at relative speeds of 400 to 600 mph are violently buffeted. Well-separated tracks in a single tunnel lead to higher costs than twin tubes, each with traffic in one direction only. Thus the twin-tube concept for HSGT is a further burden imposed by the high-speed feature.

PARAMETRIC MODEL

The previous five prerequisites, derived from the high-speed assumption for the HSGT system, ordered the components in the parametric model. The

* In analogy with other ground transportation modes by auto or urban rail, the construction of enclosures and the fixed facilities of roads, tracks, garaging and maintenance stations, and parking and terminal facilities necessitates larger expenditures than vehicle acquisition. The HSGT enclosure and facilities are no exception, representing over two-thirds of the system's financial commitments.

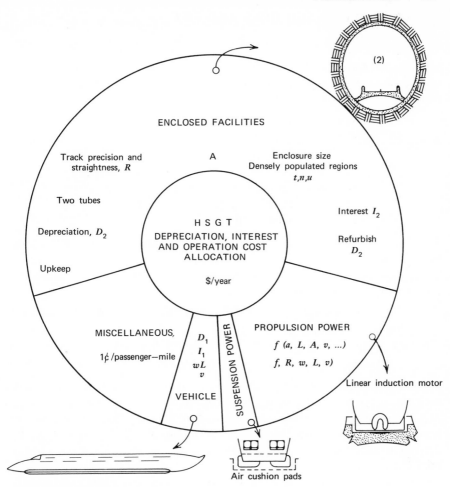

Fig. 1. Schematic of HSGT model.

topics will then be the cost definition of the power requirement for aero-dynamic drag and lift-suspension of vehicles in tunnels, the fabrication costs of ground-supported vehicles running at personal aircraft speeds, and the construction costs of enclosed guideways and power distribution lines, all these in the 1966 context of the Northeast Corridor. The parameters and allocation of the yearly costs of HSGT that resulted are shown in Figure 1.

Beyond the goal of early cost definition, the purpose of this parametric model of HSGT was the search for cheapest enclosure dimensions, guideway precision, and train operating speed.

POWER REQUIRED FOR DRAG AND LIFT

The expression for train aerodynamic resistance was based upon a single-vehicle train having well-streamlined ends, low-silhouette, and with smooth skin, flush rivets, and no gaps or protuberances. The aerodynamic drag force resisting train motion outside a tube (Hoffman, 1969) was taken to be

$$\text{aerodrag} = (9 \times 10^{-4} + 5 \times 10^{-7}L)av^2 \quad \text{lbf} \quad (1)$$

where 9×10^{-4} = coefficient for nose and tail ends profile drag, $\text{lbf}/(\text{ft}^2) \times (\text{mph})^2$

5×10^{-7} = coefficient for skin drag of a cabin, $\text{lbf}/(\text{ft}^3)(\text{mph})^2$

a = cross-sectional area enclosed by midship outer skin, ft^2

L = train length, nose tip to tail end, ft

v = train speed, mph

This empirical expression fitted the experimental data on trains designed up to the 1960s.

Formula (1), times v and the appropriate conversion factor, gives the power required to overcome airdrag of a train in the open

$$\text{aeropower} = (2.4 + 0.0013L) \times 10^{-6}av^3 \quad \text{hp} \quad (2)$$

where $2.4 \times 10^{-6} = 0.00267 \times 9 \times 10^{-4}$, $\text{hp}/(\text{ft}^2)(\text{mph})^3$

$0.0013 \times 10^{-6} = 0.00267 \times 5 \times 10^{-7}$, $\text{hp}/(\text{ft}^3)(\text{mph})^3$

0.00267 = conversion factor, $\text{hp}/(\text{lbf})(\text{mph})$

Equation (2) predicts the aerodynamic power required by a modern train and anticipated the first test results for United States trains traveling at 130 to 140 mph in open country—not in tunnels. With the HSGT need that the train be enclosed in a tube, the power consumption in that tunnel should be derived and related to the aerodynamic drag in the open. Therefore, (2) was multiplied by the ratio of the drag in a tunnel to that in the open, C. The drag amplification factor for trains in tunnels has been investigated empirically (Blaho, 1954) and analytically (Gouse, Noyes, and Swarden, 1967; Hammitt, et al. 1968) and was approximated for a smooth tunnel to be

$$C = (1 - A)^{-3} \quad (3)$$

where A = coefficient of fill = ratio of cross-sectional areas, train/tunnel = blockage ratio.

For a ribbed tunnel, the magnification factor might be 40% higher than C in expression (3). Such internally stiffened tubes are contemplated only for evacuated tunnels, while smooth-walled pipe is more probable for the first HSGT enclosure. Multiplying (3) by (2) gave the total aerodynamic power requirement, hp_a, for a train in a tunnel to be

$$\text{hp}_a = (2.4 + 0.0013L) \times 10^{-6} \times (1 - A)^{-3}av^3 \quad (4)$$

For a 100-seat vehicle running at 250 mph in a tunnel proportioned for least-cost blockage, hp_a will be between 10,000 and 15,000 hp, according to (4).

The power required to lift the vehicle and keep it suspended above the guideway, whether by an air-cushion or by a magnetic field, or to overcome the rolling resistance of wheels on rails is an order of magnitude less than hp_a. This suspension power, hp_s, is least for vehicles supported by wheels; for example, it is only 50 to 100 hp for a 100-seat train at 250 mph. The feasibility of wheeled trains speeding at 200 to 300 mph on steel rails for long runs is yet to be demonstrated. The problems are with wheels rapidly wearing out-of-round, shortened rim life, ensuing roughness and waviness of ride and escalating maintenance costs for vehicles and ways. Man's oldest transport-easing invention, the wheel, must be radically redesigned to the advanced HSGT specifications.*

On the other hand, a half-scale train has run in France on an air-cushion at 250 mph with a smooth ride (*Proceedings*, 1969). Although present thinking favors TACVs (tracked air-cushion vehicles) for USHSGT, both types of vehicle support hp_s, wheeled and air-cushioned, are calculated here.

The hp_s for a magnetically supported train has been estimated (Powell and Danby, 1966) to be between these two extremes. The suspension of a full-scale loaded vehicle with superconducting coils or permanent-magnets above a track with repelling coils has not been demonstrated. The costs of a magnetic track and of the complex of on-board equipment has been estimated to almost double the system facility costs. The acquisition and operations costs of devices necessary to achieve the magnetic fields with reasonable coil weight appeared as diseconomic alternates to the resting of the train upon wheels or air cushions.

The more feasible alternative of wheeled vehicles will be treated first. The least train rolling resistance, between 3 and 4 lb/ton of vehicle weight, is for conventional railroad steel wheels with little flange friction on straightaways of smooth, continuously welded steel rails. With a slight advance in rail support, rigidity and stiffer wear-resistant alloys for wheels, a resistance of 0.002 lbf/lb of load was assumed for HSGT.

For example, the wheel rolling resistance force in a 100-ft long train weighing 30,000 lbm can be as low as 60 lbf, as compared to its aerodynamic drag force of over 17,000 lbf at $v = 250$ mph, with $a = 100$ ft^2 and $A = 0.3$.†

* The research incentives for developing a 200–300 mph train wheel are the power and cost saving potentials. Success in reinventing a wheel for HSGT eliminates the 500 to 1000 hp on-board for sustaining the air cushions, cuts hp_a down by a noticeable amount (no bulky air pads), and simplifies guideway design.

† Low-speed train wheels also provide traction besides suspension. The transmission of propulsive force to the track by wheels is ruled out in high-speed trains. The ratio of

Thus hp_s for wheel-supported trains is far smaller than the TACVs hp_s, and may be neglected hereafter. In the following calculations the power required to separate moving vehicles from the tracks by an air-cushion is significant. The least hoverpower required to lift and stabilize a tracked air-cushion vehicle was taken from Figure A.6 of Bliss (1966) to be

$$hp_{s,\min} = wL(0.01 + 1.7 \times 10^{-7}v^2) \qquad (5)$$

for a train lineal density, w lbm/ft, typical of lightweight aircraft structural construction and of the widths anticipated for HSGT (4 to 6 seats abreast).* The assumptions for (5) were of a 6-ft pad width, 1.5 psi cushion pressure, an understructure weighing one-twentieth of the loaded vehicle, and track roughness of 3×10^{-4}. The track roughness, R, was here defined as the amplitude of deviation from mean straight line divided by the mean wavelength between inaccuracies.

However, the $R = 3 \times 10^{-4}$ implicit in (5), about 1 cm/100 ft, might give the passengers a rough ride in HSGT vehicles at their top speed (Civil Hovercraft, 1965). Combinations of two alleviations to the vibrational discomfort problem are possible:

1. Construction of a more precise track, that is, lower valued R's than the basis of (5).
2. Greater hoverheights than stipulated in (5) to absorb the track's inaccuracies in the air-cushion, requiring greater expenditures of horsepower than $hp_{s,\min}$.

For the second solution of greater hoverheight, the experimental data in Fig. A.5 of Bliss (1966) indicate that the additional hp_s beyond the minimum for lift is proportional to the increased hoverheight for small increments and that a doubling of hoverheight requires about 1.25 times the $hp_{s,\min}$. These

---

required propulsive force to weight on the wheels is 17,000/30,000 in the example single-car train or about 0.57, more than twice the coefficient of friction common for a locomotive steel wheel about to spin on a steel rail. In other words, the tractive effort of HSGT trains clearly exceeds the capability of torqued wheels and must be transmitted to the ground by other means, namely the magnet-to-magnet traction power plant represented by the linear induction motor.

* In actuality, w should be assumed to vary with v^3, since a fraction of the vehicle's weight (about one-sixth for the illustrative example) is the primary active portion of the induction motor and its controls. This propulsion weight is proportional to the operating power level of the unit, and in more refined versions of (5) and subsequent expressions, w could be formulated as a constant plus a small term related to V^3, A, a, and L. In this derivation, this second term was eliminated for conciseness, and w was later assumed at values somewhat higher than normal, to compensate for this neglected term. This simplification introduced errors of less than 20% in w, well within the uncertainties for w of HSGT trains.

proportions and the requirement that operating hoverheight be linear with the track roughness R led to augmenting $hp_{s,min}$ by

$$0.75 + \frac{0.25R}{3 \times 10^{-4}} \quad \text{for} \quad R > 3 \times 10^{-4}$$

The total hoverpower for air clearances providing a more comfortable ride then became

$$hp_s = \left(3 + \frac{R}{3 \times 10^{-4}}\right) wL(0.0025 + 0.42 \times 10^{-7}v^2) \tag{6}$$

For instance, the 250 mph illustrative vehicle with $wL = 30,000$ lbm traveling at a comfort level of $R = 6 \times 10^{-4}$ requires

$$hp_{s,air-cushion} = 770 \text{ hp}$$

whereas the same train rolling on advanced design wheels and rails consumes rolling resistance power of only

$$hp_{s,wheels} = 40 \text{ hp}$$

In addition to the power required for lift and drag (which is highest at maximum speed), power is also needed at the lower speeds for acceleration, grade climbing, on-board auxiliaries, lighting, air-conditioning, entertainment, communication, and other amenities. The nonpropulsive power requirements are negligibly small when compared to hp_a, whereas acceleration and grade negotiation use spare hp_a capability. For example, reconsider the 100-ft illustrative vehicle described earlier ($wL = 30,000$ lbm, $a = 100$ ft^2, $v = 250$ mph, $A = 0.3$) that required the 11,500 hp traction power plant. With this train the acceleration possible with full-power applied is

$$\text{acceleration} = \frac{11,500 - hp_a}{0.00267 \times 30,000v}$$

or

$$\frac{145}{v} - 9.3 \times 10^{-6}v^2, \quad g \tag{7}$$

and is plotted in Figure 2. The limit acceleration of 0.15g, consistent with human comfort in a passenger train is also shown in Figure 2. This limit of 0.15g is the mean between the 0.1g that may topple unseated passengers and the 0.2g that overstrains the elderly or very young seated person.

Equation (7) shows that the 0.15g acceleration can be kept up to $0.91v_{max}$ with the spare power and ample motor reserves up to almost top speed. This $0.91v_{max}$ is furthermore reached in less than 70 sec at 0.15g, and the study neglected hereafter the acceleration power requirements as being small compared to the sustained hp_a at cruising speed.

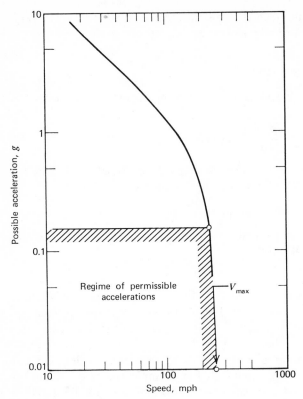

Fig. 2. Acceleration possible with unused propulsion power in illustrative train.

Grade-climbing power may also be omitted since grades in the high-speed sector of the track should be minimal for comfort, and steeper grades will occur only within a mile or two of the terminal.

The remaining calculation of the yearly total power cost of HSGT requires defining the unit cost for doing mechanical tractive work in modern vehicles, $\$_{power}/(hp)(hr)$. Piston and turbine engines for automobiles, trucks, or buses, average $\$0.02/(hp)(hr)$, ranging from $1.5¢/(hp)(hr)$ in diesels to $2.5¢/(hp)(hr)$ for passenger car engines, while train traction electric motors may go as low as $\$0.01/(hp)(hr)$. The linear induction motors in HSGT* vehicles were assumed to have electromechanical conversion efficiencies of one-half those of rotating motors, due to the larger-than-normal air gaps between primary and secondary magnets. Electric traction by linear induction was thus also costed at $\$0.02/(hp)(hr)$ in HSGT.

* The excess heat wasted by the lower-efficiency linear motors—some 10 MW per vehicle-trip—will present massive thermal pollution problems in the tubes, and the choice among

The energy cost of operating each vehicle an hour at cruising speed was then assumed to be

$$\text{hourly energy cost} = 0.02(\text{hp}_a + \text{hp}_s), \qquad \frac{\$_{\text{power}}}{\text{hr}} \qquad (8)$$

and the yearly vehicle-hours of operation at close to full power for the fleet of vehicles in the system are about

$$\frac{\text{vehicle-hr}}{\text{year}} = \frac{tn}{u} \qquad (9)$$

where t = mean trip time of individual passengers, hr/trip (roughly 1 hr for the Washington–New York leg or 2 hr for the Boston to Washington trip).

n = expected yearly number of trips taken via HSGT, passenger-trips/yr. The passenger market forecast for the 1980s is uncertain and n was left a variable here.

u = anticipated occupancy, passengers/vehicle. This equals the passenger utilization factor times the maximum capacity, and is also left as a variable.

Finally, the yearly power cost for the whole HSGT complex, the product of expressions (8) and (9), is then

$$\$_{\text{power}}/\text{yr} = \frac{tn}{u}\left[(4.8 + 0.0026L) \times 10^{-8} \times (1 - A)^{-3}av^3 + \right.$$

$$\left. + \left(3 + \frac{R}{3 \times 10^{-4}}\right)wL(5 + 0.84 \times 10^{-4}v^2) \times 10^{-5}\right] \quad (10)$$

This expression began to bring together some seemingly unrelated facets of the system, spanning from socioeconomic factors ($\$, t, n, u$) through civil construction engineering (R, A) and advanced vehicle technology (v, a, L, w).

COST OF VEHICLES

Cost-estimating relationships for predicting development, production, and acquisition by Federal agencies of aircraft designed to cruise beyond 400 mph were well established (Levenson and Barro, 1966). Reliable cost data exist about ground-supported transportation vehicles for private or public use up

---

candidate powerplants will be dictated by the relative ventilation costs for each propulsive mean. The cost of dispersing the exhaust of combustion engines in enclosures is several times that for dissipating the waste heat from linear induction motors of equal power.

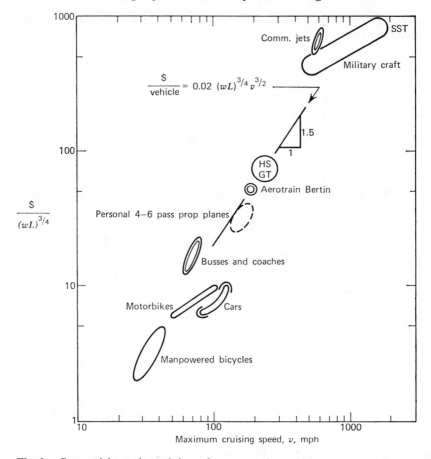

Fig. 3.   Cost, weight, and speed data of transportation vehicles.

to 140 mph. The study presumed vehicle costs by interpolation between the slower ground vehicles and the speedier airframes, since HSGT vehicles would travel at speeds between these two vehicle groupings.

The size and performance characteristics found most predictive for airframe costs are gross take-off weight, maximum cruise speed, and peak engine thrust at sea level. A representative sample of procurement cost to governmental agencies of military airframes, including fuselages, wings, empennages, and so on (calculated from weight, wL, and top speed, v) is shown as the shaded band in the upper corner of Figure 3, near the commercial jets. The slower transportation vehicles, available to consumers in mass-produced quantities, are located in the lower portions of Figure 3.

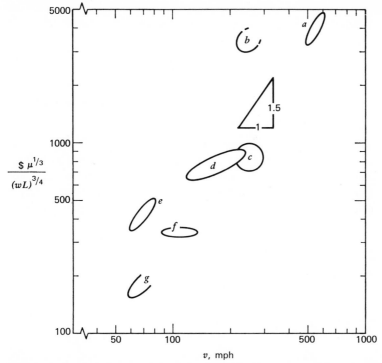

Fig. 4. Cost of quantity-produced passenger vehicles. (*a*) L/TOL, 150 seats; (*b*) metro-copter; (*c*) HSGT; (*d*) small private plane; (*e*) Bus; (*f*) automobile; (*g*) motorbike, *v*. Vehicles produced per year by manufacturer per model (one third of market).

The $\frac{3}{4}$ exponent for the vehicle weight, wL, without payload is the average of the exponents of the weight in Levenson and Barro (1966), which varied little from model to model. Greater variation was found instead in the powers for v, anywhere from $\frac{1}{2}$ to slightly over 1 for aircraft. The discrete cost regions of Figure 3 may be considered a related continuum. A multiple regression analysis of the data, weighted in favor of the collective transport vehicles shown by the doubled oval lines, suggested an exponent of 1.5 for v.

The plots in Figure 3 are in a reasonably compact band for vehicles varying by two orders of magnitude in speed, whose cost per pound ranges from under 1 \$/lb to over 100 \$/lb. Figure 4 shows some further consolidation of the data when the cost formulation includes also the production rate.

Placing the HSGT train at $200 < v < 300$ mph, and central to the data groups in Figure 3, is equivalent to costing the vehicle at about

$$\frac{\$}{\text{vehicle}} = 0.02(wLv^2)^{3/4} \tag{11}$$

The total number of vehicles in the fleet* to be initially acquired for an operational HSGT system is

$$(8760 \times 0.5)^{-1}\left(\frac{tn}{u}\right) \tag{12}$$

where $8760 = \mathrm{hr/yr}$

0.5 = anticipated vehicle utilization factor = (mean of yearly hours of vehicle in-service)/8760

Public carriers have operated at peak times with vehicle utilization factors as low as 0.2—an early value for first-generation helicopters—and as high as 0.6 for municipal coaches and highway cruisers, occasionally up to unity for buses at rush hour. The assumption of a value of 0.5 for the utilization factor was made prior to the passenger demand and market forecasting models developed since.

Finally, the yearly cost of having acquired the HSGT vehicle fleet is the product of (11), (12), and the depreciation and interest rates

$$\frac{\$_{\text{fleet}}}{\text{yr}} = 4.6 \times 10^{-6}(D_1 + I_1)\frac{tn}{u}(wLv^2)^{3/4} \tag{13}$$

where D_1 = yearly depreciation rate of vehicles

I_1 = yearly interest rate on the capital invested in vehicles

and

$$4.6 \times 10^{-6} = 0.02 \times (8760 \times 0.5)^{-1}$$

CONSTRUCTION OF FIXED FACILITIES

Amortized construction costs of the enclosure and guideway of the HSGT system have already been noted as being much greater than the yearly costs anticipated for power consumption and vehicle acquisition.

This situation is analogous to the case in all modes of transport by tracked vehicles. For instance, the yearly interest on the bonds of San Francisco's Bay Area Rapid Transit District (BARTD) is over three times the expected operating costs.

Not only are construction costs the larger portion of the total, but also the least accurately predictable in comparison to costs of moving conveyances. The final costs of the fixed facilities of BARTD were underestimated in the planning stage by a misjudgment factor of 2. This and the preceding sections

---

* As an example, the Northeastern Seaboard can be serviced by a fleet of 40 to 50 vehicles, plus spares, if tn/u were to be 2×10^5 vehicle-hr/yr.

of this cost model are the most imprecise portions of this study, and a twofold correction or conservatism factor on costs was incorporated into the construction calculations.

The expression at the bottom of Table 1 was the earliest estimate of the HSGT system's fixed facilities capital costs. The table also enumerates the assumptions of the system's location, line lengths, terrain, enclosure dimensions, and trackage (these latter being left as variables in A and R), unit costs of tunneling or excavation, and lining and power distribution lines. The construction cost was in terms of a 450-mile Northeast Corridor line, connecting Washington, New York, Boston, and the intervening cities. Of this, 100 miles of HSGT track were assumed to be deep, underground tunnels under the densely populated cities, 150 miles running below the surface of suburban sparser localities, and 200 miles in rural open country. The guideway excavation was taken to be the following.

1. Tunnels in medium to hard rock, geologically representative of the eastern littoral at 200- to 500-ft depths below the surface.
2. Cut and cover enclosures just below the surface, possibly with a new roadway on top of the segments of the HSGT guideway.
3. On-grade tubes enclosing the guideway, consisting of reinforced concrete pipes anchored to the ground.

In the model two separate tubes were assumed for travel in two directions* without defining the distance separating the twin tunnels.

The entries for the concrete work amount to about one-half of the total and are based on unit prices of centrifugally cast, steel-reinforced pipe for large-diameter (up to 20 ft) water conveyances—either for the distribution of potable water, flood waters, or sewage waste. Cost prediction of these concrete pipes was probably the most accurate of the model components, and closely correlatable to varying size (see Figure 5).

Trackage costs in Table 1 were representative of both rail and air-cushion track costs of HSGT. The 1950 book value of first-class high-speed railroad trackage was $72,000/mile, equivalent to $130,000/mile today.

If the vehicles are supported by an air-cushion on a concrete track, the basis was cost estimates of freeway overpass decking. Precision-aligned concrete flooring and structural supports, plus reinforcing on California freeways and access ramps, are being constructed for $5 to $10/ft².

The lower of these figures, applied to an air-cushion track shaped as a shallow channel, indicated track costs of 0.25×10^6/mile for a poorly

---

* Twin tubes are not the only solution to the problems of buffeting when vehicles pass at high relative speeds on two close tracks. A single tunnel, twice as wide as high, could house the two tracks separated by a concrete fence-wall, though construction costs for this scheme are probably higher than for the twin-tube design.

Character of Traversed Terrain			Single Track Length, Miles	Type of Construction	Land Acquisition Costs
Description	Symbol	Location			
Urban central core City terminals Underwater crossings	••••••••		100	Tunnel	Negligible
Suburban localities Under public right—of—ways	||||||||||||		150	Cut and cover roadway on top	Absorbed by roadway installation savings
Rural open country	——		200	On—grade	Small

Terrain	Excavation, Subgrade Preparation, Haul, Disposal			Enclosure Tube or Tunnel Lining of Steel Reinforced Concrete		Trackage, 10^6 \$/Mile	Electric Power Distribution Lines, Substations
	s/ft³	Volume Removed Per Tube		\$/ft³	ft³ × 10⁷/tube		
		ft³ × 10⁷	Type				
••••••	0.5	5.3/A	Rock	3	0.7/A	0.125 (1 + $\dfrac{0.001}{R}$)	0.2 × 10⁶ \$/mile
|||||||||||	0.03	8/A	Rock and dirt	4	1/A		
——	0.01	10.6/A	Dirt	5	1.4/A		

Table 1.   Assumed dimensions and construction costs of HSGT fixed plant facilities.

Additional Assumptions.

A = Coefficient of fill, $a/[\pi/4\ ID^2]$; $a = 100\ \text{ft}^2$

ID = Inner diameter of enclosure = 30 × (wall thickness of concrete enclosure tube)

1.05 = Factor for terminals, stations, and yard costs being 1/20 of guideways

1.01 = Factor for ground controls and guidance costs being 1/100 of guideways

1.10 = Factor for engineering and land acquisition being 1/10 of guideways

2 = Number of tubes required for full route of the HSGT summary construction costs of fixed facilities (\$)

$$\left\{ (2.65 + 0.24 + 0.1 + 2.1 + 4 + 7) \times \frac{10^7}{A} \right.$$

$$+ 450 \left[0.125 \left(1 + \frac{0.001}{R} \right) + 0.2 \right] \times 10^6 \Big\}$$

$$\times\ 1.1 \times 1.05 \times 1.01 \times 2 = \left(\frac{0.38}{A} + 0.34 + \frac{1.3 \times 10^{-4}}{R} \right) \times 10^9$$

aligned construction. The French experience with the first air-cushion track was four times as costly as this last figure, though the expense was for a more precise track.

Doubling of the construction estimates for the customary railroad trackage accounted for the advanced rolling stock requirements of HSGT. This

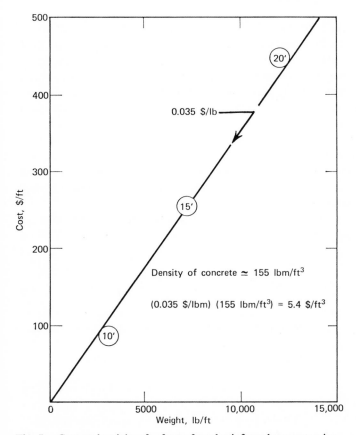

Fig. 5.   Cost and weight of a foot of steel-reinforced concrete pipe.

doubling also brought the figure close to the 0.25×10^6/mile of air-cushion channel tracks. The quarter-million dollar/mile was thus used for the cost of laying medium-precision trackage ($R = 0.001$) for either air-cushion or wheel-supported HSGT vehicles.

It was felt desirable to leave track costs in the model as a function of R, the dimensionless mean air-bag excursion in tracked air-cushion vehicles or the maximum spring traverse in conventionally sprung wheeled trains. With half of the track cost assigned to precision requirements, and the other half to train loading factors (and thus invariant with R), the HSGT track cost commitments were finally expressed as

$$\$/(\text{mile})(\text{track}) = 0.125\left(1 + \frac{0.001}{R}\right) \times 10^6$$

as indicated in Table 1. By way of comparison the single-track capital cost of laying the BARTD's rails was estimated in 1964 to be also around 0.25×10^6/mile, with $R = 0.002$. The fixed portion of the electric power collection and distribution lines were assumed at one-fifth of a million dollars per mile.

With these assumptions, the excavation, enclosure, trackage, and electrical distribution could be summed in the bracketed term at the bottom of Table 1 to obtain the guideway construction costs for the two parallel tubes of the HSGT. Construction costs were next factored upward to account for land acquisition, engineering and planning, terminals and stations, and controls. The largest of these additional cost burdens was system detail design and land acquisition, represented by the factor 1.10, while terminal stations and maintenance yards added only 0.05 to the unit construction cost.

Finally, the total construction costs were combined into the last expression in Table 1 as a function of A and R, and the yearly cost of HSGT facilities were

$$\frac{\$_{\text{facility}}}{\text{yr}} = (D_2 + I_2)\left(\frac{0.38}{A} + 0.34 + \frac{1.3 \times 10^{-4}}{R}\right) \times 10^9 \qquad (14)$$

where D_2 = yearly depreciation, plus fixed equipment and facilities replacement rate during normal service

I_2 = yearly interest rate on the invested capital in guideways

The capital costs of the Boston–New York–Washington HSGT, according to (14) and with the least-cost values of A and R, are about two billion 1966 dollars, or 4.5×10^6 $/mile. By comparison the single guideway TACV facility planned for linking Miami with its Everglades jetport 50 miles away is now estimated at 1.5×10^6 $/mile. Doubling the track and covering it would triple its unprotected, single-channel costs. These numbers were a checkpoint for HSGT's 4 to 5 million $/mile cost forecast.

The wages and administrative costs for the personnel operating the HSGT trains and facilities were formulated (Hoffman, 1969) to be

$$\frac{\$_{\text{personnel}}}{\text{yr}} = 0.01nvt \qquad (15)$$

THE RESULTING HSGT MODEL

The sum of (10), (13), (14), and (15) gave a first approximation of the total yearly cost of HSGT system operation:

$$\frac{\$_{\text{HSGT}}}{\text{yr}} = \frac{tn}{u}\left[(4.8 + 0.0026L) \times 10^{-8} \times (1 - A)^{-3}av^3 + \right.$$

$$\left(3 + \frac{R}{3 \times 10^{-4}}\right)wL(5 + 0.84 \times 10^{-4}v^2) \times 10^{-5}\right] +$$

$$4.6 \times 10^{-6}(D_1 + I_1) \times \frac{tn}{u} \times (wLv^2)^{3/4} +$$

$$(D_2 + I_2) \times \left(\frac{0.38}{A} + 0.34 + \frac{1.3 \times 10^{-4}}{R}\right) \times$$

$$10^9 + 0.01nvt \tag{16}$$

The first observation of the result equation (16) is that system and user costs can be calculated as functions of technology variables (cruising speed, vehicle suspension or lift alternatives, vehicle and tunnel geometries, and track precision), as well as in terms of socioeconomic and behavior variables $(t, n, u, \$, D, I)$. Another observation is that disparate characteristics of social-engineering system, ranging from civil and vehicle engineering to economics, can be embodied into a single model as (16).

Examples of the uses of this HSGT model follow and derive least-cost choices in some technological and funding decisions ahead for HSGT. For instance, an economically feasible speed regime will be derived, an optimum enclosure size and track alignment may be calculated. Since a variation in A and R has conflicting influences on two component terms of (16), setting to zero the differential of (16) with respect to A and R specifies the preferable geometries. The search for cost minima defining other preferable technologies (e.g., evacuated versus ambient-pressure tubes) is now also facilitated by having the parametric definitions in (16).

EXAMPLES OF THE USE OF THE COST MODEL

Least-cost Service and Cruise Speed

The cost estimate per passenger-mile of the future HSGT in present-day dollars, as affected by the cruising speed, v, assumed that the following characteristics have been fixed:

$tn = 2 \times 10^7$ to 3×10^7 yearly passenger-hours of travel at v

$u = 100$ passengers per vehicle, mean occupancy

$L = 100$ ft, $a = 100$ ft^2, $w = 300$ lb/ft, vehicle structural characteristics

$A = 0.36$, $R = 2.2 \times 10^{-3}$, enclosure and guideway characteristics

$D_1 + I_1 = D_2 + I_2 = 0.1$, discount plus interest factors

Dividing (16) by vtn and rounding off numbers gives the cost per passenger-mile to be

$$\frac{\$}{\text{passenger-mile}} = 1.9 \times 10^{-7}v^2 + 2.6 \times 10^{-6}v + 1.3 \times 10^{-5}v^{1/2}$$

$$+ \frac{7.4}{v} + 0.01 \tag{17}$$

for $tn = 20$ million yearly passenger hours and is shown in Figure 6.

The term $7.4/v$ accounts for the guideway costs and makes up about $\frac{3}{4}$ to $\frac{1}{2}$ of the total cost per passenger mile of HSGT, ($v = 200$ to 300 mph), in this example. It is evident that the prediction of facilities cost, particularly in the

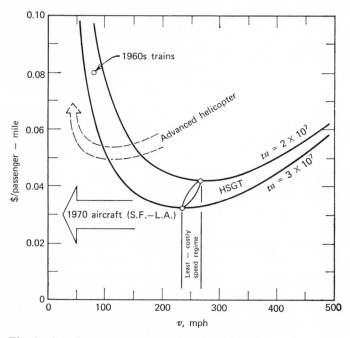

Fig. 6. Sample passenger costs as function of speed.

definition of future unit construction costs and of depreciation and interest rates, needs the greatest attention and accuracy in subsequent forecasting models, since assumption errors in these civil engineering parameters result in almost proportionate errors in prediction of service costs. Equally as important is the accuracy of forecasts for t, n, u, and I_2, the market projections for HSGT, since these descriptors of transportation demand and ridership affect travel costs in direct proportion to their stipulated values.

With the assumptions implicit in (17), the least-costly speed, V, is obtained by setting $d(17)/dv$ equal to zero, namely

$$3.8 \times 10^{-7}V + 2.6 \times 10^{-6} + \frac{0.65 \times 10^{-5}}{V^{1/2}} - \frac{7.4}{V^2} = 0$$

whose solution of interest is near $V_0 = 267$ mph. With a more optimistic anticipation for the popularity of the service, that is, if tn were to assume the higher value of 3×10^7, the $7.4/v$ term drops to $5/v$ in (17), and V_0 becomes 233 mph.

The first conclusion is that the 250-mph cruise speed (the mean of the two sample V_0's) appears as the most parsimonious technology target for HSGT. The second conclusion is that passenger costs, were service available today, would be in the neighborhood of 3 or 4¢/passenger-mile.

Another item of interest emerges from Figure 6; HSGT train service will be less costly than present-day's slow trains, but intermediate in cost between that of helicopters and airbus jetcraft. The time savings, conveniences, safety, and all-weather reliability of the HSGT will probably also be intermediate between those of the airbus and those of the helicopter. Comparative advantages of the train over aircraft will be mostly in the time-of-travel benefits accrued from locating the HSGT stations in the city centers; this will afford a sizable reduction in the 1-hr ride to and from the high-capacity airports or heliports, necessarily dispersed away from the densest-population regions.

Optimal Proportions of Facilities

The model in (16) can be directly used to find optimal facility geometries corresponding to the least-cost values of A and R. To this end, it is convenient to simplify (16) into a more manageable form by setting constant some of the economic variables that are more weakly related to the dimensioning of the enclosed guideway (e.g., D and I), and some of the vehicle physical characteristics that by now are well defined by the preceding analysis, such as a, L, w, u, and nt.

Varying these parameters over a range of plausible values affects only marginally the service cost of HSGT, as shown in Figure 7. The plots in this figure were purposely based on $A = 0.3$ in contrast to the A of 0.36 of Figure

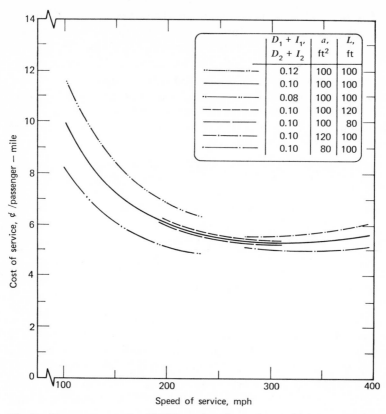

Fig. 7. Passenger costs for HSGT services for various vehicle cross-sectional areas and lengths, and selected depreciation plus interest rates. (Other parameters fixed at $A = 0.3$, $R = 10^{-3}$, $w = 300$ lb/ft, $nt = 2 \times 10^7$ passenger-hrs/yr, $u = 100$ passengers/vehicle)

6, to emphasize the leverage exerted by the blockage ratio, A, on passenger costs; the more commodious tunnels implicit in Figure 7, result in an extra cent per passenger mile vis-à-vis the tighter tubes of Figure 6.

The band width of the curves in Figure 7 is sufficiently narrow with excursions in a, L, and $D + I$, that little distortion would be introduced in the model by setting

$$D_1 + I_1 = D_2 + I_2 = 0.10$$
$$a = 100 \text{ ft}^2$$
$$L = 100 \text{ ft}$$
$$w = 300 \text{ lb/ft}$$
$$u = 100 \text{ passengers/vehicles}$$
$$nt = 2 \times 10^7 \text{ passenger-hours/yr}$$

With these values, rearranging terms and rounding off numbers, (16) becomes

$$C_0 = 5.1 \times 10^{-6} \times (1 - A)^{-3}v^2 + (0.9 + 1000R) \times$$

$$\left(\frac{5}{v} + 0.84 \times 10^{-4}v\right) + 10^{-3}v^{1/2} + \frac{500}{v} \times$$

$$\left(\frac{0.38}{A} + 0.34 + \frac{1.3 \times 10^{-4}}{R}\right) + 1 \qquad \text{¢/passenger-mile} \quad (18)$$

This expression for the cost of HSGT service is plotted in Figure 8 for $R = 10^{-3}$, again implying a 1¢/passenger-mile penalty vis-à-vis the less costly and more tolerantly imprecise $R_0 = 2.5 \times 10^{-3}$ found later. Also shown in Figure 8 are the least-costly blockage ratios, A_0, obtained from setting $dC_0/dA = 0$, namely from

$$A_0 = 1 - 0.01685v^{3/4}\sqrt{A_0} \qquad (19)$$

The value of $A_0 = 0.36$ that was used earlier in (17), is close to that for $V_0 = 250$ mph and can be used to define the inside diameter of the tunnel to be

$$\text{diameter} = \left(\frac{4}{\pi} \times \frac{100 \text{ ft}^2}{0.36}\right)^{1/2} = 19 \text{ ft}$$

This result of this use of the model might be of interest to civil engineering planners, since it states that the tunnel-liner can be similar to the 20-ft water conveyance pipe of Figure 5, now commercially available.

Substituting $A = 0.36$ into (18) and letting $dC_0/dR = 0$ gives the next result of interest to the guideway and vehicle designer, namely that for least-cost systems $R_0 = 2.5 \times 10^{-3}$. This result again forecasts that conventional technology of track alignment will suffice for HSGT, since the deviations from straightness of 2.5 ft amplitude/1000 ft of track exceed those of BARTD track bed.

Benefits and Costs of Tube Evacuation

A third use of the model in (16) is the preliminary assessment of the benefit/cost aspects of evacuated-tube HSGT, when compared to the ambient-pressure tube travel discussed so far. The widely discussed scheme of running trains in vacuo (Edwards, 1965) and thus possibly reducing the costs and technical intricacies of high-speed interurban transit can now be subjected to analysis on the basis of the preceding calculations.

Several alternative methods of propulsion and braking have been envisaged for vehicles in evacuated tunnels:

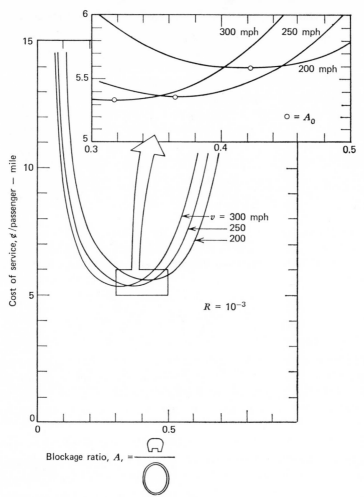

Fig. 8. Passenger costs for varying HSGT enclosure dimensions.

- Metering small amounts of air into the tubes fore and aft of the vehicle, to decelerate or accelerate it by pressing on the nose or tail section.
- Providing steep downgrades for starting away from stations and sharp upramp inclines for slowing down on approaches (proper use of gravity forces).
- Combinations and mixes of these latter two procedures.
- Electric motors. Either rotary motors driving or retarding wheels, or linear induction motors accelerating or decelerating the vehicle understructure.

In all cases, wheels are proposed for suspension rather than the now un-feasible air-cushion, in many instances torqued by electric motors for those situations where the small aerodynamic and rolling resistance still present must be overcome while coasting. It is this last powerplant configuration, namely electric motors rotating wheels that support a vehicle running in essentially level evacuated tubes, that will be considered in this benefit/cost study of vacuum ground travel.

The prime benefits of HSGT tunnel evacuation would be the following.

1. Reduction of aerodynamic drag in proportion to the reduction in air pressure.
2. Elimination of one of the two tunnels, since the buffeting problem is now removed, and two tracks can be accomodated within a single oval tube.

For example, were the tunnel to be at 0.01 atm, the air drag would be reduced to one hundredth of its former level in ambient-pressure tunnels, and a single tube with two sets of rails could be configured with ample sway clearances at $A = 0.3$ to 0.4.

The major cost increases attributable to evacuation of the HSGT system are due to:

1. Thicker lining requirements to make the tunnel more resistant to collapse from the external pressure increase of one atmosphere.
2. Massive air valving and interlocks at stations and terminals.
3. Redesign of train fuselage and passenger air-conditioning for frequent-cycle inflation and deflation.
4. Pumps and air purging provisions to maintain prescribed low-pressure levels in the tunnel.

With the two lists of merits and demerits of tube evacuation, the appro-priate components can be extracted from the parametric model and modified to give the yearly system benefits and costs of evacuated vis-à-vis ambient pressure tunnels.

The savings in power costs to overcome resistance are 0.99 of the aero-dynamic drag and 0.9 of the air-cushion power in (10), about 70×10^6 $/year, assuming that $A = 0.36$, $R = 2.5 \times 10^{-3}$, $v = 250$ mph and that the other parameters are fixed at the values set in (18). Eliminating one of the tubes and retaining only a single tunnel for two sets of conventional tracks saves about half of (14), which was for two tunnels, or roughly 80×10^6 $/year. Thus the benefits of evacuating the HSGT rail-line amount to about 150×10^6 $/year, exclusive of the costs calculated next.

A tunnel shell that must safely withstand an external pressure increment of 15 psi should be double the thickness of a conventional lining shell. The construction costs of the steel reinforced lining represented three-fifths of the total of 80×10^6 \$/yr in (14). Readapting the thickness of the shell for evacuated tubes then raises system costs by $0.6 \times 80 \times 10^6$ or some 50×10^6 \$/yr.

The large valves and interlocks at stations, outlets and termini also double that portion of the construction costs, which was 0.05 of the total of the formulation in Table 1. With this "stations" factor now becoming more nearly 1.10, the extra cost of station redesign for vacuum tunnels is $0.05 \times (80 + 50) \times 10^6$ or some 6.5×10^6 \$/yr.

A train running frequently in and out of evacuated tubes requires extensive design refinements in on-board air pumps, pressure controls and passenger-comfort safeguards, cabin pressurization and door-sealing equipment, and structural reconfiguring and beef-up to withstand the numerous daily cycles of decompression and pressurization on station arrival and departure. The full effect of these vehicle changes and improvements is to push costs up to where the HSGT vehicle, item c in Figure 4, might now be relocated closer to the aircraft group a and b in Figure 4, possibly doubling the vehicle cost. Thus the vehicle cost penalty for running in vacuum is near the value of (13), about 2×10^6 \$/yr with our earlier parameter stipulations.

Air will tend to leak continuously into the tunnels through joints, fissures, seams, and from the stations and other access holes. The cost of purging out this excess air may be estimated from current experience with sustaining the evacuation of large space simulation laboratories. In one such large installation, some 300 kW are expended for retaining a vacuum 10^4 harder than the 0.01 atm in a volume 10^{-4} times the volume of the 450-mile tube from Washington to Boston. By analogy, one would then guess at 1 to 2 MW as sufficient power for keeping the pressure in the HSGT tunnel down at 0.01 atm, representing a yearly outlay of one or two million dollars for electric power, pump depreciation and interest, tube patching and resealing, and other maintenance.

In sum, the added system construction costs for evacuation would run to some 60×10^6 \$/yr, as opposed to the system benefits in cost-reduction of 150×10^6 \$/yr. The benefit/cost ratio for evacuating the HSGT line, from this first-order estimate, is therefore 2.5, that is the concept of ground travel in vacuo appears to be very beneficial and highly economic. It is indeed a rare situation for a major innovation in transportation technology to promise such ambitious pay-offs as a 2.5 benefit/cost ratio, and the potential savings of the order of ninety millions of \$/yr delineated in the preceding analysis call for a more detailed and exhaustive scrutiny than the one shown here. The evaluation of vacuum-tube high-speed travel should have some high priority in the Nation's program to enhance its transportation capabilities.

ACKNOWLEDGMENTS

This parametric costing of fast intercity travel systems was performed in 1966, while the author was a consultant to TRW Systems Inc. The study was supported by independent research and development funds and helped by Drs. Paul Dergarabedian and George R. Pittman, Jr. of TRW, to whom the author is greatly indebted.

The opinions and conclusions expressed here are those of the author and do not necessarily reflect the views of TRW or the policies of the U.S. Department of Transportation.

REFERENCES

BLAHO, M. (1954), "Drag of Trains in Tube Tunnels," *Acta Technica Academiae Scientiarum Hungaricae*, Tomus VIII, Fasciculi 3–4, Budapest, pp. 185–206.

BLISS, D. S. (1966), "Application of Air-Cushions to High-Speed Guided Land Transport," Institution of Mechanical Engineers, Convention on Guided Land Transport, Session 4, Paper A, London, October 28.

"The Civil Hovercraft Development Program, Parts I and II" (1965). Hovercraft Development Ltd., Air Cushion Vehicles (Supplement to *FLIGHT*), Vol. 6, No. 37–38, July–August.

EDWARDS, L. K. (1965), "High Speed Tube Transportation," Scientific American, Vol. 213, No. 2, August, pp. 30–40.

GOUSE, S. W., B. S. NOYES, and M. SWARDEN (1967), "Aerodynamic Drag of A Body Traveling in a Tube," Report No. DSR 76108-3 for the U.S. Department of Transportation, Clearinghouse No. PB 177 211, October.

HAMMITT, A. G., A. S. HERSH, K. R. A. MURTHY, J. B. PETERSON, and D. B. BLISS (1968), "Drag of Vehicles Traveling in Tubes," *Proceedings of the 6th Aerospace Science Meeting of the American Institute of Aeronautics and Astronautics*, January.

HOFFMAN, G. A. (1969), "A Parametric Model of High Speed Ground Transportation," *Journal of Transportation Research*, Vol. 3, No. 3.

KIRCHNER, M. E. and J. V. FRONT (1967), "Multi-Rotor Applications in VTOL Aircraft," *ASME Publication 67-TRAN-61*.

LEVENSON, G. S., and S. M. BARRO (1966), "Cost-Estimating Relationships for Aircraft Airframes," The RAND Corporation, Memorandum RM-4845-PR, May.

PICKERELL, D. J., and R. A. CRESSWELL (1968), "Powerplant Aspects of High-Speed, Inter-city VTOL Aircraft," *Journal of Aircraft*, Vol. 8, No. 5, September–October.

POWELL, J. R., and G. R. DANBY (1966), "High-Speed Transport by Magnetically Suspended Trains," ASME Paper No. 66-WA/RR-5, December.

Proceedings of the 1969 Conference on High Speed Ground Transportation (1969), Transportation Research Institute, Carnegie-Mellon University, Schenley Park, Pittsburgh, Pa., 15213.

"Special Issue on Transportation" (1968), *Proceedings of the Institute of Electrical and Electronics Engineers*, Vol. 56, No. 4, April.

XII   Analysis of the American Education System: Alexander M. Mood

INTRODUCTION

A rudimentary model of the public school system as an input-output process is presented in this chapter. The inputs are students' own abilities and attitudes, parental support, peer support, quality of the school system, community support, and society's posture with respect to education. Outputs are various categories of academic achievement as well as social competence, responsibility, self-confidence, creativeness, ethics, and ambition. All these factors must be measured by index numbers or simple indicators. The model is a set of regression equations relating outputs to inputs. Some implementation of the model has been made possible by means of data gathered in the U.S. Office of Education's Equality of Educational Opportunity Survey.

This chapter describes the beginnings of a fairly substantial effort to build a model of the educational activities carried out by the United States public school system. The effort began in 1965 when I was serving under Francis Keppel, U.S. Commissioner of Education, and it is being continued in several places, particularly the U.S. Office of Education where able operations analysts and educators are developing basic parameters and equations for a comprehensive model. As yet the model presented is not specifically defined but the general form that it must take is reasonably clear.

The model views the educational system as an input-output process which uses various resources during the school year to transform the educational level of the incoming students to a higher level at the end of the year. Creation of the model requires the development of measures of the resources and of the educational levels and the determination of relations between them so that one can get a fairly clear understanding of how various resources contribute to increasing education. Education is an extremely complicated enterprise, and we cannot expect that a reliable model of it can be developed without a large expenditure of time and money.

It is, on the other hand, an extremely large and important enterprise that could be vastly improved by a deeper understanding of how it works. The contribution of an effective model bringing such understanding makes a large effort reasonable. Kershaw and McKean (1959) presented this potential a number of years ago in a RAND document. Two major contributions are expected. One is providing a much clearer view of how inputs to the school system may be manipulated to achieve desired outputs that would be of material assistance to educational administration and also to legislators and school board members who must make important educational budget decisions. More generally, parents and voters could also use information of this kind to help them determine what kind of local school system they wish to build and maintain.

The second major contribution of such a model is that it will provide a calibration device by means of which research workers in education can compare their experimental results with those of other research workers. Because at present there is no such device, experimental results point in all directions and appear to be highly contradictory. One reason is that experimenters cannot draw random samples of pupils, teachers, parents, and communities, but they must usually settle for a few with which their universities happen to have working agreements. It is no wonder that replication of a given experiment seldom results in replication of the result. There would be somewhat better hope of it if there existed a calibration device for adjusting pupils' abilities to an average ability, teachers' abilities to an average, parents' education and interest to an average, school facilities to an average, and so on. Of course we can never expect to get the kind of precision in comparisons between experiments in education that we get in the natural sciences, but a well-developed calibration procedure would bring pedagogy a tremendous step closer to being a science.

These considerations led me to establish a sizeable operation analysis group at the U.S. Office of Education and to begin the development of a model. The effort had the enthusiastic support of Commissioner Keppel, and it was generously funded thanks to his efforts and to the full endorsement of the effort by the Bureau of the Budget.

INPUTS AND OUTPUTS

After quite considerable exploration by operations analysts and educators at the U.S. Office of Education there was general agreement that all the inputs to the educational process could be usefully classified into six major determinants of a student's educational process; they may be characterized as follows:

1. The support of his education by his family.
2. The endorsement of educational endeavor by his peers.

3. Community support of education.
4. Properties of the educational system.
5. Society's posture with respect to education.
6. The student's own abilities and attitudes.

Figure 1 provides a very gross view of the arrangement of these forces. In it, the oval representing young persons is sliced to represent individuals; the darkened slice represents a student, in that it overlaps the school system oval; the student is also a member of a family and of the community and of society at large.

The community consists of a variety of other persons, organizations, and facilities not shown in Figure 1, which are important to learning in the large sense; some (e.g., a museum) are relevant to formal education.

These six very broad determinants of a student's educational accomplishment need to be broken down into components before an attempt is made to create quantitative measures for them. An example of such a specification is provided by the following outline:

   I. Components of family support of a student
     A. Provision of a physically and psychologically comfortable home.
     B. Pressure on the student to perform well at school.
     C. Pressure on the school to educate the student well.
     D. Provision of educational know-how.
  II. Components of peer support of a student
     A. Positive attitude toward educational achievement.
     B. High educational expectations for themselves.
     C. Mutual assistance with school work.
 III. Components of community support
     A. Healthy social climate.
     B. Belief in the value of education.
     C. Participation in school activities.
     D. Financial support.
     E. Provision of community cultural and recreational resources.
 IV. Components of society's support
     A. Freedom to pursue knowledge.
     B. Laws and policy regarding school organization, school governance, curriculum, personnel, and attendance.
     C. Provision of rewarding roles in society for educated persons.
     D. Provision of resources for education; particularly, new knowledge.
   V. The school system
     A. Teachers
       1. Belief in educability of the pupils.
       2. Competence in organizing and managing classroom.

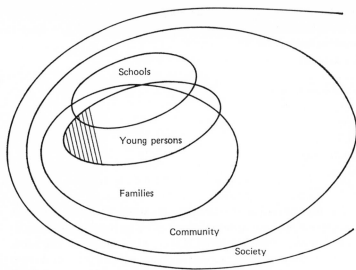

Fig. 1

      3. Knowledge of field in which teaching.
      4. Knowledge of educational technology.
      5. Ability to communicate with students.
      6. Ability to motivate students.
   B. Administration
      1. Selection of goals appropriate to the needs of students and society.
      2. Competence in creating effective organizations of teachers and students for reaching these goals.
      3. Competence in monitoring programs and in making suitable modification of them when achievement of goals is threatened.
      4. Ability to maintain clear communication between school and society.
   C. Curriculum and other aspects of school program
      1. Relation to current social and economic needs and opportunities.
      2. Appropriateness to student capabilities and desires.
      3. Adaptability to needs of individual students.
      4. Attractiveness and stimulation of the curriculum.
      5. Health and food programs.
      6. Extracurricular and recreational programs.
 VI. Components of educational state of the student
   A. Achievement of skills and knowledge
      1. Communications

    2. Mathematics and computer languages
    3. Natural sciences
    4. Social sciences
    5. Humanities
    6. Arts
  B. Personal development
    1. Social competence
    2. Responsibility
    3. Self-confidence
    4. Creativeness
    5. Ethics
    6. Ambition

These last twelve components (of the educational state of the student) are outputs as well as inputs. We may think of them as being inputs at the beginning of a school year and as being outputs at the end of the year. The other five major determinants may then be regarded as operating on the input state of the student to transform it during the course of the year to the output state.

MEASURES

Having arrived at a set of components such as those listed above, one can then begin to assemble a set of items by means of which each component might be quantified. For example, the set of items associated with a given component might be combined with appropriate weights to form an index number which will serve as a measure of the component.

Going back for illustration to the components of family support, the first was provision of a comfortable home. Items that might serve to indicate the level of that component are as follows.

- Quality of food.
- Quality of clothing.
- Quality of residence.
- Adequacy of space (uncrowded).
- Both parents living at home?
- Parents reasonably congenial?
- Parents deal fairly with children?
- Quiet place to study?
- Family has good relations with neighbors?
- Absence of serious emotional disturbances which might distract student from school work?
- Student required to augment family income?

In measuring such items one would not give any credit to luxury. That is, quality of food would mainly refer to balanced nutrition; quality of clothing would reach the top of the scale if the clothing were warm, clean, and of no embarrassment to the child.

For another illustration, the second component of family support refers to pressure to perform well; some items that might give good indication of such pressure are as follows:

- Rewards for good grades.
- Distress at low grades.
- Parents apprise homework requirements and see to it that it is done.
- Parents enforce regular attendance at school.
- Parents influence students to undertake ambitious educational programs.
- Parents influence students toward careers which demand outstanding educational performance.

An item such as the second might be measured on a simple qualitative scale using categories as severe discipline for low grades, real hostility generated on part of parents toward student, withdrawal of significant rights and privileges, minor penalties, reasoned disapproval, little concern, and entirely satisfied with barely passing grades.

None of the determinants or their primary components has a direct measure. Each of them must therefore be quantified by means of an appropriate index number or other measure. A few are already well in hand; for example, various tests for achievement in different subject matter fields have been designed and validated by educators; sociologists have developed indexes of social and economic status. Some of the other components can be readily indicated by easily available economic and financial data. Nevertheless there remains a sizable development task. For each unquantified component a list of items must be assembled out of which can be constructed a test or questionnaire which will provide the basis for a satisfactory measurement of the component.

The measures will often be the only indicators because the components are so complex or abstract that no comprehensive list of their elements is possible. It may be worthwhile to distinguish between indexes and indicators. The Cost of Living Index (maintained by the U.S. Bureau of Labor Statistics) is made up of a long list of prices of items that provide a very complete representation of things families must purchase. One could use instead a simple indicator made up of, say, prices of only four items: bread, rent, automobiles, and hospital room rates. With properly chosen weights the indicator will have very high correlation with the complete index. That is the distinction; an indicator does not pretend to be a comprehensive measure but it does give reasonable promise that it would have high correlation with a comprehensive measure if one existed. Often the "reasonable promise" will rest only on the judgment of reasonable persons; it will not be possible to verify that a high correlation exists.

It is essential, if education is to develop a widely applicable body of quantitative theory, that there be agreement among educational researchers about the construction of each index or indicator. Although many indicators will be quite arbitrary and far less satisfactory than the indexes used by economists, they must necessarily have the same standing in the field of education that the Cost of Living Index, Gross National Product, Wholesale Price Index, and so on have in the field of economics. When we do have such generally accepted measures, then research workers will be able to calibrate the subjects (students, teachers, parents, school administrators, curricula, etc.) of their experiments and surveys in the same way that other research workers do, and there will begin to be some real verification of the results of others when replication is attempted. Educational research will then be on the road to building a unifying quantitative structure.

Of course, wide agreement about formulation of measures does not mean that they must have their specifications fixed forever. They can be revised periodically (just as economic indexes are) to reflect the evolution of society and of educational goals and practices.

Of course, the existence of widely agreed upon measures does not imply that other measures will not be used. Thus in many experimental situations, special student output variables will have to be devised by research workers as is the case presently. When one is experimenting with a methodology directed toward a particular facet of achievement, then the measure may well require more emphasis on that facet than will be found in standard agreed upon measures.

MODEL

The model contemplated here is simply a set of regression equations relating the output measures to the input measures. In its briefest form, it is

$$S_1 = f(S_0, P, F, L, C, Y)$$

where S_0 is the initial state of the student and is a vector consisting of measures of components such as the twelve listed at the end of the section on inputs and outputs; S_1 is the output state of the student and is the same vector at a later time; P, F, L, C, and Y are indicators or index numbers representing, respectively, the major determinants: peers, family, school, community, and society; the function f is linear in the regression coefficients. These five measures will in turn be linear regression functions of their components which will in turn be linear regression functions of the items chosen to specify them.

As is shown in the next section, the model can also be made linear in all the independent variables as well as in the regression coefficients.

The model is constructed using the major determinants as independent variables rather than orthogonal variables derived from the components by factor analysis. The reason is that a given orthogonal variable is composed of a variety of components in a way that defies intuitive understanding of what the variable represents. This model is intended not just for research workers but for educational administrators and for laymen who sit on school boards and in legislative bodies. If they are to understand the quantitative findings of this model and to use them in their deliberations about educational activities and budgets, then it is extremely important that the terms used to describe the findings be altogether meaningful to laymen. Esoteric jargon could destroy much of the utility of the model.

No effort has been made here to combine the output measures into a single quantity; it seems not to be necessary for the primary purposes which the model is intended to serve. Economists (Becker, 1964; Schultz, 1963; Machlup, 1962; Denison, 1964; Benson, 1968; Mincer, 1962; Weisbrod, 1962; Davis, 1966) do that, in a sense, when they calculate the return on investment in education. That kind of calculation is useful for assisting governmental agencies to weigh trade-offs between expenditures for education and for other socially valuable activities, but this model is not particularly directed to that problem; it is rather concerned with assessing the educational operation.

One can, of course, construct a single output measure by combining the twelve output measures into an index number; for example, it might be done by forming a weighted average of them. The question is—what should the weights be? There are endless possibilities. A policy-making group might simply choose them arbitrarily on the basis of its own judgment of the relative importance of each of the twelve measures. Weights might be derived from results of some widely used scoring device such as the college entrance examination given each year by the Educational Testing Service. One very interesting set of weights might be derived from an economic criterion such as discounted lifetime earnings of graduates. Many educators would argue that this method would put too utilitarian a stamp on education; perhaps it would, but the resulting weights would at least give a baseline from which could be determined the "cost" of deviations from an income-effective criterion; that would be a considerable aid to policy-makers.

CRITERION SCALING

A primary purpose of the model is calibration. That is, the model is expected to make it possible to adjust data from experiments and surveys so that their results can be better compared with those of other studies. That goal can be accomplished in infinitely many ways and it may well be done in a way that simplifies as much as possible the use of the model.

The greatest simplification would occur if the model were linear in the independent variables, and it appears that no serious penalty would result from arbitrarily forcing it to be linear. A transformation device (Guttman, 1941; Weinfeld, Mayeske, and Beaton, 1967; Beaton, 1969) originated by Guttman and often called "criterion scaling" can be employed to introduce a great deal of linearity into it. An illustration will make clear how the transformation works. In the accompanying figure the horizontal axis measures an item to be scaled (years of education of the parent having the more education) and the vertical axis measures the criterion (result of an achievement test in arithmetic). The points represent individual observations. The curve shows the relationship between the criterion and the item; it might have been obtained by a curvilinear regression analysis. The item is criterion scaled by grouping the data (as by the light vertical lines in the figure) and replacing the number of years of education of each parent in a group by the average value of the achievement scores in that group. Then the regression of achievement against the transformed years of parents' education would be nearly linear and the regression coefficient would be nearly one. (It will not be exactly one because vagaries of points within a group may cause the regression to fail to pass exactly through the group average.) This transformation maximizes the

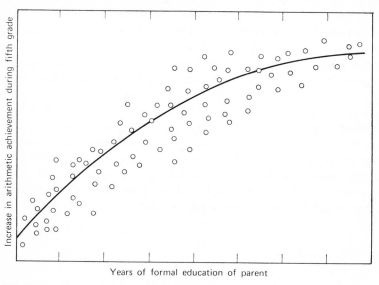

Years of formal education of parent

Fig. 2

amount of variance removed by the independent variable; in doing so it uses up as many statistical degrees of freedom as there are groups. In most educational studies there are sufficient observations that this reduction of degrees of freedom is of little consequence. Of course, once the transformations have been specified, it is not necessary to obtain data to repeat the specification of the transformation (see Figure 2).

If this kind of scaling operation were applied to every item of every component, a great deal of linearity would be built into the model. The scaling can be done equally as easily with qualitative items. Thus the horizontal axis in the figure might have been simply a list of occupations of the students' fathers arranged in ascending order of average student achievement; the scaling would be done by replacing (coding) each occupation by the average value of the achievement scores of that occupation. Similarly there is no difficulty about scaling "no response" or "don't know" to a question; the response is simply coded by the average achievement score of those students who made the response.

PARTITIONING OF VARIANCE

The major forces affecting learning appear to be confounded to an extraordinary degree. Thus far, at any rate, efforts to disentangle the effects of the different forces have had little success, and it is altogether possible that they may never be separated. Certainly there is so much interaction between home and school that we can hardly expect to separate fully their effects.

Let us suppose that index numbers for the major determinants have been developed on the basis of criterion scaling and that we are examining a set A of achievement data in fifth grade arithmetic by means of a linear regression on five indexes of the five major forces; the regression would have the form:

$$A = aP + bF + cL + dC + eY$$

in which lowercase letters are the regression coefficients. Application of the regression will reduce the raw variance V of the achievement scores to $(1 - R^2)V$ where R^2 is the multiple correlation coefficient.

As indicated above, the five indexes will turn out to be highly correlated with each other. The result is, therefore, that any four of the five will remove nearly as much variance as all five. In fact, any three will not do much worse than any four.

A device for measuring the extent to which the five forces are uniquely associated with achievement and jointly associated with achievement is a special partition of variance into unique and common parts (Newton and Spurrell, 1967; Coleman et al., 1966; Mayeske, 1969). The idea is best presented with only two independent variables. Let V be the variance of the achievement scores A. Let the regression on P alone remove the fraction $R_P{}^2$ of the variance and let the regression on F alone remove the fraction $R_F{}^2$ of the variance. Finally, let the regression on P and F jointly, that is,

$$A = aP + bF$$

remove the fraction $R_{PF}{}^2$ of the variance. This last fraction can be split into three parts as follows:

$R_{PF}{}^2 - R_P{}^2$ is the fraction of V uniquely associated with F

$R_{PF}{}^2 - R_F{}^2$ is the fraction of V uniquely associated with P

and the remainder

$$R_{PF}{}^2 - (R_{PF}{}^2 - R_P{}^2) - (P_{PF}{}^2 - R_F{}^2) = R_P{}^2 + R_F{}^2 - R_{PF}{}^2$$

is the proportion that may be associated with either P or F.

With three independent variables P, F, and L, the variance removed by all three can be partitioned into seven ($2^3 - 1$) parts: three parts unique to each of the three; three parts that may be associated with either of the elements of the three pairs PF, PL, FL; and one part that may be associated with any of the three.

In general, with n independent variables, one can define a similar partition into $2^n - 1$ parts. If we now use the integers $1, 2, \ldots, n$ to denote the variables (instead of $P, F, L, \ldots$), then a simple device for writing down formulas for the part of a variance common to a subset, say 2, 4, 7, out of 8 variables, is to expand the product

$$-(1 - x_2)(1 - x_4)(1 - x_7)x_1 x_3 x_5 x_6 x_8$$

and replace the resulting terms by R^2 with the same subscripts as appear on the x's in the term. Thus for four variables, the unique proportion of the variance associated with the second variable is

$$U_2 \sim -(1 - x_2)x_1 x_3 x_4$$
$$= R_{1234}^2 - R_{134}^2$$

and the part that may be associated with either 1 or 3 is

$$E_{13} \sim -(1 - x_1)(1 - x_3)x_2 x_4$$
$$= -R_{1234}^2 + R_{124}^2 + R_{234}^2 - R_{24}{}^2$$

In using this rule to write the formula for the part that may be associated with all the independent variables, the -1 is deleted after expansion of the appropriate product

$$-(1 - x_1)(1 - x_2)(1 - x_3) \cdots (1 - x_n)$$

Thus for two variables

$$E_{12} \sim -(1 - x_1)(1 - x_2)$$
$$= -R_{12}^2 + R_1^2 + R_2^2$$

as above in the first example used in this section in which the subscripts were P and F instead of 1 and 2.

A primary reason for using this kind of characterization of the data is that it seems reasonable to expect that these proportions may be somewhat more stable than regression coefficients or correlations might be in the early stages of trying to implement the model with actual data. That is, whatever set of items one might use to develop an indicator of a component, it is to be expected that the proportion of variance associated with the component will change little so long as the items are intelligently selected.

Another reason is that the independent variables in any social process, and certainly in education, are highly correlated among themselves and this kind of partition of variance provides measures of the extent to which they overlap each other in their association with the dependent variables.

ILLUSTRATIVE RESULTS

An opportunity to implement a model of this kind arose with the passage by Congress of the Civil Rights Act of 1964. Section 402 of the Act required the Commissioner of Education to survey the "lack of availability of equal educational opportunities for individuals by reason of race, color, religion, or national origin . . . ." The main purpose of the survey was to document the condition of components of the schools attended by children of different ethnic groups. Since, however, it seemed important not only to document the state of the components but also to estimate their relevance to educational achievement, I recommended to Commissioner Francis Keppel that we include achievement tests in the survey. I also recommended that certain sociological information about the students be obtained so that the relative importance of school and family components could be explored. These additions to the survey would, hopefully, give valuable guidance to school administrators especially in view of the impending passage of the Elementary-Secondary Education Act which would provide nearly one billion dollars per year to low-income school districts.

The educational establishment tends to guard the concept of local control of schools very zealously, hence to resist any intrusion of the Federal Government into school activities. However, the heroic efforts of Commissioner Keppel persuaded the establishment to permit this survey on the grounds that it would serve the general welfare of education. The survey was carried out in the fall of 1965 under the direction of the distinguished sociologist, James S. Coleman, of Johns Hopkins University. A massive report on the survey (Coleman et al., 1966), often called the Coleman Report, was published in July 1966.

The survey produced a large comprehensive set of school, student, family, and community data from 600,000 students in 4000 public schools. Teachers, principals, and superintendents, as well as the students, filled out personal questionnaires. Students and teachers took tests. The data were analyzed in accordance with the model described in this chapter except that criterion scaling was not used. Short deadlines required that the analysis in the official report be very hasty and directed immediately to the civil rights issues. For that reason I present here a few sample results that are more directly related to the model. They are taken from a book (Mayeske et al., 1969) soon to be published by the U.S. Office of Education containing very careful analyses of the survey data made by operations analysts at the Office under the direction of George Mayeske. These analyses used criterion scaling; they combined four achievement scores into a composite achievement criterion which was used for the scaling; the formation of index numbers from questionnaire items was done by calculating weights for the items by maximizing the correlation between the criterion and the index.

Table 1   Proportions of Variance in Achievement Between Schools Associated with Peer Quality P and School Quality L

	Third Grade	Sixth Grade	Ninth Grade	Twelfth Grade
R_P^2	.5254	.7884	.8207	.8221
R_L^2	.4901	.7322	.7601	.7865
R_{PL}^2	.5646	.8296	.8662	.8617
Unique for P	.0745	.0974	.1061	.0752
Unique for L	.0392	.0412	.0455	.0396
Either P or L	.4509	.6910	.7146	.7469

When one examines the variance of achievement scores in a large nation-wide sample he finds that about one-third of the variance lies between schools and about two-thirds lies between students in the same school. The illustrative numerical results given below refer only to the one-third of the variance between schools. Thus they refer to a regression of school averages of achievement against school averages of the indexes representing the major determinants. Table 1 gives the proportion of variance removed (squared multiple correlation coefficient) by two determinants individually (the peer index P and the school index L) in the first two lines and together in the third line.

Then in the last three lines are proportions of variance uniquely associated with P and L and the proportion that may be associated with either P or L. In the right-hand column we observe that 82% of the variance in achievement between schools is removed by a regression on the school index alone. Putting both indexes into the regression raises the percent of variance removed to 86%. Hence the proportions of variance uniquely attributable to P and L are quite small; the bulk of the variance removed can be associated with either the peers or the school characteristics.

Table 2 shows the relative importance of teachers as opposed to other

Table 2 Proportions of Variance in Achievement Associated with Peer Quality P, Teacher Quality T, and Other School Characteristics O

	Third Grade	Sixth Grade	Ninth Grade	Twelfth Grade
$R_P{}^2$	.5254	.7884	.8207	.8221
$R_T{}^2$	.4751	.7145	.7195	.7441
$R_O{}^2$	.1129	.1588	.2543	.3178
$R_{PT}{}^2$	.5569	.8197	.8449	.8399
$R_{PO}{}^2$	.5336	.8028	.8495	.8444
$R_{TO}{}^2$	.4901	.7322	.7601	.7865
$R_{PTO}{}^2$	.5646	.8296	.8662	.8617
Unique for P	.0745	.0974	.1061	.0752
Unique for T	.0310	.0268	.0167	.0173
Unique for O	.0077	.0099	.0213	.0218
Either P or T	.3462	.5466	.4891	.4514
Either P or O	.0073	.0058	.0193	.0206
Either T or O	.0005	.0045	.0075	.0005
P or T or O	.0974	.1386	.2062	.2749

school characteristics. In it the school index L was split into two indexes, T and O, with T being the index of teacher quality and O including all other aspects of school quality such as class size, age of school building, laboratories, libraries, textbooks, audiovisual and other equipment, curriculum, administration, adequacy of grounds and athletic fields, and extracurricular activities. The first seven lines of Table 2 give the squared multiple correlation coefficients for the individual regressions against P, T, and O, then for two at a time, then for all three together. In the seventh line of the twelfth grade column we find, of course, that the three together remove 86% of the variance as was the case in the third line of Table 1 because L is composed of T and O. The most striking result is seen in the second line of Table 1. Essentially the whole school effect can be associated with the teacher quality index; the other part of the school index takes out much less variance on its own and looking at the last line of Table 2, practically the whole of its regression effect overlaps both the teacher and the peer regression effects.

Using only the P and T indexes in the regression one finds the results in Table 3.

Table 3 Proportions of Variance in Achievement Between Schools Associated with Peer Quality P and Teacher Quality T

	Third Grade	Sixth Grade	Ninth Grade	Twelfth Grade
$R_P{}^2$	.5254	.7884	.8207	.8221
$R_O{}^2$	.4751	.7145	.7195	.7441
$R_{PO}{}^2$	.5569	.8197	.8449	.8399
Unique for P	.0818	.1052	.1254	.0958
Unique for O	.0315	.0313	.0242	.0178
Either P or O	.4436	.6832	.6953	.7263

Finally using only the P and O indexes, some additional interest comparisons with the other tables can be made (see Table 4).

Particularly it is revealing to compare the "unique for P" and "either P or O" rows in Table 4 with the corresponding rows in Table 2.

Other sets of data will also be extremely useful for constructing this model. The project talent data (Flanagan et al., 1962) provide comprehensive achievement and sociological information about a large sample of high school students followed over a long period of time; they are now being used by analysts at the U.S. Office of Education. Another exceptionally valuable source of data is in the immediate offing with the recent decision by the Educational Compact of the States to undertake the periodic nationwide assessment of education which has been under development for several years

Table 4 Proportions of Variance in Achievement Between Schools Associated with Peer Quality P and Other School Characteristics O

	Third Grade	Sixth Grade	Ninth Grade	Twelfth Grade
$R_P{}^2$	.5254	.7884	.8207	.8221
$R_O{}^2$	.1129	.1588	.2543	.3178
$R_{PO}{}^2$	.5336	.8028	.8495	.8444
Unique for P	.4207	.6440	.5952	.5266
Unique for O	.0082	.0144	.0288	.0223
Either P or O	.1047	.1444	.2255	.2955

in a project directed by Ralph Tyler (1965) and funded by the Carnegie Corporation and the Ford Foundation.

ACKNOWLEDGMENT

My ideas about the model presented here have been much influenced by many of my colleagues at the U.S. Office of Education. I am particularly aware of debts to Frederic Weinfeld, James Rocks, and George Mayeske. Also I have learned much about the educational process from Francis Keppel and James Coleman. I am particularly indebted to George Mayeske for keeping me thoroughly posted, after I left the office, on the progress of his expert analyses of the Educational Opportunity Survey data.

REFERENCES

BEATON, ALBERT E. (1969), "Scaling Criterion of Questionnaire Items," *Socio-Economic Planning Science*, Vol. 2, pp. 355–362.

BECKER, GARY S. (1964), *Human Capital*, Columbia University Press, New York.

BENSON, CHARLES S. (1968), *The Economics of Public Education*, Houghton Mifflin, New York.

COLEMAN, J. S. et al. (1966), *Equality of Educational Opportunity*, U.S. Office of Education, Government Printing Office Catalogue No. PS 5.238:38001, Washington, D.C.

DAVIS, RUSSELL C. (1966), *Planning Human Resource Development*, Rand McNally, Chicago, 11.

DENISON, EDWARD F. (1964), "The Contribution of Education to Economic Growth," *The Residual Factor and Economic Growth*, Organization for Economic Cooperation and Development, Paris.

FLANAGAN, J. C. et al. (1962), *Studies of the American High School*, Final Report to U.S. Office of Education, Project TALENT, University of Pittsburgh.

GUTTMAN, L. (1941), in *The Prediction of Personal Adjustment*, Paul Horst, Ed., Social Science Research Council, New York.

KERSHAW, J. A., and R. N. McKEAN (1959), *Systems Analysis and Education*, RM-2473, RAND Corporation, Santa Monica, California.

MACHLUP, FRITZ (1962), *The Production and Distribution of Knowledge in the U.S.*, Princeton University Press, Princeton, N.J.

MAYESKE, GEORGE W. (1969), "The Development of a Model for Student Achievement," *Socio-Economic Planning Science*, Vol. 2, pp. 363–372.

MAYESKE, GEORGE (1969), *A Study of Our Nation's Schools*, U.S. Office of Education.

MINCER, JACOB (1962), "On-the-Job Training: Costs, Returns and Some Implications," *Journal of Political Economics*, Supplement to Vol. 70, pp. 50–80.

NEWTON, R. G., and D. J. SPURRELL (1967), "A Development of Multiple Regression for the Analysis of Routine Data," *Applied Statistics*, Vol. 16, pp. 51–64.

SCHULTZ, THEODORE W. (1963), *The Economic Value of Education*, Columbia University Press, New York.

TYLER, RALPH W. (1965), "Assessing the Progress of Education," *Phi Delta Kappa*, Vol. 47, pp. 13–16.

WEINFELD, F. D., G. W. MAYESKE, and A. E. BEATON, JR. (1967), *Item Response of the Educational Opportunities Survey Student Questionnaire*, Analytical Note 60, U.S. Office of Education (National Center for Educational Statistics), Washington, D.C.

WEISBROD, BURTON A. (1962), "Education and Investment in Human Capital," *Journal of Political Economics*, Supplement to Vol. 70, pp. 106–124.

INDEX